21023885 9

The
Gold Plated
HOUSE PLANT
EXPERT

Contents

CHAPTER 1
PLANTS IN THE HOME

You don't need to read a book to learn about the beauty, variety and popularity of house plants — just look around you. Everywhere you will find them, the impressive indoor gardens in public buildings . . . tiny pots on windowsills . . . scores of colourful varieties offered for sale in garden shops.

The charm of house plants may be universal, but many millions of them die needlessly each year. You have to face the fact that your house is not a particularly good home for them — most plants would be much happier in the moist, bright air of a well-lit laundry! So you just can't leave them to look after themselves; each plant needs care and each variety has its own particular requirements. It is the purpose of this book to tell you the secrets of success and the special problems of all the types you are likely to find.

Forget about green fingers. Anyone can grow house plants and make them look attractive. If everything dies as soon as you take it home, then you are making a serious basic mistake and the answer is in these pages. If your plants look sickly and unattractive then it's a matter of poor choice, incorrect upkeep or lack of knowledge about house plant display. Once again the answers are here. True exotics, such as some Orchids and many Bromeliads are quite easy to grow . . . exciting displays are not difficult to make . . . increasing your stock is surprisingly simple . . . here you will find the key.

The *Golden* Rules

● DON'T DROWN THEM
Roots need air as well as water — keeping the compost soaked at all times means certain death for most plants. Learn how to water properly — see pages 226 – 227.

● GIVE THEM A REST
Beginners are usually surprised to learn that nearly all plants need a rest in winter, which means less water, less feeding and less heat than in the active growing period. See page 231.

● ACCEPT THE LOSS OF 'TEMPORARY' PLANTS
Some popular gift plants, such as Cyclamen, Chrysanthemum and Gloxinia will die down in a matter of weeks. You've done nothing wrong — these types are flowering pot plants which are only temporary residents.

● GIVE THEM EXTRA HUMIDITY
The atmosphere of a centrally-heated room in winter is as dry as desert air. Learn how to increase the air humidity — see page 229.

● TREAT TROUBLE PROMPTLY
Expert or beginner, trouble will strike sometime. One or two scale insects or mealy bugs are easily picked off; an infestation may be incurable. Overwatering is not fatal at first, but kills when prolonged. Learn to recognise the early signs of trouble.

● GROUP THEM TOGETHER
Nearly all plants look better and grow better when grouped together. Learn the how and why of plant grouping on pages 26 – 36.

● LEARN TO REPOT
After a year or two most plants begin to look sickly; in many cases the plant simply needs repotting into a larger container. Learn how on page 239.

● CHOOSE WISELY
The plant must be able to flourish in the home you provide for it. Even the expert can't make a shade-lover survive in a sunny window. Read the rules on pages 8 – 19.

● HAVE THE PROPER TOOLS
A number of tools are essential. Buy a watering can with a long, narrow spout and a mister for increasing humidity, reducing dust and controlling pests. You will need a reputable brand of compost (never use garden soil) and a collection of pots (2½, 3½, 5 and 7 in. are the most useful) plus stakes and plant-ties or string. Drip trays will keep water off the furniture — a bottle of liquid fertilizer and a safe pest killer will keep the plants looking healthy. To complete your tool kit, include a soft sponge, an old kitchen spoon and fork, and a pair of small-sized secateurs.

Choosing indoor plants

A bewildering range of plants is now available, and it's all too easy to make a mistake. Look around the homes of your friends to see which plants appear to flourish, but don't be guided by the large specimens in public buildings. These plants are often rented and returned to the nursery when the poor conditions start to have an effect.

You want to buy a plant . . . ask yourself the following six questions and the answers will give you a short list of types which will suit your purpose. Then choose the one which really appeals to you, for that is the most important requirement of all.

QUESTION 1	DO I WANT A PLANT WHICH WILL BE ON DISPLAY ALL YEAR ROUND?

If you buy a Gloxinia and it starts to die down after a couple of months, you have done nothing wrong — it is a temporary plant. If the same thing happens to an Ivy then you *are* responsible, because it is a permanent plant. Never choose a flowering pot plant if you want to have foliage all year round.

ALL YEAR ROUND DISPLAY

FOLIAGE HOUSE PLANTS are varieties which can be expected to live permanently under room conditions, provided that their particular needs are met. The foliage remains alive all year round, although some types need to overwinter in an unheated room and a few others lose their display value with age.
See A – Z guide — pages 41 – 115

ALL YEAR ROUND DISPLAY

FLOWERING HOUSE PLANTS are varieties which can be expected to live permanently under room conditions, provided that their particular needs are met. After flowering, the foliage remains alive but may not be attractive. Some types need to overwinter in an unheated room and a few need to spend part of the summer outdoors.
See A – Z guide — pages 121 – 160

TEMPORARY DISPLAY

FLOWERING POT PLANTS are varieties which provide a temporary floral display under room conditions and are moved away when the flowering period is over. Most are discarded, but some can be stored indoors as leafless plants or bulbs whilst others can be put in the greenhouse or garden.
See A – Z guide — pages 165 – 199

ALL YEAR ROUND DISPLAY

CACTI are a family of succulent plants which bear small patches of woolly tufts (areoles) on their thickened stems. Practically all Cacti are leafless and most of them bear spines. They will live permanently under room conditions and many can be made to flower.
See A – Z guide — pages 203 – 212

ALL YEAR ROUND or TEMPORARY DISPLAY

MISCELLANEOUS INDOOR PLANTS are varieties which cannot be fitted into any of the 4 basic groups described above. There may be a distinctive growth habit or a unique cultural requirement. Listed here are plants grown for food and those raised from pips.
See A – Z guide — pages 213 – 222

QUESTION 2 — HOW MUCH TIME AND SKILL DO I HAVE?

EASY FOLIAGE HOUSE PLANTS

Asparagus, Aspidistra, Bromeliads, Cissus antarctica, Chlorophytum, Coleus, Cyperus, Dracaena marginata, Fatshedera, Fatsia, Ficus elastica decora, Grevillea, Hedera (mist leaves in winter), Helxine, Howea, Monstera, Neanthe, Philodendron scandens, Rhoicissus rhomboidea, Sansevieria, Saxifraga sarmentosa, Succulents, Tolmiea, Tradescantia, Zebrina.

Some plants have the reputation of being almost as indestructible as plastic. These 'cast-iron' plants include Sansevieria, Cissus antarctica, Fatsia, Fatshedera, Aspidistra, Cacti and other Succulents (if kept dry) and Cyperus (if kept wet). A much larger group are classed as 'easy' — they can tolerate a wide range of conditions and will stand a considerable amount of neglect and poor management. Choose here if you are a beginner or if you have little time to spare for house plant care.

At the other end of the scale is the 'delicate' group. These plants require carefully controlled conditions, which may mean constant temperature, very careful watering or high humidity at all times. Examples are Acalypha, Caladium, Calathea, Codiaeum, Dizygotheca, Ixora and Gardenia. Leave these plants to the experienced house plant grower.

QUESTION 3 — DO I WANT A POPULAR PLANT OR A RARITY?

POPULAR INDOOR PLANTS

Azalea, Begonia, Bromeliads, Bulbs in Bowls, Cacti & Succulents, Chlorophytum, Cissus antarctica, Codiaeum, Cyclamen, Dieffenbachia, Dracaena, Ferns, Ficus, Hedera, Impatiens, Kalanchoe, Monstera, Palms, Pelargonium, Philodendron scandens, Poinsettia, Pot Chrysanthemum, Saintpaulia, Sansevieria, Schefflera, Tradescantia, Yucca.

Most people choose the old favourites which have stood the test of time and are available everywhere. Included in this book there are also plants you have never seen — the rarities. They are worth trying if you like a challenge, but remember that the reason for their unpopularity may be a delicate constitution, high price or lack of attractive features.

There are many exceptions. Some rarities are stunning — others (e.g Abutilon, Beaucarnea, Carex and Pentas) are easier to grow than most popular ones. Another reason for rarity status may be their recent arrival — Radermachera, the New Guinea Impatiens Hybrids and Pot Gerberas were unknown a few years ago.

QUESTION 4 — HOW MUCH DO I WANT TO SPEND?

There is no such thing as an average price — the variation is enormous. The usual way of obtaining a plant is to buy one in a 3−5 in. pot, but even here one type may be much dearer than another. The expensive ones have one or more factors against them — these drawbacks include slowness of growth, special requirements during development, difficulty in propagation and lack of popular appeal.

If you want lots of foliage and money is limited then there is no point in looking at mature palms or tall specimen trees. Buy instead rooted cuttings or young plants of quick-growing varieties — feed and pot on regularly. An even less expensive plan is to sow seed or strike cuttings at home.

QUESTION 5 — WHAT SIZE AND SHAPE DO I WANT?

Both size and shape are extremely important considerations when choosing a plant. A small, low-growing variety can look completely out-of-place against a large, bare wall . . . a tall, tree-like plant can look distinctly unsafe on a narrow windowsill. Remember that you may be buying a young specimen — in your home a small neat Dracaena or Ficus can become a man-sized tree in a few seasons. There are six basic plant shapes and nearly all indoor plants fit into one or other of these groups. But there are borderline cases, and a few plants will change with age from one shape type to another.

GRASSY PLANTS

GRASSY PLANTS have long, narrow leaves and a grass-like growth habit. Very few true grasses are offered as house plants because their leaf form has never been generally accepted for indoor decoration. Several grass-like plants with long and extremely narrow leaves are listed as indoor plants, but they are not often seen.

Examples: Acorus
Carex
Ophiopogon
Scirpus

Broad-leaved Grassy Plants are much more popular; Chlorophytum comosum is one of the most widely grown of all foliage house plants. Several flowering plants have grassy leaves of this type — good examples are Billbergia nutans, Vallota, Tillandsia lindenii and Narcissus.

BUSHY PLANTS

BUSHY PLANTS are a vast collection of varieties which do not fit into the other groups. The standard pattern is an arrangement of several stems arising out of the compost, with a growth habit which is neither markedly vertical nor horizontal. They may be small and compact like Peperomia or tall and shrubby like Aucuba. Some plants are naturally bushy, regularly producing side shoots; others must be pinched out regularly to induce bushiness. The Secrets of Success listed for each bushy plant will tell you if pinching out is necessary.

Examples: Achimenes
Begonia rex
Coleus
Hypocyrta
Maranta
Pilea

UPRIGHT PLANTS

UPRIGHT PLANTS bear stems with a distinctly vertical growth habit. They vary in height from an inch to the tallest house plants available. Medium-sized upright plants are an essential component of the mixed group, providing a feeling of height to offset the horizontal effect created by rosette plants, trailing plants and low bushes. Tall, upright plants are often displayed as solitary specimens, serving as effective focal points.

Column Plants have thick vertical stems which are either leafless or bear leaves which do not detract from the column effect. Many Cacti and some Succulents have this growth habit.

Examples: Cereus peruvianus
Cleistocactus straussii
Haworthia reinwardtii
Kleinia articulata
Notocactus leninghausii
Trichocereus candicans

Trees are an extremely important group, providing spectacular specimen plants for large displays and the basic centrepiece in collections. All trees have the same basic form — a central branched or unbranched stem bearing leaves with relatively small leaf bases. Some are quite small, such as miniature Succulent 'trees' or a young Croton; others are capable of growing many feet tall.

Examples: Aphelandra
Citrus
Codiaeum
Ficus benjamina
Ficus elastica decora
Laurus
Schefflera

False Palms have stems which are completely clothed by the elongated stem bases when the plant is young. In a mature plant usually only the upper part of the stem is covered by leaves and the characteristically palm-like effect is created. Large false palms are often used as specimen plants in public buildings.

Examples: Beaucarnea
Dieffenbachia
Dracaena
Pandanus
Yucca

CLIMBING & TRAILING PLANTS

CLIMBING & TRAILING PLANTS bear stems which, when mature, are either provided with support to grow upwards or are left to hang downwards on the outside of the container. Many (but not all) varieties can be used in both ways. As climbers they are trained on canes, strings, trellis-work, wire hoops or vertical poles; they can be grown in wall-mounted pots to frame windows or they can be trained up stout supports to serve as room dividers. As trailers they can be used to spread horizontally as ground cover in indoor gardens or left to trail over the sides of pots or hanging baskets.

Climbers are always grown as upright plants. Twining varieties are allowed to twist around the supports provided. Clinging varieties bearing tendrils must be attached to the supports at frequent intervals; if left to grow unattended the stems will soon become tangled together. Varieties bearing aerial roots are best grown on a moss stick (see page 114).

Examples: Dipladenia
Passiflora
Philodendron hastatum
Stephanotis

Climber/Trailers are extremely useful house plants and many popular varieties belong to this group. When growing them as climbers it is usually advisable not to tie all the stems to a single cane — it is more attractive to spread out the stems on a trellis or on several canes inserted in the pot. When growing them as trailers it is sometimes necessary to pinch out the growing tips occasionally to prevent straggly growth.

Examples: Ficus pumila
Hedera
Philodendron scandens
Scindapsus

Trailers are always grown as pendent plants, with stems hanging downwards, or as creeping plants, with stems growing along the soil surface. Many trailers have striking foliage or attractive flowers and are best grown in hanging baskets or stood on high pedestals.

Examples: Begonia pendula
Campanula isophylla
Columnea
Fittonia
Helxine
Nertera
Sedum morganianum
Senecio rowleyanus
Zygocactus

ROSETTE PLANTS

ROSETTE PLANTS bear leaves which form a circular cluster around the central growing point. Most rosette plants are low-growing and combine well with bushy and upright plants in Pot Groups and Indoor Gardens.

Flat Rosette Plants have large leaves which lie almost horizontally, forming a loose rosette. African Violet is the best known example; Gloxinia and some Primulas have a similar growth habit.

Succulent Rosette Plants have fleshy leaves borne in several layers and often tightly packed together. The leaves may be horizontal or nearly upright. This arrangement helps to conserve moisture in the natural desert habitat.

Examples: Aloe humilis
Aeonium
tabulaeforme
Echeveria setosa
Haworthia fasciata
Sempervivum
tectorum

Funnel Rosette Plants are common among the Bromeliads. The basal area of the strap-like leaves forms a 'vase' which holds rainwater in the natural tropical habitat. Plants are usually large and spreading.

Examples: Aechmea
Guzmania
Nidularium
Vriesea

BALL PLANTS

BALL PLANTS are leafless and have a distinctly globular shape. They are all Cacti, and the stem surface may be smooth or covered with hair and spines.

Examples: Astrophytum
Echinocactus
grusonii
Ferocactus
Mammillaria
Parodia
Rebutia miniscula

QUESTION 6 — WHAT WILL THE GROWING CONDITIONS BE LIKE?

Most people choose a house plant which has the right shape, appearance and price. It is essential, however, that it should also be right for the light and warmth it will receive in its new home. There are three important points to remember.

- **Each plant has its own likes and dislikes.** Some plants need an unheated room in winter, and a few will grow quite happily in full sun, but many would die under such conditions. Don't guess — look up your plants' special needs in the A−Z guides.
- **A new plant gets homesick even in good conditions.** Many varieties suffer a distinct shock when they are moved from their well-lit and humid glasshouse home to your walled-in and dry living room. Don't assume that the conditions must be wrong if the plant looks jaded for the first few weeks — read page 20.
- **An established plant may adapt to poor conditions.** The Secrets of Success given for each plant in the following pages describe the *ideal* growing conditions; here the plant will flourish. But many plants are capable of slowly adapting to a poorer environment.

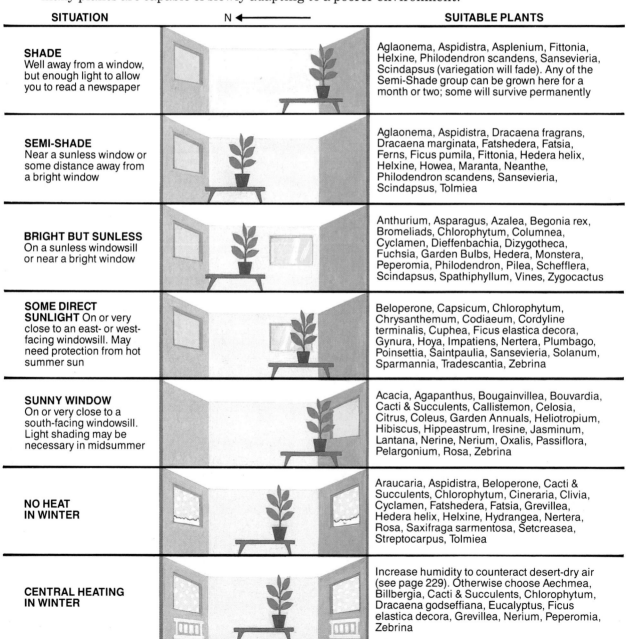

SITUATION	N ←	SUITABLE PLANTS
SHADE Well away from a window, but enough light to allow you to read a newspaper		Aglaonema, Aspidistra, Asplenium, Fittonia, Helxine, Philodendron scandens, Sansevieria, Scindapsus (variegation will fade). Any of the Semi-Shade group can be grown here for a month or two; some will survive permanently
SEMI-SHADE Near a sunless window or some distance away from a bright window		Aglaonema, Aspidistra, Dracaena fragrans, Dracaena marginata, Fatshedera, Fatsia, Ferns, Ficus pumila, Fittonia, Hedera helix, Helxine, Howea, Maranta, Neanthe, Philodendron scandens, Sansevieria, Scindapsus, Tolmiea
BRIGHT BUT SUNLESS On a sunless windowsill or near a bright window		Anthurium, Asparagus, Azalea, Begonia rex, Bromeliads, Chlorophytum, Columnea, Cyclamen, Dieffenbachia, Dizygotheca, Fuchsia, Garden Bulbs, Hedera, Monstera, Peperomia, Philodendron, Pilea, Schefflera, Scindapsus, Spathiphyllum, Vines, Zygocactus
SOME DIRECT SUNLIGHT On or very close to an east- or west-facing windowsill. May need protection from hot summer sun		Beloperone, Capsicum, Chlorophytum, Chrysanthemum, Codiaeum, Cordyline terminalis, Cuphea, Ficus elastica decora, Gynura, Hoya, Impatiens, Nertera, Plumbago, Poinsettia, Saintpaulia, Sansevieria, Solanum, Sparmannia, Tradescantia, Zebrina
SUNNY WINDOW On or very close to a south-facing windowsill. Light shading may be necessary in midsummer		Acacia, Agapanthus, Bougainvillea, Bouvardia, Cacti & Succulents, Callistemon, Celosia, Citrus, Coleus, Garden Annuals, Heliotropium, Hibiscus, Hippeastrum, Iresine, Jasminum, Lantana, Nerine, Nerium, Oxalis, Passiflora, Pelargonium, Rosa, Zebrina
NO HEAT IN WINTER		Araucaria, Aspidistra, Beloperone, Cacti & Succulents, Chlorophytum, Cineraria, Clivia, Cyclamen, Fatshedera, Fatsia, Grevillea, Hedera helix, Helxine, Hydrangea, Nertera, Rosa, Saxifraga sarmentosa, Setcreasea, Streptocarpus, Tolmiea
CENTRAL HEATING IN WINTER		Increase humidity to counteract desert-dry air (see page 229). Otherwise choose Aechmea, Billbergia, Cacti & Succulents, Chlorophytum, Dracaena godseffiana, Eucalyptus, Ficus elastica decora, Grevillea, Nerium, Peperomia, Zebrina

The Living Room

The living room is the area where the family gathers. It is here that the adults relax, the children play and everyone seeks comfort. It is also the spot where most people keep indoor plants.

Virtually every living room can be improved by the thoughtful use of plants, but not if you merely scatter a few pots of nondescript greenery around — a couple on the windowsill, one on the mantlepiece, another on the piano and so on. The interior designer sets out to create a number of *plant stations*, each one of which is bold enough and attractive enough to be admired. The next chapter describes the four types of plant station — the Specimen Plant which consists of a single plant, and the groups — the Pot Group, the Indoor Garden and the Terrarium.

Each type of plant station has its own advantages and its own special role to play. Decide on the number and types of plant stations and then pick plants from the A-Z guides to provide the effect you desire. If the room is cosily warm in winter then you have created a problem for some plants. It may be too warm for most flowering pot plants and the air will be too dry for many house plants. Don't worry — there are still a large number of plants which will flourish with proper care in the centrally-heated living room.

How you display your plants is a matter of taste, provided that their cultural needs are met and that they do not obstruct the movement of people around the room. Perhaps the only general rule is that you must keep a sense of proportion — a potted Pilea may look pathetic in a large open area — a tall Dracaena could certainly overpower a tiny, crowded room.

The Hall

Indoor plants are a vital feature of the well-furnished hall, for it is here that visitors gain their first impression of the inside of your home. Beautiful leaves and flowers are an immediate indication of a well-tended house. If the hall is large, well-lit and heated in winter you are indeed fortunate — you can have a bold Specimen Plant or an impressive Indoor Garden, and you can choose from an enormous list of varieties.

Unfortunately, most halls are quite different. They are poorly lit, subject to draughts and wide fluctuations in temperature, and tend to be narrow passageways rather than square or rectangular rooms. Flourishing but unexciting plants will look better than struggling exotics, so choose from the 'easy' group listed on page 9.

The favourite site is a table near the front door — make sure that plants are kept out of the line of traffic at this congested spot. Plants in the hall must never be an obstacle to easy movement from room to room — consider a wall-mounted plant trough where the passageway is narrow.

A well-lit spot near the hall window or at the top of the stairs is often the best hallway environment. Garden Bulbs, Azalea, Chrysanthemum, Erica, Cineraria and Primulas will usually last longer on a hall or landing windowsill than in a warm living room. Keep the size of the plant in keeping with the space — a large plant in a small hall will make the area look even smaller. Consider using the same varieties of plants in both the hall and landing in order to link the two areas together.

The Kitchen

More than half the kitchens in this country contain one or more pots — this room is second only to the living room as the most popular place for indoor plants. Some members of the family may spend much of the day here, and the somewhat clinical appearance of white units, steel sink etc can be considerably softened and enlivened by the presence of colourful plants.

By far the most popular spot for kitchen plants is the windowsill. There is usually a hotch-potch of types — African Violets next to recently-rooted cuttings, pots of Cacti and Succulents next to Bulbs in bowls, sick plants taken from other rooms next to Primulas and Herbs in pots. This is a good spot — you cannot help but keep an eye on them when working at the sink, water is readily to hand and the equipment for removing and disposing of dead leaves and flowers is right there. The windowsill in front of the sink is generally a reasonably good environment — the air is moister than in other rooms and the light is usually good. Natural gas is not a problem but splashing foliage with hot soapy water can be troublesome.

Kitchens can be an undesirable residence for plants with a delicate constitution. Draughts occur near outside doors and large temperature changes occur near the cooker. So pick colourful workaday plants rather than expensive temperamental ones. Begonias, Impatiens, Scindapsus, Zebrina, Hypoestes and Pelargoniums are good examples.

The kitchen is a busy area and plants should be kept out of the way. Space on work surfaces is usually too limited to devote to plants — choose instead pots on shelves, a wall display or a hanging display above the sink.

The Dining Room

Only one in four dining rooms contains house plants, and yet these areas would seem to be ideal for living greenery. Ample horizontal surfaces, a location close to the kitchen for easy watering and a somewhat sparse decor which would benefit from attractive leaves and bright flowers.

The problem is one of space — most dining rooms are quite small and it would be a mistake to have plants which obstruct easy passage around the chairs. But even in the most compact room, a centrepiece of house plants on the dining table is an excellent idea . . . with three provisos.

Firstly, the plants must be low-growing so as not to interfere with conversation with the person opposite. Good examples are Saintpaulia, Begonia semperflorens, Peperomia, Pilea and small-leaved Ivy. Secondly, the plants must be in good condition — dust, dead leaves and live greenfly are distinctly distasteful.

Finally, avoid strong-smelling plants — this means heavily fragrant ones such as Hyacinth which can mask the taste of the food, and unpleasantly pungent ones like Exacum in full flower.

If you have a large dining room then house plants can make a splendid contribution to the general decor. A tall Dracaena in the corner, a Boston Fern on a pedestal, a bold Pot Group on the sideboard etc. Indoor plants can provide a living screen between the separate functions in a combined living/dining room. Use vigorous climbers growing up an attractive framework, the plants being stood in pots or a waterproof trough placed at ground level. Pots of colourful hanging plants can be used to soften the lines of a wooden island unit which may be used to divide the dining area from the rest of the room.

The Bedroom

The bedroom is the least popular spot for indoor plants. Some interior designers feel that bedrooms are in use for too short a time during the waking hours to make a house plant display worthwhile. Others take the opposite view — they consider the bedroom an important place for plants, with types chosen to reflect the character of both the room and its occupants. One wakes to the sight of green foliage and before going to sleep you can enjoy the fragrance of Jasmine, Stephanotis or Hyacinths. Whatever your own view, you need not worry about the old wives' tale that plants are unhealthy in a bedroom.

The conditions in a centrally-heated bedroom really are too good to waste. It is an excellent spot for plants which hate too much heat in winter and tend to suffer in a centrally-heated living room. Examples are Cyclamen, Heliotrope, Beloperone, Hydrangea, Campanula, Buxus, Bougainvillea, Yucca and Abutilon.

Perhaps the best plan is to have one or two really eye-catching Specimen Plants rather than aiming for the group displays which belong in the living room or kitchen. A floor-standing architectural plant is the designer's choice for a large bedroom — in a smaller one you can have a hanging display or set the pot holders on windowsills or a dressing table. An unused fireplace can be masked by a foliage plant display.

Bedrooms which are heated for all or part of the night make good house plant hospitals. Put off-colour plants here until they recover, and overwinter plants which need a rest during the non-flowering season. The bedroom can be a place of relaxation and recuperation for you, the Fuchsias and the Pelargoniums.

The Bathroom

A plant display in the bathroom is more likely to be seen in a magazine than in the home, but with a little thought plants can be used to add a touch of luxury. The problem bathroom is small, unheated in winter and has a tiny window with frosted glass. Choose a tough, glossy-leaved foliage plant such as Philodendron scandens (often called the Bathroom Plant in the U.S.), Cissus antarctica or Scindapsus aureus. Place the pot on the windowsill or put it in a wall-mounted pot holder.

In the larger bathroom with a decent-sized window you have a much larger choice of plants and display types. A Display Window (see page 27) makes an attractive feature, or you can create a Pot Group or Indoor Garden containing Ferns, Palms, Ivies, Heptapleurum, Asparagus, Ficus benjamina and so on. The moist air will keep the plants flourishing and steamy conditions provide a tonic for many varieties. Bath surrounds are usually too narrow to support plant pots — this precarious placing is best avoided, especially if there are children around.

The large, well-lit bathroom really comes into its own when it is centrally heated. It then becomes the best room in the house for the cultivation of delicate exotic plants — Anthurium, Calathea, Maranta, Adiantum, Caladium and the rest.

Finally, a few points on bathroom plant care. Misting should not be necessary if the room is in regular use but the leaves will need sponging at fairly frequent intervals — talcum powder and hair lacquer aerosols are the plant enemies in the bathroom.

The Garden Room

The dividing lines between *greenhouse*, *conservatory* and *garden room* are vague, and experts disagree over the definitions. Regard a greenhouse as a glass or mainly glass (or plastic) structure which is entered from the garden and is almost exclusively used for the comfort of the plants rather than the people who tend them. A conservatory is basically similar in physical appearance, although it may be more ornate. It differs from the greenhouse by being entered through the house and although the plant display remains dominant there is generally some provision for people to sit and relax within its glass roof and walls. The garden room (other names: sun room, plant room, growing room) is also entered through the house, but the main consideration here is human comfort with the extensive plant displays serving as an attractive background. The ceiling may or may not be transparent.

Impressive plant displays are essential to transform a glass-walled extension into a garden room. Bold Specimen Plants, Pot Groups, Terraria and Indoor Gardens — the choice is up to you. The plants you can grow will depend on the amount of heat you provide in winter. A minimum of 55°F means that nearly all house plants will be suitable for your garden room. Don't just fill it with common-or-garden varieties — separate plain types with tropical beauties.

You must provide a number of things apart from a heater in winter. Shading will be needed to protect plants from the hot summer sun, and there must be some way of ventilating the room. Cane and cast iron are the popular furnishing materials and the floor should be covered with a rot-proof surface such as tiles or polypropylene carpeting. If possible have a water tap fitted in a corner of the room.

Buying indoor plants

Indoor plants are raised in glasshouses in which the air is warm and humid. The world outside is far less accommodating, so always buy from a reputable supplier who will have made sure that the plants have been properly hardened off. In this way the shock of moving into a new home will be reduced to a minimum.

House plants can, of course, be bought at any time of the year, but it is preferable to purchase delicate varieties between late spring and mid-autumn. But some plants can only be bought in winter, and you should be extra careful at this time of the year. Plants stood outside the shop or on a market stall will have been damaged by the cold unless they are hardy varieties — avoid buying delicate plants which are stood in the open as 'bargain' offers.

Now you are ready to buy. If you are shopping for flower seeds, choose F1 hybrids if available. If you are picking bulbs, make sure that they are firm, rot-free and without holes or shoots. When buying house plants, ensure that the specimen is not too big for the space you have in mind and then look for the danger signs. None present? Then you have a good buy.

Danger signs

All flowers open; no sign of developing buds

Signs of disease or pests

Plant not evenly clothed with leaves

Floppy leaves

Space can be seen between compost and inside of the pot

Green slime covering pot and top of compost

Roots growing out of the pot

Taking plants home

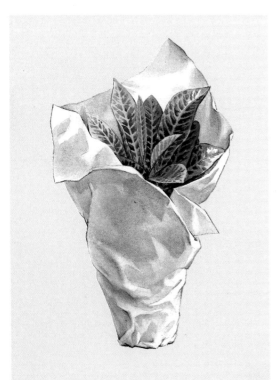

Make sure the plant is properly wrapped before leaving the shop or nursery. The purpose of this wrapping is twofold — to protect stray leaves from damage and to keep out draughts. In winter the protecting cover should be closed at the top.

Much has been written about the danger of walking home with a delicate house plant in the depths of winter, but just as much damage is done by putting plants in the boot of a car in the height of summer . . . plants can be killed by baking as well as freezing. When taking a plant home by car the best plan is to secure it in a box and place it on a seat.

Once your new plant is home it will need a period of acclimatisation. For a few weeks keep it out of direct sunlight and draughts, and be careful not to give it too much heat or water. It is quite normal for a delicate variety to lose a leaf or two during this settling-in period, and the worst thing you can do is to keep on moving it from one spot to another in order to find the 'proper' home. Just leave it alone in a moderately warm spot out of the sun.

Flowering pot plants (such as Azalea, Chrysanthemum and Cyclamen) which are purchased in flower during the winter months require different treatment; put them in their permanent quarters immediately and give them as much light as possible.

CHAPTER 2
DISPLAYING INDOOR PLANTS

There are between six and ten plants in the average home, and they are treated in one of two basic ways. You may regard them as green pets to be kept apart, carefully tended when alive and mourned when dead. Here you will try to find the right environment to fit the plant, whereas the modern trend is to regard indoor plants as living decor. Here you find the right plants to fit the environment — they may be stood singly or massed together, and the temporary pot plants are no more mourned than cut flowers when their final hour arrives.

To understand the principles of indoor plant display, look out of the window. The garden is brought alive by its contrasting shapes and colours — bold specimens may stand on their own but bedding plants need to be massed in order to produce a bold display.

There are very few rules to tell you how to arrange plants correctly. They should be in keeping with their surroundings — large architectural plants in spacious rooms, small pots on tiny windowsills. Let dramatic ones stand on their own as specimens, but always group insignificant and below-par ones in a group. Pick up ideas from magazines, TV and other people's homes, but above all create displays which please *you*.

Stand it on its own

A Specimen Plant is a flowering or foliage plant grown as a solitary feature. It may be retained in its pot or transplanted into a container.

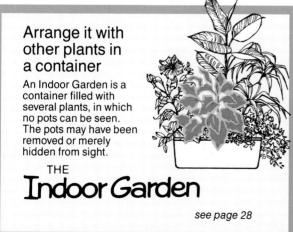

THE
Specimen Plant

see page 22

Place it alongside several other pots

A Pot Group is a collection of plants in pots or individual containers closely grouped to create a massed effect. The pots remain visible as separate units.

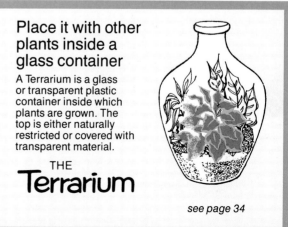

THE
Pot Group

see page 26

Arrange it with other plants in a container

An Indoor Garden is a container filled with several plants, in which no pots can be seen. The pots may have been removed or merely hidden from sight.

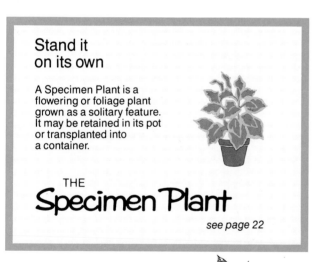

THE
Indoor Garden

see page 28

Place it with other plants inside a glass container

A Terrarium is a glass or transparent plastic container inside which plants are grown. The top is either naturally restricted or covered with transparent material.

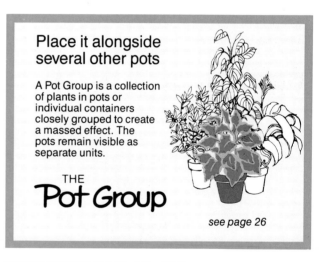

THE
Terrarium

see page 34

THE Specimen Plant

The purpose of a plant display is to provide an attractive focal point in the room. Most ordinary plants need to be grouped together to achieve this effect, but some are best seen on their own in a prominent place. These are the Specimen Plants. Of course, correct plant choice is all-important, but you must also pay attention to the position, receptacle, lighting and background provided for the plant if you want to achieve the maximum effect.

You may want a large specimen which will cover an area of several square feet. Unfortunately the cost of a mature floor-standing house plant which can dominate a corner or wall could well be prohibitive. A good plan is to buy a young plant, repot regularly and then place it in its permanent position once it has reached the required height. Alternatively stand a hanging plant on a pedestal or grow a vigorous climber to clothe the required area.

It makes good design sense to display fine examples of dramatic plants as solitary specimens. Small and medium-sized foliage types, however, are usually best grouped together and not kept as a collection of isolated pots on shelves and windowsills.

The Right Receptacle

Receptacles for indoor plants are available in all sorts of shapes and sizes. Unfortunately the words 'receptacle', 'container' and 'pot' are used interchangeably and this leads to confusion. Use the word **Receptacle** to describe *any* type of housing for one or more plants. Leaving out the oddities (bark for Staghorn Fern, driftwood and coral for Air Plants etc), there are 3 basic types of receptacle:

Pot
A receptacle with a drainage hole or holes at the base. It is used for potting one or more plants. A pot holder or drip tray is necessary

Pot Holder
(Other names: Pot Hider, Cachepot)
A waterproof receptacle with no drainage holes. It is used for holding and hiding a single pot

Container
A receptacle with no holes at the base. It is used for potting one or more plants or for holding several pots

Some people enjoy the natural look of a clay pot, but most Specimen Plants are improved by being placed in a pot holder. This should be taller than the pot and the space between them should be filled with damp peat. Pot holders come in many forms — you can buy ones made of wire, plastic, pottery, wood, glass fibre, cane or metal and you can use ordinary household objects, such as copper bowls and pans. Make sure that the size of the pot and its holder if present is in keeping with the plant — a large Palm in a small pot would look distinctly top-heavy. Never use multicoloured pot holders for multicoloured plants and remember that mobility is important — large floor-standing receptacles should have castors where possible.

The Right Background

Light-coloured walls without a pattern are the ideal backcloth, although strongly variegated specimens are best displayed against a dark wall. If the background is highly coloured and intricately patterned, choose a plant with all-green, simple leaves. Deeply cut leaves (such as Monstera) and delicate flowers (such as Stephanotis) need a plain background.

The Right Lighting

For life-giving illumination the plants must rely on daylight or fluorescent lighting. For display purposes the light of an ordinary bulb directed on to the foliage or flowers will greatly enhance the appearance of a Specimen Plant in the evening. The best type of bulb to use is a spotlight or floodlight, but overheating can be a problem. Switch on the light and place your hand just above the leaves nearest the bulb. If you can feel the warmth then the plant is too close.

The Right Plant

ARCHITECTURAL PLANTS

An Architectural plant (also called a Decorator, Accent or Statement plant) has a shape which is large, distinctive and attractive. Its basic use is to act as a focal point, although it may be used to either clothe a bare space or divide off a section of the room. Palms, false palms and tree-like plants are the types most frequently used, and interior decorators usually choose tall specimens from the following list:

> Araucaria heterophylla
> Cyperus
> Dieffenbachia
> Dracaena
> Fatsia japonica
> Ficus benjamina
> Ficus elastica decora
> Ficus lyrata
> Grevillea robusta
> Palms
> Philodendron bipinnatifidum
> Schefflera actinophylla
> Yucca

CLIMBING PLANTS

Many climbers make excellent Specimen Plants, and the more vigorous ones can be used to provide a large, leafy specimen at the lowest possible cost. You can choose a foliage type (Philodendrons, Vines, etc) or a flowering climber (Hoya, Thunbergia, etc). Good examples are

> Cissus
> Monstera
> Passiflora
> Philodendron hastatum
> Philodendron panduraeforme
> Rhoicissus
> Scindapsus
> Stephanotis

HANGING PLANTS

Some hanging plants are showy enough to be displayed on their own in hanging baskets or on pedestals rather than as part of a Plant Group. Good examples are

> Chlorophytum
> Columnea
> Nephrolepis
> Zygocactus

MULTICOLOURED FOLIAGE PLANTS

Many popular house plants have multicoloured foliage, and the most dramatic varieties are frequently used as Specimen Plants. Good examples are

> Begonia rex
> Caladium
> Codiaeum
> Cordyline terminalis
> Nidularium
> Rhoeo

FLOWERING POT PLANTS

Some flowering pot plants are so colourful that they are best displayed on their own. Good examples are

> Azalea indica
> Begonia tuberhybrida
> Cyclamen
> Garden Bulbs
> Gloxinia
> Hydrangea
> Pelargonium
> Poinsettia

The Right Position

HANGING FROM THE CEILING There is no finer way of displaying a trailing plant than suspending it in a container attached to the ceiling or a wall bracket. Nothing impedes the cascading stems, and the sight of living plants in mid-air has a special attraction. We notice the plants in a hanging basket on the wall of a house and we wouldn't give them a second glance if they were growing in the bed below. A hanging Specimen Plant can be used to add height to a floor-standing display or to add interest and colour to a dull side or alcove window. There is, unfortunately, a rather long list of warnings. Don't have a hanging display in the line of traffic if the ceiling is low — plants must never be part of an obstacle course. Choose the container with care (see page 32) and make sure that the attachment to the ceiling or wall is strong enough to withstand the weight of the container and the compost just after watering. The plant must be a fine specimen and in peak condition — a bedraggled Ivy or a trailing stem or two of Philodendron scandens may actually diminish the beauty of the environment. Plant care is not easy — it is obviously more difficult to water a hanging display than its floor-standing or windowsill-sitting counterpart — yet high displays need more frequent watering than low ones.

SITTING ON A WINDOWSILL People who regard their house plants as green pets rather than display material generally choose the windowsill as the favourite place to house them. Here they can be watched, watered and carefully tended. This does not mean that plants in the window do not fit into the interior decorator's scheme of things, but the line of several separated pots neatly placed along the sill is neither one thing nor the other. From the display point of view it is much better to use an eye-catching Specimen Plant — low and bushy if sited in the middle of the window or tall and narrow if placed on one side. Choose a type with leaves which are enhanced by light shining through or on them — examples are Caladium and Iresine. Of course you must keep the plant in keeping with its surroundings — a small and insignificant plant in a large window has little display value. Choose the plant with care — if the window faces east, south or west you will need one which can withstand some direct sun — a south-facing window will need some form of screen against the hot summer sun. Check the compost frequently — with the sun in summer and the radiator below in winter, watering can be a never-ending chore! If the view from the window is not important and you don't need the light, consider having a hanging plant above and a sill-borne one below. Alternatively you can make a Display Window (see page 27).

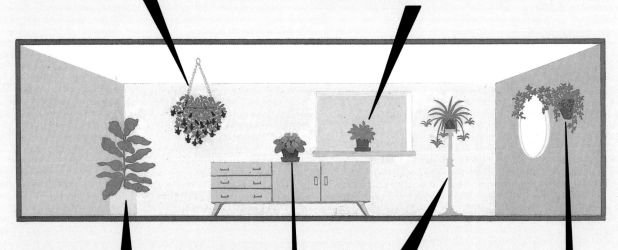

STANDING ON THE FLOOR The place for the large Specimen Plant is on the floor — placing a heavy pot on a table can make it look unsafe. Bold Architectural plants are the usual choice, but there are other possibilities. Flowering standards (see page 177) are best displayed in this way. Tall climbers with large leaves (Philodendron, Monstera etc) also make excellent floor-standing specimens — use a moss stick (see page 114) to support climbers with aerial roots. Interior designers love floor-standing Specimen Plants. A matched pair on either side of a door adds symmetry in a large room — a pot stood near a patio door brings the garden indoors. A floor-standing plant must be chosen with care. Narrow, upright plants can make the ceiling look higher — low, spreading ones have the opposite effect. It is important to choose the right receptacle — remember it can damage the carpet so place a piece of wood or cork below it.

STANDING ON FURNITURE Small Specimen Plants need to be raised off the ground so that they can be enjoyed at close range. The usual way to do this is to place the pot on a windowsill, shelf or piece of furniture. You must use a drip tray which is deep enough to protect the surface of the furniture — mop up any spillage immediately.

STANDING ON A PEDESTAL A number of indoor plants produce long pendulous stems or arching leaves and the display is often spoilt if the pot is stood on a sideboard or windowsill. The place for such plants is in a hanging container or on a pedestal. You can buy a reproduction antique pedestal if your home is decorated in this style, but for modern surroundings it is extremely simple to make a wooden pillar with straight sides. To house several pots in a pedestal-like arrangement you can buy a metal or cane plant stand. See page 27 for details of this type of Pot Group.

GROWING AGAINST A WALL The plants most usually grown against a wall are flowering types (to provide a splash of colour against a pastel wall) and trailers (to frame windows, pictures, etc). There are a number of difficulties — it is not easy to create moist conditions, the pot is often small which means that constant watering is essential, and it is difficult to tell when the plant requires watering in a high-mounted display. Choose a receptacle which is soundly made, not too ornate and with a saucer which is both large and deep.

One plant — Nine impressions

Dusty leaves

Washed leaves

Polished leaves

Plain background

Mirrored background

Patterned background

Uplighting

Spotlighting

Backlighting

THE Pot Group

The simple step of bringing together several isolated plants to make a Pot Group can add a new dimension to your indoor display. There are three basic reasons for this transformation:

- The overall effect is much bolder than can be achieved with individual pots. Plants at the rear of the group can be raised to give added height.
- Small-leaved plants such as Ficus pumila, Adiantum, Helxine and Tradescantia can seem insignificant and uninteresting when grown in isolated pots, but suddenly come to life when grouped with large-leaved varieties and so add an important ingredient to the overall effect.
- Individual perfection, so important with the Specimen Plant, is not vital. Bare stems, lop-sided growth and damaged leaves can all be easily hidden by surrounding them with other plants.

The advantage of grouping is not just a matter of appearance; there are also cultural benefits. Watering is an easier task when plants are collected together rather than scattered around the room. The close proximity of other plants and a large expanse of moist compost means that the air humidity around the foliage is increased, and this can be vitally important for a delicate variety.

The house plant owner has the satisfaction of creating an individual arrangement. Various groupings are shown on these two pages, but there are no hard and fast rules except that plants should, wherever possible, have the same basic light and warmth requirements. At first glance the Pot Group would seem to be less desirable than the more natural-looking Indoor Garden, where the pots are either removed or hidden. But the groupings on this page have an important advantage — pots can be treated separately which means that water-loving plants such as Chlorophytum can be grown alongside desert plants such as Cacti and Succulents.

THE STANDARD GROUP

Between four and a dozen clay or plastic pots are closely grouped together to produce a pleasing arrangement in which both shapes and tints are varied. In the most usual grouping foliage plants are used to provide the permanent framework and flowering pot plants are used to provide splashes of colour. The taller plants, the darker greens and the larger leaves are placed at the back of the group.

It is a basic error to assume that you *must* create a riot of different colours and a wide variety of shapes in order to give your Pot Group a professional touch. The skilled interior decorator will sometimes use only foliage plants, relying on different leaf forms and variegation to produce an attractive display.

THE PROFESSIONAL GROUP

This type of display, much loved by interior designers, is the big brother of the Standard Group. Although it is usually found in public buildings, a simple version is worth considering for a bare corner in your home. Pot Holders are an important feature of the Professional Group — they are decorative and of different heights. The one at the back of the group is either much taller than the others or is raised on a block of wood to display to the maximum the pinnacle plant it contains — a Kentia Palm in the illustration above. The pot holder at the front of the group holds a large flowering pot plant which is replaced when its display is finished. A trailing plant is grown in one of the middle containers and its stems are allowed to drape over the base unit.

THE PEBBLE TRAY

Grouping plants within a shallow tray is a useful technique for maintaining plants which need high humidity in a centrally-heated room. If you have difficulty in growing African Violets then try them in a Pebble Tray. The tray should be about 2 in. high, and can be made of any waterproof material. The dimensions are up to you, but avoid a dangerously wide overhang if the tray is to be stood on a windowsill.

Place 1 in. of gravel in the bottom of the tray and keep the bottom of this layer wet at all times. The water level, however, must not be allowed to cover the top of the gravel. Group the plants on the surface.

A favourite place for a Pebble Tray is on a radiator shelf below a windowsill. In this situation the humidity around the plants in winter will be trebled. Watering plants is a simple matter — allow excess water to run out of the pots and into the gravel.

THE COLLECTION

A group of pots containing closely related plants can be found in the homes of people at both ends of the house plant knowledge scale. The young beginner often starts with a collection of Succulents and Cacti, grouped neatly on a windowsill . . . in the home of the keen indoor gardener you will often find a prized collection of his or her speciality — Ferns, African Violets, Orchids, etc. In the U.K. collections are usually housed in a spot exposed to natural light; in the U.S. the fluorescent-lit plant table is popular — see page 225.

Collections, big and small, have one feature in common. Unlike the Standard Group where the overall decorative effect is all-important, the basic purpose of the Collection is to highlight the individuality, rarity or beauty of each plant.

THE DISPLAY WINDOW

The Display Window turns an ordinary window into a tiered arrangement of flowers and greenery. Shelves of glass or transparent plastic are fixed across the window opening at convenient heights, and the pots are arranged along each shelf. You will either love or hate the Display Window — to some it is an excellent way to show off their Cacti and Succulents, or their range of flowering plants and other sun lovers. To others this type of Pot Group is far too regimented, with several rows of pots one above the other standing at attention. If you do go ahead, go all the way and make sure that the whole of the glass area is used for display purposes. A thing of beauty for you, perhaps, but a nightmare for the window cleaner!

THE VERTICAL DISPLAY

The Pot Group is nearly always a horizontal display, although the pots are sometimes set at different heights. The Vertical Group, however, is both easily arranged and can be extremely effective. The traditional version is a corner shelf unit with a pot on each shelf — use the same variety of colourful trailing plant to produce a column of foliage or flowers. A series of hanging baskets attached to each other can be used to give the same effect — the metal or cane plant stand which carries pots at different heights has the advantage of portability.

THE
Indoor Garden

Find a container which is large enough to hold several indoor plants — it should be attractive in shape, colour and design. Now plant out the specimens into potting compost you have placed inside the container; alternatively stand the pots on a layer of peat, sand, gravel or pebbles and surround each pot with damp peat so that the clay or plastic is no longer visible. You now have an Indoor Garden.

Your Indoor Garden may be five small plants in a bowl or it may be a forest of greenery and flowers in a multi-tiered Planter, but the basic advantages and principles of construction remain the same. Some of the advantages of the Indoor Garden are similar to those of the Pot Group — the creation of a bold effect, the proper utilisation of insignificant foliage and flowers, the hiding of ugly bare stems and damaged leaves, the ease of watering and the creation of moist conditions around the foliage. But the 'natural' effect is much more dramatic than with the Pot Group — here you are truly gardening.

Surprisingly, indoor gardening remains an unusual concept because there is still a strange reluctance to growing house plants in groups rather than as individual specimens. Colourful plants such as Begonia semperflorens and Coleus can be bedded out in the home as they are in the garden, but they are nearly always grown indoors as single plants in solitary pots. As every gardener knows, most ordinary shrubs, perennials and roses look best when grown with other plants in a bed or border, but very rarely do we find a bed or border indoors. The Multiple Planter (see page 30) undoubtedly offers the greatest scope for a bold display, but any large Planter will do. The fact remains that many house plants look better and thrive better when grown in the company of others.

There are several reasons why most plants grow much better in an Indoor Garden than in a solitary pot. Higher humidity, insulation of the roots from sudden changes in temperature and the water reservoir below each pot are amongst the most important benefits. But there are dangers, and you should be on your guard against them. Close planting means reduced ventilation, and so the chance of pest and disease attack is increased. Prune or remove plants to avoid overcrowding and cut off mouldy leaves or flowers immediately they are seen.

The Ingredients of the Indoor Garden

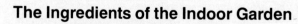

PLANT
All the plants in a container will receive approximately the same conditions of moisture and warmth. Light conditions will also be similar across a small Indoor Garden, but the plants at the back of a corner unit or in the centre of a large square unit may receive appreciably less light than the unshaded plants at the edges. For planting suggestions see page 33 — the standard pattern is to have a permanent foliage background with splashes of colour provided by flowering plants.

POT
It is much better to leave the plants in their pots rather than planting them directly into the compost. In this way plants can be occasionally turned to prevent one-sided growth and to stop them rooting into the surrounding peat. Plants can also be easily removed when flowering is over or when repotting is necessary. The individual pots must have drainage holes.

PEAT
Make sure that the peat reaches to the rim of each pot and keep it moist but not saturated. This damp peat will provide a moisture reserve beneath each pot, which means that a plant will survive much better in an Indoor Garden than in an isolated pot if regular watering is interrupted at holiday time.

CONTAINER
There is an almost limitless range of watertight containers from which you can take your choice — plastic tubs, ornate jardinières, old copper steamers, home-made boxes and so on. If the container is made of wood, the inner surface and corners must be waterproof. You can use polyurethane varnish, good quality sealant, a polythene liner but never creosote.

SOAKAWAY
A soakaway is not essential but it is a good idea to place a layer of gravel, small pebbles or coarse sand at the bottom of the container before adding peat. Include lumps of charcoal if you have this material available.

THE PLANTER

The single Planter is the most popular of all Indoor Gardens. Until recently long troughs of metal, wood or plastic were the only popular containers, but there is now a wide range of cylindrical and cubic containers in every shade of tough plastic. A black or white Planter is recommended for modern decor.

Water carefully so that the surrounding peat does not become waterlogged. If the pots are stood on a thick layer of peat, the roots can be allowed to grow through the drainage holes and into the moist peat so that the Planter becomes a self-watering one. The usual recommendation where the pots stand on a shallow layer of gravel or peat is to lift or turn the pots occasionally to prevent rooting.

The size of Planters varies enormously. Egg-cups have been used for tiny Succulents — at the other end of the scale Indoor Gardens draining into the hardcore of the house have been built into the floors of the homes of the rich and design-conscious.

Whatever the size, the effect will be enhanced if you choose the right background for your Planter. Plain wood and mirror or mirror tiles are ideal.

THE MULTIPLE PLANTER

Flowering Pot Plants

Foliage House Plants

Bedding with one variety of flowering plants

The simplest form consists of two or more ordinary containers pushed together to form a Multiple Planter. The best form is a tailor-made garden designed to fit the allotted space. The average handyman can quite easily construct a Multiple Planter from plastic-coated board — for maximum effect the planting units should be on different levels. The cracks between the boards must be sealed.

Each planting unit can be treated individually from both the planting and cultural standpoint. In the illustration flowering pot plants are grown in the unit closest to the window, the lowest unit is used for indoor bedding (Wax Begonia, Coleus, Crocus, etc) which changes with the season and finally the tallest units provide a permanent backcloth of foliage house plants. An added advantage is that each unit can be individually watered so that moisture-lovers can be grown alongside Cacti and Succulents.

Several proprietary types of vertical Multiple Planter are available. Each unit is clipped on to the one below to form a tower — plants are potted into the open side of each unit.

THE POT-ET-FLEUR

The Pot-et-Fleur is essentially a small Planter in which a group of foliage house plants is grown. During its construction a glass tube or metal florist tube is sunk into the peat between the pots. Subsequently this tube is filled with water and used for arranging cut flowers. In this way flowers from the garden or florist can be used to produce ever-changing and colourful displays.

At the beginning of the year 3 or 4 Daffodils against a living green backcloth look most attractive. During summer a few blooms from the flower garden or shrub border — Roses are excellent. Do not aim for a skilled arrangement — just a few points of colour to add interest to a group of house plants. The obvious favourite for Christmas time is a sprig or two of berried Holly.

Surprisingly the idea has never become popular — flower arrangers find the Pot-et-Fleur too limiting for their skills. The mistake is regarding it as a hybrid of pot plant culture and flower arranging — it is in fact a house plant display with a few seasonal flowers to brighten it up.

THE HANGING BASKET

A group of attractive indoor plants in a hanging basket will indeed provide a beautiful display, but do not rush into hanging a container from a hook in the ceiling or a bracket on the wall until you have carefully studied the difficulties.

The air will be warmer and drier than at floor or windowsill level. The height of the display usually makes watering difficult, and when water is applied too liberally the basket may drip on to the floor.

You must choose a container which is suitable for indoors. The standard wire basket lined with sphagnum moss is ideal for outdoors, but in the home you will have the problem of water dripping on to the floor. You can line the basket with polythene sheet, but waterlogging may then be a problem. The best answer is to put the pots of plants in a larger waterproof container which bears the holding wires, chains or cords. The space between the pots and the hanging container should be filled with moist peat. A variation is a plastic hanging pot with a built-in drip tray. Always use a peat-based potting compost rather than a soil one — excess weight can be a problem.

To make watering and misting an easier task place the display at eye-level or if you must suspend it over head-high then have a pulley arrangement instead of an ordinary hook. You can buy a pump-action watering can if the display cannot be lowered. Ensure that the hook is securely fixed to a ceiling joist or the bracket is firmly attached to the wall, and finally make sure that your choice of plants is suited to the light available — flowering plants and variegated foliage house plants will need a spot near a window.

Good hanging basket plants:

Aporocactus	Chlorophytum	Hoya	Setcreasea
Asparagus	Episcia	Lobelia	Tradescantia
Begonia	Fuchsia	Pelargonium	Zebrina
Campanula	Hedra	Scindapsus	Zygocactus

THE MIXED BOWL

One of the simplest of all Indoor Gardens, in which a small selection of foliage plants and one or two flowering plants are removed from their pots and planted in a peat-based compost. The traditional pattern is to have a large pinnacle plant towards the back of the bowl, several compact bushy plants in the middle and a trailing plant at the front. The container is usually a bulb bowl, but any waterproof bowl will do.

A Mixed Bowl is always a welcome present to receive, but it is not a *permanent* Indoor Garden. When the flowers fade the best plan is to break up the arrangement and repot the individual plants before the roots become hopelessly intertwined. Explain to the donor, if necessary, that you are not destroying her present — you are preserving it.

Planting suggestions for an Indoor Garden

You will be able to make your selection from scores of different varieties — let the A-Z sections later in this book be your guide. Aim for closely-matched requirements for heat, light and water whenever you can. Remember that you have to live with the Indoor Garden, so choose colour and form which you find pleasing.

The next step is to make sure that the height and shape of the plants are in keeping with the size of the container. Aim for a variation in height, a contrast in leaf shape and texture, and a controlled use of colour.

First of all, the tall plant or plants ('pinnacle' plants) which give height to the display. Be careful in small Indoor Gardens that you don't choose a wide-spreading giant which dwarfs and shades all others. Sansevieria provides height without spread, and feathery-leaved plants such as Grevillea and Dizygotheca avoid the shading effect of large leaves. The choice of pinnacle plants for a large Planter is of course much easier — Palms, Dracaena, Ficus, Monstera and Philodendron are all widely used.

For most displays it is the medium-sized range of plants which form the basic framework. If you don't want to rely on flowering pot plants for colour you can use some non-green foliage varieties — red-leaved Cordyline terminalis, yellow Scindapsus, variegated Chlorophytum and Ivies, and the multicoloured Croton, Coleus and Begonia rex.

Finally, don't forget the trailers which are needed to soften the hard line of the edge of the container. The popular four are Ivy, Tradescantia, Ficus pumila and Zebrina, but there are others. Gynura, Asparagus sprengeri, Plectranthus or Pelargonium peltatum can be used as alternatives.

THE MINIATURE GARDEN

This special type of Indoor Garden is an attempt to reproduce an outdoor garden on a small scale. Paths, pools, figurines, etc, are used for decoration and mossy turfs plus tiny-leaved plants are used for landscaping. Japanese styles are popular, and the Miniature Garden is usually kept on a trolley so that it can be wheeled outside in fine weather and into the kitchen for watering. This style of Indoor Garden is really for the keen hobbyist, as upkeep is difficult and without a high degree of artistry the result can appear distinctly amateurish.

THE DISH GARDEN

A small Indoor Garden made in a shallow dish using carefully-chosen Succulents. Unlike other Indoor Garden containers the dish usually has drainage holes. For further details see page 104.

THE LIVING SCREEN

The eating area in a combined living/dining room can be separated in many ways. A wooden divider unit is sometimes used — a few pots in the open spaces will help to enliven such a unit. A living screen is preferred by many plant-lovers. A deep and reasonably wide trough is placed on the floor and a trellis or series of decorative poles secured in the compost so the support runs from floor to ceiling. Pots are then inserted in the compost — suitable plants are Cissus, Syngonium, Hedera, Ficus benjamina, Scindapsus, Philodendron scandens and Ficus pumila.

THE Terrarium

A Terrarium has two basic features. It surrounds the plants completely or almost completely with glass or some other transparent material, and access to the outside air is either strictly limited or non-existent. As a result plant-killing draughts are excluded and the air within is always moister than the room atmosphere. The result is that a wide range of delicate plants can be grown which would fail miserably if grown outside the Terrarium under ordinary room conditions.

Planting suggestions for a Bottle Garden

The range of plants you can grow in a Bottle Garden with a restricted or closed top is strictly limited. Do not use flowering plants, quick-growing foliage plants, Cacti or Succulents.

Choose from the following list and buy small specimens:

Acorus	Hedera helix (small-leaved var.)
Begonia rex (small-leaved var.)	Maranta
Calathea	Neanthe bella
Cryptanthus	Pellionia
Dracaena sanderana	Peperomia
Ferns	Pilea
Ficus pumila	Saxifraga sarmentosa
Fittonia	Selaginella

The varieties to choose depend, of course, on where you place the Terrarium. If placed well away from the light it can be used to house Ferns and other green-leaved plants. When part of a window, the Terrarium is an excellent home for Orchids, Bromeliads, exotic foliage plants and all the dazzling flowering plants listed in the A-Z guides as needing some direct sun and moist air.

The reason why the Terrarium has remained the Cinderella of indoor plants is hard to understand. It cannot be a matter of cost, because suitable containers are to be found in most homes. All you need is a goldfish bowl, fish tank, large bottle or even a large glass mixing bowl. The only requirements are transparent sides and either a restricted neck or an opening which can be covered with glass or transparent plastic. Nor can this lack of general acceptance be due to the newness of the idea. Fern-cases were all the rage in the 1850s — these were ornate examples of the Wardian Case (see page 163) used to house Ferns and other delicate foliage plants in Victorian parlours. Also in Victorian times the noted horticultural author Shirley Hibberd actively promoted the idea of a glass extension for plants built out from an ordinary window — his *hortus fenestralis*.

So it has been a story of ups and downs for Terraria. After the Victorian boom the idea was neglected in Britain, but the Plant Window became popular in some countries during the 20th century. For the U.K. it was the Bottle (Carboy) Garden which first reached some degree of popularity, but it is the shop-bought version of the Fishtank Garden, made from soldered metal strips and glass panes, which is now beginning to overtake the glass carboy.

THE PLANT WINDOW

The most successful of all Terraria is the Plant Window. It is essentially a window with an external pane or panes of glass (double-glazed to provide winter insulation) and an internal fully-glazed door which can be opened to get to the space within. At the base of this space is a tray filled with gravel in which the pots are housed and then hidden with damp peat.

Plant Windows are a feature of many homes in Germany, Scandinavia, Holland and parts of the U.S. — but are a rarity in British houses. This type of display is generally built at the time of house construction — it is a difficult task to construct one on to an existing building. The Plant Window floor is generally 1½ – 2½ ft wide and there are a number of basic features which must be provided. Some form of shading will be needed if the window faces south, and a ventilator is usually essential. There are all sorts of optional extras — fluorescent lighting, piped water supply, underfloor heating, automatically controlled humidifiers and ventilators, etc.

A Plant Window can truly be a thing of beauty. The atmosphere is even better than that in a conservatory for jungle plants. Here you can grow Orchids, Anthuriums, Bougainvilleas, Columneas, Caladiums and Acalyphas to perfection, but a lot of work is involved. Careful watering is essential and ventilation must be regularly adjusted to prevent misting. Plants must be groomed and the glass must be cleaned at regular intervals.

THE FISHTANK GARDEN

A glass-cased garden which opens at the top is known as a Fishtank Garden — the many attractive glass cases which open at the side are sold simply as Terraria.

The treatment of both is the same. Begin by placing a layer of gravel and charcoal at the bottom of the container and then add a 2 in. layer of seed and cutting compost. You can landscape the 'ground' into hills and valleys — use stones and pebbles if you wish but do not incorporate wood.

There is an extensive range of plants which are suitable for the Fishtank Garden or shop-bought Terrarium. It is a pity to waste such a good home on commonplace plants. Delicate Ferns, Crotons, Fittonia, Maranta, Cryptanthus, Calathea, Selaginella and Rhoeo will all flourish. Between the foliage add flowering varieties to provide splashes of colour — African Violets and small Orchids are ideal. Two warnings — never use Cacti or Succulents and always leave room between the plants so that they will be able to spread without becoming cramped.

After planting cover the top with a sheet of glass with bevelled edges. Close the door of a standard Terrarium. Stand it in a well-lit spot out of direct sunlight. If excessive condensation appears, slide open the lid or door for a few hours, but keep it shut at other times. There is little else to do — remove dead or diseased leaves and water every few months. This portable mini-jungle is the easiest way to grow exotic plants.

THE BOTTLE GARDEN

It is curious that until recently the only popular type of Terrarium in Britain was the Carboy or Bottle Garden. It is difficult to make, requiring special tools and some dexterity. First of all, make sure that the bottle is clean and dry. Insert a stiff paper cone in the mouth and pour in a 2 in. layer of gravel. Add a thin layer of charcoal and finally a thick layer of Seed and Cutting Compost. Firm the compost with a tamper (a cotton reel at the end of a bamboo cane) and then build up the compost to form the back of the garden.

Now introduce the plants — for planting suggestions, see page 34. You will need about six, including one tree-like specimen and at least one trailer. The planting tools are a dessert spoon at the end of one cane and a fork at the end of another. Firm the compost around each plant with the tamper.

Your Bottle Garden is now finished and is ready for watering. Use a long-necked watering can and train a gentle stream of water against the glass. Use very little water — just enough to clean the glass and moisten the surface. Insert the stopper; if the glass clouds over later, then remove the stopper until the condensation disappears. Re-insert the stopper — you will probably never have to water again.

CHAPTER 3

THE HISTORY OF INDOOR PLANTS

It is probably right and proper that books on house plants should be filled with down-to-earth advice on growing and displaying the varieties we buy. Care, problems and propagation are dealt with at length, but one subject is missing. The history of plants in the home is usually ignored or outlined very sketchily. The Victorians loved them, the between-the-Wars people ignored them and the post-1950 houseowners rediscovered them.

There is much more to the house plant story than that, and the plot has its fair share of surprises. The starting point, however, is hazy and we can only guess at who began it all. Most historians think it was the Chinese — there is some evidence that plants were grown in palace gardens in the East about 5000 years ago.

We know that plants were grown in containers in Ancient Egypt, and it seems that Rameses III began the European potted plant story about 3000 years ago. The most breathtaking example of container planting in the Ancient World was in the Hanging Gardens of Babylon created by Nebuchadnezzar for his wife Amytis in about 580 BC. Along the towering terraces were 4 ft wide columns made of sun-baked brick and filled with earth. These were planted with large trees — a pot plant display which has hardly ever been rivalled. The Ancient Greeks had roofs and courtyards filled with plants in terracotta pots, but once again there is scant evidence that the pots were actually moved inside.

As we move forward in history the evidence for indoor plant culture becomes stronger. The Romans brought Roses from Rhodes and Egypt and induced winter blooming by growing them in structures with thin sheets of mica forming the roofs. Heated greenhouses — an idea which was lost with the fall of Rome and did not reappear for 1500 years! Not everyone at the time liked this brilliant idea which was the starting point of growing under glass — the writer Seneca wrote "Do not those live contrary to nature who require a rose in

House plants in Ancient Rome — an atrium (open-ceiling room) in Pompeii

winter and who, by the excitement of hot water and an appropriate modification of heat, force from winter the late blooms of spring?"

Forcing Roses to bloom before their natural season is not the same as growing plants for interior decoration. The city of Pompeii was buried under lava in 79 AD — its excavation has given us a detailed picture of how the Romans lived. The larger houses had an atrium — a room with a partly open roof. It seems quite clear that pots of terracotta or stone were kept here — pots filled with Laurel, Myrtle or Pomegranate.

The indoor plant picture grows dim again as we move from the Roman Empire to the Dark Ages in the early centuries of the Christian Era. There is little doubt that pots of herbs and sweet-smelling plants were kept in cottages and monasteries, but written or painted records on the subject are almost non-existent. The Crusaders are assumed to have brought back some exotic plants from Asia Minor in the 11th and 12th centuries, but we know nothing of their fate. In both the 13th and 14th centuries there were isolated instances of both flowers and fruits being forced under glass, but the start of the house plant story was still to come.

We have so far seen a number of firsts — the first pot plants at the start of recorded history, the first greenhouse in Ancient Rome and in Chapter 7 the first movement of plants from one country to another at the time of the Pharaohs in Egypt. But we still haven't seen the first 'house plant' as we popularly understand the term — a plant which will grow and look attractive indoors and which in a temperate climate is not suitable for all-the-year-round outdoor cultivation. In nearly all cases such plants are exotics originally imported from tropical or sub-tropical areas.

The house plant story began at the beginning of the 15th century when trading ships brought back to Venice and Genoa exotic plants from Asia — plants such as Hibiscus and Jasmine. Wealthy Italian merchants bought them and placed the plants both outside and inside their grand houses — the house plant story had begun.

First the Dutch and then the British, French and Germans turned to this idea of growing tender exotic plants in the 16th century. For them there was only one plant — the Orange. Aristocrats everywhere planted them in large tubs and placed them in groves along the pathways during the summer months. In the winter the tubs were moved into wooden sheds which were heated by coal fires — dismal places in which many plants died. Correspondence by Lord Burghley in 1561 described this early cultivation of the Orange in England, but there was no 'indoor plant' aspect to it — the Oranges were merely hibernated over winter.

The interior of the orangery at Saltram (Devon). It was built in 1773 – 1775, and is still used for overwintering Orange trees

With the start of the 17th century things began to change. These Orange shelters became permanent stone or brick buildings and from about 1620 onwards glass was introduced into the walls. The age of the orangery had arrived, and many fine examples were built between 1675 and 1775. You can see them today at Longleat, Hampton Court, Woburn, Saltram, Charlecote Park, Kew, Powis Castle, Burghley and many other stately homes. The trees came from abroad and so did the information — *The Management, Ordering, and use of the Lemon and Orange Trees* (1683) was translated from the Dutch original.

Before the arrival of the 18th century a new type of structure began to be erected — the greenhouse. It is believed that the word was coined by John Evelyn in his *Kalendarium Hortense* in 1664. At first the difference between the greenhouses and the orangeries of the day was slight — the only point of variance was that the greenhouse was designed for the protection of a wide range of plants. No longer was it just a matter of Oranges — thousands of exotic plants had been introduced to Europe from India, America and Asia. In 1677 the catalogue of William Lucas, Nurseryman, offered plants of Orange, Lemon, Olive, Pomegranate, Oleander, Jasmine and Jerusalem Cherry. Thus the greenhouse was designed to protect a wide range of frost-sensitive exotics, but it remained an inefficient structure until the start of the 19th century.

There were two problems. The first one was heating, and the first attempt with open fires, wood-burning stoves and pans of hot charcoal led to disastrous losses as the plants succumbed to the fumes from the burning fuel. Things improved greatly when it was discovered that heat could be generated by heaping dung and the wood bark used in tanning ('tan bark') within the house. Hot air passing through pipes leading from sealed furnaces was a further improvement, but it was not until the hot water system with a boiler and external stove took over in the 19th century that a clean atmosphere free from plant-killing fumes was possible. The second problem was the absence of light — for most of the 18th century greenhouses continued to have one or more glazed walls and a solid roof — it was not until the end of the century that the greenhouse turned into a glasshouse with a glazed roof and glass walls.

So far we have been concerned with the cultivation of frost-sensitive plants in temperate countries. This involved the use of orangeries and then greenhouses by the aristocracy, botanical gardens and keen amateur horticulturalists so that they could grow their 'exotiks'. This activity was important in the history of house plants as it enabled thousands of delicate varieties to be grown. It also stimulated plant collectors to roam the world to look for new specimens . . . but it had nothing to do with growing plants purely for decoration in the living rooms of ordinary houses.

Few books touched on this humble subject before the 19th century. Sir Hugh Platt's *Garden of Eden* (1594) was the first, describing the cultivation of herbs (Rosemary, Basil, Marjoram) and Carnations in the house. Fairchild's *City Gardener* (1722) recommended the use of Vines, Aloes and some Cacti for indoor display. But there was very little written on the subject when the House Plant Craze started in about 1820. Of course, this does not mean that plants were unknown in

*Teatime in a Victorian country cottage.
No Palms and no ornate pot holders — just a line
of terracotta flower pots on the windowsill*

the living room before the start of the 19th century. For generations pots of herbs, Lychnis, Campanula etc had been kept on windowsills, and before the start of the House Plant Craze there were pots of Chlorophytum, Pelargonium, Cacti, Aloe and so on in the rooms of cottages, farmhouses etc. The basic point is that these plants were part of the rural domestic scenery — they were not fashionable.

Things changed quite dramatically in the 1820s — the interest in having plants indoors grew and grew until no self-respecting parlour would be without its pedestal and every villa had its Palm. This Victorian phase did not begin with the foliage plants associated with it — the Palm, the Aspidistra and the Fern. The early years were a time for Cacti and Succulents, together with a wide range of flowering plants.

Then something happened — gas was introduced in the urban areas during the 1840s, and many flowering house plants were no longer able to survive. In the middle-class villas with coal-gas illumination the Palms, Rubber Plants and the Aspidistras of the 1850s took over, because these foliage plants were able to withstand the effect of gas fumes. But the Victorian scene was not all Palms and Aspidistras.

Firstly there was the fern-case — an ornate terrarium which housed ferns and occasionally other delicate plants. The enclosed specimens were protected from fumes, and 'pteridomania' gripped Britain from 1855 to 1870. This love of ferns and the fanciful glass, brass and wooden structures which housed them spread to the U.S. but not to other countries in Europe. It came suddenly, and died just as quickly, in Britain.

*Teatime in a fashionable Victorian house.
The large conservatory is filled with foliage and flowering
plants — Palms, Strelitzia, Monstera, Ferns, Musa, Aloe . . .*

A much grander structure than the simple fern-case was the conservatory. These glass structures appeared all over the country during the 1850s. The conservatory was attached to the house, and its purpose was to display plants picturesquely, like the 'winter gardens' which preceded them, rather than serve merely as a home for exotics, like the greenhouse in the garden.

Several factors combined to make the conservatory boom possible. Hot-water boiler systems had been introduced, which meant the end of plant-killing coal-fire fumes. Sheet glass was introduced in 1832 and the Glass Tax was lifted in 1845. By 1851 glass was a cheap building material and so the conservatory craze began.

This was the hey-day of the Victorian house plant boom, and it is nonsense to think of it as a time of dull foliage plants. More than half the plants being introduced from abroad were now conservatory plants, and the range grown was enormous. A partial list includes Aloe, Anthurium, Araucaria, Aspidistra, Beaucarnea, Begonia, Browallia, Caladium, Calceolaria, Camellia, Canna, Celosia, Cineraria, Cuphea, Cycas, Cyperus, Datura, Dianthus, Dracaena, Eucalyptus, Ferns, Ficus, Fuchsia, Grevillea, Hedera, Heliotropium, Musa, Nerium, Palms, Passiflora, Pelargonium, Rohdea, Saxifraga . . . the conservatories of a hundred years ago were places of delight.

At work in a Victorian conservatory,
with neither a Palm nor an Aspidistra in sight

So the larger houses had their conservatories and the middle-class villas had Palms, Aspidistras, Rubber Plants and Cyperus in the heavily-curtained parlours. But in the cottages of Britain pots of flowering plants still lined the windowsills and the working classes grew their 'mechanics' plants' such as the Auricula and Pot Leek.

Towards the end of the 19th century there was a craze for collecting Orchids, and some fetched huge prices. But it was the beginning of the house plant decline in Britain — a new century dawned and the 1914–1918 War changed many things. One of the casualties was the House Plant Craze.

Between 1920 and 1945 Britain turned to cut flowers. In most homes the potted plant was scorned as a symbol of the over-ornate Victorian Age. Not all were lost — Palms and a few Ferns continued to adorn hotels and a few public buildings, and pots of flowers appeared on the windowsills of country cottages. A few Aspidistras were retained for sentimental reasons (some flourish to this day as a memory of great-grandmother) but the popular appeal of the house plant had gone.

The United States also suffered a reaction away from indoor plants in the 1920s, but a recovery started in the 30s. Philodendron scandens caught the popular imagination and the African Violet was beginning its phenomenal success story. Europe never lost interest to the same extent as Britain and the U.S. — the house plant light never went out in Scandinavia, Holland or Germany.

Since 1950 there has been a rebirth of interest in the U.K. and a great increase in plant numbers in other countries. The British renaissance was led by Thomas Rochford III, first with Ivies and Rubber Plants and then with a host of foliage and flowering varieties. House plants are once again present in nearly every home, and the choice is enormous. The boom is set to continue because we have things which the Victorians never enjoyed. Rooms are lighter and warmer, and a host of varieties can be purchased on the High St. Popular plants such as Poinsettia, Rubber Plant, Begonia and so on have been bred to take out their temperamental nature and a wide array of colourful new ones such as Pot Chrysanthemums have appeared. The history of house plants is a continuing story — we may have only just reached the most interesting chapter.

CHAPTER 4
FOLIAGE HOUSE PLANTS

Foliage house plants make up the permanent framework of an indoor plant collection. Here are the plants which remain green throughout the year, their attraction arising from the beauty of each individual leaf (e.g Monstera deliciosa and Begonia rex) or from the overall effect of the foliage (e.g Asparagus and Chlorophytum).

A few of these plants, such as Zebrina and Sansevieria occasionally produce small flowers, but it is for their leaves and general growth habit that specimens of this group are grown. This does not mean that they can only provide a dull green background — Coleus, Croton, Gynura, Begonia, Maranta and many others offer a multicoloured display. Even more types have foliage which is lined, splashed or spotted with white or cream — Tradescantia, Dieffenbachia, Chlorophytum, Scindapsus and Ivy are just a few examples.

These plants *belong* indoors. Some of them appreciate a winter holiday in an unheated room away from the family but not for them the fate of flowering pot plants — the end-of-season dustbin, the enforced summer outdoors or a stemless winter indoors. With proper care many varieties are capable of outliving their owners, but a few do deteriorate with age. Coleus tends to become unattractive after a year or two and so do Gynura and Hypoestes. The answer is to raise cuttings and replace the parent plant. The only 'temporary' foliage house plant is Caladium, which spends each winter as a dormant tuber.

It is impossible to generalise about the proper care of foliage house plants; a few are extremely delicate and some have cast-iron constitutions. The popular types which have all-green, large, shiny leaves are usually extremely tolerant of poor conditions. Variegated types need more care; fleshy-leaved varieties need less frequent watering. But each plant has its own personality, and in the following A-Z guide you will find your plant and a list of its needs.

ABUTILON

Abutilon striatum thompsonii

The Spotted Flowering Maple is a shrub for a large room, where its vigorous stems and yellow-splashed leaves can be allowed to spread. Orange blooms appear in summer as an extra bonus.

There are no special cultural problems, and mealy bug is the only pest which is likely to be a nuisance. Prune the shoots in spring to encourage bushiness and cut back the shrub to half its size in autumn.

SECRETS OF SUCCESS

Temperature: Average warmth; keep cool in winter (50°–60°F).

Light: Choose a partially shady spot.

Water: Water liberally from spring to late autumn. Water sparingly in winter.

Air Humidity: Mist leaves occasionally.

Repotting: Repot in spring.

Propagation: Stem cuttings or seeds in spring.

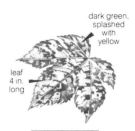
dark green, splashed with yellow

leaf 4 in. long

ABUTILON STRIATUM THOMPSONII
Spotted Flowering Maple

TYPE

The Flowering Maples are generally grown for their blooms (see page 123) but **A. striatum thompsonii** is best known for its variegated leaves. Quick-growing — can reach 5 ft or more.

ACALYPHA

Acalypha wilkesiana

It is difficult to overwinter Copper Leaf in the average room. The problem is the high humidity requirement, which can be readily satisfied in the greenhouse but not in the home. For this reason it is more usual to raise new plants from cuttings each year rather than trying to maintain a permanent shrub.

Keep in a well-lit spot or the red and brown mottling will be lost. Watch for red spider mite.

SECRETS OF SUCCESS

Temperature: Keep the shrub warm; 65°–75°F during the day, minimum 60°F at night.

Light: Bright, indirect light or some sun.

Water: Keep the compost fairly dry at all times.

Air Humidity: Moist air is vital. Surround pot with damp peat and mist leaves frequently.

Repotting: Repot annually in spring.

Propagation: Stem cuttings in spring or summer.

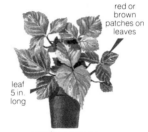
red or brown patches on leaves

leaf 5 in. long

ACALYPHA WILKESIANA
Copper Leaf

TYPES

A. wilkesiana is a colourful shrub which can reach 4 ft or more. There are several fine varieties — **godseffiana** (green edged with white) and **musaica** (red, orange and copper).

ACORUS

Acorus gramineus variegatus

The white-striped leaves of this grassy plant form fan-shaped tufts. Its great advantage as a background plant among more spectacular specimens is that it will withstand poor conditions — it is not affected by waterlogging, draughts or cold winter nights. It suffers from few problems, but leaf tips will turn brown if the compost is short of water. Watch for red spider mite if the air is warm and dry.

SECRETS OF SUCCESS

Temperature: Prefers cool conditions — keep in an unheated room in winter.

Light: Bright light or semi-shade; not direct sun.

Water: Keep compost wet at all times.

Air Humidity: Misting is not necessary.

Repotting: Repot, if necessary, in spring.

Propagation: Divide plants at any time of the year.

leaf 15 in. long

narrow, leathery leaves

ACORUS GRAMINEUS
Sweet Flag

TYPE

Only one variety is offered — **A. gramineus variegatus**. This is the white-striped form — not particularly showy, but useful in a terrarium. It is an uncommon house plant and is not widely available.

AGLAONEMA

leathery leaf
attached to
a long stalk

short, bare
stem may form
when plant
is mature

AGLAONEMA MODESTUM

AGLAONEMA COMMUTATUM SILVER SPEAR

AGLAONEMA PICTUM

AGLAONEMA SILVER QUEEN

AGLAONEMA PSEUDOBRACTEATUM

AGLAONEMA COMMUTATUM

AGLAONEMA
Chinese Evergreen

The spear-shaped decorative leaves of Aglaonema, the Chinese Evergreen, have the virtue of thriving in poorly lit locations. This is only true of green-leaved varieties — white and yellow ones need brighter conditions.

According to some European authorities the shade tolerance of this slow-growing plant is its *only* virtue — it has even been described as being far too difficult for growing in the home. In the United States, however, it is regarded as one of the most tolerant and reliable of house plants.

The best advice is to treat it as a moderately easy plant with a few special needs. Grow it in a shallow pot and keep it well away from draughts and smoky air. In winter it requires warm and moist air.

SECRETS OF SUCCESS

Temperature: Warm in summer; at least 60°F in winter.

Light: Semi-shade. Keep well away from direct sunlight.

Water: Water sparingly in winter. For the rest of the year water thoroughly.

Air Humidity: Moist air is necessary. Mist leaves regularly, but never use a coarse spray. Surround pot with damp peat.

Repotting: Every 3 years transfer to a larger pot in spring.

Propagation: In spring or summer pot up basal shoots with a few leaves and roots attached. Air layering is an alternative.

SPECIAL PROBLEMS

LEAVES SHRIVELLED BROWN TIPS
Cause: Air too dry.

LEAVES CURLED. BROWN EDGES
Cause: Air too cool, or cold draughts.

INSECTS: Mealy bugs at the base of the leaf stalks can be a serious problem; so can red spider mite if the light is too bright. See Chapter 15.

TYPES

Aglaonema Silver Queen

The Aglaonemas are popular house plants — the arum-like flowers which appear in summer are not particularly showy, so they are grown primarily for their large and colourful foliage. Aglaonemas tolerate shade, but the variegated ones are usually chosen and the need for light increases as the green area of the leaf decreases. Near-white varieties need a well-lit situation. The baby of the group is **A. pictum** (6 in. speckled and velvety leaves) — the giant is **A. nitidum** (18 in. plain green leaves). The usual plain green species is **A. modestum**, but it is the variegated types which are generally chosen. **A. commutatum** has silver bands — **A. pseudobracteatum** (Golden Evergreen) is blotched with yellow, cream and pale green. **A. commutatum Silver Spear** is an attractive variety, but perhaps the best of all the Aglaonemas are the hybrids **A. Silver Queen** and **A. Silver King** with foliage which is almost entirely silvery-grey.

Aglaonema pseudobracteatum

ALOCASIA

The Alocasias are distinctly uncommon — you will find them in few textbooks and even fewer shops. They certainly arouse attention — the erect, thick stems bear enormous arrow-shaped leaves with pale-coloured or white veins. Unfortunately these spectacular specimen plants are not really happy in the living room and need to return to greenhouse or conservatory conditions after a few months. A rest period is required in winter — do not feed and keep the compost on the dry side.

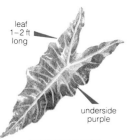

leaf
1–2 ft
long

underside
purple

ALOCASIA SANDERIANA
Kris Plant

TYPES

A. sanderiana has metallic green leaves with scalloped edges — **A. amazonica** is easier to find and the leaves are darker, contrasting sharply with the bold white veins. A showpiece in any room.

SECRETS OF SUCCESS

Temperature: Warm; above 70°F. A lower temperature (minimum 65°F) is acceptable in winter.
Light: Bright in winter, semi-shade in summer.
Water: Give a little water every few days to keep the compost moist at all times, but water very sparingly in winter.
Air Humidity: Mist leaves very frequently.
Repotting: Repot annually in early spring.
Propagation: Divide plants at repotting time.

Alocasia amazonica

ANTHURIUM

The Crystal Anthurium is neither easy to care for nor easy to obtain, but it is one of the most eye-catching of all foliage house plants. It is not impossible to keep this jungle plant in an ordinary room for years, but it will need careful attention. Don't plant too deeply, keep the air moist and satisfy its special watering needs. Finally a vital tip — make sure that the aerial roots are placed in the damp compost.

Anthurium crystallinum

SECRETS OF SUCCESS

Temperature: Average warmth; minimum temperature 60°F in winter.
Light: Bright in winter; away from direct sun in summer.
Water: Give a little water every few days to keep the compost moist at all times.
Air Humidity: Mist leaves very frequently.
Repotting: Repot annually in spring.
Propagation: Divide plants at repotting time.

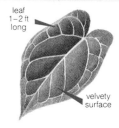

leaf
1–2 ft
long

velvety
surface

ANTHURIUM CRYSTALLINUM
Crystal Anthurium

TYPE

There is a single foliage species — **A. crystallinum.** The leaf colour changes from bronzy-purple to deep green with age — the foliage hangs vertically, displaying the silvery veins.

ARAUCARIA

A handsome and easy-to-grow conifer with many uses — seedlings for the terrarium, small plants for table display and tall trees as bold specimens in halls or large rooms. It flourishes in cool and light conditions, and will grow to about 5 ft. Keep it pot-bound to restrict growth. The major problem is leaf drop and loss of lower branches. The main cause is either hot, dry air or drying out of the compost. Too much sun or waterlogging can also be the culprit.

Araucaria heterophylla

SECRETS OF SUCCESS

Temperature: Average warmth; keep cool in winter (night temperature 50°F).
Light: Bright light or semi-shade; avoid direct sun in summer.
Water: Water regularly from spring to autumn. Water sparingly in winter.
Air Humidity: Mist leaves occasionally, especially if room is heated in winter. Ventilate in summer.
Repotting: Repot every 3 – 4 years in spring.
Propagation: Difficult — best to buy plants.

needles
½ in.
long

branches
arranged
in tiers

ARAUCARIA HETEROPHYLLA
(ARAUCARIA EXCELSA)
Norfolk Island Pine

TYPE

A. heterophylla is the only species sold as a house plant. It is a slow-growing tree bearing stiff branches covered with prickly needles. Best grown as a specimen plant to ensure symmetrical growth.

ASPARAGUS

The two popular Asparagus Ferns (A. plumosus and A. densiflorus sprengeri) are grown for their graceful feathery foliage, which is often used in flower arrangements. But all is not what it seems; they are not ferns, and the 'leaves' are really needle-like branches.

Asparagus Fern is an easy plant to grow, much easier than most true ferns, because it will adapt to wide variations in light, heat and frequency of watering. It does not demand a humid atmosphere and can be easily propagated. For maximum effect make sure that the arching or trailing branches are not impeded by other plants — a hanging basket is the ideal home.

The flat-leaved variety called Smilax by florists is A. asparagoides. It is more difficult to grow indoors than the ferny varieties, but it is sometimes recommended for hanging displays.

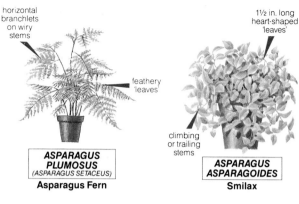

horizontal branchlets on wiry stems

feathery 'leaves'

ASPARAGUS PLUMOSUS
(ASPARAGUS SETACEUS)
Asparagus Fern

1½ in. long heart-shaped 'leaves'

climbing or trailing stems

ASPARAGUS ASPARAGOIDES
Smilax

SECRETS OF SUCCESS

Temperature: Average warmth; not less than 50°F at night. Constantly high temperature can be harmful.

Light: Can adapt to bright or semi-shady conditions. Keep away from direct sunlight.

Water: Water regularly from spring to autumn. Occasionally water from below (see page 227). In winter water sparingly.

Air Humidity: Mist occasionally, especially in winter if room is heated.

Repotting: Repot annually in spring.

Propagation: Divide plants at any time of the year. Sow seeds in spring.

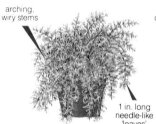

arching, wiry stems

1 in. long needle-like 'leaves'

ASPARAGUS DENSIFLORUS SPRENGERI
Asparagus Fern
(Emerald Fern)

climbing stems

2 in. long strap-like 'leaves'

ASPARAGUS FALCATUS
Sicklethorn

'leaf' 1 in. long

dense needle-like foliage

ASPARAGUS MEYERI
Plume Asparagus
(Foxtail Fern)

SPECIAL PROBLEMS

YELLOWING FOLIAGE, BROWN-EDGED OR SCORCHED. LEAF DROP
Cause: Too much sun, or compost has been allowed to dry out.

YELLOWING FOLIAGE, NO SCORCH. LEAF DROP
Cause: Temperature too high or not enough light.

PLANT DEATH
Cause: Root rot disease is the likely culprit, caused by faulty watering. For more details see page 245.

TYPES

The Asparagus species which have become popular as house plants have needle-like 'leaves'. They have a ferny look — **A. plumosus** is a compact plant with graceful, spreading branches when young but the thin stems become straggly with age. Berries sometimes appear and the smallest type is **A. plumosus nanus. A. densiflorus sprengeri** has trailing stems with bright green 'leaves' (hence the common name Emerald Fern) and red berries. Less well known but more attractive is the Plume Asparagus — **A. meyeri**. The erect and stiff stems are 15 – 18 in. long and densely covered with needles — a green bottle-brush plant which serves as a useful contrast to large-leaved plants in pot groups. There is nothing fern-like about **A. falcatus** — the sickle-shaped leaves are large and the 3 ft high stems are distinctly prickly. Finally there is the old fashioned Smilax — **A. asparagoides**. A vigorous plant with trailing stems which can reach 5 ft or more — the shiny foliage remains fresh for a long time after cutting.

Asparagus plumosus

Asparagus densiflorus sprengeri

ASPIDISTRA

Aspidistra elatior variegata

A Victorian favourite, once much-maligned but now regaining some of its former popularity. The common name of Cast Iron Plant indicates its ability to withstand neglect, draughts and shade. The leaves are both slow growing and long lasting. The plant can withstand periods of dryness at the roots if the temperature is not too high, but it does have two strong dislikes — it will die if the soil is constantly saturated and it will be harmed by frequent repotting.

SECRETS OF SUCCESS

Temperature: Average warmth; keep cool but frost-free in winter.

Light: Extremely tolerant, but not of direct sun.

Water: Water regularly from spring to autumn. Water sparingly in winter.

Air Humidity: Wash leaves occasionally, but can stand dry air.

Repotting: Repot every 4 – 5 years in spring.

Propagation: Divide plants in spring or summer.

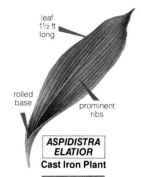

leaf 1½ ft long — rolled base — prominent ribs

ASPIDISTRA ELATIOR
Cast Iron Plant

TYPES

The dark green leaves of **A. elatior** withstand both air pollution and neglect but are scorched by sunlight. A cream-striped variety (**A. elatior variegata**) is available — it is more attractive but less hardy.

AUCUBA

Aucuba japonica variegata

A useful plant for rooms which are not heated in winter and where adequate light is a problem. It is not suitable for hot and dry locations as serious leaf fall will occur. Brown edges in summer mean that you are not watering frequently enough. When small, the Spotted Laurel can be stood on a windowsill or table. It will produce a woody shrub reaching 5 ft or more, but it can be kept in check by pruning in the spring.

SECRETS OF SUCCESS

Temperature: Average warmth; keep cool in winter (night temperature 40° – 45°F).

Light: Bright light or shade; avoid direct sun in summer.

Water: Water regularly from spring to autumn. Water sparingly in winter.

Air Humidity: Mist plant frequently, especially in winter. Wash leaves occasionally.

Repotting: Repot annually in spring.

Propagation: Stem cuttings root easily. Late summer is the best time.

serrated leaves — leaf 5 in. long

AUCUBA JAPONICA VARIEGATA
Spotted Laurel

TYPES

A. japonica is an outdoor shrub with leathery, glossy foliage. Only the variegated types are used indoors. **Variegata** is the most popular — **goldiana** (almost all-yellow) is the most colourful.

BEAUCARNEA

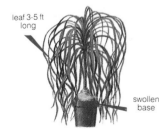

leaf 3-5 ft long — swollen base

BEAUCARNEA RECURVATA
(NOLINA TUBERCULATA)
Pony Tail
(Elephant Foot)

TYPE

One species is sold — **B. recurvata**. A shaggy-looking false palm which makes a talking point. It grows slowly, but with time the trunk will grow to 6 ft or more and the base will be swollen like a huge bulb.

A curiosity rather than a thing of beauty, the Pony Tail is still very useful if you want a tall specimen plant which will not require a lot of attention. The swollen bulb-like base stores water, so occasional dryness at the roots will do no harm. The plume of long strap-like leaves gives the plant its common name. It is a rarity in Britain but is popular in the U.S., where it flourishes and reaches ceiling height in the warm, dry atmosphere of centrally heated rooms.

SECRETS OF SUCCESS

Temperature: Average warmth; minimum temperature 50°F in winter.

Light: Brightly lit spot; some sun is beneficial.

Water: Water thoroughly, then leave until compost is moderately dry. Avoid overwatering.

Air Humidity: Misting not necessary.

Repotting: Repot, when necessary, in spring.

Propagation: Plant up offsets at repotting time. Not easy; best to buy plants.

Beaucarnea recurvata

BEGONIA

Begonias are an essential part of any worthwhile house plant collection, but the range of types available is bewildering. Most Begonias are grown for their floral display (see pages 127 – 128) although these varieties may also have attractive foliage. The situation with the types described here is reversed — they are grown for their foliage display although some have flowers as a bonus. The original Begonia rex came from India, but the species no longer exists. All our colourful plants are hybrids. Its off-centre heart-shaped leaves are easy to recognise, but the foliage Begonias include many other shapes — stars, ovals, spears etc. Surfaces range from waxy and smooth to dull and deeply puckered. If you cannot generalise about appearance you can about cultivation. All detest overwatering and direct summer sun, and are not difficult as long as there is some room heat in winter. Do not expect foliage Begonias to become part of the family like Monstera, Palms and Chlorophytum — even with care these foliage varieties usually last for only a year or two under ordinary room conditions. But take heart — new plants can be easily raised from leaf cuttings.

SECRETS OF SUCCESS

Temperature: Average warmth; not less than 55°F.

Light: A bright spot away from direct sunlight. A few hours of morning or evening sun in winter are beneficial. Turn pots occasionally.

Water: The compost should be kept moist from spring to autumn; allow surface to dry between waterings. Water sparingly in winter.

Air Humidity: Moist air needed — surround pots with damp peat. Mist surrounding air, but never wet the leaves.

Repotting: Repot annually in spring. Leaves of pot-bound plants lose colour.

Propagation: Leaf cuttings root easily (see page 236). Plants can be divided at repotting time.

SPECIAL PROBLEMS

Diseases are a menace. See page 245.

TYPES

The types described and illustrated on these 2 pages are grown primarily or solely for their foliage. This group is dominated by the many hybrids of **B. rex**, so widely used in plant groups where a contrast to plain green varieties is required. Scores of varieties are available — old favourites include **President Carnot** (green and silver), **Helen Teupel** (red, green and pink) and **King Edward IV** (purple and red). Miniature Rex Begonias are available. Similar to the familiar Rex but with puckered leaves and a dark cross-shaped heart is **B. masoniana**. **B. maculata** is quite different — cane-like stems several feet high bear 9 in. long leaves, white-spotted above and red below. **B. metallica** is another tall-growing species, metallic green above and red-veined below. The Beefsteak Begonia (**B. feastii** or **B. erythrophylla**) has fleshy round leaves which are shiny green above and red below — the variety **bunchii** has leaves with crested and frilly margins. Where space is limited grow the compact **B. boweri** (6 – 9 in. high) or its hybrid **B. Tiger**. **B. Cleopatra** is a small bushy plant (6 – 9 in. high) grown for its glistening bronzy leaves. The underside of the foliage bears white hairs, and the shape of the leaf is much more like a Maple or Sycamore than a Begonia — hence the common name (Mapleleaf Begonia). Most of the above Begonias and varieties produce small flowers in winter or summer, depending on the species.

Trailing Begonias are generally grown for their floral display (see page 127) but a few trailing foliage types are occasionally seen. Examples include **B. solanthera** (waxy foliage) and **B. imperialis** (velvety foliage). You would never guess that **B. foliosa** was a Begonia — its pendent stems clothed with tiny oval leaves have a distinctly fern-like appearance.

Begonia solanthera

Begonia masoniana

Begonia Cleopatra

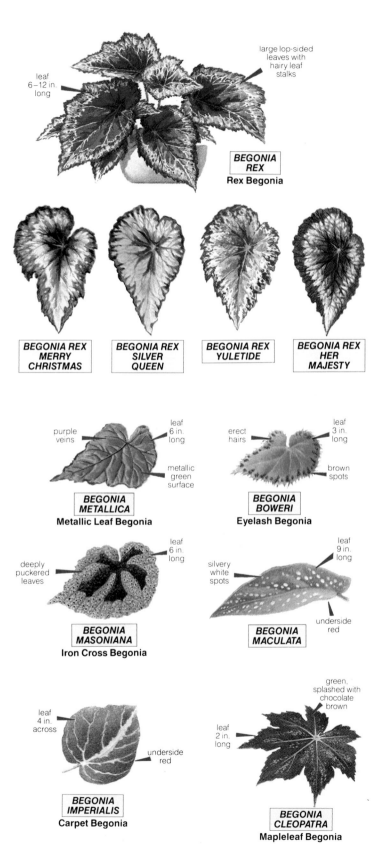

leaf 6–12 in. long

large lop-sided leaves with hairy leaf stalks

BEGONIA REX
Rex Begonia

BEGONIA REX MERRY CHRISTMAS

BEGONIA REX SILVER QUEEN

BEGONIA REX YULETIDE

BEGONIA REX HER MAJESTY

purple veins

leaf 6 in. long

metallic green surface

BEGONIA METALLICA
Metallic Leaf Begonia

erect hairs

leaf 3 in. long

brown spots

BEGONIA BOWERI
Eyelash Begonia

deeply puckered leaves

leaf 6 in. long

BEGONIA MASONIANA
Iron Cross Begonia

silvery white spots

leaf 9 in. long

underside red

BEGONIA MACULATA

leaf 4 in. across

underside red

BEGONIA IMPERIALIS
Carpet Begonia

green, splashed with chocolate brown

leaf 2 in. long

BEGONIA CLEOPATRA
Mapleleaf Begonia

Begonia rex Bettina Rothschild

Begonia feastii bunchii

Begonia Tiger

BOWIEA

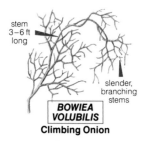

stem
3–6 ft
long

slender,
branching
stems

**BOWIEA
VOLUBILIS**
Climbing Onion

TYPE

One variety only — **B. volubilis**. The large above-ground bulb produces thin and straggly stems in winter. A few short-lived leaves and small greenish flowers appear before the stems die down in late spring.

So many of the plants in this book can be classed as both popular and attractive. The Sea Onion or Climbing Onion is neither — it is both rare and repulsive. It is grown only as a novelty, so that visitors can express their surprise. Easier to find in the U.S. than in Britain — look for it in the catalogues of specialist nurseries. Plant the bulbs in Seed & Cutting Compost during the dormant season (summer – autumn).

SECRETS OF SUCCESS

Temperature: Cool or average warmth; tolerates 50°F quite happily.

Light: Moderately well-lit but away from direct sunlight.

Water: Water sparingly for most of the year. Keep compost moist when stems start to grow in winter — do not water in summer.

Air Humidity: Misting not necessary.

Repotting: Repot when offsets fill the pot.

Propagation: Plant up offsets at repotting time.

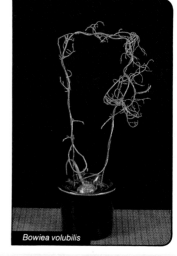

Bowiea volubilis

BREYNIA

Breynia nivosa roseopicta

You will find this plant in a number of garden centres and department stores but in very few textbooks. It is basically a greenhouse plant which was introduced as a house plant in the 1980s. Under glass it will grow into a shrub — in the living room it is grown as a small bush, with slender branches densely clothed with colourful leaves. Humidity is the problem — it needs a moist atmosphere.

SECRETS OF SUCCESS

Temperature: Average warmth; not less than 55°F in winter.

Light: Bright light; not direct sun.

Water: Keep compost moist at all times; reduce watering in winter.

Air Humidity: Mist leaves frequently.

Repotting: Repot every 2 years in spring.

Propagation: Stem cuttings in summer. Make sure each cutting has a heel at the base.

oval leaf
1 in. across

**BREYNIA NIVOSA
ROSEOPICTA**
Leaf Flower

TYPES

B. nivosa has green leaves marbled with white. The variety **roseopicta** is the usual choice. The pink, white and green variegated leaves have a flower-like appearance — hence the common name.

National Expenditure on Indoor Plants

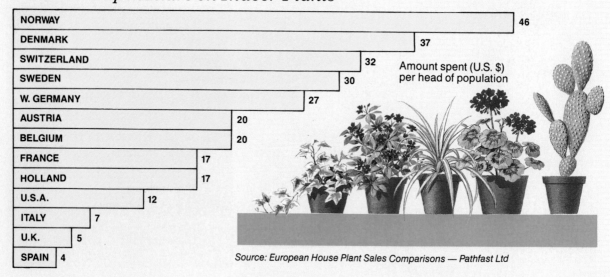

Country	Amount spent (U.S. $) per head of population
NORWAY	46
DENMARK	37
SWITZERLAND	32
SWEDEN	30
W. GERMANY	27
AUSTRIA	20
BELGIUM	20
FRANCE	17
HOLLAND	17
U.S.A.	12
ITALY	7
U.K.	5
SPAIN	4

Source: European House Plant Sales Comparisons — Pathfast Ltd

BROMELIADS

showy flowers produced by many varieties

leaves usually leathery and strap-like

central water-holding 'vase' present in most varieties

The Bromeliads are full of surprises. Interior designers look upon them as almost essential for their modern decor schemes, yet beginners often feel that these spectacular and often brightly-coloured plants must be too difficult for them to grow. The first surprise is that few plants are easier to care for.

Another surprise is the method of watering — into the central rosette rather than into the compost. Then there is the flowering habit — as the flower-head opens the parent rosette begins to die, although it may survive for a further year or two. So propagation after flowering is necessary to preserve your collection.

The native home of the Bromeliads is the American jungle, where they dwell among the orchids in the trees or on the forest floor. A novel way of growing and showing your plants is to build a Bromeliad tree. Otherwise keep them in small pots with drainage holes and a peat-based compost. Remember that they all have a tiny root system so overpotting or overwatering can be fatal.

Some Bromeliads, such as Aechmea, Vriesea and Guzmania, are grown for the beauty of their flower-heads as well as for the attractiveness of their foliage. Two others (Tillandsia and Billbergia) are grown mainly for their colourful blooms. For details of the flowering Bromeliads, see pages 130 – 131. A group of Bromeliads do not need watering at all — see page 214 for details of these Air Plants.

HOW TO MAKE A BROMELIAD TREE

Leafy Bromeliad:
Choose plants with a well pronounced 'cup' in the heart of the rosette. Remove from pot, wrap roots with sphagnum moss and then tightly attach with plastic-covered wire to branch

Tillandsia usneoides (Spanish Moss): a unique Bromeliad which grows as grey-green strands in moist air.
No watering required

Keep cup filled with water and syringe sphagnum moss weekly

Pebbles

Branch set in Plaster of Paris and stones

Leafy Bromeliad

Sphagnum moss

Container

SECRETS OF SUCCESS

Temperature: High temperatures (above 75°F) may be required to bring plants into flower, but average warmth (minimum 50°F) is satisfactory for foliage types or plants in flower.

Light: Most Bromeliads require a brightly-lit spot away from direct sunlight. Pineapple and the Earth Stars will thrive in full sun.

Water: Never overwater, and ensure that there is good drainage. Keep the 'vase' filled with water — use rainwater in hard water areas. Empty and refill 'vase' every 1 – 2 months. Water the compost only when it dries out. With non-vase varieties keep the compost moist, but never wet.

Air Humidity: Mist the leaves in summer. Feeding through the leaves is the natural method of nutrition, so occasionally use dilute liquid fertilizer instead of water in the sprayer.

Repotting: Rarely, if ever, necessary.

Propagation: Offsets appear at the base of the plant. When the offset is several months old remove it with some roots attached and plant shallowly in Seed & Cutting Compost. Keep warm until established.

SPECIAL PROBLEMS

LEAVES WITH PALE BROWN PATCHES
Cause: Sun scorch. Move plant away from direct sunlight.

LEAVES WITH BROWN TIPS
Cause: Dry air is a likely reason — mist during the summer months. Other possibility is failure to fill 'vase' with water or use of hard water.

PLANT DEATH
Cause: Overwatering if plant has not yet flowered. If it has flowered then rotting and death of the rosette which bore the flower stalk is natural.

INSECTS
Scale and mealy bug can be troublesome — see page 244.

BROMELIAD TYPES

large
saw-edged
leaves

AECHMEA FASCIATA
(AECHMEA RHODOCYANEA)
Urn Plant
(Vase Plant)

The Urn Plant is good enough to be the showpiece of any living room or florist window. The arching 2 ft grey-green leaves are banded with silvery powder and the floral spike which appears when the plant is a few years old is striking (see page 130). There are other Aechmeas — **A. chantinii** is grown for its large banded leaves and bright flowers, **A. fulgens discolor** for its purple-backed foliage plus decorative berries, and where space is limited there are dwarfs like **A. Foster's Favorite**.

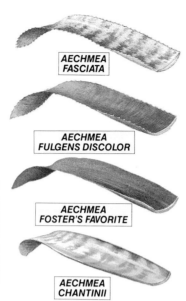

AECHMEA FASCIATA

AECHMEA FULGENS DISCOLOR

AECHMEA FOSTER'S FAVORITE

AECHMEA CHANTINII

Aechmea Foster's Favorite

smooth-edged
leaves

VRIESEA SPLENDENS
(VRIESEA SPECIOSA)
Flaming Sword

The usual Vriesea is **V. splendens** — dark-banded foot-long leaves and a brilliant red flower-head. There are others. **V. hieroglyphica** has interestingly-marked leaves but it rarely flowers and does not deserve its common name — King of the Bromeliads. **V. fenestralis** is also a foliage variety, grown for its finely-netted leaves rather than its blooms.

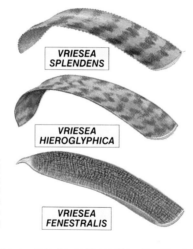

VRIESEA SPLENDENS

VRIESEA HIEROGLYPHICA

VRIESEA FENESTRALIS

Vriesea fenestralis

saw-edged
leaves

NEOREGELIA CAROLINAE TRICOLOR
Blushing Bromeliad

The favourite variety, **Neoregelia carolinae tricolor**, blushes at the centre when about to flower, whereas the Fingernail Plant reddens at the leaf tips. The glossy leaves are about a foot long, and with age the foliage of the **tricolor** variety becomes suffused with pink.

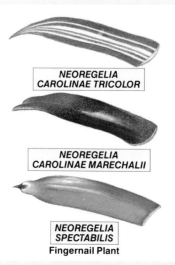

NEOREGELIA CAROLINAE TRICOLOR

NEOREGELIA CAROLINAE MARECHALII

NEOREGELIA SPECTABILIS
Fingernail Plant

Neoregelia spectabilis

ANANAS
Pineapple

sharply saw-edged leaves

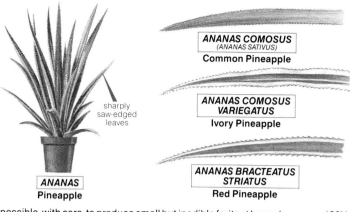

ANANAS COMOSUS
(ANANAS SATIVUS)
Common Pineapple

ANANAS COMOSUS VARIEGATUS
Ivory Pineapple

ANANAS BRACTEATUS STRIATUS
Red Pineapple

Ananas bracteatus striatus

It is possible, with care, to produce small but inedible fruits at home (see page 130) but the Pineapple Plant is generally grown for its foliage. The leaves are narrow and fiercely spined, so take care. The Common Pineapple is rather dull and too large for the living room — a much better choice is its smaller and more colourful variety **Ananas comosus variegatus**. Best of all is **A. bracteatus striatus**, bearing stiff and arching 1 – 2 ft leaves brightly striped with green, cream and pink.

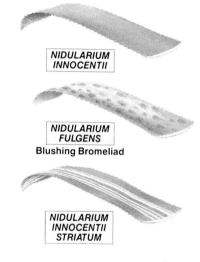

saw-edged leaves

underside purple

NIDULARIUM INNOCENTII
Bird's Nest Bromeliad

NIDULARIUM INNOCENTII

NIDULARIUM FULGENS
Blushing Bromeliad

NIDULARIUM INNOCENTII STRIATUM

Nidularium fulgens

Not often seen — differs from the more popular and rather similar Neoregelia by having a central rosette of very short leaves. This 'bird's nest' turns bright red at flowering time. Leaves below the bird's nest are about 1 ft long and 2 in. wide.

CRYPTANTHUS
Earth Star

small, wavy-edged leaves

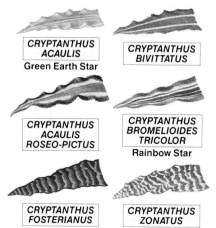

CRYPTANTHUS ACAULIS
Green Earth Star

CRYPTANTHUS BIVITTATUS

CRYPTANTHUS ACAULIS ROSEO-PICTUS

CRYPTANTHUS BROMELIOIDES TRICOLOR
Rainbow Star

CRYPTANTHUS FOSTERIANUS

CRYPTANTHUS ZONATUS

These low-growing plants are best kept in a glass container. There is a wide range to choose from — plain, striped and banded in green, red, brown and yellow. Leaf sizes range from **Cryptanthus bivittatus** (4 in.) to **C. fosterianus** (15 in.). The brightest (and most difficult to grow) is **C. bromelioides tricolor**.

Cryptanthus fosterianus

BROMELIAD TYPES continued

large, smooth-edged leaves

very wide rosette base

GUZMANIA LINGULATA
Scarlet Star

The Guzmanias are grown for their showy flower-heads as well as their leaves. **G. lingulata** (leaves 1½ ft long) is popular — the variety **minor** (pale green leaves 4 in. long) is preferred where space is limited. The most colourful foliage belongs to **G. musaica** (green banded with mahogany) but plants are usually chosen for the size and colour of their flower-heads — many hybrids are available (see page 131).

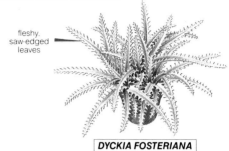

fleshy, saw-edged leaves

DYCKIA FOSTERIANA

Dyckia is certainly the least popular of the Bromeliads described in this section. Its stiff and barbed leaves are fleshy, and the rosettes have two unusual features. Daughter rosettes are freely produced so that a cluster of plants is produced with age, and the flower-heads arise from the side and not the centre of each rosette. There is the green **Dyckia brevifolia** (leaves 4 in. long) and the bronzy **D. fosteriana** (leaves 9 in. long).

BUXUS

leaf
1 in.
long

glossy,
leathery
leaves

**BUXUS
SEMPERVIRENS**
Common Box

The popular **B. sempervirens** (Common Box) can be grown, but the Small-leaved Box (**B. microphylla**) is a better choice. Slow growing — prune to keep in shape. Can be trimmed to decorative shapes — balls, cones, standards etc.

Box is a favourite shrub outdoors, but has only recently been accepted as a house plant. It is tolerant of cool conditions and draughts, producing a dense screen of shiny small leaves. There is an essential requirement — good light, especially in winter. Stand the pot outdoors in summer. These shrubs can be clipped and trained at any time of the year. The only danger is overwatering.

SECRETS OF SUCCESS

Temperature: Average or below average warmth; keep cool in winter.

Light: A well-lit spot; some direct sunlight is beneficial.

Water: Water thoroughly but let compost become dryish between waterings — do not keep compost constantly moist.

Air Humidity: Mist leaves occasionally.

Repotting: Repot, if necessary, in spring.

Propagation: Stem cuttings in late summer.

Buxus microphylla

CALADIUM

A unique foliage house plant, both in appearance and cultivation. The striking arrow-shaped leaves are spectacular — paper thin and beautifully marked and coloured. Long stalks bear these foot-long leaves above the pots, which are best set amongst other plants. The dazzling foliage, however, is not permanent and lasts only from late spring to early autumn.

Plant Caladium tubers in Potting Compost in spring and keep moist at 75°F or more. When shoots appear mist daily and slowly adjust to living room temperature. Warmth at all times is vital — at no stage should the temperature fall below 60°F. If you buy a Caladium plant, protect from cold on the way home.

SECRETS OF SUCCESS

Temperature: Warm; above 70°F whenever possible, never below 60°F.

Light: Moderately well-lit but away from direct sunlight.

Water: Water freely during the growing season.

Air Humidity: Mist frequently, especially in spring.

After Care: Foliage dies down in autumn. Stop watering; keep tubers at about 60°F in pots or in peat. Replant tubers in spring — small 'daughter' tubers can be potted up separately.

paper-thin
decorative
leaves

CALADIUM
Angel's Wings
(Elephant's Ears)

**CALADIUM
HORTULANUM
CANDIDUM**

**CALADIUM
HORTULANUM
MRS HALDERMAN**

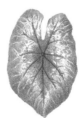

**CALADIUM
HORTULANUM
ROSEBUD**

**CALADIUM
HORTULANUM
FRIEDA HEMPLE**

**CALADIUM
HORTULANUM
LORD DERBY**

There are scores of varieties available but they are usually sold unnamed. The textbooks can't agree whether these hybrids should be listed under **C. bicolor** or **C. hortulanum** — obviously naming a Caladium is not easy! Several are illustrated here — **C. hortulanum candidum** is easily recognised (white with green veins) and so is its reverse image **Seagull** (green with white veins). Easier to grow than the showy hybrids is the smaller **C. humboldtii** (green blotched with white).

Caladium hortulanum candidum

Caladium hortulanum Arno Nehrling

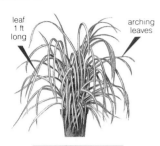

leaf
1 ft
long

arching
leaves

CAREX

From the vast family of Sedges only one or two are suitable as house plants. The Japanese Sedge is not often seen but is extremely easy to look after indoors. Its white-striped leaves make it a useful specimen for a terrarium or for growing among other plants in an indoor garden. It is one of the most durable of foliage plants, growing happily in sun or shade, low temperatures and in wet or dryish compost. Producing more specimens is a simple job as divided-up plants root very easily.

Carex morrowii variegata

CAREX MORROWII VARIEGATA
Japanese Sedge

TYPE

C. morrowii variegata has a cast-iron constitution and the foliage is much narrower than the leaves of Chlorophytum. An excellent choice for a small mixed bowl or trough — but hardly anyone sells it.

SECRETS OF SUCCESS

Temperature: Average or below average warmth; keep cool in winter.

Light: Not fussy; semi-shade, well-lit or sunny.

Water: Keep the compost moist but it should not be kept waterlogged.

Air Humidity: Ventilate on warm days.

Repotting: Repot every 2 years in spring.

Propagation: Divide plants at any time of the year.

---

green,
banded with
creamy-white

leaf
9 in.
long

CHLOROPHYTUM COMOSUM VITTATUM
Spider Plant
(St. Bernard's Lily)

TYPES

C. comosum is available everywhere. Arching leaves form an attractive rosette, and the long stalks bear plantlets. Several varieties are available. **Vittatum** is the usual one — **variegatum** has green leaves edged with white.

CHLOROPHYTUM

The Spider Plant has been grown indoors for 200 years, and it is now one of the most popular of all house plants. This popularity is not surprising — it is quick-growing with attractive arching leaves, and in spring and summer the cascading wiry stems produce small white flowers followed by tiny plantlets. Left on the mother plant, these plantlets grow to give an attractive display, especially in a hanging basket. Removed from the mother plant they can be used to produce new plants. Above all the Spider Plant has the prime requirement for popularity — it is extremely adaptable. It will grow in hot or cool rooms, sunny windows or shady corners and it doesn't mind dry air.

Chlorophytum comosum vittatum

SECRETS OF SUCCESS

Temperature: Average warmth; not less than 45°F in winter.

Light: Not fussy; a well-lit spot away from direct sunlight is best.

Water: Water liberally from spring to autumn; sparingly in winter.

Air Humidity: Misting occasionally in summer is beneficial.

Repotting: Repot in spring if plant has started to lift out of the pot.

Propagation: Peg down plantlets in compost — cut stem when rooted. Alternatively divide plants at repotting time.

SPECIAL PROBLEMS

INSECTS
Chlorophytum is virtually pest-free. Aphid may attack if plants are weak.

LEAVES WITH BROWN TIPS
Cause: Most likely reason is underfeeding — don't forget to feed with every watering. Other possible causes are bruising and excessively hot air. Cut off damaged tips and correct the fault.

LEAVES PALE & LIMP IN WINTER. SOME YELLOWING & LEAF FALL
Cause: Too much heat and too little light.

LEAVES WITH BROWN STREAKS IN WINTER
Cause: Too much water under cool conditions when the plant is not growing. Water sparingly in winter.

LEAVES CURLED WITH BROWN SPOTS & EDGES. SOME YELLOWING & LEAF FALL
Cause: The soil around the roots has dried out. Chlorophytum needs a plentiful supply of water when it is actively growing.

NO STEMS
Cause: The plant is too young; stems bearing plantlets will not form until the plant is mature. If it is mature, then lack of space is the most likely cause; avoid overcrowding.

CLEYERA

In contrast to the many universal favourites in this book, Cleyera japonica tricolor is a rarity in Britain. It deserves to be more popular as it is easy to grow and does not drop its leaves at the first change in conditions — an annoying habit of some other variegated-leaved shrubby plants. It is slow growing and it can be kept compact by occasionally removing the shoot tips. The leaves are edged with yellow and small white flowers may appear as a bonus.

leaves reddish when young

leaf 3 in. long

CLEYERA JAPONICA VARIEGATA

TYPES

C. japonica is an unusual shrub which grows about 2 ft tall — you will certainly not find it at your local garden centre. The glossy-leaved variegated form — **C. (or Eurya) japonica variegata** is the one to look for.

SECRETS OF SUCCESS

Temperature: Average warmth; keep cool in winter (minimum temperature 50°F).

Light: Well-lit but away from direct sunlight.

Water: Keep the compost moist at all times. Use rainwater if tap water is hard.

Air Humidity: Mist leaves occasionally.

Repotting: Repot, when necessary, in spring.

Propagation: Stem cuttings in summer. Rooting hormone and bottom heat are necessary.

Cleyera japonica variegata

COCCOLOBA

Coccoloba is a plant for the lover of rarities — it will grow in the house but it is more suited to the conservatory or greenhouse. As an indoor plant it is grown for its stiff, olive-green leaves — the red veins turn pale cream with age. Under natural conditions fragrant white flowers appear and these are followed by red grape-like fruits — unfortunately the plant won't flower indoors. Not really a difficult plant, but it does need moist air and some warmth in winter.

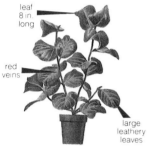

leaf 8 in. long

red veins

large leathery leaves

COCCOLOBA UVIFERA

Sea Grape

TYPE

C. uvifera is commonly grown in semi-tropical regions of the world but is not often seen indoors. It needs space — grow it in a large tub so that it can show off its striking kidney-shaped leaves.

SECRETS OF SUCCESS

Temperature: Average warmth; minimum winter temperature 55°F.

Light: Well-lit but away from direct sunlight.

Water: Keep the compost moist at all times.

Air Humidity: Mist leaves regularly.

Repotting: Repot, when necessary, in spring.

Propagation: Stem cuttings in summer; rooting hormone and bottom heat are necessary.

Coccoloba uvifera

COFFEA

The Coffee Tree won't disappoint you if you expect an attractive bush with dark, shiny, wavy-edged leaves for decoration. It will disappoint you if you expect coffee beans for breakfast. It is an undemanding plant, but the compost must never be allowed to dry out, and draughts are positively harmful. It can reach 4 ft or more in height, but you can keep it in check by pruning in spring.

Coffea arabica

leaf 6 in. long

wavy-edged leaves

COFFEA ARABICA

Coffee Tree

SECRETS OF SUCCESS

Temperature: Average warmth; minimum winter temperature 50°F.

Light: Well-lit but away from direct sunlight.

Water: Keep the compost moist at all times.

Air Humidity: Mist leaves occasionally.

Repotting: Repot every 2 years in spring.

Propagation: Stem cuttings in summer; rooting hormone and bottom heat are necessary. Plants can be raised from unroasted coffee beans.

TYPES

The true Coffee Tree **(C. arabica)** can be grown indoors and the shrub may even flower after a few years. The variety **nana** is a smaller plant but it flowers more readily.

CODIAEUM (CROTON)

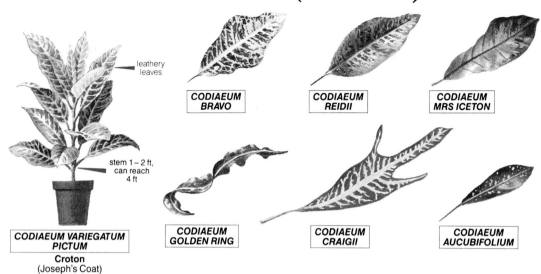

leathery leaves

stem 1 – 2 ft, can reach 4 ft

CODIAEUM BRAVO

CODIAEUM REIDII

CODIAEUM MRS ICETON

CODIAEUM GOLDEN RING

CODIAEUM CRAIGII

CODIAEUM AUCUBIFOLIUM

CODIAEUM VARIEGATUM PICTUM

Croton
(Joseph's Coat)

The attraction of the Crotons is obvious — vivid foliage colours and varied leaf shapes. But before you buy one of these hybrids of Codiaeum variegatum pictum make sure that you can satisfy its difficult requirements. It will need a fairly constant temperature which will not drop below 60°F and it will need moist air. The compost will have to be kept moist at all times with tepid water, and you will have to keep the pot away from draughts. Your reward for creating the right conditions will be a colourful bush which will have the clear sign of the expert . . . the lower stem of a Croton fully clothed with leaves.

SECRETS OF SUCCESS

Temperature: Warm; not less than 60°F in winter.

Light: Good light is necessary; an east- or west-facing windowsill is ideal.

Water: Water liberally from spring to autumn. Water sparingly in winter.

Air Humidity: Air must be moist. Mist leaves regularly — daily if possible. Wash leaves frequently.

Repotting: Repot, when necessary, in spring.

Propagation: Stem cuttings in spring. Rooting hormone and bottom heat are necessary.

SPECIAL PROBLEMS

LOSS OF LOWER LEAVES
Cause: If brown tips are present — air or compost is too dry.
If brown edges are present — temperature is too low.

LOSS OF LEAF COLOUR
Cause: Not enought light.

INSECTS
Red spider mite and scale can be a problem — see Chapter 15 for details.

Codiaeum Norma

TYPES

The basic variety is **C. variegatum pictum**, and over the years hundreds of different named types have appeared. Most have laurel-like foliage, but there are also forked leaves, long ribbons, lobed leaves, twisted and curled types. Identification is not easy — the colour often changes with age, a pink or red hue taking over from the yellows and greens. Examples of well-known varieties include **Appleleaf** and **Vulcan** (yellow with red edges and green veins), **Norma** (green with red veins and splashes of yellow), **aucubifolium** (green with yellow spots), **Bravo** (green splashed with yellow and red). **Reidii** is popular — so are the lobed varieties such as **craigii** and **holuffiana**. There are many, many others, such as **Mrs Iceton**, **Excellent**, **Gold Finger**, **Gold Sun** and **Julietta**.

Codiaeum Gold Finger

COLEUS

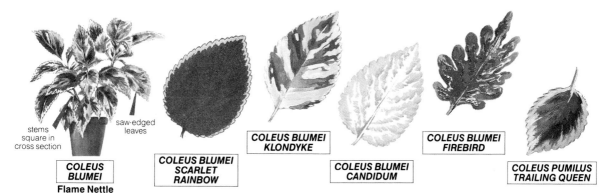

stems square in cross section

saw-edged leaves

COLEUS BLUMEI
Flame Nettle

COLEUS BLUMEI SCARLET RAINBOW

COLEUS BLUMEI KLONDYKE

COLEUS BLUMEI CANDIDUM

COLEUS BLUMEI FIREBIRD

COLEUS PUMILUS TRAILING QUEEN

The poor man's Croton. Coleus thoroughly deserves this nickname as it is the cheapest and easiest way to add brightly-coloured foliage to a house plant collection. The soft-stemmed bush should be kept at about 1 ft high by pinching the tips, and flower stalks should be removed as they appear. Plants are obtained by sowing seed, taking cuttings or buying nursery-grown stock. They can be over-wintered, but Coleus soon becomes leggy and defoliated. The best plan is to treat it as an annual by sowing seed or taking cuttings each spring. Care is easy; just remember to keep it in a sunny spot, use soft water and never let the compost dry out.

SECRETS OF SUCCESS

Temperature: Average warmth; not less than 50°F.

Light: Give as much light as possible, but shade from summer noonday sun.

Water: Keep compost moist at all times; reduce watering in winter. Use rainwater if tap water is hard.

Air Humidity: Keep air moist; mist leaves in winter and summer.

Repotting: Cut back and repot in early spring.

Propagation: Stem cuttings in spring or summer. Alternatively sow seeds in early spring.

Coleus Scarlet Poncho

SPECIAL PROBLEMS

LEGGY STEMS
Cause: Young plants — not enough light or failure to pinch out tips. Old plants — normal effect, nothing can be done.

LEAF DROP
Cause: Not enough water; in summer it may be necessary to water every day.

Coleus Salmon Lace

TYPES

The usual height is 1–2 ft, but dwarf varieties such as **Sabre** are available. New plants are raised from seed or cuttings and there is a bewildering choice of **Coleus blumei** hybrids. Most (but not all) have nettle-like leaves — there are also ruffled ones (e.g **The Chief**), frilly ones (e.g **Firebird**) and wavy-edged ones (e.g **Butterfly**). There is no basic colour — almost every conceivable mixture can be found. There are some attractive single-coloured varieties, such as **Golden Bedder** (yellow) and **Volcano** (deep red), but the usual choice is for a multicoloured Coleus. There is a trailing species — **C. pumilus** (**C. rehneltianus**). Several varieties (e.g **Scarlet Poncho**) can be grown from seed.

Coleus Sabre Mixed

CUPRESSUS

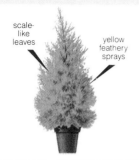

scale-like leaves

yellow feathery sprays

CUPRESSUS MACROCARPA GOLDCREST

Once it was unthinkable to grow Cupressus indoors, but there are now a couple of types which have proved to be successful and are becoming increasingly popular. There are the upright C. macrocarpa Goldcrest and the weeping C. cashmeriana. These trees will grow 4 – 6 ft high — prune in early spring if necessary to keep the plant in bounds.

SECRETS OF SUCCESS

Temperature: Average warmth; not less than 45°F in winter.
Light: A well-lit spot away from direct sunlight.
Water: Water liberally from spring to autumn; sparingly in winter.
Air Humidity: Mist leaves occasionally.
Repotting: Repot every 2 years in spring.
Propagation: Stem cuttings in spring.

CYPERUS

There is just one golden rule for success with the Umbrella Plant — keep the roots constantly wet. Place the pot in a saucer or outer container which should always contain water. This plant is grown for its overall shape rather than the beauty of its foliage — thin stems topped by radiating strap-like leaves, with small grass-like flowers in summer. It is best grouped with other plants or grown in a bottle garden; choose the dwarf-growing C. diffusus if space is limited. Cut out yellowing stems to encourage new growth.

SECRETS OF SUCCESS

Temperature: Not fussy, but keep at 50°F or above in winter.
Light: Well-lit or shade, but avoid direct summer sunlight.
Water: Keep it soaked and restrict free drainage.
Air Humidity: Mist leaves frequently.
Repotting: Repot every year in spring.
Propagation: Divide plants at repotting time.

palm-like leaves

CYPERUS DIFFUSUS
Umbrella Plant

grass-like leaves

CYPERUS ALTERNIFOLIUS
Umbrella Plant

thread-like leaves

CYPERUS PAPYRUS
Papyrus

Cyperus alternifolius

TYPES

C. papyrus (6 – 8 ft), the source of both paper and Moses' cradle in biblical times — too tall and difficult for most homes. The popular ones are **C. diffusus** (1 – 2 ft) and **C. alternifolius** (3 – 4 ft). C. alternifolius has two interesting varieties — **C. alternifolius gracilis** (1½ ft, dark green leaves) and **C. alternifolius variegatus** (3 ft, white-striped leaves).

DICHORISANDRA

Dichorisandra reginae

An indoor plant in the rarity class. Large-leaved and shrub-like when staked, but on close inspection it is clearly very similar to its close relative, the lowly but ever-popular Tradescantia (page 112). The leaves are colourful and clasping, and small starry flowers appear in late summer. But there is an important difference — Dichorisandra requires high air humidity.

SECRETS OF SUCCESS

Temperature: Average warmth; not less than 55°F in winter.
Light: A well-lit spot away from direct sunlight.
Water: Water liberally from spring to autumn; sparingly in winter.
Air Humidity: Stand in a pebble tray — mist leaves regularly.
Repotting: Repot, when necessary, in spring.
Propagation: Very easy — stem cuttings in spring, summer or autumn.

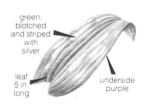

green, blotched and striped with silver

leaf 5 in long

underside purple

DICHORISANDRA REGINAE
Queen's Spiderwort

TYPES

There is an all-green Dichorisandra (**D. thyrsiflora**) but the only one grown as a house plant is **D. reginae**. This latter plant is bushy at first, but fully-grown stems (2 ft) need support.

DIEFFENBACHIA

large, fleshy leaves on stout stalks

fleshy, upright stem — bare at base when mature

DIEFFENBACHIA
Dumb Cane
(Leopard Lily)

DIEFFENBACHIA AMOENA

DIEFFENBACHIA OERSTEDII

DIEFFENBACHIA PICTA EXOTICA

DIEFFENBACHIA PICTA MARIANNE

DIEFFENBACHIA PICTA RUDOLPH ROEHRS

A splendid plant, much beloved by interior decorators on both sides of the Atlantic. Its common name, Dumb Cane, is derived from the unpleasant effect of its poisonous sap on the mouth and throat. Wash hands after taking cuttings.

A well-grown Dieffenbachia will reach 5 ft or more, but under ordinary room conditions some of the lower leaves will fall to give a false palm effect. It is not an easy plant to grow; it will not tolerate low winter temperatures or cold draughts. Dry air and fluctuating temperatures can be fatal to some delicate varieties, but the most popular type (D. picta exotica) is fairly tolerant and not at all difficult to grow in the centrally heated home. With age or bad management the plant may become leggy and unattractive. Cut off the cane, leaving a 4 in. stump. The crown of leaves can be used as a cutting; the stump will resprout to produce a new plant.

SECRETS OF SUCCESS

Temperature: Average or above average warmth. Not below 60°F in winter.

Light: Partial shade in summer; bright light in winter.

Water: Water regularly from spring to autumn; sparingly in winter. Let soil surface dry between waterings.

Air Humidity: Mist frequently. Surround pot with damp peat. Wash leaves occasionally.

Repotting: Repot annually in spring.

Propagation: There are several methods to choose from. Remove and pot up top crown of leaves; use rooting hormone and bottom heat. Pieces of stem, 2 or 3 in. long, can be used as cane cuttings (see page 237). Some varieties produce daughter plants at the base; remove and use as cuttings.

SPECIAL PROBLEMS

INSECTS
Keep watch for scale and red spider mite; see Chapter 15.

STEM BASE SOFT & DISCOLOURED
Cause: Stem rot disease. This condition is encouraged by overwatering and low temperatures. If damage is slight — cut out diseased area, spray with carbendazim and repot. If damage is severe — discard plant: use top as a cutting.

LOWER LEAVES YELLOW & WILTED
Cause: Low winter temperatures or cold draughts are the most likely reason. Plants will survive at 50°–55°F but lower leaves will suffer.

LOSS OF COLOUR
Cause: Direct sunlight or excessive brightness will give leaves a washed-out appearance. Move to a shadier spot.

LOSS OF LEAVES
Cause: Most likely reasons are temperature too cool, dry air or cold draughts if leaves are young. Old leaves tend to drop naturally with age.

LEAVES WITH BROWN EDGES
Cause: Compost has been allowed to dry out: it should be kept moist but not soggy at all times. Cold air can have a similar effect.

TYPES

The giant-leaved types with foliage 2–2½ ft long are **D. bowmannii** and **D. imperialis**. Another large species is **D. amoena** — the 18 in. long leaves are dark green striped with white bars. This striped effect is most striking in the variety **Tropic Snow**. The most popular species is **D. picta**, sometimes sold as **D. maculata**. The leaves are about 10 in. long, and they range from nearly all-green to practically all-cream. **Exotica** is heavily splashed with ivory — **Marianne** is even paler. For a compact plant, choose **compacta** or **Camilla**. All-green Dieffenbachias are hard to find — there are **D. humilis** and **D. oerstedii** . . . if you can locate a supplier.

Dieffenbachia amoena Tropic Snow

Dieffenbachia picta Camilla

DIZYGOTHECA

Dizygotheca elegantissima

A graceful plant with leaves divided into finger-like serrated leaflets which are dark green or almost black. The bush has a splendid lacy effect when well grown. It has the usual problems of so many delicate plants — it detests soggy compost but it drops its leaves if the soil ball is allowed to dry out. It does not like sudden changes in temperature and the air must be moist. If lower leaves fall, cut off the stem in spring and the stump will shoot again.

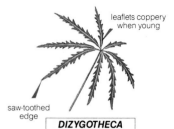

leaflets coppery when young

saw-toothed edge

DIZYGOTHECA ELEGANTISSIMA
(ARALIA ELEGANTISSIMA)
False Aralia
(Finger Aralia)

SECRETS OF SUCCESS

Temperature: Average warmth; minimum temperature 60°F in winter.

Light: Bright, but away from direct sunlight.

Water: Water moderately from spring to autumn; sparingly in winter.

Air Humidity: Mist leaves frequently.

Repotting: Repot every 2 years in spring.

Propagation: Difficult. Try stem cuttings in spring; use rooting hormone and bottom heat.

TYPES

D. elegantissima is the popular species — delicate in both appearance and constitution. This plant can grow up to 6 ft high, but the dark green leaves lose their lacy effect in old specimens. **D. veitchii** has wider leaves with wavy (not serrated) edges.

EUCALYPTUS

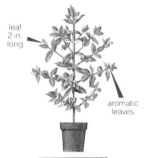

leaf 2 in. long

aromatic leaves

EUCALYPTUS GLOBULUS
Blue Gum

TYPES

E. globulus (Blue Gum) grows too tall for indoor cultivation — it is better to choose either the slower-growing **E. gunnii** (Cedar Gum) or **E. citriodora** (Lemon-Scented Gum).

Young plants of these giant Australian trees have attractive grey-green leaves which produce a distinctive aroma when crushed. They will flourish under ordinary room conditions if kept well-lit and cool. Pots can be stood outdoors in summer. Pinch out tips to keep growth in check and to maintain the production of juvenile foliage — old leaves are much less attractive. Eucalyptus is a fast-growing plant — seeds sown in spring will produce a large shrub in autumn. Plants are usually discarded after a couple of years.

SECRETS OF SUCCESS

Temperature: Cool or average warmth; keep at 45° – 50°F in winter.

Light: Bright light; some direct sun is beneficial.

Water: Water regularly from spring to autumn. Water sparingly in winter.

Air Humidity: Misting is not essential.

Repotting: Repot annually in spring.

Propagation: Sow seeds in spring — keep at 65°F.

Eucalyptus gunnii

EUONYMUS

leaf 2 in. long

leathery leaves

EUONYMUS JAPONICA MEDIOPICTUS

TYPES

E. japonica is the species grown as a house plant. There are several varieties, differing in the distribution of green and yellow (or white) on the leaves. Grow the dwarf **microphyllus** where space is limited.

Several variegated types are available; two popular varieties are illustrated here. These shrubby plants have oval, leathery foliage — E. japonicus microphyllus leaves are less than 1 in. long. Small white flowers may appear in late spring. Euonymus is a useful specimen for a bright unheated room, and will happily spend the summer outdoors. In a heated room, however, it will probably shed its leaves in winter. Keep the plant in check by pruning in spring, and remove all-green shoots as soon as they appear.

SECRETS OF SUCCESS

Temperature: Average warmth; keep cool in winter.

Light: Bright, indirect light or some sun.

Water: Water regularly from spring to autumn; sparingly in winter.

Air Humidity: Mist the leaves occasionally.

Repotting: Repot every year in spring.

Propagation: Stem cuttings in summer.

Euonymus japonica microphyllus albus

The DRACAENA Group

HOW TO GROW A TI TREE
Ti Trees are grown by planting pieces of mature cane cut from Dracaena, Cordyline or Yucca. The crown of leaves which appears at the top of the cane gives an 'instant palm' effect. Nursery-raised Ti Trees can be obtained but you can also grow your own — Ti Canes (cut from outdoor tropical plants and dried before shipment) are becoming increasingly available.

Crown of leaves appears at the side of the cane once rooting has taken place

Dry cane planted firmly in Seed & Cutting Compost. Keep compost moist but not wet

An old Dracaena, after its top has been removed and used as a cutting, will grow as a Ti Tree.

SPECIAL PROBLEMS

LEAVES WITH BROWN TIPS AND YELLOW EDGES
Cause: The most likely reason is dry air. Most Dracaenas need high air humidity — surround pot with moist peat and mist regularly. Cold draughts can have a similar effect, and so can underwatering. If dryness at the roots is the cause there will also be brown spotting on the foliage — see below.

LEAVES SOFT & CURLED WITH BROWN EDGES
Cause: Temperature too low. Delicate Dracaenas will quickly show these symptoms if kept close to a window on cold winter nights.

YELLOWING LOWER LEAVES
Cause: If this effect occurs slowly it is the natural and unavoidable process of old age. Dracaenas are false palms, with a characteristic crown of leaves on top of a bare stem. This growth habit is due to the limited life span of the foliage, each leaf turning yellow and dying after about 2 years.

LEAVES WITH BROWN SPOTS
Cause: Underwatering. The soil ball must be kept moist.

PLANT DEATH
Cause: One of 2 fatal faults — either too much water has been given in winter or the plant has been kept too cold.

LEAVES WITH BLEACHED DRY PATCHES
Cause: Too much sun. Move to a shadier spot.

Dracaena is becoming increasingly popular as a specimen plant, providing a bold and attractive focal point for a living room or hallway. Tall specimens are much in demand for public buildings, and the choice is much larger than it was a few years ago.

Most Dracaenas are false palms — the leafless woody trunk and crown of leaves giving a distinct palm-like appearance, but in fact they are unrelated to the true palms. These stately plants are ideal for the contemporary or hi-tech living room, but they are not new to the house plant scene. The Dracaena was much admired in Victorian times, but only recently has it reached the bestseller lists. It now outsells nearly every other large foliage plant, except for the Palms and the Rubber Plant.

There is some confusion over the naming of plants in this group. There is also some confusion over the ease (or difficulty) of growing these false palms, with their cane-like stems and crown of leaves. The simple answer is that they can be easy or difficult; it all depends on which variety you choose.

There are three easy ones — Dracaena marginata, D. draco and Cordyline australis. These will stand some shade, some neglect and quite low winter temperatures. The remainder of the group need more care — higher winter temperatures, careful watering to ensure moist but not soggy compost, and frequent misting.

Not all the Dracaenas are palm-like — D. godseffiana is a shrub which bears no similarity to its relatives. It is a robust plant, withstanding lower winter temperatures and drier air than the delicate varieties.

SECRETS OF SUCCESS

Temperature: Average warmth; not less than 55°F in winter. The easy types listed below can withstand lower temperatures.

Light: Light shade is the best general position — close to an east or west window is an ideal spot. Some varieties, such as C. terminalis, must have good light; but two — D. marginata and D. fragrans — will grow in shade.

Water: Keep the compost moist at all times. Reduce watering in winter but do not let it dry out.

Air Humidity: Mist leaves regularly. Only D. draco and D. godseffiana can grow happily in dry air.

Repotting: Every 2 years transfer to a larger pot in spring.

Propagation: There are several methods to choose from. Remove crown from old leggy canes and plant in Potting Compost; use rooting hormone and bottom heat. Alternatively, air layer the crown before potting up. Pieces of stem, 2 or 3 in. long, can be used as cane cuttings (see page 237).

HOW TO CHOOSE A DRACAENA

Easiest to grow	*C. australis* *D. marginata* *D. draco*
Smallest leaves	*D. sanderiana*
Largest leaves	*D. fragrans massangeana*
Most attractive leaves	*C. terminalis* *D. marginata tricolor* *D. deremensis bausei*
Tallest stems	*D. fragrans*

DRACAENA GROUP TYPES

Dracaena marginata tricolor

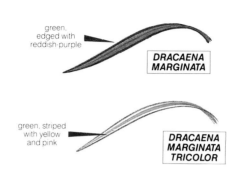

green, edged with reddish-purple

DRACAENA MARGINATA

green, striped with yellow and pink

DRACAENA MARGINATA TRICOLOR

D. marginata has a branching, snake-like trunk which can grow up to 10 ft high — its crown of shiny narrow leaves is much loved by interior decorators. The variety **tricolor** is more colourful and is an established favourite — **colorama** is a more recent introduction and is quite widely available.

leaf 2 ft long

narrow leaves

narrow stem, often branched and twisted

DRACAENA MARGINATA

Madagascar Dragon Tree

Dracaena godseffiana Florida Beauty

glossy leaves

leaf 3 in. long

wiry stems

DRACAENA GODSEFFIANA

Gold Dust Dracaena

D. godseffiana is a much-branched shrub with cream-splashed leaves. The amount of spotting depends on the variety — the foliage of **Florida Beauty** is often more cream than green.

leaf 9 in long

green, edged with white

DRACAENA SANDERANA

Ribbon Plant

Where space is limited, the usual choice is **D. sanderana**. The grey-green twisted leaves are not wide-spreading and the maximum height is 2–3 ft.

Dracaena sanderana

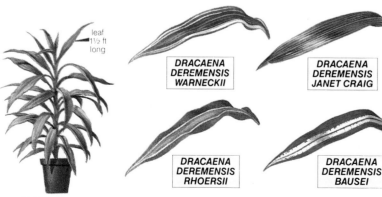

leaf 1½ ft long

DRACAENA DEREMENSIS WARNECKII

DRACAENA DEREMENSIS JANET CRAIG

DRACAENA DEREMENSIS RHOERSII

DRACAENA DEREMENSIS BAUSEI

DRACAENA DEREMENSIS

D. deremensis has many varieties but only a few are widely available. You should be able to find the species and its varieties **warneckii** and the dwarf-growing **compacta**. The tall **D. hookeriana** (narrow green leaves edged with white) is listed in some books but is rarely seen for sale.

Dracaena deremensis warneckii

Dracaena fragrans massangeana

leaf 2 ft long

broad leaves

DRACAENA FRAGRANS

green, banded with yellow

DRACAENA FRAGRANS MASSANGEANA
Corn Palm

green, edged with yellow

DRACAENA FRAGRANS LINDENII

leaf 1½ ft long

tough, sword-shaped leaves — resin ('dragon's blood') exudes from trunk

DRACAENA DRACO
Dragon Tree

D. fragrans is a solid-looking plant. On top of the stout trunk there is a crown of glossy leaves which are about 4 in. wide. Several varieties such as **lindenii** and **Victoria** (broad yellow stripe) are available, but **massangeana** with its corn-colour central band outsells all the others.

D. draco is a giant (50 ft or more) in its natural habitat but grows to only 4 ft indoors. Leaves are red-edged if kept in good light — old foliage arches downwards. The thick trunk develops slowly with age — young plants are practically stemless.

Dracaena or Cordyline?

The species and varieties of Cordylines are often confused with and sold as Dracaenas. You may find the popular Cordyline terminalis labelled as Dracaena terminalis and its favourite English name is Red Dracaena.

Despite the confusion there are clear-cut differences. Cordyline has a creeping rootstock and its roots are white and knobbly. Dracaena has a non-creeping rootstock and the smooth-surfaced roots are deep yellow or orange.

Cordyline terminalis Kiwi

leaf 1 ft long

green, splashed with red, pink and cream

CORDYLINE TERMINALIS TRICOLOR

leaf 9 in. long

green, streaked with red

CORDYLINE TERMINALIS REDEDGE

leaf 1 ft long

plain green

CORDYLINE TERMINALIS TI

4–6 ft high

dull, rough-edged leaves

CORDYLINE STRICTA

C. terminalis (often sold as **Dracaena terminalis**) is the only popular one and has many common names — Goodluck Plant, Ti Plant, Red Dracaena, Polynesian Ti and so on. The leaves are usually tinged or splashed with red and there are many varieties of this compact 1–2 ft false palm. **Rededge** is the favourite one — you can buy many others such as **Prince Albert** (green and red), **Firebrand** (bronze), **amabilis** (green and white) and **baptistii** (green, pink and yellow). **Ti** is all-green and is the 'grass' used for hula skirts in Hawaii — most all-green varieties are not suitable for ordinary room conditions but **volckaertii** is a tolerant exception. New varieties of C. terminalis continue to appear — look for **Atom** and **Kiwi**.

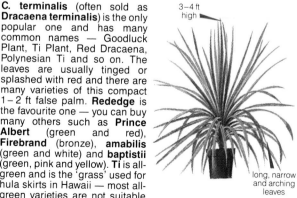

3–4 ft high

long, narrow and arching leaves

CORDYLINE AUSTRALIS
(DRACAENA INDIVISA)
Cabbage Tree
(Grass Palm)

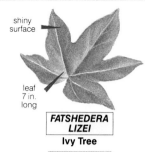

shiny surface

leaf 7 in. long

FATSHEDERA LIZEI
Ivy Tree

FATSHEDERA

This easy-to-grow hybrid of Hedera and Fatsia deserves its popularity. It prefers cool conditions, but it can be grown in a heated room as long as the winter temperature is kept below 70°F and the light is reasonably bright. It can be grown as a shrub, like its Castor Oil Plant parent — all you have to do is to pinch out the growing tips each spring. Or you can grow it as a climber like its Ivy parent — train it to a stake or trellis. For maximum effect grow about three plants in each pot and occasionally wash the attractive, dark green leaves.

Fatshedera lizei variegata

TYPES

F. lizei was introduced about 80 years ago. The stems can reach 6 ft or more. Support is needed, or you can pinch out the tips and grow it as a bush. The white-blotched form (**variegata**) is more difficult to grow.

SECRETS OF SUCCESS

Temperature: Average warmth; not less than 35°F in winter.
Light: Bright or light shade; keep well-lit in winter.
Water: Water regularly from spring to autumn; sparingly in winter.
Air Humidity: Mist the leaves frequently.
Repotting: Repot every year in spring.
Propagation: Stem cuttings in summer.

FATSIA

An excellent specimen plant for living room or hallway, reaching a height of 4 ft or more. It prefers a cool, well-ventilated and bright situation but it is extremely durable, accepting a wide range of conditions. For economy buy a small plant — it will grow quickly, especially if it is fed regularly and repotted annually. Cut back the growing tips each spring to keep it bushy. Wash the leaves occasionally and remove the flower buds which may appear. If leaves become disfigured, cut back the stalk and the plant will quickly sprout again.

leaf 1 ft across

shiny surface

pointed tip

FATSIA JAPONICA
(ARALIA SIEBOLDII)
Japanese Aralia
(Castor Oil Plant)

Fatsia japonica

SECRETS OF SUCCESS

Temperature: Average warmth; if possible keep cool in winter. Avoid temperatures above 70°F.
Light: Bright or light shade. Keep well-lit in winter.
Water: Water regularly from spring to autumn; sparingly in winter.
Air Humidity: Mist leaves frequently.
Repotting: Repot every year in spring.
Propagation: Stem cuttings in summer, or sow seeds in spring.

TYPES

F. japonica is an old favourite, with large deeply-lobed leaves and a tough constitution. There are several varieties, including **variegata** (cream-edged foliage) and **moseri** (compact growth habit).

SPECIAL PROBLEMS

LEAVES TURN YELLOW AND THEN DROP
Cause: Two quite separate culprits can cause this trouble; look for other symptoms. If leaves are wilted and soft — overwatering is the reason. If leaves are dry and brittle — too much heat is the cause.

LEAVES SHRIVELLED
Cause: The air is too dry or the leaves have been exposed to hot summer sun. Remember to mist the foliage regularly and to provide some shade in summer.

LEAVES PALE & SPOTTED, LEAF EDGES BROWN & BRITTLE
Cause: Underwatering. A large plant will need frequent watering in summer.

In the window of the front parlour, which was never opened, Mrs Pipchin kept a collection of plants in pots, which imparted an earthy flavour of their own to the establishment... There were half a dozen specimens of the cactus, writhing round bits of lath like hairy serpents; another specimen shooting out broad claws like a green lobster; several creeping vegetables, possesser of sticky and adhesive leaves; and one uncomfortable flower pot hanging to the ceiling, which appeared to have boiled over, and tickling people underneath, with its long green ends...

Charles Dickens
Dombey and Son (1848)

FERNS

Ferns are making a comeback. In Victorian times they were extremely popular and large collections were grown in conservatories and in specially constructed glass cases. But very few varieties were grown as ordinary living room plants, because gas fumes and coal fire smoke are extremely toxic to nearly all ferns. It was the advent of central heating with its freedom from fumes which led to the revival of interest, but radiators in turn have their problems. Few ferns can tolerate hot dry air, so air humidity has to be artificially increased (see Secrets of Success).

Most ferns are not really difficult to grow in the modern home, but they will not tolerate neglect. The compost must never be allowed to dry out, and the surrounding air needs to be kept moist.

There is a bewildering choice of varieties. Nearly two thousand are suitable for growing indoors, but comparatively few are available commercially. The classical picture of a fern is a rosette of much divided, arching leaves (correctly referred to as 'fronds') but there are also ferns with spear-shaped leaves, holly-like leaflets and button-like leaflets. There is also a wide choice of ways to display your collection. Many of them are ideal for a hanging basket and some, such as Boston Fern and Bird's Nest Fern, are large enough and bold enough to be displayed as specimen plants on their own. Delicate ferns, such as Delta Maidenhair, are best planted in a terrarium. When grouping ferns with other plants make sure that they are not crushed — the fronds are fragile and need room to develop. In addition ensure that all dead and damaged fronds are removed so that new ones can grow.

HOW TO CHOOSE A FERN

Easiest to grow	*Cyrtomium* *Davallia* *Pteris cretica* *Nephrolepis* *Asplenium nidus* *Pellaea rotundifolia*
For hanging baskets	*Nephrolepis* *Adiantum*
For bold display as a specimen plant	*Nephrolepis* *Asplenium nidus* *Blechnum gibbum*

SECRETS OF SUCCESS

Temperature: Average warmth; cool but not cold nights are desirable. The best temperature range is 60° – 70°F; the minimum for most types is about 50°F and ferns may suffer at more than 75°F.

Light: Despite popular opinion, ferns are not shade lovers indoors as most varieties originated in the dappled brightness of tropical woodland. Good indirect light is the proper location; an east- or north-facing windowsill is ideal.

Water: Compost must be kept moist at all times and never allowed to dry out. This does not mean constantly soggy compost — waterlogging will lead to rotting. Reduce watering in winter.

Air Humidity: Moist air is necessary for nearly all ferns. Spray plants regularly and use one or other of the techniques described on page 229.

Repotting: Repot in the spring when the roots fill the pot — most young specimens will probably require annual repotting. Do not bury the crown of the plant.

Propagation: The simplest way is to divide the plant into 2 or 3 pieces in early spring if it produces rhizomes. Some ferns produce young plants at the ends of runners (example — Boston Fern) or on fronds (example — Mother Fern). It is possible, but not always easy, to raise plants from spores obtained from the underside of mature fronds — see page 235.

SPECIAL PROBLEMS

BROWN DOTS OR LINES REGULARLY ARRANGED ON UNDERSIDE OF FRONDS
Cause: These are spore cases — an indication that the frond is mature and healthy. The spores produced inside these spore cases can be used for propagation — see page 235.

BROWN SHELLS IRREGULARLY SCATTERED ON FRONDS
Cause: Scale — the Bird's Nest Fern is particularly susceptible to this pest. For control, see page 244.

YELLOWING FRONDS, BEGINNING AT BASE OF PLANT. MATURE FRONDS DEVELOP BROWN SPOTS AND FALL
Cause: Air too warm — a common complaint when ferns are stood too close to radiators. Few ferns can tolerate very high temperatures. If the plant is also limp and wilting, then the cause is incorrect watering.

YELLOWING FRONDS, BROWN TIPS. NO NEW GROWTH
Cause: Air too dry. See Secrets of Success.

PALE FRONDS, SCORCH MARKS ON SURFACE
Cause: Too much sun. Ferns must be protected from midday sunshine in summer.

PALE FRONDS, WEAK GROWTH
Cause: Not enough fertilizer. Ferns need feeding, little and often, during the growing season.

FRONDS DYING BACK
Cause: Two most likely culprits are dry air and dry compost.

FERN TYPES

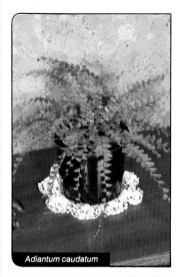
Adiantum caudatum

leaflets ½ in. long

young fronds coppery-pink

black stems

filmy leaflets

fronds forked at base

ADIANTUM RADDIANUM
(ADIANTUM CUNEATUM)
Maidenhair Fern
(Delta Maidenhair)

ADIANTUM HISPIDULUM
Australian Maidenhair
(Rose Maidenhair)

The Maidenhair Ferns have wiry stems, delicate leaves and a delicate constitution. They need moist air, warmth and shade — plants for the terrarium or shaded conservatory rather than the living room. **A. raddianum** is perhaps the easiest to grow — the arching **A. tenerum farleyense** is the most attractive. **A. hispidulum** is quite distinctive and **A. capillus-veneris** grows wild in Britain.

Adiantum capillus-veneris

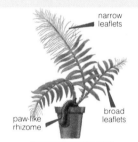

narrow leaflets

paw-like rhizome

broad leaflets

AGLAOMORPHA MEYENIANA
Bear's Paw Fern

A. meyeniana is a fern you will find in few textbooks and even fewer homes — it's one for the specialist. It has 2 unusual features — a creeping furry rhizome and fronds with both narrow and broad leaflets.

large palm-like crown of stiff fronds; trunk develops with age

BLECHNUM GIBBUM

The Blechnum Ferns develop a distinct trunk with age — the handsome crown has a 3 ft spread. The most popular species is **B. gibbum** — in a large collection you might find the Brazilian Tree Fern (**B. braziliense**).

pale green lacy fronds

CIBOTIUM SCHIEDEI
Mexican Tree Fern

Cibotium, like other Tree Ferns, is much more likely to be seen in the U.S. than in Britain. **C. schiedei** is the favourite one, extremely graceful with arching fronds and capable of producing an 8 ft trunk under glass.

holly-shaped leaflets, glossy dark green

CYRTOMIUM FALCATUM ROCHFORDIANUM
Holly Fern

Cyrtomium is an excellent fern to buy — unlike so many others it can withstand dry air and draughts. **C. falcatum** (Fishtail Fern) has smooth-edged leaflets — the variety **rochfordianum** is holly-like.

Asplenium nidus

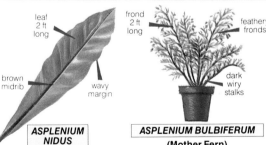

leaf 2 ft long

brown midrib

wavy margin

frond 2 ft long

feathery fronds

dark wiry stalks

ASPLENIUM NIDUS
Bird's Nest Fern

ASPLENIUM BULBIFERUM
(Mother Fern)
(Hen-and-Chicken Fern)

The Aspleniums or Spleenworts need shade and a moist atmosphere. There are 2 basic types which are cultivated as house plants, and they look nothing like each other. Firstly there is the Bird's Nest Fern — **A. nidus**. Its spear-like undivided leaves surround the fibrous 'nest' at the centre. Not difficult, but you must not handle the young fronds. The other type of Asplenium is the Mother or Hen-and-Chicken Fern. The fronds are finely divided and when mature bear numerous tiny plantlets. **A. bulbiferum** is the usual one — **A. viviparum** is smaller and the fronds more arching.

Asplenium bulbiferum

tiny leaflets on small fronds — wiry stems

creeping rhizome ('hare's foot')

DAVALLIA CANARIENSIS
Hare's Foot Fern

Davallia is grown for its thick and hairy rhizomes which grow over the edge of the pot. Common names for the various species include Hare's Foot, Squirrel's Foot and Rabbit's Foot. Grow **D. canariensis** (carrot-like foliage) or the larger but less hardy **D. fejeensis**.

dull green leathery leaflets — black trunk

DICKSONIA SQUARROSA
New Zealand Tree Fern

Dicksonia is the true Tree Fern. This native of Australasia belongs in a large conservatory and not in the living room. It produces a 10–20 ft high trunk when mature — grow it in the border or a large tub. **D. squarrosa** is a pretty pot plant when small, but forms a tall tree when mature. **D. antarctica** is the best one.

leathery brownish-green fronds

DIDYMOCHLAENA TRUNCATULA
Cloak Fern

The large **D. truncatula** fronds bear shiny leaflets in a double herringbone pattern. It is, however, a rarity which requires a humid atmosphere. There are two virtues — it will grow in quite dense shade and plants can be raised from spores.

Didymochlaena truncatula

plain leaf edges

erect fronds

NEPHROLEPIS EXALTATA
Sword Fern

graceful, arching fronds

NEPHROLEPIS EXALTATA BOSTONIENSIS
Boston Fern

ruffled leaflet edges

NEPHROLEPIS EXALTATA FLUFFY RUFFLES
Feather Fern

lacy leaflet edges

NEPHROLEPIS EXALTATA WHITMANII
Lace Fern

If you can only have one fern, choose a variety of Nephrolepis. In Victorian times **N. cordifolia** with its 1–2 ft erect fronds and the larger **N. exaltata** were very popular. The basic leaf pattern was a herringbone, with long leaflets (the 'bones') arranged on either side of the midrib (the 'backbone'). These stiff species of Nephrolepis are now not often grown — about a hundred years ago a gracefully drooping mutation was discovered in Boston — **N. exaltata bostoniensis**. This variety has become the popular variety on both sides of the Atlantic and there are now scores of different types. Examples are **rooseveltii** (large with wavy leaflets), **maassii** (compact with wavy leaflets) and **scottii** (compact with rolled leaflets).

There are varieties with a double herringbone pattern — each leaflet being divided up like a herringbone. The leaflets are sometimes divided even further, to give a feathery or lacy effect. Examples are **Fluffy Ruffles** (feathery leaflets in a double herringbone pattern), **whitmanii** (lacy leaflets in a triple herringbone pattern) and **smithii** (fine lacy leaflets in a quadruple herringbone pattern).

Nephrolepis cordifolia

Nephrolepis exaltata bostoniensis

Nephrolepis exaltata Gloriosa

FERN TYPES continued

Pellaea rotundifolia

round, leathery leaflets on low-growing fronds

fronds darken with age

black stalks

PELLAEA ROTUNDIFOLIA
Button Fern

PELLAEA VIRIDIS
Green Brake Fern

Pellaea viridis macrophylla

Pellaea has an unusual feature for a fern — it prefers dry surroundings to the moist conditions required by the vast majority of the group. **P. rotundifolia** is easy to grow — foot long arching fronds arise from a creeping rootstock. Pairs of shiny leaflets grow along the wiry stalk. These ½ in. leaflets are round at first — later oval. **P. viridis** is also easy to grow but is much more fern-like — its variety **macrophylla** has paler and much larger leaflets.

FERN LEAF LANGUAGE

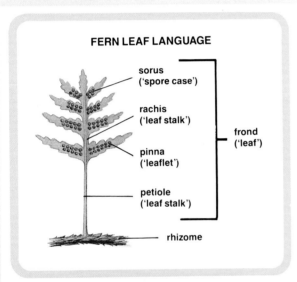

sorus ('spore case')

rachis ('leaf stalk')

pinna ('leaflet')

petiole ('leaf stalk')

frond ('leaf')

rhizome

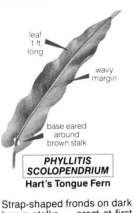

leaf 1 ft long

wavy margin

base eared around brown stalk

PHYLLITIS SCOLOPENDRIUM
Hart's Tongue Fern

Strap-shaped fronds on dark brown stalks — erect at first and then arching with age. The frond edges are wavy — the varieties **crispum** and **undulatum** have frilly margins.

Phyllitis scolopendrium undulatum

Platycerium bifurcatum

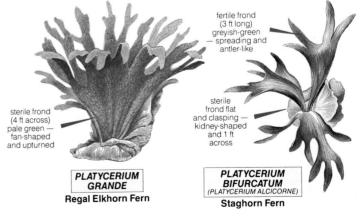

fertile frond (3 ft long) greyish-green — spreading and antler-like

sterile frond (4 ft across) pale green — fan-shaped and upturned

sterile frond flat and clasping — kidney-shaped and 1 ft across

PLATYCERIUM GRANDE
Regal Elkhorn Fern

PLATYCERIUM BIFURCATUM
(PLATYCERIUM ALCICORNE)
Staghorn Fern

The Staghorn and Elkhorn Ferns bear large and spectacular fronds, usually divided at their ends into antler-like lobes. The fronds are of two distinct types — there are sterile fronds at the base and spore-bearing fertile fronds above. **P. bifurcatum** is the popular and easy-to-grow species — the fertile fronds are the showy ones. **P. grande** is larger, and here it is the sterile fronds rather than the fertile ones which provide the display.

HOW TO MAKE A FERN COLUMN

If you have a large glass bell jar you can make a Fern Column, an attractive adaptation of the Victorian Fern Case for growing delicate specimens. Use miniature ferns bought from a specialist supplier — it is illegal to dig up ferns growing in the countryside.

Set the plastic-mesh tube in the dish using Plaster of Paris; place small pebbles over the surface. Pour some Potting Compost into the tube; insert the roots of a fern and then secure in place by adding more moist compost. Carry on adding compost and planting until the column is full. Press compost down, water from top and syringe surface. Place bell jar over the Fern Column.

HOW TO MAKE A FERN PLAQUE

Platycerium bifurcatum (Staghorn Fern) grows on tree trunks in its natural home in Australia. An ideal way to display this plant in the home is to make a Fern Plaque.

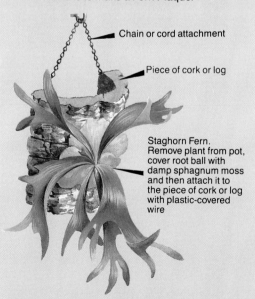

Chain or cord attachment

Piece of cork or log

Staghorn Fern. Remove plant from pot, cover root ball with damp sphagnum moss and then attach it to the piece of cork or log with plastic-covered wire

Watering is simple. Once a week immerse plant and plaque in a bucket of water for a few minutes. Allow it to drain before rehanging

frond up to 2 ft long

stalk 1½ ft long

deeply divided frond

POLYPODIUM AUREUM
(PHLEBODIUM AUREUM)
Hare's Foot Fern

P. aureum has deeply cut leaves (1 – 2 ft long) on thin stalks. There are a number of unusual features — the thick rhizome creeps along the surface and this fern will grow in the dry air of the living room. The most attractive variety is **mandaianum** — blue-green leaflets with wavy edges.

Polypodium aureum mandaianum

upright, pointed fronds

POLYSTICHUM AURICULATUM
Prickly Shield Fern

The most popular species is **P. tsus-simense**, the Tsussima Holly Fern. It is a small plant, less than 1 ft high, with dark green fronds. An excellent house fern because it does not mind dry air — the larger and stiffer **P. auriculatum** needs a humid atmosphere.

Polystichum tsus-simense

A collection of ferns planted in a Victorian fern-case. The Fern Craze was at its height in the 1860s — one catalogue listed 818 species

Pteris ensiformis victoriae

FERN TYPES continued

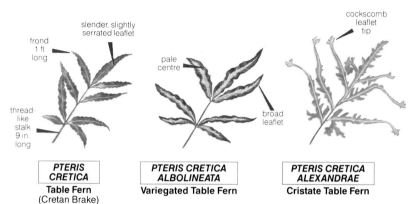

frond 1 ft long

slender, slightly serrated leaflet

thread-like stalk 9 in. long

PTERIS CRETICA
Table Fern
(Cretan Brake)

pale centre

broad leaflet

PTERIS CRETICA ALBOLINEATA
Variegated Table Fern

cockscomb leaflet tip

PTERIS CRETICA ALEXANDRAE
Cristate Table Fern

Pteris tremula

Most types of Pteris are easy to grow, producing handsome fronds in a range of shapes and sizes. The most popular types are varieties of **P. cretica** which are available in an assortment of leaflet colours and forms — all-green or variegated, plain or crested. These varieties include **albolineata**, **alexandrae**, **wilsonii** (compact with feathery leaflet tips) and the cockscomb-tipped **wimsettii**. **P. ensiformis** is similar to P. cretica, but the leaves are darker. Its variety **victoriae** (silver band along the midrib) is the prettiest of all the Table Ferns.

P. tremula (Australian Brake Fern) is quite different. The 3 ft long fronds are borne on upright stalks, each leaflet being much divided to produce a feathery effect. The third type of Pteris (**P. vittata**) is not often seen — its common name (Ladder Fern) aptly describes its shape. Long leaflets are borne like the rungs of a ladder on either side of the midrib of each frond. It is a large plant, with arching fronds growing 2–3 ft long.

Pteris vittata

FICUS

In the Ficus or Ornamental Fig family are found house plants which vary from stately trees to lowly creepers, and since Victorian times the unchallenged head of the family has been the Rubber Plant. Once only the narrow-leaved F. elastica was grown, but this old-fashioned variety has now been replaced by the much more attractive F. elastica decora and F. elastica robusta. The all-green Rubber Plants are much easier to grow than the variegated ones, and by far the most important danger is overwatering. Wash leaves occasionally.

The Weeping Fig is increasing in popularity because it is a splendid specimen plant for the modern home. Its leaves are not large, but it is so much more tree-like and graceful than the Rubber Plant.

At the other end of the scale are the trailing types, which are much smaller . . . and more difficult to grow. This is because they need moist air and are fussy about their requirement for evenly moist compost.

SECRETS OF SUCCESS

Temperature: Average warmth; not less than 55°F in winter.
Light: A bright spot for tree types, a partially shaded site for others. A Rubber Plant will adapt to a few hours' sunshine each morning, but this would be fatal to a Creeping Fig.
Water: Water with care. With tree types the compost must dry out to some extent between waterings. The trailing types require more frequent watering. Use tepid water and apply very little in the winter months.
Air Humidity: Mist occasionally in summer. Misting is essential for trailing types.
Repotting: Avoid frequent repotting. Repot every 2 years in spring until the plant is too large to handle.
Propagation: Stem cuttings in summer if stems are non-woody; rooting hormone and bottom heat are necessary. Air layer woody varieties. (See page 235).

SPECIAL PROBLEMS

SUDDEN LOSS OF LEAVES
Cause: The most likely reason depends on the type of Ficus. Rubber Plant — overwatering is the usual culprit; carry out standard remedial treatment (see page 246). Other possibilities are low winter temperatures, too little light, too much fertilizer and cold draughts. Weeping Fig — most likely cause is too little light or movement of the plant from one environment to another.

LOSS OF LOWEST LEAF
Cause: The bottom leaf of tree types will turn yellow and drop with age — this is a natural process and some degree of legginess is usual after a few years.

YELLOWING LEAF EDGES, SOME LOSS OF LOWER FOLIAGE
Cause: An early sign of more serious trouble, or the effect of underfeeding. Feed at the recommended rate throughout the growing season.

DRY SHRIVELLED LEAVES
Cause: A common problem with trailing types — the most likely reason is exposure to direct sunlight, failure to mist the leaves regularly and allowing the compost to dry out.

INSECTS
Both red spider mite and scale can be troublesome.

TYPES

● BUSHY TYPE

small olive-like berries

leathery, dark green leaves

FICUS DIVERSIFOLIA
Mistletoe Fig

Ficus diversifolia (F. deltoidea) is a slow-growing bush, eventually reaching a height of about 3 ft. The leaves bear small brown spots and the pea-sized fruits appear all year round — quite attractive but inedible.

Ficus diversifolia

● TRAILING TYPES

leaf 1 in. long

thin heart-shaped leaves

thin wiry stem

FICUS PUMILA
(FICUS REPENS)
Creeping Fig

leaf ½ in. long

thin heart-shaped leaves

FICUS PUMILA MINIMA
Creeping Fig

leaf 3 in. long

thin wiry stem

leathery pointed leaves

wiry stem

FICUS RADICANS VARIEGATA
Trailing Fig

Ficus pumila

The word 'Ficus' conjures up a picture of Rubber Plants and other tree-like specimens, but there are two lowly species which are useful as trailers or climbers. **Ficus pumila** produces a dense green carpet and is one of the best of all indoor ground covers — the stems will cling to any damp surface and so it is an excellent climbing subject for a moss stick (see page 114). The variety **minima** has smaller leaves and **variegata** has white-spotted foliage. **F. radicans** has larger leaves with wavy edges — the popular type is the cream-edged **variegata**.

FICUS TYPES continued

● TREE TYPES

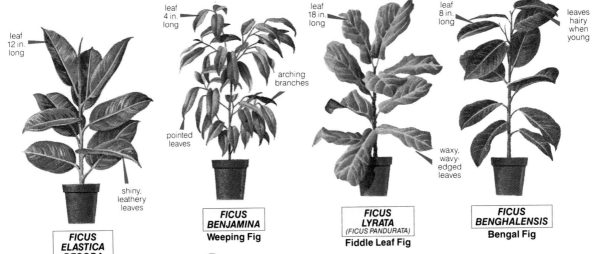

leaf 12 in. long

shiny, leathery leaves

FICUS ELASTICA DECORA
Rubber Plant

leaf 4 in. long

arching branches

pointed leaves

FICUS BENJAMINA
Weeping Fig

leaf 18 in. long

waxy, wavy-edged leaves

FICUS LYRATA
(FICUS PANDURATA)
Fiddle Leaf Fig

leaf 8 in. long

leaves hairy when young

FICUS BENGHALENSIS
Bengal Fig

FICUS ELASTICA BLACK PRINCE

FICUS ELASTICA TRICOLOR

FICUS TRIANGULARIS

FICUS RUBIGINOSA VARIEGATA
Rusty Fig

FICUS RELIGIOSA
Bo Tree

The low-growing Ficus species are dealt with on the previous page — here we are concerned with the ever-popular Rubber Plant and its relatives. The **Ficus elastica** of earlier days had narrow, drooping leaves and a rather fussy nature — it has been replaced by a number of varieties. **Decora** is the favourite one, **robusta** has even larger, wider leaves and **Black Prince** is just like robusta but with near-black foliage. There are also variegated types with yellow- or cream-splashed leaves — look for the pink midrib of **doescheri**, the complicated marbling of **schrijvereana**, the pink flush of **tricolor** and the cream edges of **variegata**. F. benjamina is increasing in popularity because it is a splendid specimen plant for the modern home. The variety **nuda** has narrow leaves — other varieties include **Hawaii, Starlight** and **Gold Princess**. F. benjamina is a weeping tree growing about 6 ft high — F. rubiginosa (**F. australis**) is a low-spreading tree with 4 in. long leaves. Its common name (Rusty Fig) is derived from the brown colouration of the underside of the leaves. Other species with 3–4 in. leaves include **F. triangularis** (triangular), **F. retusa** (oval) and **F. religiosa** (heart-shaped with a tail-like tip). Even smaller is the foliage of the shrub-like **F. buxifolia** — the brown stems bear 1 in. triangular leaves. But the spectacular species are the large-leaved ones — **F. benghalensis** (the Banyan Tree of India) bears leaves of the standard Rubber Plant type but which are hairy when young. The largest-leaved popular Ficus is **F. lyrata** — violin-like foliage in both shape and size.

Ficus elastica robusta

Ficus benjamina variegata

Ficus elastica schrijvereana

FITTONIA

Fittonia is a low-growing creeper with extremely attractive leaves. Prominent veins form a delicate tracery over the green surface, and many people have bought a specimen to add novelty to their collection . . . only to find that the plant has died within weeks. Unfortunately the standard large-leaved types are very difficult to grow under ordinary room conditions; they demand constant warmth and abundant moisture around the leaves. The usual advice is to grow them in a terrarium or bottle garden. A dwarf-leaved variety of F. argyroneura has been introduced and the textbooks will have to be changed. This Fittonia is quite easy to grow in the living room. It is just as attractive as its large-leaved parent, but it will flourish in dry air provided it is kept away from sunlight, given some winter heat and occasionally misted with water.

SECRETS OF SUCCESS

Temperature: Average warmth; not less than 60°F in winter.

Light: Choose a partially shaded spot. Direct sunlight must be avoided.

Water: Water liberally from spring to autumn; sparingly in winter. Use tepid water.

Air Humidity: Moist air is vital. Surround pot with damp peat and mist leaves frequently.

Repotting: Repot annually in spring.

Propagation: Creeping stems will root in surrounding compost — remove and pot up rooted cuttings. Divide plants in spring.

SPECIAL PROBLEMS

SUDDEN DEATH IN WINTER
Cause: Cold and wet conditions are always fatal. The plant needs winter warmth and the compost should be kept slightly moist but never soggy at this season of the year.

STRAGGLY GROWTH
Cause: Fittonia is a creeping plant and straggly growth is natural. Cut back stems in spring.

SHRIVELLED LEAVES
Cause: Air too dry or too much light. See Secrets of Success.

YELLOWING, WILTING LEAVES
Cause: Overwatering. Carry out standard remedial treatment (see page 246).

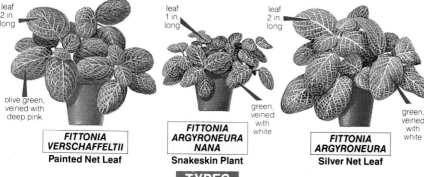

leaf 2 in. long — olive green, veined with deep pink

FITTONIA VERSCHAFFELTII
Painted Net Leaf

leaf 1 in. long — green, veined with white

FITTONIA ARGYRONEURA NANA
Snakeskin Plant

leaf 2 in. long — green, veined with white

FITTONIA ARGYRONEURA
Silver Net Leaf

Fittonia argyroneura nana

TYPES

Fittonia is easily recognised — the leaves bear a network of white, pink or red veins. This pattern is responsible for all the common names — Net Plant, Lace Leaf, Snakeskin Plant and so on. The large-leaved **F. verschaffeltii** has pink veins — for bright red veins grow the variety **pearcei**. The white-veined **F. argyroneura** is even more distinctive, but both are difficult to grow under ordinary room conditions. Choose instead the less-demanding dwarf **F. argyroneura nana**.

GEOGENANTHUS

Geogenanthus produces frilly-edged mauve flowers in summer, but it is grown for its unusual foliage rather than for the short-lived blooms. Each leaf is striped from base to tip and the surface is puckered — hence the common name. Geogenanthus is neither an easy plant to locate in the shops nor an easy type to care for — it needs both warmth and moist air.

leaf 4 in. long — leathery leaves

GEOGENANTHUS UNDATUS
Seersucker Plant

TYPE

Only one species is available — **G. undatus** (alternative name — **Dichorisandra musaica undata**). A compact plant, rarely exceeding 1 ft. The stems are unbranched — the leaves dark green with silvery stripes.

SECRETS OF SUCCESS

Temperature: Warm; above 65°F at all times.

Light: Brightly lit spot, away from direct summer sun.

Water: Keep compost moist at all times; reduce watering in winter.

Air Humidity: Mist frequently in spring and summer.

Repotting: Repot, when necessary, in spring.

Propagation: Stem cuttings in spring; use rooting hormone and bottom heat.

Geogenanthus undatus

pale green leaf, blotched or edged with white

hairy surface

GLECHOMA HEDERACEA VARIEGATA

Ground Ivy

TYPE

G. **hederacea variegata** (sometimes sold as **Nepeta hederacea**) is the only type grown as a house plant. Use it for ground cover or in a hanging basket — the stems must be cut back drastically each winter.

GLECHOMA

Glechoma is an excellent trailing plant — quick growing, easy to propagate, undemanding and with the added bonuses of pale blue flowers and fragrant 1 in. leaves. It does have a major drawback — hardly any house plant suppliers in Britain offer it for sale or have even heard of it! Like Ivy it is one of the very few house plants which originated in Europe, and it is hardy outdoors. This means that cool winter conditions are required.

SECRETS OF SUCCESS

Temperature: Average warmth; if possible keep cool in winter.

Light: Well-lit but away from direct sunlight.

Water: Water liberally from spring to autumn; sparingly in winter.

Air Humidity: Mist occasionally in summer.

Repotting: Repot in spring, but not usually necessary.

Propagation: Very easy — use trimmings as stem cuttings.

Glechoma hederacea variegata

GREVILLEA

Large indoor trees are expensive to buy, but with nearly all suitable varieties buying a seedling will mean a wait of several years before it becomes a specimen tree. Grevillea may be the answer for a cool and bright spot — it can be grown easily from seed and will reach 1 ft high in the first season and reach the ceiling in four or five years. Grevillea is an easy and reliable plant to grow with no special requirements.

SECRETS OF SUCCESS

Temperature: Cool or average warmth; not less than 45°F in winter.

Light: Brightly lit spot; some sun is acceptable but protect from midday summer sunlight.

Water: Water liberally from spring to autumn; sparingly in winter.

Air Humidity: Mist leaves occasionally.

Repotting: Repot annually in spring.

Propagation: Raised easily from seed. Sow in spring or summer.

Grevillea robusta

tree-like growth

underside silky

GREVILLEA ROBUSTA

Silk Oak

TYPE

G. **robusta** is the only type grown. The lacy, fern-like effect of the foliage tends to disappear with age, so it is usual to cut back or discard plants once they reach 2–3 ft.

GYNURA

An extremely useful climber or trailer for a well-lit spot. It grows quickly, it has no special needs and its foliage is covered with shiny purple hairs. This attractive colouring requires good light for development. Both varieties of Gynura produce small dandelion-like flowers in spring; these should be removed at the bud stage as most people find the flower scent offensive. Pinch out the tips occasionally to stimulate new leaf production; after a couple of years discard the plant and replace by rooted cuttings.

SECRETS OF SUCCESS

Temperature: Average warmth; not less than 50°F in winter.

Light: Brightly lit spot; some direct sunlight is beneficial.

Water: Water liberally from spring to autumn; sparingly in winter.

Air Humidity: Mist leaves occasionally.

Repotting: Repot in spring, but not usually necessary.

Propagation: Stem cuttings root very easily.

Gynura sarmentosa

dark green, covered with purple hairs

leaf 3 in. long

GYNURA SARMENTOSA

Velvet Plant

TYPES

G. **sarmentosa** is a popular trailer. The foliage has a velvety look — gleaming purple in bright light. G. **aurantiaca** has larger leaves, but it is more upright and less attractive.

HEDERA

stems not self supporting

leaves not succulent

The Ivies thoroughly deserve their high reputation as decorative plants. As climbers they can quickly clothe bare surroundings, provided you choose a vigorous Hedera helix variety. The stems bear aerial roots which cling to wallpaper, woodwork etc. The larger leaved, slower growing Canary Island Ivy does not possess these clinging aerial roots, so adequate support is necessary.

Ivies are just as useful as trailers in hanging baskets or as ground cover between larger plants, and it is here that the smaller bushy varieties come into their own. Examples of suitable types are Little Eva, Glacier and Needlepoint Ivy.

On the other hand the Ivies no longer deserve their past reputation as easy plants. They flourished in the unheated rooms of yesterday, but they do suffer in the hot, dry air of the centrally heated homes of today. Regular misting of the leaves is necessary when the radiators are switched on in winter. Expect brown leaf tips if you don't.

SECRETS OF SUCCESS

Temperature: Cool but frost-free. Ideally the room should be unheated in winter. Night temperatures above 60°F can lead to problems.

Light: Bright conditions in winter. Avoid direct sunlight in summer.

Water: Keep compost moist in summer by regular watering. In winter water sparingly, but never let the compost dry out.

Air Humidity: Mist frequently in summer, especially if the room is warm and dry. Mist in winter if the room is heated. Wash leaves occasionally.

Repotting: Every 2 years transfer to a larger pot in spring.

Propagation: Occasional removal of tips is necessary to promote bushiness. Use these trimmings as stem cuttings.

HOW TO MAKE AN IVY TREE

Cut the side shoots from a specimen of Fatshedera lizei and stake the stem. When it has reached 3 ft high remove the top growth with a horizontal cut. Make crossed cuts on stem top as shown below.

4 Ivy cuttings inserted into cut stem and bound with raffia

1 inch-deep cuts

SPECIAL PROBLEMS

LEAF EDGES BROWN & DRY. BARE SPINDLY GROWTH
Cause: Too warm. Look for red spider mite (see page 244). Cut back bare stems. Move to a cooler site.

LEAVES UNDERSIZED. BARE SPINDLY GROWTH
Cause: Too little light, although it is natural for mature leaves at stem base to drop with age. Cut back bare stems.

LEAVES ALL GREEN
Cause: Too little light. Variegated types revert to all-green habit in shady conditions. Another possibility is the need for repotting.

LEAF TIPS BROWN & DRY. STUNTED GROWTH
Cause: Air too dry. Look for red spider mite (see page 244). Remove dead growth. Mist leaves regularly.

HEDERA HELIX GREEN RIPPLE

HEDERA HELIX
English Ivy

HEDERA HELIX CHICAGO

HEDERA HELIX LITTLE EVA

HEDERA HELIX HARALD

HEDERA HELIX CRISTATA
Parsley Ivy

HEDERA HELIX GLACIER

HEDERA HELIX LUTZII

HEDERA TYPES

The general form of ivy needs no description — it is grown in homes throughout Europe and America. Less well known, however, is the extent of the variations on the basic pattern. Nearly all the True Ivies are varieties of the Common or English Ivy (**Hedera helix**) which bears characteristically lobed leaves. These varieties range in leaf form from simple shields (**scutifolia**) to long-pointed stars (**sagittaefolia**). Edges are smooth or ruffled, and colours vary from simple green to complex mixtures of white, cream, grey, green and yellow.

The largest-leaved ivy is **H. canariensis**. The green-leaved species is not popular — the type seen everywhere is the variegated **Gloire de Marengo**. Most True Ivies can be grown as either climbers or trailers — for a compact ground cover choose a small-leaved variety and pinch out the growing tips 2 or 3 times each year.

HEDERA HELIX JUBILEE
Goldheart Ivy

HEDERA HELIX SCUTIFOLIA

HEDERA HELIX SAGITTAEFOLIA
Needlepoint Ivy

HEDERA HELIX IVALACE
Lacyleaf Ivy

HEDERA CANARIENSIS GLOIRE DE MARENGO
Canary Island Ivy

HEDERA HELIX MARMORATA

Hedera helix Dorth

Hedera helix Kholibra

Hedera canariensis Gloire de Marengo

HELXINE

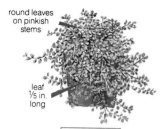

round leaves on pinkish stems

leaf 1/5 in. long

HELXINE SOLEIROLII

Mind Your Own Business
(Baby's Tears)

TYPES

The mossy mounds of **H. soleirolii** (**Soleirolia soleirolii**) were being used for ground cover in conservatories long before the start of the present boom in house plants. The variety **argentea** has silvery leaves.

Unlike nearly all other house plants, new pots of Helxine are raised at home rather than on professional nurseries. A small clump is removed from an established plant and placed on the surface of moist compost in a pot; in a short time tiny green leaves start to cover the surface.

Helxine is excellent in hanging baskets or for covering the soil around tall plants. But a word of warning — in an indoor garden it can easily smother low-growing plants and if used in a bottle garden the leaves wither in the stuffy atmosphere.

SECRETS OF SUCCESS

Temperature: Average warmth; not less than 45°F in winter.

Light: Extremely adaptable; bright indirect light is best but will survive almost anywhere.

Water: Keep the compost evenly moist at all times.

Air Humidity: Mist the leaves frequently.

Repotting: Repot, if necessary, in spring.

Propagation: Very easy — pot up small clumps at any time of the year.

Helxine soleirolii argentea

HEMIGRAPHIS

Hemigraphis alternata

A climbing plant, popular in some parts of the U.S. for hanging baskets but a rarity in Britain. Red Ivy (H. alternata) has coloured leaves — silvery in the absence of sunshine, metallic purple when exposed to a few hours' sunshine. Hemigraphis is not an easy plant to grow, but it is not quite as difficult as indicated by some textbooks. It needs winter warmth, occasional misting, and pruning when stems become straggly. Small white flowers occasionally appear.

SECRETS OF SUCCESS

Temperature: Average warmth; not less than 55°F in winter.

Light: Bright light or semi-shade; some direct sun will enhance colour.

Water: Water liberally from spring to autumn; sparingly in winter.

Air Humidity: Mist leaves regularly.

Repotting: Repot annually in spring.

Propagation: Stem cuttings in late spring or summer.

purple metallic sheen

stalk and underside wine red

HEMIGRAPHIS ALTERNATA
(HEMIGRAPHIS COLORATA)

Red Ivy

TYPES

H. alternata is not worth searching for unless you can provide winter warmth. Despite its name, this plant is quite different from a True Ivy — growth is limited to 1 – 1½ ft and the 3 in. leaves are oval. **H. exotica** (Waffle Plant) has puckered leaves.

HEPTAPLEURUM

Heptapleurum arboricola variegata

A fast-growing tree-like plant with about ten leaflets radiating from each leaf-stalk. The Parasol Plant is a fairly recent introduction, and it is still less popular than its much larger close relative, Schefflera actinophylla. Its main advantage over Schefflera is that it will happily grow as a bush if the growing point of the main stem is removed. Heptapleurum is quite easy to grow if you provide winter warmth, good light and mist regularly when the room is centrally heated. Leaf fall may occur if there is a sudden change in conditions; blackened tips indicate overwatering.

SECRETS OF SUCCESS

Temperature: Average warmth; not less than 60°F in winter.

Light: Bright light; not direct sun.

Water: Water liberally from spring to autumn; sparingly in winter.

Air Humidity: Wash leaves occasionally. Mist plant frequently.

Repotting: Repot annually in spring.

Propagation: Take stem cuttings or sow seeds in spring.

glossy leaflets

leaf-stalk attached to tree-like stem

HEPTAPLEURUM ARBORICOLA

Parasol Plant

TYPES

Remove growing point of **H. arboricola** for a quick-growing bush or stake to produce a 6 ft unbranched tree. Named varieties are available — **Hayata** (greyish leaves), **Hong Kong** (dwarf growing) and **variegata** (yellow-splashed leaves).

HYPOESTES

Freckle Face is grown for the colourful nature of its leaves. In a well-lit spot with some direct sunshine the leaf colouring will be vivid; in a shady site the foliage will be all-green. Young plants make attractive small bushes, but they must be regularly pruned to keep them 1 – 2 ft high.

Lavender flowers appear in summer, but they are insignificant and should be pinched out. After flowering, the plant sometimes becomes dormant and watering should be reduced until new growth starts.

SECRETS OF SUCCESS

Temperature: Average warmth; not less than 55°F in winter.

Light: Bright light; some direct sun will enhance colour.

Water: Keep soil evenly moist. Water liberally from spring to autumn; more sparingly in winter.

Air Humidity: Mist the leaves frequently.

Repotting: Repot annually in spring.

Propagation: Sow seeds in spring or take stem cuttings in spring or summer.

leaf 2 in. long

pink spots

HYPOESTES SANGUINOLENTA
Freckle Face
(Polka Dot Plant)

TYPES

The downy leaves of **H. sanguinolenta** (**H. phyllostachya**) are covered with pale pink spots — they are at their showiest in the variety **Splash**. Pinch out tips to maintain bushiness.

Hypoestes sanguinolenta Splash

IRESINE

The Iresines are unusual plants. Chicken Gizzard has a most unusual common name and Bloodleaf has remarkable wine red leaves and stems. They are rarities in Britain but are quite widely grown in the U.S. Iresines are sun-lovers — away from a south-facing window the colours tend to fade and growth becomes lank and straggly. Even under ideal conditions the plants become leggy with age. Nip out growing tips occasionally to maintain bushiness.

SECRETS OF SUCCESS

Temperature: Average warmth; not less than 55°F in winter.

Light: Give as much light as possible; shade from summer noonday sun.

Water: Keep compost moist at all times; reduce watering in winter.

Air Humidity: Mist leaves regularly.

Repotting: Repot, if necessary, in spring.

Propagation: Stem cuttings in spring or summer.

leaf 3 in. long

wine red leaves

IRESINE HERBSTII
Bloodleaf
(Beefsteak Plant)

TYPES

I. herbstii grows about 2 ft high, its red stems bearing notched leaves. The variety **aureoreticulata** (Chicken Gizzard) is more colourful — red stems, green leaves and yellow veins.

Iresine herbstii aureoreticulata

JACARANDA

An elegant plant, lacy-leaved and tree-like. It is an excellent choice, but specimens are not easy to obtain. Under good conditions it grows rapidly and will reach 3 ft high, but Jacaranda cannot be expected to produce its beautiful blooms indoors. It is therefore grown as a foliage house plant, and despite its rarity it is by no means difficult to grow in a heated sunny room. Remember to use tepid soft water and to mist the leaves when the air is dry.

SECRETS OF SUCCESS

Temperature: Average or above average warmth; not less than 55°F in winter.

Light: Bright light; some direct sun is beneficial.

Water: Water moderately from spring to autumn; sparingly in winter.

Air Humidity: Mist leaves frequently.

Repotting: Repot, when necessary, in spring.

Propagation: Stem cuttings in summer. Sow seeds in spring.

ferny foliage

JACARANDA MIMOSIFOLIA
Jacaranda

TYPE

Only one species is grown indoors — **J. mimosifolia**. It will not flower, but the delicate leaves make Jacaranda an attractive house plant. Plants lose their lower leaves with age.

Jacaranda mimosifolia

LAURUS

The Laurel or Bay Tree is not often referred to in house plant books, but it was first grown inside Roman villas more than 2,000 years ago. This popular patio shrub will thrive under ordinary room conditions if it is kept in a sunny spot, given plenty of fresh air (it doesn't mind draughts) and watered with care. Overwatering in winter is the usual cause of failure. Keep the shrub trimmed to 3 – 4 ft high and the pot can be stood outdoors in summer.

leaf 3 in. long

aromatic leaves

LAURUS NOBILIS
Bay Tree

SECRETS OF SUCCESS

Temperature: Cool or average warmth; keep cool but frost-free in winter.

Light: Bright light; some direct sunlight is beneficial.

Water: Water moderately from spring to autumn; sparingly in winter.

Air Humidity: Mist leaves regularly.

Repotting: Repot, when necessary, in spring.

Propagation: Stem cuttings in spring or autumn.

TYPE

The leaves of **L. nobilis** are the 'bay leaves' sold for kitchen use. The plant can be trimmed into a geometric or fanciful shape (ball, cone, pyramid etc) — excellent in some settings but horrible in others.

Laurus nobilis

The MARANTA Group

oblong leaves

underside usually purple

The Maranta group contains four closely-related members — Maranta, Calathea, Ctenanthe and Stromanthe. The outstanding feature of all of these plants is their spectacular foliage, bearing coloured veins or prominent blotches on a background which ranges from near white to almost black. The plants in the Maranta group have a number of requirements in common — protection from the direct rays of the sun, a need for high air humidity, a hatred of cold draughts and a vital need for warmth in winter.

The Marantas and Stromanthe are low-growing, rarely exceeding 8 in. high. The two popular varieties — M. leuconeura kerchoveana and M. tricolor are not at all difficult to grow, although in general the Maranta group is not for the beginner. The common name of Prayer Plant describes their curious habit of folding and raising their leaves at night.

The Calatheas and Ctenanthe are generally taller and more difficult to care for. In expert hands they can be grown as uncovered specimens but they are much more suitable for the terrarium or bottle garden.

SECRETS OF SUCCESS

Temperature: Average warmth — sudden fluctuations can harm delicate varieties. Maintain minimum winter temperature of 50°F for Maranta, 60°F for Calathea.

Light: Partial shade — colours fade in bright light. Do not expose to direct sunlight. Move to a well-lit but sunless spot in winter.

Water: Keep compost moist at all times; reduce watering in winter. Use tepid soft water.

Air Humidity: Mist leaves regularly. Surround pot with damp peat.

Repotting: Repot every 2 years in spring.

Propagation: Divide plants at repotting time. Cover pots with polythene and keep warm until new plants are established.

SPECIAL PROBLEMS

LEAF TIPS BROWN & DRY. STUNTED GROWTH
Cause: Air too dry. Look for red spider mite (see page 244). Remove dead growth. Mist leaves regularly.

LEAVES CURLED & SPOTTED. LOWER LEAVES YELLOW
Cause: Underwatering. Compost should be kept moist at all times — unlike many house plants it should not be allowed to dry out slightly between watering when the plant is actively growing.

LEAF FALL
Cause: Air too dry. The plant is particularly sensitive to low air humidity and should be surrounded with damp peat or planted in a bottle garden.

LIMP, ROTTING STEMS
Cause: Air too cool and compost too wet in winter. See Secrets of Success.

LEAVES DISCOLOURED OR SCORCHED
Cause: Too much light, especially direct sunlight. The plant should be moved immediately; delay could be fatal.

MARANTA GROUP TYPES

Maranta tricolor

prominent
red
veins

MARANTA TRICOLOR
*(MARANTA LEUCONEURA
ERYTHROPHYLLA)*
Herringbone Plant

brown
blotches
turning
green
with
age

**MARANTA
LEUCONEURA
KERCHOVEANA**
Prayer Plant
(Rabbit's Foot)

blackish-
green
leaf
with
silvery
veins

**MARANTA
LEUCONEURA
MASSANGEANA**

Maranta leaves are about 6 in. long. **M. bicolor** is available — the dark green leaves are blotched with brown. All the popular varieties belong to the species **M. leuconeura** — easily distinguished from M. bicolor by the tubers which form below the surface and by the smaller leaves. For red veins buy the variety **erythrophylla** (sold as **M. tricolor**) or **Fascinator**. For white veins pick **massangeana** and for dark patches on bright green leaves the usual choice is **kerchoveana**.

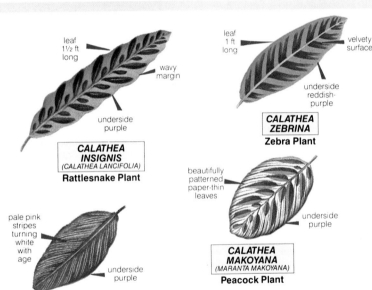

leaf
1½ ft
long

wavy
margin

underside
purple

**CALATHEA
INSIGNIS**
(CALATHEA LANCIFOLIA)
Rattlesnake Plant

leaf
1 ft
long

velvety
surface

underside
reddish-
purple

**CALATHEA
ZEBRINA**
Zebra Plant

beautifully
patterned
paper-thin
leaves

underside
purple

**CALATHEA
MAKOYANA**
(MARANTA MAKOYANA)
Peacock Plant

pale pink
stripes
turning
white
with
age

underside
purple

**CALATHEA
ORNATA**

Calathea makoyana

The showiest Calathea is undoubtedly **C. makoyana**. With 1 ft long papery leaves borne upright on long stalks, its decorative tracery gives rise to one of its common names — Cathedral Windows. The leaves of **C. ornata** are smaller — choose the variety **roseolineata** or **sanderana**. Much less usual are **C. picturata argentea** (silvery grey edged with green) or **C. louisae** (dark green with yellowish-green centre). There are a few Calatheas with lance-like leaves — **C. insignis** and the smaller **C. lindeniana** bear their leaves upright — the leaves of **C. zebrina** and the smaller **C. bachemiana** are held horizontally.

leaf
1½ ft
long

velvety
surface

underside
reddish-
purple

**CTENANTHE
OPPENHEIMIANA
TRICOLOR**
Never Never Plant

The Ctenanthes are closely related to the Calatheas — both are eye-catching and difficult to grow. They have a long list of hates — direct sunlight, temperatures below 60°F, cold or hard water and feeding after repotting. There are several species, but the only one you are likely to find is **C. oppenheimiana tricolor** with cream-coloured blotches covering a large part of the leaf surface.

Stromanthe is compact and low-growing like Maranta, but the foliage is marked with the distinct tracery of Calathea with which it is easily confused. The usual species is **S. amabilis**, but it is hard to find a supplier and even harder to grow. Don't waste your money unless you have a heated greenhouse or terrarium — it needs a minimum temperature of 65°F and the atmosphere must be moist.

underside
grey-green

**STROMANTHE
AMABILIS**

MONSTERA

Monstera deliciosa has been a favourite for many years. With proper care young specimens (sometimes mistakenly sold as Philodendron pertusum) soon develop large adult leaves which are perforated and deeply cut. Sturdy support is essential, and stems can reach a height of 20 ft or more. If your aim is to grow a tall plant with giant leaves you must care for the aerial roots — push them into the compost or use a moss stick. Winter brightness is essential — Monstera produces small leaves and spindly leaf-stalks when there is not enough light. The plant stops growing altogether in deep shade.

The Monsteras are easy to grow and have no special requirements. However, the white lily-like flowers and edible fruits are only likely to appear on conservatory or greenhouse plants.

moss stick: tube of rolled plastic netting filled with damp moss or peat (see page 114)

aerial roots

foliage on young plant undivided — later cut and often perforated

MONSTERA DELICIOSA
(PHILODENDRON PERTUSUM)
Swiss Cheese Plant
(Splitleaf Philodendron)

SECRETS OF SUCCESS

Temperature: Average warmth; not less than 50°F in winter. Active growth starts at 65°F.

Light: Keep out of direct sunlight. Choose a spot in light shade or moderate brightness.

Water: During winter keep the soil just moist — make sure it is not waterlogged. For the rest of the year water thoroughly, but allow compost to become dryish between waterings.

Air Humidity: Mist if room is heated. Occasionally wash and polish mature leaves.

Repotting: Every 2 years transfer to a larger pot in spring.

Propagation: When too tall remove tip in summer at a point just below an aerial root. Plant the cutting — the severed parent will continue to grow. Air layer as an alternative.

TYPES

M. deliciosa is the species grown as a house plant. With proper care giant leaves 1½ ft or more across will be produced. The form **variegata** has white and cream lines or patches on the leaves — more colourful but not necessarily more attractive. Where space is limited grow the compact variety **borsigiana**.

SPECIAL PROBLEMS

LEAVES WEEPING AT EDGES
Cause: Compost too wet. Allow to dry out and increase time between waterings.

ROTTING STEMS
Cause: Stem rot disease. This is usually a winter problem as the fungus is encouraged by too much moisture and too little heat. It may be possible to save the plant by repotting and keeping the compost dry and warm.

YELLOWING LEAVES
Cause: Overwatering is the most likely reason if many leaves are affected and if there are signs of wilting and rotting. If there is no wilting or rotting, underfeeding is the probable cause. If only lower leaves are affected, look for brown spots and for small and dark new leaves — the signs of underwatering. Pale leaves with straw-coloured patches indicate too much sunlight.

LOSS OF LEAVES
Cause: It is normal for the lowest leaves to drop with age. If there is abnormal leaf fall then any serious upset in conditions could be the cause — always look for other symptoms on upper leaves. If the leaves turn brown and dry before falling then too much warmth is the cause. This is a common winter problem when the pot is kept near a radiator.

LEGGY GROWTH, SMALL PALE LEAVES
Cause: Too little light is the first thing to look for. Monstera will not thrive in deep shade.

BROWN SPOTS ON UNDERSIDE OF LEAVES
Cause: Red spider mite — see page 244.

LEAVES WITH BROWN AND PAPERY TIPS & EDGES
Cause: Dry air is the most probable cause. Mist the leaves or surround the pot with damp peat. A pot-bound plant will show similar symptoms. Brown tips are also a symptom of overwatering, but general yellowing will also be present if waterlogging is the cause.

NO HOLES IN LEAVES
Cause: It is normal for the leaves in young plants to be uncut and not perforated. In mature leaves the most likely causes are lack of light, cold air, too little water and underfeeding. In tall plants the most likely reason is failure of water and food to reach the uppermost leaves. Aerial roots should be pushed into the compost or allowed to grow into a moist support.

MIMOSA

Mimosa pudica

Although this plant makes an attractive feature, its main claim to fame is its peculiar habit of rapidly folding up its leaves and drooping its branches when touched during the day — at night the leaves fold naturally. It is an easy plant to raise from seed or cuttings and it is easy to care for, with the added benefit of bearing ball-like pink flower-heads during the summer months.

SECRETS OF SUCCESS

Temperature: Average warmth, not less than 60°F in winter.

Light: Bright light; some direct sunlight is beneficial.

Water: Keep compost moist at all times; reduce water in winter.

Air Humidity: Mist leaves regularly.

Repotting: Not usually necessary.

Propagation: Stem cuttings in spring or summer. Sow seeds in early spring; pour hot water over seeds before sowing.

leaves fold when touched

MIMOSA PUDICA
Sensitive Plant

TYPE

M. pudica is a 2 ft branching plant bearing delicate branches and feathery leaves. The stems are spiny and the sensitive leaves take about ½ – 1 hour to recover after being touched.

MIKANIA

Mikania ternata

Mikania is a quick-growing trailing plant which has entered the shops but is found in hardly any textbooks. It is colourful — the veins are purple and the leaf surface has a distinctly red or purple appearance when the plant is kept in a brightly-lit spot. Mikania is not really happy in the living room — it needs moist air, but misting can damage the leaves.

SECRETS OF SUCCESS

Temperature: Average warmth; not less than 50° – 55°F in winter.

Light: Bright with some direct sunlight.

Water: Keep compost moist at all times; reduce water in winter.

Air Humidity: Mist with care — tepid water, very fine spray and keep misted plants away from sunshine.

Repotting: Repot, when necessary, in spring.

Propagation: Stem cuttings in spring.

leaflet 2 in. long
underside purple

MIKANIA TERNATA
Plush Vine

TYPE

There is a single species sold as a house plant — M. ternata. The palmate leaves are green with a purplish sheen, slightly hairy above and densely hairy below.

NICODEMIA

oak-like leaves 1 – 2 in. long

NICODEMIA DIVERSIFOLIA
Indoor Oak

TYPE

There is a single species — N. diversifolia, also called Buddleia indica. This leafy shrub grows about 1½ ft high. It needs to rest in winter — water sparingly and do not feed.

The Indoor Oak is a rarity in Europe, but it is gaining popularity in the U.S. where it was introduced from Africa some years ago. The common name relates to the shape of its leaves, but the similarity with the familiar oak tree ends there. Nicodemia foliage is dark green and glossy with a quilted surface; the growth habit is shrubby and definitely not tree-like. This indoor plant would add an unusual note to any house plant collection, but it is no more attractive than many of the popular shrubs described elsewhere in this book. It is not difficult to care for, but winter warmth is essential. Pinch out tips occasionally to maintain bushiness.

SECRETS OF SUCCESS

Temperature: Average warmth; not less than 55°F in winter.

Light: Bright light or semi-shade; avoid direct sun in summer.

Water: Keep compost moist at all times; reduce water in winter.

Air Humidity: Mist leaves occasionally.

Repotting: Repot, if necessary, in spring.

Propagation: Stem cuttings in spring or summer.

Nicodemia diversifolia

OPHIOPOGON

Lily Turf is not often seen indoors, but it is an undemanding durable plant for an unheated room. It will grow in sun or shade and has the added benefit of producing small white or mauve flowers in summer. Lily Turf is an apt name for Ophiopogon — although a member of the Lily family its long green, green-and-white striped, or purplish-black leaves are distinctly grass-like and spread quite rapidly to form a turf. Brown leaf tips indicate too much heat in winter or too little water in summer.

SECRETS OF SUCCESS

Temperature: Average warmth; keep cool but frost-free in winter.

Light: Bright light or semi-shade; avoid direct sun in summer.

Water: Keep compost moist at all times; reduce watering in winter.

Air Humidity: Mist leaves frequently.

Repotting: Repot every year in spring.

Propagation: Divide plants at repotting time.

Ophiopogon jaburan variegata

leaf 8 in. long
blackish-green leaves
OPHIOPOGON JAPONICUS
Dwarf Lily Turf

TYPES

O. japonicus is the Dwarf Lily Turf, bearing short leaves and insignificant mauve flowers. **O. jaburan** or White Lily Turf is taller (2 ft) and the clusters of white flowers in summer are more prominent.

OPLISMENUS

Basket Grass is an excellent alternative to the ever-popular Tradescantia in hanging baskets and wall pots. Its slender stems spread rapidly and trail gracefully. Oplismenus is sometimes recommended as a ground cover for use between other plants, but it can be a menace if allowed to get out of hand. One of the main blessings of this trailer is the simplicity of raising new plants — just snip off a piece and plant in Potting Compost. It is not usually worthwhile keeping old plants — plant several cuttings in a pot each spring to maintain the display of fresh young plants.

SECRETS OF SUCCESS

Temperature: Average warmth; not less than 45°F in winter.

Light: Bright light, but avoid direct sun.

Water: Water liberally from spring to autumn; sparingly in winter.

Air Humidity: Mist leaves occasionally.

Repotting: Not usually necessary. If plant is to be retained, repot in spring.

Propagation: Very easy. Divide plants or take stem cuttings between spring and autumn. Self-rooted cuttings may be found around the plant; remove and pot up.

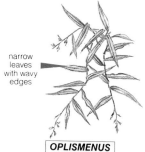
narrow leaves with wavy edges
OPLISMENUS HIRTELLUS
Basket Grass

TYPES

The house plant species is **O. hirtellus**. The variety you are most likely to see is **variegatus (Panicum variegatum)**. Its 3–4 in. leaves on branching stems are gaily striped with white and pink.

Oplismenus hirtellus variegatus

OSMANTHUS

If you like the idea of having living Holly growing in your home at Christmas time, then choose Osmanthus (False Holly) rather than Ilex — the True Holly. Osmanthus will flourish quite happily indoors all year round, provided that you keep it in an unheated room and let it receive some direct sunlight. The bush is slow growing and the leaves are hard and prickly. The textbooks talk about fragrant tubular flowers in autumn, but these rarely appear when the plant is grown indoors.

SECRETS OF SUCCESS

Temperature: Cool but frost-free. Night temperatures above 60°F can lead to problems.

Light: Brightly lit spot; some direct sun is beneficial.

Water: Water moderately from spring to autumn; sparingly in winter.

Air Humidity: Mist leaves occasionally.

Repotting: Repot, when necessary, in spring.

Propagation: Stem cuttings in spring.

Osmanthus heterophyllus variegatus

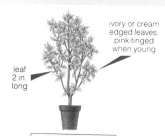
ivory or cream edged leaves; pink-tinged when young
leaf 2 in. long
OSMANTHUS HETEROPHYLLUS VARIEGATUS
False Holly

TYPES

O. heterophyllus is the species grown, and **variegatus** is the most popular variety. The plant grows about 3 ft high — trim back occasionally. The variety **purpureus** has near-black leaves.

PALMS

Palms are attractive . . . and expensive. It is not the nurseryman's fault; they are difficult and costly to raise. They are still well worth the investment for two special purposes. For a bottle garden or terrarium the Parlour Palm is unrivalled as a centrepiece, and the old 'Palm Court' favourite, the Kentia Palm, is ideal if you want an elegant specimen plant with a cast-iron constitution.

Both of these well-known palms are remarkably easy to look after in an average room, provided you don't regard them as lovers of tropical sunshine and desert-dry air. In fact they require cool winters, moist summers and protection from direct sunlight. The Parlour Palm produces tiny ball-like flowers while the plant is still quite small.

Palms come in a range of leaf types and sizes, but there is a basic common feature. The only growing point is at the tip of each stem. If you try to cut a stem back you will kill it.

SECRETS OF SUCCESS

Temperature: Average warmth; not less than 50°F in winter. Winter night temperature should not exceed 60°F for Parlour and Kentia Palms.

Light: A few delicate palms revel in sunshine, but the popular varieties should be kept in partial shade. Both Parlour and Kentia Palms can thrive in low light conditions.

Water: The first need is for good drainage; all palms detest stagnant water at the roots. During winter keep the soil slightly moist. Water more liberally in spring and summer.

Air Humidity: Mist if room is heated. Occasionally sponge mature leaves. Avoid draughts.

Repotting: Only repot when the plant is thoroughly pot-bound, as palms dislike disturbance. Compact the compost around the soil ball.

Propagation: From seed. A temperature of 80°F is required, so propagation is difficult.

SPECIAL PROBLEMS

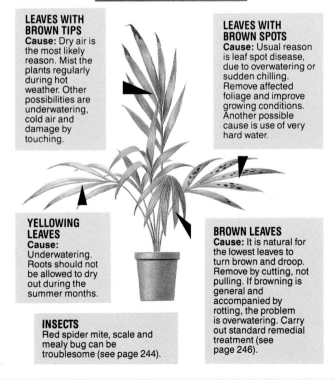

LEAVES WITH BROWN TIPS
Cause: Dry air is the most likely reason. Mist the plants regularly during hot weather. Other possibilities are underwatering, cold air and damage by touching.

LEAVES WITH BROWN SPOTS
Cause: Usual reason is leaf spot disease, due to overwatering or sudden chilling. Remove affected foliage and improve growing conditions. Another possible cause is use of very hard water.

YELLOWING LEAVES
Cause: Underwatering. Roots should not be allowed to dry out during the summer months.

BROWN LEAVES
Cause: It is natural for the lowest leaves to turn brown and droop. Remove by cutting, not pulling. If browning is general and accompanied by rotting, the problem is overwatering. Carry out standard remedial treatment (see page 246).

INSECTS
Red spider mite, scale and mealy bug can be troublesome (see page 244).

PALM TYPES

● FEATHER PALMS

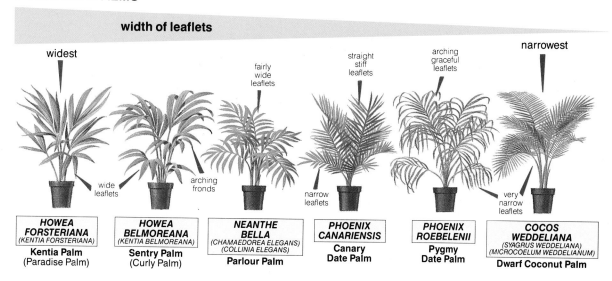

width of leaflets

widest

wide leaflets

arching fronds

fairly wide leaflets

straight stiff leaflets

arching graceful leaflets

narrowest

narrow leaflets

very narrow leaflets

| *HOWEA FORSTERIANA* *(KENTIA FORSTERIANA)* **Kentia Palm** (Paradise Palm) | *HOWEA BELMOREANA* *(KENTIA BELMOREANA)* **Sentry Palm** (Curly Palm) | *NEANTHE BELLA* *(CHAMAEDOREA ELEGANS)* *(COLLINIA ELEGANS)* **Parlour Palm** | *PHOENIX CANARIENSIS* **Canary Date Palm** | *PHOENIX ROEBELENII* **Pygmy Date Palm** | *COCOS WEDDELIANA* *(SYAGRUS WEDDELIANA)* *(MICROCOELUM WEDDELIANUM)* **Dwarf Coconut Palm** |

Fronds are divided on either side of the midrib into leaflets — these leaflets may be soft and drooping or stiff and erect. **Neanthe bella**, the most widely grown of all indoor palms, belongs to this group. It may be listed as **Collinia elegans** or **Chamaedorea elegans Bella** in the textbooks, but all these names refer to the old favourite Parlour Palm which is usually bought as a 6–12 in. specimen. After a few years it will reach its adult height of about 2 ft and tiny yellow flowers and small fruit appear if grown in good light. The dwarf nature of Neanthe makes it ideal for small rooms and bottle gardens — for a much bolder display the usual choice is one of the Howea (Kentia) palms. These are the traditional Palm Court plants which grow up to 8 ft tall. It is not too easy to distinguish between the 2 species — **Howea forsteriana** is the British favourite and is quicker growing but less arching than **H. belmoreana**.

The true Date Palm (**Phoenix dactylifera**) is less attractive though quicker growing than the species of Phoenix sold as house plants — **P. canariensis** (6 ft) and **P. roebelenii** (3 ft). The true Coconut Palm (**Cocos nucifera**) unfortunately dies after a couple of years indoors. Its near relative **Cocos weddeliana** (more correctly **Syagrus weddeliana**) is sold as a house plant and is thought by some experts to be the most attractive of all the indoor palms. But it has none of the hardiness of the popular types and needs the warmth and humidity of a conservatory.

Howea forsteriana

Neanthe bella

PALM TYPES continued

● FISHTAIL PALMS

wedge-shaped leaflets

CARYOTA MITIS

Burmese Fishtail Palm

The Fishtail Palms get their name from the shape of the leaflets, which are about 6 in. long and 4 in. wide. **Caryota mitis** is the favourite one — lots of ragged-edged leaflets on arching fronds. **C. urens** (Wine Fishtail Palm) is less popular and less attractive — its leaflets are more triangular but there are fewer of them. Both types form stems — mature height 6–8 ft.

Caryota urens

● SAGO PALMS

ball-like base

CYCAS REVOLUTA

Sago Palm

The Sago Palms (cycads) are distinctly palm-like in appearance but they are not closely related to the true palms. You will find only one species at the garden centre — **Cycas revoluta**. It is an extremely slow-growing plant, putting out just one leaf per year. In time an attractive, dark green rosette of stiff arching foliage is formed — mature height 2 ft.

Cycas revoluta

● CANE PALMS

deep green narrow leaflets

yellowish green leaflets

deep green broad leaflets

cane-like stems

CHAMAEDOREA SEIFRIZII

Reed Palm

CHRYSALIDOCARPUS LUTESCENS
(ARECA LUTESCENS)

Areca Palm
(Butterfly Palm)

CHAMAEDOREA ERUMPENS

Bamboo Palm

A small group of palms produce tall reed-like stems which look rather like bamboo canes when mature. These plants are popular with interior decorators in the U.S., providing bold focal points for large rooms. Reed and Bamboo Palms can grow 6–10 ft tall under good conditions and the fronds of the Areca Palm may reach 3 ft or more. Rhapis excelsa (page 89) and the closely related R. humilis are sometimes called Bamboo Palms as their slender stems can grow 5–7 ft high.

Chrysalidocarpus lutescens

● FAN PALMS

Trachycarpus fortunei

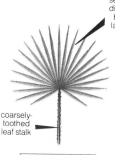

segments divided to base of large fan

coarsely-toothed leaf stalk

CHAMAEROPS HUMILIS
European Fan Palm

segments not divided to base of large fan

finely-toothed leaf stalk

TRACHYCARPUS FORTUNEI
(CHAMAEROPS EXCELSA)
Windmill Palm

segments not divided to base of large fan

drooping tips

toothed leaf stalk

LIVISTONA CHINENSIS
(LATANIA BORBONICA)
Chinese Fan Palm

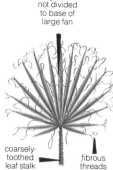

segments not divided to base of large fan

coarsely-toothed leaf stalk

fibrous threads

WASHINGTONIA FILIFERA
Desert Fan Palm

Fronds are split into numerous segments radiating from a point at the base of each frond — these segments may be entirely or only partly divided. The leaf stalks are long, up to 2 ft or more, and are generally toothed. The Fan Palms are not widely grown as house plants — the large leaves can be dramatic in the right situation but have none of the graceful effect associated with palms. Some are easy — **Chamaerops humilis** (the only native European palm) is quite hardy indoors, but others are difficult to grow — **Washingtonia filifera** is short lived. The large-leaved ones are too wide-spreading for the average room — it is only the smaller-leaved **Rhapis excelsa** with its upright stems which is widely sold.

segments divided to base of small fan — leaflets 8 in. long

RHAPIS EXCELSA
Little Lady Palm

> **❝**In tasteful homes, where there are ladies, the window-gardening may be safely left in their hands. It is surprising the progress that the dear, nimble-fingered creatures make in this delightful art.**❞**
>
> F.W. Burbidge
> **Domestic Floriculture (1875)**

leaf 2–3 ft long

saw-edged leaves

leaves spirally arranged on stem

PANDANUS VEITCHII
Screw Pine

TYPES

P. veitchii is wide-spreading and reaches a height of about 4 ft. The serrated leaf edges are sharp — grow the variety **compacta** to keep the foliage out of harm's way. **P. baptistii** has smooth-edged leaves.

PANDANUS

The spiny-edged narrow leaves are quite similar to those of the Pineapple plant and they are arranged spirally around the stem — hence the common name Screw Pine. It is a slow-growing plant, but with proper treatment it will develop into a showy false palm several feet high, with a corkscrew-like trunk and long, arching leaves. Thick aerial roots will appear; these should not be removed. Grow Pandanus as a specimen plant, away from easy contact with people — the spines are sharp! Winter warmth is necessary and so is moist air. Keep the compost almost dry in winter — the most common cause of death is water standing at the base of the leaves when the air is cold.

SECRETS OF SUCCESS

Temperature: Average warmth; not less than 55°F in winter.

Light: Bright light; avoid direct sun in summer.

Water: Water liberally from spring to autumn; very sparingly in winter. Use tepid water.

Air Humidity: Mist leaves frequently.

Repotting: Repot every 2 or 3 years in spring. Use thick gloves.

Propagation: Remove basal suckers when they are about 6 in. long and treat as stem cuttings. Use rooting hormone and bottom heat.

Pandanus veitchii

PELARGONIUM

Pelargoniums, commonly known as Geraniums, are among the most popular of all house plants. It is, of course, the flowering varieties which are responsible for this popularity, but there is a small group which are grown for their foliage rather than their indifferent flowers. These are the Scented-leaved Geraniums, and the common names describe the aroma when the leaves are gently crushed. Keep the plants cool and fairly dry in winter and prune back the stems in spring to maintain bushiness.

SPECIAL PROBLEMS

See Flowering Geraniums, page 152.

SECRETS OF SUCCESS

Temperature: Average warmth; keep cool (45°–55°F) in winter.

Light: Bright with some direct sunlight, but protect from midday summer sun.

Water: Water liberally from spring to autumn; sparingly in winter.

Air Humidity: Do not mist the leaves.

Repotting: Repot, when necessary, in early spring.

Propagation: Stem cuttings in summer. Do not use a rooting hormone and do not cover the pot containing cuttings.

PELARGONIUM CAPITATUM
Rose Geranium

PELARGONIUM CRISPUM
Lemon Geranium

PELARGONIUM GRAVEOLENS
Rose Geranium

PELARGONIUM TOMENTOSUM
Mint Geranium

Pelargonium crispum

TYPES

Rose, citrus and mint aromas are amply covered by the Scented-ieaved Geraniums. Some examples are shown here — **P. capitatum** (3 ft, pink flowers), **P. crispum** (2 ft, pink flowers), **P. graveolens** (3 ft, rose-red flowers) and **P. tomentosum** (2 ft, white flowers). There are other aromas, such as **P. fragrans** (nutmeg), **P. Prince of Orange** (orange) and **P. odoratissimum** (apple). Cut back occasionally to maintain bushiness.

PELARGONIUM COOKERY

The foliage of scented-leaved Geraniums can be used in all the standard roles for fragrant leaves — pot-pourri, scented pillows, linen bags etc. In addition the foliage can be used in the kitchen to add zest to a wide variety of dishes. Make sure that the plants have not been recently treated with a pesticide, and wash the leaves before use.

The scent determines the recommended use. Citrus-scented varieties are used in fruit salad, herb butter and egg custard — rose-scented types are added to green salads and all sorts of desserts. These leaves can be crystallised by painting with beaten egg white, covering with caster sugar and then drying in a warm airing cupboard.

Use mint-scented geraniums as a herb when cooking lamb dishes — apple-scented types are recommended for veal, and nutmeg-scented varieties for chicken.

PELLIONIA

The two types of Pellionia make useful additions to the terrarium or bottle garden, but when used in a hanging basket or as ground cover between other plants they are more demanding than easy trailers like Tradescantia. The Pellionias require moist air and winter warmth. They are not too fussy about the amount of light they receive but they are unusually sensitive to draughts. The low-growing stems root into the compost as they grow over the surface.

oval, green leaf with pale central area

PELLIONIA DAVEAUANA

TYPES

There are two species. **P. daveauana** (Watermelon Pellionia) bears a pale central band on each leaf — the outer margin may be olive or bronzy-green. The other is **P. pulchra** (Satin Pellionia) — look for the very dark veins on the upper surface and purple colour below.

SECRETS OF SUCCESS

Temperature: Average warmth; not less than 55°F in winter.

Light: Semi-shade or bright indirect light. Protect from direct sunlight.

Water: Keep compost moist at all times; reduce watering in winter. Use soft water.

Air Humidity: Mist leaves frequently.

Repotting: Repot every 2 years in spring.

Propagation: Divide plants at repotting time. Stem cuttings root easily.

Pellionia pulchra

PEPEROMIA

Peperomias are widely used in dish gardens, bottle gardens and other situations where space is limited. They are slow growing, compact and some species produce curious 'rat-tail' flower-heads made up of tiny greenish flowers on an upright spike. Despite these common characteristics, there really is no way of knowing whether an unknown plant in a house plant display is a Peperomia. There are three which have been popular favourites for many years — P. caperata, P. hederaefolia and P. magnoliaefolia. The experienced indoor gardener will have no difficulty in recognising that trio, but there are scores of other species. Trailing, bushy and upright types are available, and the foliage may be fleshy, quilted, corrugated, smooth or hairy, green or variegated . . . or even striped like a watermelon.

The Peperomias are easy to care for under average room conditions, but do remember that their natural home is either the tree trunks or mossy floor of the tropical rain forests in America. Use a peat-based compost rather than soil and the leaves will fall if allowed to wilt through lack of water. Despite their jungle home, however, Peperomias do not need a constantly moist atmosphere for success and will grow in a centrally-heated room.

SPECIAL PROBLEMS

LEAVES WITH BROWN TIPS & EDGES
Cause: Sudden drop in temperature. Remove all damaged leaves; keep plants out of draughts and away from cold windowsills.

SUDDEN LOSS OF LEAVES FROM SUCCULENT VARIETIES
Cause: Foilage has been allowed to wilt before watering. Remember to water when the compost is dryish but *before* leaves wilt.

LEAVES WILTED & DISCOLOURED. STEM OR LEAF ROT PRESENT. CORKY SWELLINGS UNDER LEAVES
Cause: Overwatering, especially in winter. Carry out standard remedial treatment (see page 246).

SUDDEN LOSS OF LEAVES IN WINTER
Cause: Temperature too cool. Move to a spot where a minimum of 50°F can be maintained.

SECRETS OF SUCCESS

Temperature: Average warmth; not less than 50° — 55°F in winter.

Light: A bright or semi-shady spot, away from direct sunlight. Peperomias will thrive in fluorescent light.

Water: Water with care. The compost must dry out to some extent between waterings, but never wait until the leaves wilt. Use tepid water and apply very little in the winter months.

Air Humidity: Mist occasionally in summer; never in winter.

Repotting: Avoid frequent repotting. If necessary after several years transfer to a slightly larger pot in spring.

Propagation: Cuttings root easily. Between spring and late summer take stem cuttings from upright and trailing varieties; leaf cuttings from bushy varieties.

● TRAILING TYPES

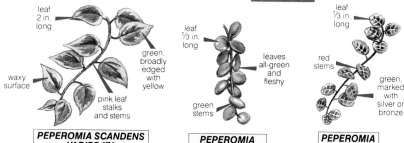

TYPES

leaf 2 in. long

waxy surface

green, broadly edged with yellow

pink leaf stalks and stems

PEPEROMIA SCANDENS VARIEGATA

Cupid Peperomia

leaf 1/3 in. long

leaves all-green and fleshy

green stems

PEPEROMIA ROTUNDIFOLIA

leaf 1/3 in. long

red stems

green, marked with silver or bronze

PEPEROMIA PROSTRATA

Creeping Peperomia

The bushy Peperomias are much better known than the trailing ones, although the brightly coloured Cupid Peperomia has become quite popular. Its stems grow about 3 ft long, and this plant can be used as either a climber or trailer. The other Peperomia trailers are not widely available. Both **P. prostrata** and **P. rotundifolia** have tiny round leaves, and the experts argue about their identification.

Peperomia scandens variegata

PEPEROMIA TYPES continued

● BUSHY TYPES

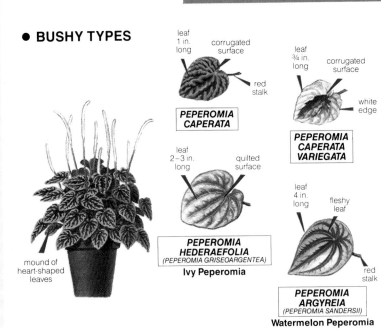

leaf 1 in. long — corrugated surface — red stalk

PEPEROMIA CAPERATA

leaf ¾ in. long — corrugated surface — white edge

PEPEROMIA CAPERATA VARIEGATA

leaf 2–3 in. long — quilted surface

PEPEROMIA HEDERAEFOLIA
(PEPEROMIA GRISEOARGENTEA)
Ivy Peromia

leaf 4 in. long — fleshy leaf — red stalk

PEPEROMIA ARGYREIA
(PEPEROMIA SANDERSII)
Watermelon Peperomia

mound of heart-shaped leaves

Peperomia caperata variegata

The bushy Peperomias grow about 4–6 in. high, and the familiar small-leaved species is **P. caperata**. Dwarf varieties such as **Little Fantasy** and the white-edged **variegata** are available. There are several out-of-the-ordinary small-leaved bushes — **P. orba Astrid** bears pale green, spoon-shaped leaves and **P. fraseri** stands out from other Peperomias by producing round and sweetly-scented flower-heads. The large-leaved bushes are more popular — you will have no trouble finding the metallic-leaved **P. hederaefolia**, but the striped-leaved **P. argyreia** is harder to find in the shops than in the books.

● UPRIGHT TYPES

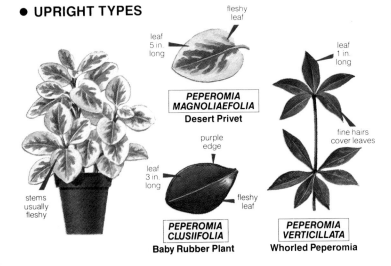

fleshy leaf
leaf 5 in. long

PEPEROMIA MAGNOLIAEFOLIA
Desert Privet

purple edge
leaf 3 in. long — fleshy leaf

PEPEROMIA CLUSIIFOLIA
Baby Rubber Plant

leaf 1 in. long
fine hairs cover leaves

PEPEROMIA VERTICILLATA
Whorled Peperomia

stems usually fleshy

The upright Peperomias have more distinct stems which grow vertically for part or all of the plant's life. Unfortunately there is much confusion over naming — the textbooks and the plant labels rarely agree! The small fleshy-leaved variety blotched with yellow is **P. glabella variegata** — much more popular is the large-leaved **P. magnoliaefolia**. The other fleshy-leaved varieties on upright stems are all types of the Baby Rubber Plant — **P. obtusifolia** has all-green leaves, **P. Green Gold** has yellow-blotched leaves and **P. clusiifolia** has all-green leaves edged with purple. **P. verticillata** is unmistakable (1 ft stems and whorls of leaves) and so is **P. pereskiaefolia** — look for the zig-zagged stems.

Peperomia argyreia

Peperomia magnoliaefolia

PHILODENDRON

Philodendrons have been used as house plants since Victorian times, and their popularity has increased in recent years. The conditions they need for healthy growth are those which they enjoyed in their ancestral home within the American tropical forests — no direct sunlight and moist surroundings when the air is warm.

There are two basic types of Philodendron. The first group, the climbers, are well suited to the average room, as long as you provide firm support for the stems. The Sweetheart Plant is the smallest and it is also the easiest to look after, with its ability to withstand both neglect and poor conditions. A feature of many climbing Philodendrons is the production of aerial roots from the stems, and these roots have an important part to play. Push them into the compost to provide moisture for the upper leaves.

Most of the second group, the non-climbers, are capable of growing into immense plants with large, deeply-lobed leaves. They are therefore more suitable for public buildings than for the average home.

SECRETS OF SUCCESS

Temperature: Average warmth; not less than 55°F in winter. P. scandens will endure lower temperatures (minimum 50°F) but P. melanochrysum needs higher than average warmth (minimum 65°F).

Light: All Philodendrons should be kept out of direct sunlight. P. scandens will succeed in shady conditions, but the usual requirement is light shade or moderate brightness. Both P. melanochrysum and variegated-leaved forms should be kept in a well-lit spot.

Water: During winter keep the soil just moist — make sure it is not waterlogged. For the rest of the year water thoroughly and regularly.

Air Humidity: Keep the air moist in summer and in heated rooms in winter — surround pots with damp peat or mist leaves regularly.

Repotting: Every 2 or 3 years transfer to a larger pot in spring.

Propagation: Cuttings require warm conditions. In summer take stem cuttings or air layer the climbing varieties. With a non-climbing variety, shoots taken from the base of the stem should be used as cuttings.

SPECIAL PROBLEMS

See Monstera, page 83.

TYPES

● **CLIMBING TYPES**

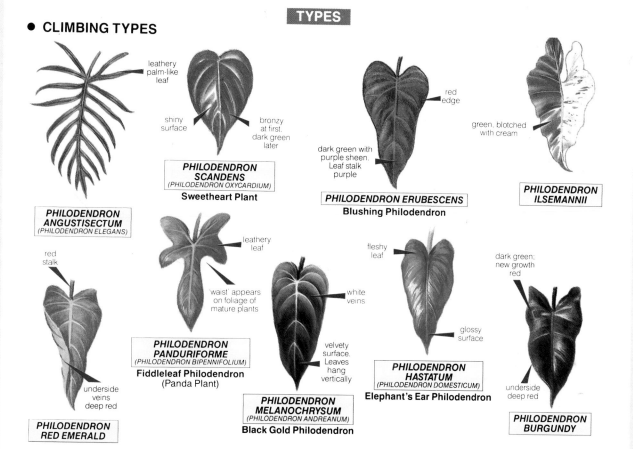

leathery palm-like leaf

shiny surface

bronzy at first, dark green later

PHILODENDRON SCANDENS
(PHILODENDRON OXYCARDIUM)
Sweetheart Plant

red edge

dark green with purple sheen. Leaf stalk purple

PHILODENDRON ERUBESCENS
Blushing Philodendron

green, blotched with cream

PHILODENDRON ILSEMANNII

PHILODENDRON ANGUSTISECTUM
(PHILODENDRON ELEGANS)

red stalk

leathery leaf

'waist' appears on foliage of mature plants

PHILODENDRON PANDURIFORME
(PHILODENDRON BIPENNIFOLIUM)
Fiddleleaf Philodendron
(Panda Plant)

white veins

velvety surface. Leaves hang vertically

PHILODENDRON MELANOCHRYSUM
(PHILODENDRON ANDREANUM)
Black Gold Philodendron

fleshy leaf

glossy surface

PHILODENDRON HASTATUM
(PHILODENDRON DOMESTICUM)
Elephant's Ear Philodendron

dark green; new growth red

underside deep red

PHILODENDRON BURGUNDY

underside veins deep red

PHILODENDRON RED EMERALD

PHILODENDRON TYPES continued

● CLIMBING TYPES continued

The Philodendrons and closely-related Monsteras live in the tropical rain-forests of America. In their native home they grow 60 ft or more, clinging to the trunks of trees by means of aerial roots. Indoors they will grow 6 – 15 ft if the aerial roots are not removed.

These plants are the most spectacular of all the house plant climbers. A moss stick (see page 114) is the ideal support and the leaves of some varieties exceed 2 ft in length. The leathery foliage varies widely in shape (entire to deeply cut), colour (pale green to rich red) and texture (glossy to velvety). Some grow quickly — **P. imbe** can increase by 7 ft in 2 – 3 years, whereas **P. Burgundy** will grow less than 1 ft in the same length of time.

P. scandens (the Sweetheart Plant or Heart-leaf Philodendron) is extremely popular and is one of the easiest plants to grow. Thin stems bear 3 – 5 in. shiny leaves. Grow as a trailer — pinch out tips to keep plant bushy. Or grow as a climber — retain aerial roots and use a moss stick for maximum effect.

The general foliage pattern for the large-leaved Philodendrons is a 6 – 15 in. arrow-shaped leaf with a glossy surface. Popular varieties include **P. hastatum** and its more branching hybrid **P. Tuxla. P. erubescens** and its hybrids such as **Red Emerald** and **Burgundy** are more colourful, and the dramatic two are the velvety **P. melanochrysum** and the variegated **P. ilsemannii.**

Philodendron melanochrysum

Philodendron scandens

Philodendron Red Emerald

● NON-CLIMBING TYPES

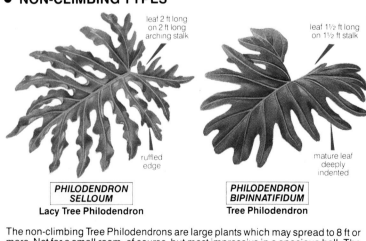

leaf 2 ft long on 2 ft long arching stalk

leaf 1½ ft long on 1½ ft stalk

ruffled edge

mature leaf deeply indented

PHILODENDRON SELLOUM
Lacy Tree Philodendron

PHILODENDRON BIPINNATIFIDUM
Tree Philodendron

The non-climbing Tree Philodendrons are large plants which may spread to 8 ft or more. Not for a small room, of course, but most impressive in a spacious hall. The two types are quite similar — large, deeply-cut leaves on long stalks with stems which become trunk-like with age. **Philodendron selloum** is the one seen in the U.S. — **P. bipinnatifidum** is shorter (mature height 4 ft) and is the species sold in Britain.

Philodendron bipinnatifidum

PILEA

A wide variety of bushy and trailing Pileas are available, and they are generally quite easy to grow, even for the beginner. Easiest of all is the popular Aluminium Plant with its white-splashed leaves. The list of dangers is a small one — move pots off windowsills on frosty nights, pinch out growing tips occasionally to keep plants bushy, and keep pots away from draughts. Even in expert hands the bushy Pileas tend to become leggy and unattractive with age. As cuttings root easily it is a good idea to start new plants each spring rather than retaining old specimens. Except for the Artillery Plant all of the bushy varieties are grown for the beauty of their individual leaves.

SECRETS OF SUCCESS

Temperature: Average warmth; not less than 50°F in winter.
Light: Bright light or semi-shade; protect from direct sun in summer.
Water: Water liberally from spring to autumn, allowing compost to dry out slightly between waterings. Water sparingly in winter. Use tepid water.
Air Humidity: Mist leaves regularly.
Repotting: Repot in spring if the plant is to be retained.
Propagation: Stem cuttings in late spring or summer.

SPECIAL PROBLEMS

INSECTS
Red spider mite can be troublesome; see page 244.

LEAF FALL IN WINTER
Cause: Cold air and wet compost can cause serious leaf fall, but even a healthy plant may shed a few leaves in winter. Cut back affected stems in spring to induce new healthy growth.

LEAVES WILTED & DISCOLOURED. STEM ROT PRESENT. SOME LEAF FALL
Cause: Overwatering, especially in winter. Carry out standard remedial treatment (see page 246).

LEAVES DISCOLOURED WITH BROWN TIPS & EDGES
Cause: Too much shade is the most likely reason. Move to a brighter spot. If the plant is well-lit, the probable cause is a sudden drop in temperature.

TYPES

silvery patches on quilted surface

leaf 3 in. long

PILEA CADIEREI
Aluminium Plant

leaf 3 in. long

dull bronzy-green, silver centre

underside red

PILEA BRONZE
(PILEA SILVER TREE)

leaf 3 in. long

deeply quilted surface, vein areas brown

PILEA MOON VALLEY
(PILEA MOLLIS)

bronzy when grown in sunlight, green when grown in shade

leaf 2 in. long

underside red

PILEA NORFOLK

leaf 1 in. long

glossy surface, dark green or coppery

underside purple

PILEA REPENS
Black Leaf Panamiga

quilted surface

reddish stems

leaf 1 in. across

PILEA NUMMULARIIFOLIA
Creeping Charlie

leaf ⅛ in. long

feathery stems with pale green leaves

PILEA MICROPHYLLA
(PILEA MUSCOSA)
Artillery Plant

The small-leaved Pileas include the trailing **P. nummulariifolia** (Creeping Charlie) and **P. depressa** (Creeping Jenny) and the fern-like **P. microphylla** which puffs out smoke-like pollen when tapped in summer.

Over the years the naming of the large-leaved Pileas has become quite confused. There is no problem with either recognising or naming the most popular species — **P. cadierei** grows about 1 ft tall and becomes leggy and unattractive with age. The variety **nana** is more compact. The species **P. spruceana** has given rise to 2 popular varieties — **P. Norfolk** and **P. Bronze,** with oval or rounded leaves in which bronze and silver dominate the quilted surface when grown in bright light. **P. involucrata,** the original Pan-American Friendship Plant is not sold as such — the popular form is **P. Moon Valley. P. repens** is smaller than the popular varieties, a low and spreading plant with coppery leaves.

Pilea Norfolk

Pilea Moon Valley

PIPER CROCATUM
Ornamental Pepper

PIPER

Several varieties of Ornamental Pepper are grown as house plants, but they are not easy to obtain. They are climbers, and with support they will reach 5 ft high. Their leaves are several inches long and highly decorative, but the plants do not bear fruit. Growing Piper should not be too much of a problem if the winter temperature can be maintained at 55°F or more and if you are prepared to mist the leaves regularly. Leaf fall is the sign that conditions are wrong; pearly drops of liquid under the leaves are quite normal.

Piper crocatum

TYPES

The waxy, dappled leaves (3 – 5 in. long) make Ornamental Pepper much more eye-catching than the Sweetheart Plant (page 94) but it is more difficult to find. Two varieties are available — **P. crocatum** (underside dark red) and **P. ornatum** (underside light green). Both may be grown as trailers as well as climbers.

SECRETS OF SUCCESS

Temperature: Average warmth; not less than 55°F in winter.
Light: Bright light; not direct sun.
Water: Keep compost moist at all times; reduce water in winter.
Air Humidity: Mist leaves regularly.
Repotting: Repot every 2 years in spring.
Propagation: Stem cuttings in spring or summer. Use rooting hormone and bottom heat.

PISONIA

PISONIA UMBELLIFERA VARIEGATA
Birdcatcher Tree

A leaf of **P. umbellifera variegata** is almost indistinguishable from a variegated Rubber Plant one, but the growth habit is rather different. The stems branch readily and the leaves bear a sticky resin — hence the common name. Grow it in the same way as Ficus — see page 73.

PSEUDERANTHEMUM

PSEUDERANTHEMUM KEWENSE
(ERANTHEMUM ATROPURPUREUM)

P. kewense is a colourful but straggly shrub which can grow 3 ft high. The leaves are marked with purple, and varieties such as **tricolor** and **variegatum** are splashed with white, cream and pink. Mature plants bear red-spotted white flowers in spring. High humidity is essential — Pseuderanthemum must be grown in a greenhouse, conservatory or a plant window (see page 34).

PLECTRANTHUS

Three species are known as Swedish Ivy. This common name indicates their popularity in Scandinavia, where they are found in hanging baskets or on windowsills.

It is a pity that Swedish Ivy is not more popular in other countries as it has many good points. It will survive in dry air, it will withstand occasional dryness at the roots and it will sometimes flower. Pinch out the stem tips occasionally to keep the plant bushy, and use these tips as cuttings which will root very easily.

SECRETS OF SUCCESS

Temperature: Average warmth; not less than 50°F in winter.
Light: Bright light or semi-shade; avoid direct sunlight.
Water: Keep compost moist at all times; reduce water in winter.
Air Humidity: Mist leaves occasionally.
Repotting: Repot every 2 or 3 years in spring, but best grown as an annual.
Propagation: Very easy. Take stem cuttings in spring or summer.

Plectranthus australis

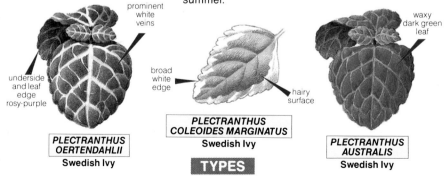

PLECTRANTHUS OERTENDAHLII
Swedish Ivy

PLECTRANTHUS COLEOIDES MARGINATUS
Swedish Ivy

PLECTRANTHUS AUSTRALIS
Swedish Ivy

TYPES

The advantages of these creeping plants as ground cover and for clothing the edges of pots and hanging baskets are well known in Scandinavia. They flourish in dry air where True Ivies would fail, and there is the added bonus of occasional flowers. The foliage of the most popular type **(P. oertendahlii)** is especially colourful. Its leaves measure 1 in. across — the largest are borne by **P. coleoides marginatus** (2 – 2½ in.).

Podocarpus macrophyllus

PODOCARPUS

Many plants suffer if they are not kept moderately warm on cold winter nights, but Podocarpus demands an unheated room if it is to live successfully for many years indoors. This durable plant does not mind a draughty situation, and there are few better trees for a cold hallway. The upright stems bear narrow, glossy strap-like leaves about 3 in. long. Buddhist Pine can be kept as a compact shrub by regular pruning, but its slow-growing habit means that it requires little attention. Hard to obtain, but well worth looking for.

SECRETS OF SUCCESS

Temperature: Average warmth, but prefers cool conditions. Minimum temperature 40°F in winter.

Light: Brightly lit spot, some sun is beneficial.

Water: Keep compost fairly moist at all times; reduce watering in winter. Do not overwater.

Air Humidity: Mist leaves occasionally.

Repotting: Repot, when necessary, in spring.

Propagation: Stem cuttings in summer. Use rooting hormone and bottom heat.

leaf 3 in. long

strap-like leaves

PODOCARPUS MACROPHYLLUS
Buddhist Pine

TYPES

In its oriental home **P. macrophyllus** grows 30 – 40 ft high — indoors it will reach about 6 ft. The house plant variety is **Maki** (Southern Yew) — the leaves are smaller and the growth habit more compact.

POLYSCIAS

Varieties of Polyscias are attractive oriental trees with twisted stems and decorative foliage. Large specimens are prohibitively expensive; buy a small plant if you can and look after it carefully. The leaves are usually ferny, but the most popular Polyscias is the Dinner Plate Aralia with large rounded leaflets. Unfortunately Polyscias is not easy to grow under room conditions, and it will readily drop its leaves if the environment is wrong. It will need good light, moist air, even moisture at the roots, and warmth in winter.

SECRETS OF SUCCESS

Temperature: Warm or average temperature; minimum temperature 55° – 60°F in winter.

Light: Bright, but away from direct sun. Will adapt to light shade.

Water: Water moderately from spring to autumn; sparingly in winter.

Air Humidity: Mist leaves frequently.

Repotting: Repot every 2 years in spring.

Propagation: Not easy. Take stem cuttings in spring; use rooting hormone and bottom heat.

leaflet 3 in. across

leathery leaves

POLYSCIAS BALFOURIANA
Dinner Plate Aralia

leaf 8 in. long

feathery leaves

POLYSCIAS FRUTICOSA
Ming Aralia

Polyscias balfouriana marginata

TYPES

Polyscias is a branched tree or shrub with decorative foliage. **P. balfouriana** bears dark green, rounded leaflets which are speckled with grey or pale green. The variety **pennockii** is yellow-veined — **marginata** has white-bordered foliage. **P. fruticosa** is quite different — the leaves are much longer and are divided into many irregular and saw-edged leaflets. This tree with its twisted stems and ferny foliage is popular with American interior decorators when an oriental look is required.
P. guilfoylei victoriae (Wild Coffee, Lace Aralia) has feathery white-edged leaves.

PLEOMELE

Pleomele is closely related to and is sometimes described as Dracaena (page 63). It has the same false palm effect — a crown of leaves on top of a cane-like stem when mature. The Pleomele stem is very narrow — it will require staking once the lower leaves have fallen. It is not an easy plant to grow — moist air is essential which means that pots should ideally be surrounded by moist peat or stood in a pebble tray (page 27).

Pleomele reflexa variegata

leaf 6 in. long

green, edged with yellow

PLEOMELE REFLEXA VARIEGATA
Song of India

SECRETS OF SUCCESS

Temperature: Average warmth; not less than 55°F.

Light: Bright light but not direct sunlight.

Water: Keep the compost moist at all times; water sparingly in winter.

Air Humidity: Mist leaves regularly.

Repotting: Repot every 2 years in spring.

Propagation: See Dracaena (page 63).

TYPES

Several types can be seen in specialist collections, such as the green-leaved **P. thalioides.** Only one is grown as a house plant — **P. reflexa variegata.**

RADERMACHERA

A house plant of the eighties — it was introduced to Europe from Taiwan at the beginning of the decade, and its popularity as a specimen indoor tree is increasing. It may be labelled simply as 'foliage plant', but you can't mistake the large compound leaves bearing shiny, deeply-veined leaflets with long tapering points. Central heating is no problem because it tolerates dry air, but it is prone to attack by whitefly and scale.

leaflet 1 in. long

RADERMACHERA DANIELLE

TYPE

There is much confusion over the naming of the Radermachera grown as a house plant. It is **R. Danielle**, which seems to be the same as **R. sinica** and **Stereospermum chelonoides.**

SECRETS OF SUCCESS

Temperature: Average warmth; not less than 50°–55°F in winter.

Light: Bright, but protect from midday summer sun.

Water: Keep compost moist at all times — avoid waterlogging.

Air Humidity: No need to mist the leaves.

Repotting: Repot, when necessary, in spring.

Propagation: Stem cuttings in summer.

Radermachera Danielle

RHOEO

The short stem bears fleshy, lance-shaped leaves. Their colouring is unusual — glossy green or green-and-yellow above, purple below. An added feature of interest is the presence of small white flowers in purple 'boats' at the base of the lower leaves. Remove side shoots if Boat Lily is to be grown as a specimen plant. It needs winter warmth, freedom from draughts and moist air. Remove dead leaves and flowers.

Rhoeo discolor vittata

leaf 1 ft long

boat-shaped bracts containing tiny flowers

underside purple

RHOEO DISCOLOR
Boat Lily

SECRETS OF SUCCESS

Temperature: Average warmth; not less than 50°–55°F in winter.

Light: Bright or semi-shade, no direct sun in summer.

Water: Keep compost moist at all times; reduce watering in winter.

Air Humidity: Mist leaves frequently.

Repotting: Repot every year in spring.

Propagation: Use side shoots as cuttings in spring or summer. Alternatively bushy plants can be divided at repotting time.

TYPES

R. discolor is the only species — the popular variety is **vittata** which bears green leaves with bold yellow stripes. The 'boat' flowers are responsible for one of the common names — Moses in the Cradle.

SANSEVIERIA

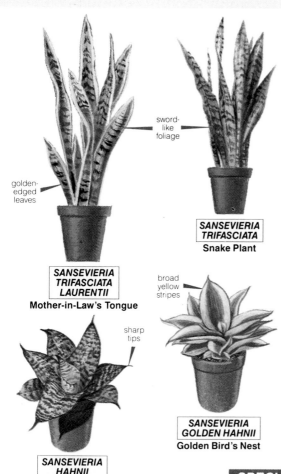

sword-like foliage

golden-edged leaves

SANSEVIERIA TRIFASCIATA
Snake Plant

SANSEVIERIA TRIFASCIATA LAURENTII
Mother-in-Law's Tongue

broad yellow stripes

sharp tips

SANSEVIERIA GOLDEN HAHNII
Golden Bird's Nest

SANSEVIERIA HAHNII

If all else fails, grow Sansevieria. This tough plant, known as Mother-in-Law's Tongue in Britain and Snakeskin Plant in the U.S., deserves its reputation for near-indestructibility. It will grow in bright sunshine or shade, withstand dry air, draughts and periods without water, and it rarely needs repotting. It can, however, be quite easily killed by prolonged overwatering in winter and prolonged exposure to near freezing temperatures.

The favourite variety is S. trifasciata laurentii. Its erect, fleshy, sword-like leaves, cross-banded with distinct golden edges, are a common sight everywhere. This bold foliage provides an excellent background for plants with ferny foliage or small flowers — Mother-in-Law's Tongue is an almost essential ingredient for the Pot Group. Grow this plant in a clay pot and treat it properly — under good conditions sprays of small, fragrant flowers will appear. The low-growing rosette varieties are much less popular, but are useful for a sunny or shady windowsill.

SECRETS OF SUCCESS

Temperature: Average warmth; not less than 50°F in winter.

Light: Bright light with some sun preferred, but will grow in shade.

Water: From spring to autumn water moderately, allowing compost to dry out slightly between waterings. In winter water every 1 – 2 months. Avoid wetting the heart of the plant.

Air Humidity: No need to mist the leaves.

Repotting: Seldom required — repot when growth cracks the pot.

Propagation: Remove offset by cutting off at base; allow to dry before inserting in compost. Alternatively divide up plant. Leaf cuttings can be used for all-green varieties (see page 236).

SPECIAL PROBLEMS

ROT AT BASE. LEAVES YELLOW AND DYING BACK
Cause: Basal rot disease. The cause is generally overwatering in winter. If the whole of the base is affected, use the upper foliage as leaf cuttings and then discard the plant. If only part of the plant is affected, remove it from the pot and chop off the diseased section. Dust cut surface with sulphur and repot. Keep dry and move to a warmer spot.

ROT AT BASE IN WINTER; NOT OVERWATERED
Cause: Cold damage. Sansevieria can be quickly damaged at 40°F or below; 50°F is the minimum temperature for safe winter care.

BROWN BLOTCHES ON LEAVES
Cause: A non-infectious disorder which starts at the tips and works downwards along the leaf. The cause is unknown and there is no cure.

TYPES

Sansevieria trifasciata laurentii

Sansevierias are one of the most popular of all house plants, due to the universal appeal of **S. trifasciata laurentii**. It is seen everywhere — the leaves reaching 3 ft or more. The basic species **S. trifasciata** (sometimes wrongly sold as **S. zeylanica**) is smaller, plainer and much less popular, but there are other colourful varieties in addition to the overworked Mother-in-Law's Tongue. **Moonshine** is small and finely modelled in light and dark green, **Bantel's Sensation** is cross-banded with cream and **craigii** is broadly-edged with cream. The tall one (5 ft) is **S. cylindrica**. Not all species of Sansevieria are tall and upright — there is the compact **S. hahnii** which produces a rosette of fleshy leaves. These leaves are about 4 in. long with pale horizontal stripes. **Golden hahnii** has vertical yellow bands along the leaf margins — **Silver hahnii** has silvery green leaves with darker stripes.

Sansevieria hahnii

leaf 1 ft long

ROHDEA JAPONICA MARGINATA

Sacred Manchu Lily

TYPES

The house plant species is **R. japonica**. It is all-green — its varieties are more colourful. **Marginata** leaves are near-black edged with white; the foliage of **variegata** bears pale yellow bands.

ROHDEA

The popularity of some house plants varies greatly from one country to another. Rohdea is an excellent example of this variation in taste — it is a great favourite in Japan but it is hardly ever grown in Europe or the U.S. The thick, leathery leaves arch downwards and in spring a flower stalk grows about 1 ft tall — the pale blooms are tiny and are followed by small fruits in summer.

SECRETS OF SUCCESS

Temperature: Cool or average warmth; not less than 45° – 50°F in winter.

Light: Bright light or semi-shade; not direct sun.

Water: Water liberally from spring to autumn; sparingly in winter.

Air Humidity: Mist leaves frequently.

Repotting: Repot annually after flowering.

Propagation: Divide plants when repotting.

Rohdea japonica

leaf 1 ½ in. across

green, edged with white and pink

underside red

SAXIFRAGA SARMENTOSA TRICOLOR

Mother of Thousands
(Magic Carpet)

TYPES

Saxifraga sarmentosa (**S. stolonifera**) bears olive green leaves with distinct silvery veins, and is more vigorous and larger than its colourful variety **tricolor**. These somewhat bristly plants grow about 9 in. high, and the pendent runners can reach 2–3 ft.

SAXIFRAGA

The outstanding feature of Mother of Thousands is the production of long, slender red runners which bear miniature plants at their ends. These runners should be allowed to hang freely, so the plant is best grown in a hanging basket or wall display. Clusters of insignificant flowers appear in summer. You can choose from two varieties — S. sarmentosa is easy to care for and is easy to propagate. S. sarmentosa tricolor is more attractive, with red-edged green-and-white leaves, but it is unfortunately slow growing and more tender.

SECRETS OF SUCCESS

Temperature: Cool or average warmth; not less than 40°–45°F in winter.

Light: Brightly lit spot, away from direct sunlight.

Water: Water liberally from spring to autumn; sparingly in winter. Allow surface to dry out slightly between waterings.

Air Humidity: Mist leaves occasionally.

Repotting: Repot every year in spring.

Propagation: Very easy. Peg down plantlets in compost — cut stem when rooted.

Saxifraga sarmentosa

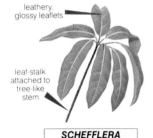

leathery, glossy leaflets

leaf-stalk attached to tree-like stem

SCHEFFLERA ACTINOPHYLLA
(BRASSAIA ACTINOPHYLLA)

Umbrella Tree

TYPES

S. actinophylla is an attractive bush when young, tall (6–8 ft) tree when mature. The number of leaflets per stalk increases from 4 to 12 with age. In specialist collections you might find the smaller **S. digitata** and the distinctly-veined **S. octophyllum**.

SCHEFFLERA

In subtropical gardens it is known as the Octopus Tree because of its spectacular tentacle-like flowers. Unfortunately it does not bloom under room conditions and the indoor plant form is known as the Umbrella Tree, which refers to the finger-like glossy leaflets radiating like umbrella spokes. Schefflera is not difficult to grow, provided it is kept moderately warm and protected from cold draughts. It becomes lanky with age due to the loss of lower leaves.

SECRETS OF SUCCESS

Temperature: Average warmth; not less than 55°F in winter. If possible avoid temperatures above 70°F.

Light: Bright light, away from direct sunshine. Will adapt to light shade.

Water: Water liberally from spring to autumn; sparingly in winter.

Air Humidity: Mist leaves frequently.

Repotting: Repot every 2 years in spring.

Propagation: Difficult. Stem cuttings in summer; use rooting hormone and bottom heat.

Schefflera actinophylla

SCINDAPSUS

The most popular species of Scindapsus is S. aureus — the Devil's Ivy or Golden Pothos. Although it is sometimes described as a difficult plant to grow there is no reason why it should not do well if you follow the Secrets of Success. In some varieties the yellow or white variegation takes up more leaf area than the green background — such varieties are difficult indoors and are best confined to the conservatory or greenhouse.

Scindapsus is a climber with aerial roots — a moss stick makes an ideal support. The stems are sometimes allowed to trail from a hanging basket or wall display. Pinch out tips to induce bushiness; keep the plant well away from draughts.

SECRETS OF SUCCESS

Temperature: Average warmth; not less than 50°–55°F in winter (60°F for S. pictus).

Light: Well-lit but sunless spot. Variegation will fade in poor light.

Water: Water liberally from spring to autumn; let compost dry out slightly between waterings. Water sparingly in winter.

Air Humidity: Mist leaves frequently.

Repotting: Repot, when necessary, in spring.

Propagation: Stem cuttings in spring or summer; use rooting hormone. Keep compost rather dry and leave in dark until rooted.

SPECIAL PROBLEMS

YELLOWING & FALLING LEAVES; ROTTING STEMS
Cause: Overwatering, especially in winter. Scindapsus cannot survive in waterlogged soil. Carry out standard remedial treatment (see page 246).

BROWN & SHRIVELLED LEAF TIPS
Cause: Air too dry. Mist the leaves regularly.

BROWN LEAF EDGES; BROWN SPOTS ON LEAF SURFACE
Cause: Underwatering during the growing season. Surface of compost should become dry between waterings, but root ball must not be allowed to dry out.

CURLED LIMP LEAVES; ROTTING STEMS
Cause: Cold air damage. Scindapsus is extremely sensitive to a sudden drop in temperature below 50°F.

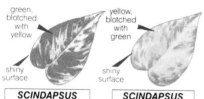

green, blotched with yellow — shiny surface

SCINDAPSUS AUREUS
(EPIPREMNUM AUREUM)
Devil's Ivy
(Golden Pothos)

yellow, blotched with green — shiny surface

SCINDAPSUS AUREUS GOLDEN QUEEN

white, blotched with green — shiny surface

SCINDAPSUS AUREUS MARBLE QUEEN

green, blotched with silver — thin white line around edge — dull surface

SCINDAPSUS PICTUS ARGYRAEUS
Silver Vine

Scindapsus aureus

TYPES

Devil's Ivy is similar to but more colourful than Philodendron scandens — the Sweetheart Plant. The easiest to grow is **S. aureus** — it can be treated as a trailer or climber, reaching 6 ft or more under good conditions. The near-white and near-yellow varieties are not easy to grow. Usual leaf size of S. aureus is 4–6 in. — **S. pictus** is smaller and more difficult.

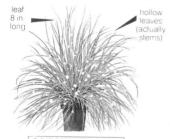

leaf 8 in long — hollow leaves (actually stems)

SCIRPUS CERNUUS
(ISOLEPIS GRACILIS)
Miniature Bulrush

TYPE

S. cernuus is the house plant species. The glossy, thread-like 'leaves' are bright green, upright at first and arching when mature. At any time of the year tiny white flowers may appear at the tips of the leaf-like stems.

SCIRPUS

There are not many grassy house plants, especially fine-leaved ones like the Miniature Bulrush. It is easy to grow but hard to find in the shops or garden centres. This rarity is unfortunate because it can be used in many ways — drooping over a hanging basket, softening the edge of a plant trough, adding variety to a terrarium or forming a miniature standard with the help of a narrow tube as in the photograph.

SECRETS OF SUCCESS

Temperature: Average warmth; not less than 50°F in winter.

Light: Brightly lit spot; protect from midday sun.

Water: Keep compost very moist (not waterlogged) at all times.

Air Humidity: Mist leaves regularly.

Repotting: Repot, when necessary, in spring.

Propagation: Divide plants when repotting.

Scirpus cernuus

SELAGINELLA

Selaginella, or Creeping Moss, was a Victorian favourite. Today it has lost much of this early popularity, but it is still an excellent choice for the bottle garden or terrarium. It is much less happy away from this protection, the tiny leaves shrivelling in hot rooms, draughty rooms or in dry air. To increase your chance of success grow it in a shallow, well-drained pot in semi-shade some distance away from the window. Surround the pot with damp peat and use soft water for watering and misting.

Temperature: Average warmth; not less than 55°F in winter.

Light: Semi-shade.

Water: Keep compost moist at all times; reduce watering in winter. Use soft water.

Air Humidity: Moist air is essential. Mist leaves regularly; avoid soaking leaves.

Repotting: Repot, when necessary, in spring.

Propagation: Stem cuttings in spring or summer.

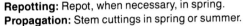

leaves blue-green

leaves pale green

SELAGINELLA UNCINATA

SELAGINELLA MARTENSII

Selaginella martensii watsoniana

Selaginella kraussiana aurea

TYPES

Trailing Selaginellas include **S. uncinata** (the blue-green Peacock Fern), **S. apoda** (pale green and moss-like) and **S. kraussiana aurea** (the yellow-green Spreading Clubmoss). The Resurrection Plant belongs here — see page 220. Not all Selaginellas trail — **S. martensii** has 1 ft high upright stems and aerial roots grow down from the stems into the compost — the variety **watsoniana** has silvery tips. **S. emmeliana** is another erect species with 6 in. high stems and lacy leaves.

SENECIO

At first glance both the Cape Ivy and German Ivy can be mistaken for one of the True Ivies described on page 78. The leaves are lobed and the stems either trail or are trained up canes. On closer inspection the lobes of Senecio leaves are found to be fleshier and generally more pointed, and if the small flowers appear the difference is immediately obvious. There are also cultural differences — Senecios are less affected by dry air than the Hedera varieties. Pinch out tips to maintain bushiness.

Temperature: Average warmth; not less than 50°F in winter.

Light: Bright; some direct sun is beneficial in winter. Will tolerate semi-shade.

Water: Keep compost moist at all times; reduce watering in winter.

Air Humidity: Mist leaves occasionally.

Repotting: Repot every 2 years in spring.

Propagation: Easy. Take stem cuttings in spring or summer.

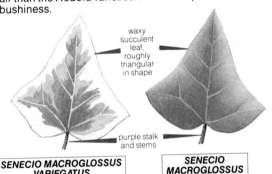

waxy succulent leaf, roughly triangular in shape

purple stalk and stems

semi-succulent leaf, 5–7 sharply pointed lobes

sunken veins

SENECIO MACROGLOSSUS VARIEGATUS
Cape Ivy
(Wax Vine)

SENECIO MACROGLOSSUS
Cape Ivy
(Wax Vine)

SENECIO MIKANIOIDES
German Ivy
(Parlour Ivy)

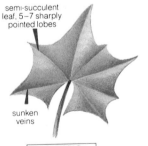

Senecio macroglossus variegatus

TYPES

It is surprising that the Senecio Ivies are not more widely grown. They are more vigorous than the True Ivies and are less affected by the warm and dry conditions in a centrally-heated room in winter. Small daisy-like flowers appear if kept in a well-lit spot. They are tall growing — pinch out tips to induce bushiness. **Senecio macroglossus** is rarely grown — you are more likely to find the yellow-blotched form (**variegatus**).

SONERILA

A bushy, colourful plant from Java — red stems bear leaves which are patterned with silver above and coloured purple below. It will grow quite happily in a carboy or terrarium, but Sonerila is a real challenge to your skill under ordinary room conditions. It is a hot house plant needing warmth, constant moisture around the leaves and careful watering. Surround the pot with damp peat and mist the leaves each day with tepid water. Dry leaf tips indicate that the air is too dry; leaf drop means that the air is too cold.

leaf 3 in. long

underside purple

SONERILA MARGARITACEA
Frosted Sonerila

Sonerila margaritacea

SECRETS OF SUCCESS

Temperature: Warm or average warmth; not less than 60°F in winter.

Light: Semi-shade; keep away from direct sunlight.

Water: Keep compost moist at all times; reduce watering in winter. Avoid overwatering.

Air Humidity: High air humidity essential. Mist leaves regularly.

Repotting: Repot every 2 years in spring.

Propagation: Stem cuttings in spring or summer. Use rooting hormone and bottom heat.

TYPE

Sonerila margaritacea is a low-growing plant with beautifully marked leaves. The surface is green or coppery green lined and spotted with silver — pink flowers appear in summer.

STENOTAPHRUM

Stenotaphrum is used as a lawn grass in tropical countries — in more temperate regions its variegated form is occasionally used to add variety to a group of house plants. The flattened stems creep for a foot or more and so it is a trailing plant with cream-banded leaves cascading downwards. A good choice (if you can find it) for a hanging basket — easy to grow under all ordinary conditions, including outdoors in summer.

green, banded with creamy-white

leaf 5 in. long

STENOTAPHRUM SECUNDATUM VARIEGATUM
Buffalo Grass
(St. Augustine's Grass)

TYPES

The all-green **S. secundatum** is rarely grown as a house plant — the variety **variegatum** is used. The foliage is quite distinctive — each leaf has a uniform width along its whole length.

Stenotaphrum secundatum variegatum

SECRETS OF SUCCESS

Temperature: Average warmth; not less than 45°F in winter.

Light: A well-lit spot is needed to maintain the cream-coloured variegation.

Water: Water liberally from spring to autumn; sparingly in winter.

Air Humidity: Misting occasionally in summer is beneficial.

Repotting: Repot, if necessary, in spring.

Propagation: Divide plants at any time of the year.

STROBILANTHES

Strobilanthes is a lovely foliage plant when it is young. The long, pointed leaves are dark green with a silvery purple sheen. Unfortunately this appearance declines with age — old plants look straggly and the colour fades from the foliage, which becomes silvery with dark veins. Discard the plants once the purple colouring goes, replacing them with new stock raised from cuttings. Not easy — a humid atmosphere is needed.

leaf 5 in. long

underside purple

STROBILANTHES DYERANUS
Persian Shield

Strobilanthes dyeranus

SECRETS OF SUCCESS

Temperature: Average warmth; not less than 55°F in winter.

Light: Brightly-lit spot, away from direct sunlight in summer.

Water: Water moderately from spring to autumn; sparingly in winter.

Air Humidity: Mist leaves frequently.

Repotting: Repot, when necessary, in spring.

Propagation: Stem cuttings in spring or summer.

TYPE

Only one species is grown — **S. dyeranus**. It is an erect shrub bearing finely-toothed leaves which are coloured purple below and with a purple blotch above extending almost to the edges.

SUCCULENTS

Three or four tiny pots of succulents and a small cactus or two are the usual starting point for a life-long interest in house plants.

The succulents are indeed a good starting point for children as these plants are easy to care for, can withstand a great deal of neglect and mismanagement, and are amongst the easiest of all plant groups to propagate.

Succulents are easily defined as plants with fleshy leaves or stems which can store water; the cacti (page 203) are a distinct group of succulents. Much less distinct is the dividing line between 'succulents' and 'house plants with fleshy leaves'. Sansevieria and other fleshy-leaved types which have different requirements to other succulents are treated as ordinary house plants in this book. Those succulents which are grown mainly for their blooms (Hoya, Rochea, Kalanchoe blossfeldiana etc.) are treated as flowering house plants or flowering pot plants.

Hundreds of succulents with widely differing shapes and sizes are commercially available. Most of them have a rosette shape, as the tightly-packed leaf arrangement helps to conserve water in their desert habitat. With age some of these types become 'rosette trees' with leaf clusters at the ends of woody stems. The remainder grow as trailing or bushy plants.

Despite the wide variety of shapes, the succulents are remarkably consistent in their needs. They evolved in the dry areas of the world and their general requirements are related to this habitat — free-draining compost, sunshine, fresh air, water in the growing season and a cold and dry resting period. Winter dormancy is vital if you want your plants to bloom and last for many years; another requirement for top quality plants is a period outdoors in summer.

SECRETS OF SUCCESS

Temperature: Average warmth from spring to autumn; succulents (unlike most house plants) relish a marked difference between night and day temperatures. Keep cool in winter; 50°–55°F is ideal but no harm will occur at 40°F.

Light: A windowsill is the right spot, as some sunshine is vital. Choose a south-facing windowsill if you can, but some shade in summer may be necessary. Haworthia and Gasteria need a bright but sunless site.

Water: Treat as an ordinary house plant from spring to autumn, watering thoroughly when the compost begins to dry out. In winter water very infrequently, once every 1–2 months.

Air Humidity: No need to mist the leaves. The main requirement is for fresh air; open windows in summer.

Repotting: Only repot when essential — then transfer to a slightly larger container in spring. Use a shallow pot rather than a deep one.

Propagation: Cuttings root easily. Take stem cuttings, offsets or leaf cuttings in spring or summer. It is vital to let the cuttings dry for a few days (large cuttings for 1–2 weeks) before inserting in compost. Water very sparingly and do not cover with polythene or glass. Another propagation method is seed sowing — germination temperature 70°–80°F.

SPECIAL PROBLEMS

STEM ELONGATED & MISSHAPPEN
Cause: Too much water in winter or too little light in summer. Refer to Secrets of Success; turn pots occasionally to ensure even growth.

BROWN DRY SPOTS
Cause: Underwatering. Remember that succulents require generous watering in summer.

BROWN SOFT SPOTS
Cause: Leaf spot disease. Water with systemic fungicide. Improve ventilation.

LEAVES WILTED & DISCOLOURED
Cause: Overwatering, especially in winter. Carry out standard remedial treatment (see page 246).

SUDDEN LOSS OF LEAVES
Cause: Very cold water straight from the tap; use tepid water in future. Another possibility is underwatering in summer.

ROT AT BASE FOLLOWED BY STEM COLLAPSE
Cause: Basal stem rot disease, due to overwet conditions in winter. Use upper stem for propagation. Next time avoid overwatering in winter, and cover compost surface with a layer of stone chippings.

HOW TO MAKE A DISH GARDEN

Succulents are ideal plants for a dish garden. Choose carefully and aim for an attractive landscape. Once made it will require very little attention and should last for a number of years on a windowsill.

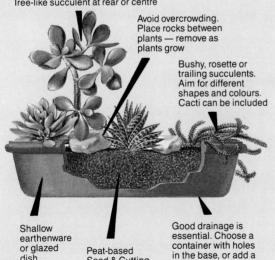

Tree-like succulent at rear or centre

Avoid overcrowding. Place rocks between plants — remove as plants grow

Bushy, rosette or trailing succulents. Aim for different shapes and colours. Cacti can be included

Shallow earthenware or glazed dish

Peat-based Seed & Cutting Compost

Good drainage is essential. Choose a container with holes in the base, or add a thick layer of charcoal

SUCCULENT TYPES

fleshy, spoon-like leaves

ADROMISCHUS COOPERI

A. cooperi has thick leaves with wavy tips. The grey-green foliage is splashed with purple and the reddish hairs which appear at the base are really aerial roots.

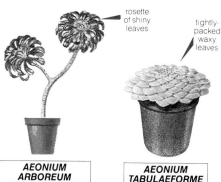

rosette of shiny leaves

AEONIUM ARBOREUM ATROPURPUREUM

tightly-packed waxy leaves

AEONIUM TABULAEFORME
Saucer Plant

The Aeoniums bear rosettes of leaves ranging in colour from yellow to almost black. The rosettes may be flat saucers of densely-packed leaves, as in **A. tabulaeforme**, or a looser arrangement on top of branched stems as found in **A. arboreum**. The latter species is all-green — more popular is the purple-brown leaved variety **atropurpureum** which can reach 3 ft or more. Even more dramatic is the variety **Schwarzkopf** which has near-black foliage.

Aeonium arboreum atropurpureum Schwarzkopf

saw-edged leaves

AGAVE AMERICANA
Century Plant

AGAVE AMERICANA MEDIOPICTA

fine threads

AGAVE FILIFERA
Thread Agave

black spines at leaf tips

AGAVE VICTORIAE-REGINAE

Agave americana marginata

The most popular Agave is the Century Plant, so-called because of the mistaken belief that it flowers only once every 100 years. There are two colourful varieties — **A. americana marginata** (green leaves edged with yellow) and **A. americana mediopicta** (cream leaves edged with green). With time these plants produce leaves 3 or 4 ft long, and both size and sharp spines make them unsuitable for a small room. **A. filifera** (upward-turned leaves 1 ft long) is more compact — even smaller is **A. parviflora**, another Agave with filament-bearing leaves. Experts usually recommend **A. victoriae-reginae** as the best choice — its 6 in. triangular leaves are dark green edged with white. Much more colourful but much rarer is **A. parrasana** — blue-grey leaves edged with bright red thorns.

Agave victoriae-reginae

SUCCULENT TYPES continued

white warts on leaves

ALOE ARISTATA
Lace Aloe

toothed leaves

ALOE HUMILIS
Hedgehog Aloe

white edges

thick triangular leaves

ALOE VARIEGATA
Partridge-breasted Aloe

toothed leaves

ALOE MITRIFORMIS

Aloe jacunda

Aloes come in all shapes and sizes, and many form stemless rosettes of fleshy leaves. Only two of them are popular as house plants. **A. variegata** is immediately recognisable — the upright 6 in. leaves are triangular with prominent white banding and edging on the dark green or purplish surface. **A. aristata** is smaller — the 4 in. long leaves form a globular rosette which when mature readily produces a large number of offsets. There are several other attractive Aloes — **A. jacunda** is the small one, forming 3 in. rosettes of spiny, cream-blotched leaves. **A. humilis** is another dwarf, with incurving blue-green leaves. **A. mitriformis** is the thorny one.

Aloes are usually stemless rosettes but there are a few stemmed forms, including the Tree Aloe **A. arborescens** (9 in. spiny leaves on tall trunks) and **A. ferox** (18 in. spiny and warty leaves). Both species are unsuitable for small rooms.

Aloe ferox

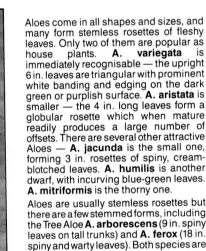

leaf 3 in. long

cylindrical leaf with furrow along upper surface

green, blotched with brown

BRYOPHYLLUM TUBIFLORUM
(KALANCHOE TUBIFLORA)
Chandelier Plant

leaf 4 in. long

fleshy, shiny leaves

underside blotched with purple

BRYOPHYLLUM DAIGREMONTIANUM
(KALANCHOE DAIGREMONTIANUM)
Devil's Backbone

leaf ¾ in. long — heart-shaped and fleshy

dark green, blotched with silver

underside purple

CEROPEGIA WOODII
Rosary Vine
(String of Hearts)

The Bryophyllums belong to the small group of house plants which bear plantlets on their leaves. **B. tubiflorum** has a series of tubular leaves encircling the stem, and at the tip of each fleshy leaf a small group of plantlets appear. It grows 3 ft high and in spring bell-shaped orange flowers appear. **B. daigremontianum** is an erect, unbranched 2–3 ft succulent with triangular leaves. These leaves are held stiffly at an angle to the stem with the serrated edges curled inwards. At these edges tiny plantlets develop.

An unusual succulent for a hanging basket or a pot standing on a shelf. The wiry stems grow about 3 ft long. It is an easy plant to grow, but the foliage is unfortunately sparse and the 1 in. tubular flowers are insignificant.

Ceropegia woodii

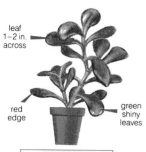

leaf 1–2 in. across

red edge

green shiny leaves

CRASSULA ARGENTEA
(CRASSULA PORTULACEA)
Jade Plant
(Money Tree)

scale-like triangular leaves

CRASSULA LYCOPODIOIDES
Rat Tail Plant

leaf 1 in. across

paired leaves surrounding the stem

CRASSULA PERFORATA
String of Buttons

propeller-shaped leaves

leaf 4 in. long

rough surface

CRASSULA FALCATA
(ROCHEA FALCATA)
Propeller Plant

Crassula ovata Hummel's Sunset

There are no typical foliage or growth characteristics to help you identify a plant as a Crassula. Leaves range from scale-like to several inches long, growth habit from sprawling to stiffly erect and leaf colour from grey to red. One of the most popular species is **Crassula argentea** with its tree-like trunk growing 3 ft or more. **C. arborescens** is rather similar, but the leaves are less rounded and are greyish in colour. There are several Crassulas with stems which seem to grow through the fused leaves — **C. perforata** (2 ft tall) and the very similar **C. rupestris** are the usual ones. **C. falcata** has larger leaves than any other common Crassula — this grey-leaved, red-flowering species is easy to grow. It reaches 2 – 3 ft — much taller than the upright branching stems of **C. lycopodioides** which are completely clothed with minute fleshy scales. A specialist supplier will offer many others.

Crassula rupestris

Cotyledon orbiculata

silvery surface

wavy-edged leaves

COTYLEDON UNDULATA
Silver Crown

The best known Cotyledon is **C. undulata** — 1–2 ft stems bearing wavy-edged and bloom-covered leaves. **C. orbiculata** is a larger shrub with red-edged leaves. The tubular flowers of Cotyledon appear in summer.

leafless stems

milky sap

EUPHORBIA TIRUCALLI
Milk Bush
(Pencil Euphorbia)

Euphorbias come in many shapes and forms. Some (e.g **E. grandicornis** and **E. resinifera**) are cactus-like — thornless succulent ones include the globular **E. obesa** (Turkish Temple) and the pencil-stemmed **E. tirucalli**.

Euphorbia obesa

SUCCULENT TYPES continued

brown-tipped pointed leaves

ECHEVERIA AGAVOIDES

flat-topped leaves

ECHEVERIA DERENBERGII

Painted Lady

waxy leaves

ECHEVERIA GLAUCA

Blue Echeveria

red-tipped leaves

fine white hairs on leaves

ECHEVERIA SETOSA

Firecracker Plant

Echeveria gibbiflora carunculata

pinky-bronze leaves

ECHEVERIA GIBBIFLORA METALLICA

surface covered with fine hairs

ECHEVERIA HARMSII
(OLIVERANTHUS ELEGANS)

Red Echeveria

Echeveria elegans

There are 2 popular Echeverias which grow as rosette-topped trees. The red-tipped leaves of **E. harmsii** form a loose rosette above the branching stems. The stout trunk of **E. gibbiflora** is taller (2 ft or more) and the leaves are larger (4 – 6 in. long) — varieties include **cristata** (wavy edged) and **metallica** (bronzy lustre).

Other Echeverias grow as flattened rosettes — the short and tightly-packed leaves are covered with a white bloom, short hairs or a waxy coating. There is an exception — **E. agavoides** bears plain-surfaced, 2 in. long green leaves. Echeveria leaves are 1 – 3 in. long and each popular species has its own distinctive feature — the ball-like silvery rosettes of **E. elegans,** the pinkish-tinged leaves of **E. carnicolor**, the waxy, hollow-spoon leaves of **E. glauca**, the furry foliage of **E. setosa** and the red-tipped grey leaves of **E. derenbergii.**

Faucaria tigrina

toothed jaw-like leaves

FAUCARIA TIGRINA

Tiger Jaws

The fleshy leaves of **F. tigrina** are 2 in. long 'jaws' complete with teeth. These spines are quite soft and so the plant is not as vicious as it looks. Yellow flowers appear in summer.

white warts on leaves

GASTERIA VERRUCOSA

Ox Tongue

Gasteria leaves are arranged in two rows — with age an untidy rosette is usually formed. **G. verrucosa** is the warty one — **G. maculata** has similar-sized leaves (5 – 6 in. long) but they are wart-free.

Gasteria maculata

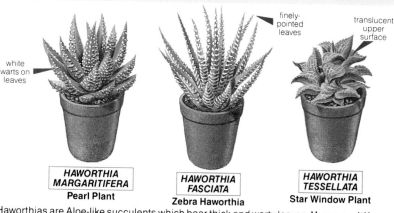

white warts on leaves

finely-pointed leaves

translucent upper surface

HAWORTHIA MARGARITIFERA	HAWORTHIA FASCIATA	HAWORTHIA TESSELLATA
Pearl Plant	**Zebra Haworthia**	**Star Window Plant**

Haworthias are Aloe-like succulents which bear thick and warty leaves. **H. margaritifera** forms a ball-like rosette about 5 in. across. The white tubercles which cover the backs of the leaves give the plant a pearly appearance — **H. papillosa** is similar. The warts on **H. fasciata** are arranged in horizontal bands — this 'zebra striping' is also a feature of **H. attenuata**. Some Haworthias have semi-transparent 'windows' instead of warts on the upper leaf surface — examples are **H. tessellata** and **H. cuspidata**.

Haworthias are generally low-growing rosettes but **H. reinwardtii** (Wart Plant) forms an erect 8 in. stem which is completely clothed with thick triangular leaves.

Haworthia attenuata

Kalanchoe tomentosa

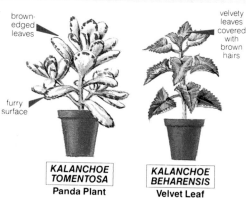

brown-edged leaves

velvety leaves covered with brown hairs

grey-green leaves

furry surface

KALANCHOE TOMENTOSA	KALANCHOE BEHARENSIS	GRAPTOPETALUM PARAGUAYENSE
Panda Plant	**Velvet Leaf**	**Ghost Plant**

There are many Kalanchoe varieties which are grown for their flowers and a few for their striking leaves. **K. tomentosa** is perhaps the most popular of the foliage ones — 1½ ft tall with woolly leaves. There is also **K. marmorata** (Pen Wiper) with scalloped and brown-blotched leaves, and **K. beharensis** grown for its large velvety foliage.

The Graptopetalums are grey-leaved, low-growing relatives of Echeveria. **G. paraguayense** has 2 in. long leaves on 3 in. stems. **G. pachyphyllum** is a miniature tree with 1 in. high stems — the rosettes are about 1 in. across.

grey-green stems

tightly-packed pointed leaves

leaf 1 in. long

silvery-white bloom

zig-zag stems

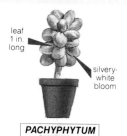

KLEINIA ARTICULATA (SENECIO ARTICULATUS)	OROSTACHYS SPINOSUS	PACHYPHYTUM OVIFERUM	PEDILANTHUS TITHYMALOIDES
Candle Plant		**Sugar Almond Plant** (Moonstones)	**Jacob's Ladder**

K. articulata is grown for its 2 ft bloom-coated stems — pale yellow flowers appear in summer. Even more dramatic is the Cocoon Plant (**K. tomentosa**) with its stems and tubular leaves covered in white wool.

O. spinosus is a saucer-like rosette of packed leaves which looks rather like Aeonium tabulaeforme. Look for the differences — this plant has spines at the ends of the leaves, and the centre folds upwards in winter.

Pachyphytum is closely related to Echeveria. You can see the family likeness in the mauve-tinged **P. amethystinum** but the popular one is quite different — **P. oviferum** bears rosettes of egg-like leaves.

P. tithymaloides is unmistakable — the fleshy stems zig-zag sharply, reaching about 2 ft. The variety **variegatus** is the popular one — oval, waxy leaves edged with white and pink. The milky sap is an irritant, so take care.

SUCCULENT TYPES continued

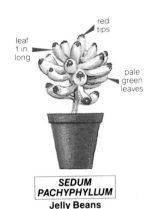

red tips
leaf 1 in. long
pale green leaves

SEDUM PACHYPHYLLUM
Jelly Beans

leaf ½ in. long
leaves turn red in sun

SEDUM RUBROTINCTUM
(SEDUM GUATEMALENSE)
Christmas Cheer

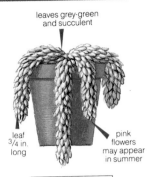

leaves grey-green and succulent
leaf ¾ in. long
pink flowers may appear in summer

SEDUM MORGANIANUM
Donkey's Tail

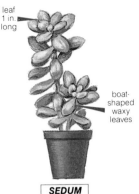

leaf 1 in. long
boat-shaped waxy leaves

SEDUM ADOLPHI
Golden Sedum

Sedum rubrotinctum

Sedums are generally low growing with branching stems and an abundance of fleshy leaves which are either cylindrical or boat-shaped. There are, of course, exceptions — **Sedum praealtum** is a vigorous 2 ft shrub with shiny 3 in. long leaves. **S. pachyphyllum** is a typical and popular Sedum — the erect, branching stems grow about 1 ft tall and the succulent leaves are cylindrical. The tips are red and so it is easily distinguished from **S. allantoides** (leaves all-green and coated with a greyish bloom) and the compact **S. rubrotinctum** (leaves suffused with red in strong light). Species with boat-shaped leaves include **S. adolphi** and **S. bellum**.

The two trailing Sedums do not look like sisters. **S. morganianum** bears 2–3 ft long stems, completely clothed with cylindrical leaves. The thin stems of **S. sieboldii mediovariegatum** bear leaves in clusters of three. Each ¾ in. leaf is cream-hearted and edged blue-green.

Sedum sieboldii mediovariegatum

Sempervivum soboliferum

dense cover of threads

SEMPERVIVUM ARACHNOIDEUM
Cobweb Houseleek

dark red tips

SEMPERVIVUM TECTORUM
Common Houseleek

Sempervivum is an old favourite both indoors and out. They are completely hardy — they seem to thrive on neglect and should not be overwatered, overfed or repotted unnecessarily. The Cobweb Houseleek is the one usually chosen — red flowers appear in summer. Many colourful varieties of both **S. tectorum** and **S. soboliferum** are available. Offsets form around the base of Sempervivum plants — hence the Hens and Chickens common name.

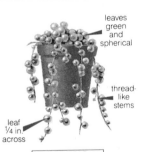

leaves green and spherical
thread-like stems
leaf ¼ in. across

SENECIO ROWLEYANUS
String of Beads

This group of Senecios is strange indeed — pendent threads bearing bead-like leaves. **S. rowleyanus** (pea-like foliage) **S. herreianus** (oval foliage) **S. citriformis** (lemon-shaped foliage).

SYNGONIUM

Syngonium requires warmth, moist air and protection from direct sunlight. Aerial roots are produced by the adult plant and a moss stick (see page 114) makes an excellent support for this attractive climbing plant.

An unusual feature of the Goosefoot Plant is the dramatic change in leaf shape which takes place as the plant gets older. The young leaves are arrow-shaped and borne on erect stalks. At this stage the variegation is boldest and brightest. With age the stems acquire a climbing habit and need support; at the same time the leaves become lobed. The juvenile form can be retained by cutting off the climbing stems as they form.

SECRETS OF SUCCESS

Temperature: Average warmth; at least 60°F in winter.
Light: Well-lit but sunless spot for variegated types, semi-shade for all-green varieties.
Water: Keep compost moist at all times; reduce watering in winter. Avoid overwatering.
Air Humidity: Mist leaves regularly.
Repotting: Every 2 years in spring.
Propagation: Take stem cuttings bearing aerial roots in spring or summer. Use rooting hormone.

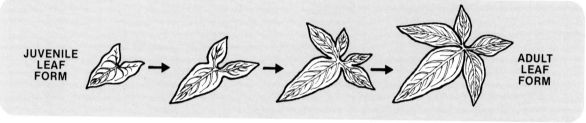

JUVENILE LEAF FORM → → → ADULT LEAF FORM

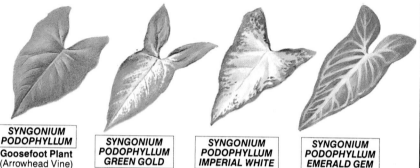

SYNGONIUM PODOPHYLLUM
Goosefoot Plant (Arrowhead Vine)

SYNGONIUM PODOPHYLLUM GREEN GOLD

SYNGONIUM PODOPHYLLUM IMPERIAL WHITE

SYNGONIUM PODOPHYLLUM EMERALD GEM

Syngonium podophyllum Emerald Gem

TYPES

The Goosefoots or Syngoniums are closely related to the climbing Philodendrons and require the same growing conditions. The most popular species is **S. podophyllum** — it is sometimes sold under the name **Nephthytis podophyllum**. Many varieties are available — the variegated types are the popular ones, ranging from almost entirely green to practically all-white or yellow. Less frequently seen are the species **S. auritum** and **S. angustatum**.

Tolmiea menziesii

TOLMIEA

This novelty plant gets its common name from the plantlets which form at the base of mature leaves. It forms a compact mound of downy, bright green leaves about 9 in. high. Tolmiea is one of the hardiest of all house plants and actually relishes a cold, well-ventilated and sunless environment. Its enemy is hot, dry air which can quickly lead to red spider mite attack and plant deterioration. It prefers a brightly lit spot but will adapt to shade.

SECRETS OF SUCCESS

Temperature: Cool to average warmth; not less than 40°F in winter.
Light: Bright light preferred, but will grow in shade.
Water: Keep compost moist at all times; reduce watering in winter.
Air Humidity: Mist leaves occasionally.
Repotting: Repot every year in spring.
Propagation: Peg down plantlets in compost — cut stems when rooted.

leaf 2 in. across

leaf stalk 4 in. long

TOLMIEA MENZIESII
Piggyback Plant

TYPE

T. menziesii is the most popular of the types which bear plantlets on their leaves — it is easy to grow even in poor conditions where little else will survive. The long leaf stalks give the plant a trailing appearance.

The TRADESCANTIA Group

By far the most important members of this group are the Inch Plants or Wandering Jews — Tradescantia, Zebrina and Callisia. Their leaves clasp the creeping or trailing stems and this group are perhaps the most popular of all hanging basket plants. Pinch out the growing tips regularly to encourage bushiness, and remove all-green shoots as soon as they appear. Winter warmth is not essential.

Setcreasea is also easy to grow and trails like a Wandering Jew, but its leaves are much longer. The Teddy Bear Vine has succulent leaves, densely covered with fur. All members of the Tradescantia family may occasionally flower indoors, but the blooms are generally insignificant. As with most families there is one difficult member. Brown Spiderwort has broad, colourful leaves borne in a rosette and this plant needs skill and a great deal of air humidity.

SECRETS OF SUCCESS

Temperature: Average warmth; not less than 45°–50°F in winter (Siderasis — 55°F).

Light: Bright light is essential. Some direct sunlight is beneficial for Zebrina, Setcreasea and Cyanotis. Grow Siderasis in semi-shade.

Water: Water liberally from spring to autumn; sparingly in winter.

Air Humidity: Mist occasionally — Siderasis regularly.

Repotting: Repot, when necessary, in spring.

Propagation: Very easy; stem cuttings in spring, summer or autumn. Propagate Siderasis by division.

SPECIAL PROBLEMS

BARE SPINDLY GROWTH
Cause: Too little light, too little water or too little fertilizer. All stems become straggly and bare with age. Cut back spindly growth; replace old plants.

LEAVES ALL GREEN
Cause: Too little light. Variegated types revert to all-green form in shady conditions.

STEMS LIMP, LEAVES YELLOW & SPOTTED
Cause: Underwatering. Water liberally during the growing season; allow surface to dry between waterings.

LEAF TIPS BROWN & SHRIVELLED
Cause: Air too dry. Look for red spider mite (see page 244). Remove dead growth. Mist leaves frequently.

TYPES

Tradescantia fluminensis Quicksilver

leaf 2–3 in. long
pale purple sap
underside pale purple

TRADESCANTIA FLUMINENSIS VARIEGATA
Wandering Jew (Inch Plant)

leaf 2–2½ in. long
shiny surface
colourless sap

TRADESCANTIA ALBIFLORA ALBOVITTATA

leaf 3–4 in. long
dull surface
hairy stem
underside purple

TRADESCANTIA BLOSSFELDIANA VARIEGATA
Flowering Inch Plant

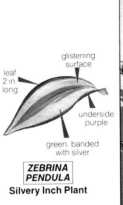

leaf 2 in. long
glistening surface
underside purple
green, banded with silver

ZEBRINA PENDULA
Silvery Inch Plant

leaf 2½ in. long
glistening surface
underside purple

ZEBRINA PENDULA PURPUSII
Bronze Inch Plant

Zebrina pendula quadricolor

T. **fluminensis** is perhaps the most popular Tradescantia — the varieties grown are **variegata** (cream striped) and **Quicksilver** (white striped). T. **albiflora** is similar, but neither the sap nor the underside of the foliage is mauve. The usual varieties are **albovittata** (white striped), **tricolor** (white and mauve striped) and **aurea** (yellow with green stripes). T. **blossfeldiana variegata** is the popular large-leaved type.

Zebrina is closely related to Tradescantia but it is more colourful. The leaves are glistening and multicoloured above and purple below. The surface colours may be green and silver (**Z. pendula**), green and purple (**Z. pendula purpusii**) or green, silver, pink and red (the showy but difficult **Z. pendula quadricolor**). Zebrina bears small purplish flowers in spring and summer.

Callisia elegans

leaf 1–1½ in. long

underside purple

CALLISIA ELEGANS
Striped Inch Plant

C. elegans (sometimes sold as **Setcreasea striata**) has small leaves and long stems — the upper surface of the foliage is dull and boldly striped with white lines. The leaves of **C. fragrans** turn pink in bright light.

leaves covered with brown hair

underside red

SIDERASIS FUSCATA
Brown Spiderwort

Siderasis differs from its relatives in 3 distinct ways. The 6 – 8 in. leaves form a rosette, it needs a terrarium for success and it bears attractive flowers (purple, 1 in. across). One species is grown — **S. fuscata**. A plant for the rarity collector.

Siderasis fuscata

Setcreasea purpurea

leaf 5 in. long

leaves and stems purple

SETCREASEA PURPUREA
Purple Heart

A straggly plant which makes up for its untidiness by its attractive colour — a rich purple when grown in good light. The leaves are slightly hairy and pink flowers appear in summer.

leaf 1 in. long — fleshy and covered with fur

underside purple

CYANOTIS KEWENSIS
Teddy Bear Vine

Unlike the closely related Tradescantia, Cyanotis bears hairy leaves. **C. kewensis** foliage has rusty brown hairs — the leaves of **C. somaliensis** (Pussy Ears) are larger and the hairs are pale grey.

Cyanotis somaliensis

Yucca elephantipes

YUCCA

A mature Yucca bears a crown of sword-like leaves on top of a stout trunk — a fine false palm for a hallway or large room. A large Yucca is expensive and should be treated properly. It will need a deep, well-drained container which can be moved outdoors in summer. In winter it will need an unheated and well-lit spot. At all times it should be kept in a sunny spot when indoors. White bell-shaped flowers may appear after a number of years.

SECRETS OF SUCCESS

Temperature: Average warmth; keep cool in winter (minimum 45°F).

Light: Provide as much light as possible.

Water: Water liberally from spring to autumn; sparingly in winter.

Air Humidity: Misting is not necessary.

Repotting: Repot every 2 years in spring.

Propagation: Remove and pot up offsets, or root cane cuttings.

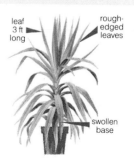

leaf 3 ft long

rough-edged leaves

swollen base

YUCCA ELEPHANTIPES
Spineless Yucca

TYPES

The 3–5 ft woody trunk bears a crown of long, leathery leaves. Choose **Y. elephantipes** — safer than **Y. aloifolia** (Spanish Bayonet) with sword-like leaves.

tendrils present

quick-growing stems

VINES

Many climbers are commonly referred to as 'vines' but the true vines are all members of the Grape family. They cling to supports by means of tendrils and two of them (Grape Ivy and Kangaroo Vine) are extremely popular and easy to grow.

The most important use of the popular vines is to clothe poles, screens and trellis work. Chestnut Vine is useful for covering large areas, Vines can also be employed for hanging baskets and as ground cover. The general requirement is for semi-shade or good light (without direct sunshine), cool conditions and occasional misting; but individual requirements vary. At one end of the scale Grape Ivy is one of the most tolerant of all house plants, surviving sun or shade, hot or cold air, dry or moist surroundings. Kangaroo Vine is a little less tolerant, suffering in bright sun and in hot, stuffy rooms. At the other end of the scale Cissus discolor is a delicate plant needing warmth and constant moisture around the leaves. All vines need good drainage; pinch out stem tips to induce bushy growth.

SPECIAL PROBLEMS

GLASSY BLOTCHES ON LEAVES WHICH LATER FALL
Cause: Direct sunlight; move plant away from the window.

LEAF TIPS BROWN & SHRIVELLED
Cause: Air too dry; mist leaves occasionally. If other symptoms (wilting, rotting, leaf fall) are present, the cause is overwatering.

SPOTTED & CURLED LOWER LEAVES WHICH LATER FALL
Cause: Underwatering. Compost must not be allowed to dry out.

MILDEW ON LEAVES
Cause: Poor drainage. Remove diseased leaves, spray with systemic fungicide and repot into a container with adequate drainage. Improve ventilation.

SECRETS OF SUCCESS

Temperature: Cool or average warmth; not less than 45° – 55°F in winter (Cissus discolor — 60°F).

Light: Brightly lit spot away from direct sunlight. Semi-shade for Cissus discolor and Rhoicissus capensis.

Water: Water liberally from spring to autumn; sparingly in winter.

Air Humidity: Mist leaves occasionally.

Repotting: Repot, when necessary, in spring.

Propagation: Stem cuttings in spring or summer.

TYPES

Cissus antarctica

C. antarctica is a great favourite for covering screens and other large areas, growing about 10 ft tall and clothing the supports with its leathery leaves. Where space is limited, grow the variety **minima**. The smallest-leaved Cissus is the dainty **C. striata** — red-stemmed, quick-growing and best grown as a trailer. The tender Cissus is **C. discolor** its green leaves blotched with silver and pale purple — the unusual one is **C. gongylodes** which bears red aerial roots.

leaf 4 in. long

glossy surface

CISSUS ANTARCTICA
Kangaroo Vine

leaf 6 in. long

underside red

CISSUS DISCOLOR
Begonia Vine

leaflets 1 in. long

leaflets pink when young

CISSUS STRIATA

HOW TO MAKE A MOSS STICK
A moss stick (U.S. name — totem pole) is a valuable aid for growing Vines, Monstera, Philodendron and Ivies. It serves a double purpose for plants with aerial roots such as Monstera — it provides support for the weak stem and it provides moisture through the aerial roots to the upper leaves.

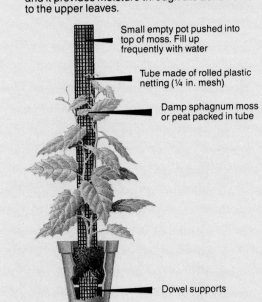

Small empty pot pushed into top of moss. Fill up frequently with water

Tube made of rolled plastic netting (¼ in. mesh)

Damp sphagnum moss or peat packed in tube

Dowel supports

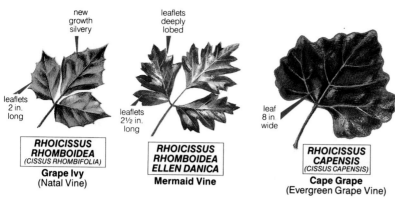

new growth silvery

leaflets 2 in. long

RHOICISSUS RHOMBOIDEA
(CISSUS RHOMBIFOLIA)
Grape Ivy
(Natal Vine)

leaflets deeply lobed

leaflets 2½ in. long

RHOICISSUS RHOMBOIDEA ELLEN DANICA
Mermaid Vine

leaf 8 in wide

RHOICISSUS CAPENSIS
(CISSUS CAPENSIS)
Cape Grape
(Evergreen Grape Vine)

Rhoicissus rhomboidea Ellen Danica

Grape Ivy (**R. rhomboidea**) is one of the most popular of all climbing house plants. Each leaf is made up of 3 leaflets, silvery at first and dark green and glossy when mature. It is extremely tolerant of poor conditions, and its only drawback is that it has become commonplace. For something a little different choose the variety **Ellen Danica** (lobed leaflets) or **Jubilee** (large, dark green leaflets). **R. capensis** is quite different to Grape Ivy and its varieties. Each large leaf is undivided — the surface is glossy and brown-edged, the underside brown and furry.

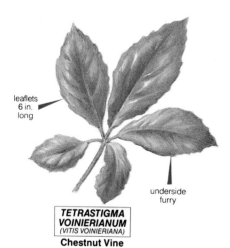

leaflets 6 in. long

underside furry

TETRASTIGMA VOINIERIANUM
(VITIS VOINIERIANA)
Chestnut Vine
(Lizard Plant)

The Chestnut Vine (**T. voinierianum**) is the giant of the group. Each leaf measures more than 1 ft across when mature — the 5 leaflets which make up each leaf are glossy and saw-edged. This plant is a rampant grower in the greenhouse or conservatory — useful if you want to cover a bare wall but a menace if delicate plants are nearby. It has never become really popular as a house plant as it is too large for most situations and is too unpredictable under room conditions. It is distinctly unhappy in warm, dry air — keep it in a cool place if you want to grow it indoors. Stout supports are necessary and so is space — it can grow 5 – 8 ft in a year.

Tetrastigma voinierianum

The Yucca and Aloe in Folk Medicine

The Yucca (page 113) has been used in a variety of ways for thousands of years by the American Indian. Leaves, twigs, buds and fruit provided food and the crushed roots were used to provide soap which was claimed to be 'as cleansing as any bought in the shops'. The fibres were used for rope making and basket weaving, and the juice of the plant was used in folk medicine. There are claims that arthritis and rheumatism have been relieved when the extracts have been tried by modern-day Yucca users, but scientific proof is rather thin.

The evidence for the beneficial properties of Aloe vera (Medicine Plant) is much stronger and this plant has been widely used for many years to bring about rapid healing of skin complaints, including radiation burns. The leaves are turned into a paste in a blender and the cream used to heal burns, reduce bleeding, rejuvenate skin, soothe sunburn and so on. With a few leaves from this succulent house plant and a lot of faith it may work for you.

ALOE VERA
Medicine Plant

CHAPTER 5

THE GEOGRAPHY OF INDOOR PLANTS

Each of the inhabited Continents has made some contribution to the list of indoor plants. The representatives from Europe and Oceania do not figure too prominently, whereas the native floras of Central and South America, the outer edges of Asia and the outer edges of Africa have each provided a vitally important part of the indoor plant kingdom.

Desert, rain forest, swamp, dry grassland — nearly all types of environment and climate have yielded indoor plants. Some of these plants occur naturally on only a tiny spot on the globe, such as the Howea Palm from Lord Howe Island and Scindapsus aureus from the Solomon Islands. Others have vast areas across several Continents as their native home — Ficus, Begonia and Pilea are examples.

When seeing an old favourite in the wild it is often immediately recognisable — Scindapsus or Monstera climbing a tree in the Tropics or Bromeliads growing in Equatorial America. Most Ferns look the same as they do indoors, and so do many flowering house plants.

So often, however, the plant in its natural habitat looks quite different to its puny descendant forced to live in a pot. Outdoors Schefflera is a noble tree, and so is Ficus elastica, Grevillea, Eucalyptus and the Palms.

Another important point to remember is that the varieties we grow are often unknown in the wild. For example, the Boston Fern is a mutation of a much plainer plant, and the named varieties of African Violet, Dieffenbachia, Fuchsia, Begonia, Coleus and Caladium bear little similarity to the rather dull species from which they were developed.

Europe

Buxus • Campanula isophylla • Carex • Chamaerops humilis • Chionodoxa • Convallaria • Crocus • Cyclamen • Cytisus • Galanthus • Hedera helix • Helxine • Hyacinthus • Laurus • Narcissus • Nerium • Phyllitis • Primula acaulis • Scilla • Scirpus • Sempervivum

As described in Chapter 3, the first plants grown indoors in Europe were varieties normally grown in the garden. They were brought inside for use in medicine, food or decoration. With the growth of serious interest in house plant culture there came a strong desire to grow exotics — plants from other Continents which were showier and more suitable for the conditions which prevail indoors.

This means that the European contribution to the World house plant collection has been limited — some Ivies, Helxine, Primroses, Italian Bellflower and a few others. There is, however, one major exception — the range of Garden Bulbs which are planted by the million in bowls each year. Crocus, Narcissus, Scilla, Lily of the Valley, Chionodoxa, Snowdrop, Hyacinth and so on are all natives of Europe.

The Americas

UNITED STATES

Beaucarnea • Ferocactus • Guzmania • Opuntia • Pteris • Selaginella • Stenotaphrum • Tolmiea • Tradescantia • Yucca

CENTRAL & SOUTH AMERICA

Abutilon • Achimenes • Adiantum • Aechmea • Agave • Allamanda • Ananas • Anthurium • Aphelandra • Aporocactus • Araucaria • Beaucarnea • Begonia (many species) • Beloperone • Billbergia • Blechnum • Bougainvillea • Bouvardia • Browallia • Brunfelsia • Caladium • Calathea • Calceolaria • Callisia • Capsicum • Cattleya • Celosia • Cephalocereus • Chamaecereus • Chamaedorea • Cleistocactus • Cleyera • Columnea • Cryptanthus • Ctenanthe • Cuphea • Dieffenbachia • Dipladenia • Echeveria • Echinocactus • Echinocereus • Epiphyllum • Episcia • Espostoa • Euphorbia • Ferocactus • Fittonia • Fuchsia • Guzmania • Gymnocalycium • Haageocereus • Hamatocactus • Hippeastrum • Hypocyrta • Iresine • Jacaranda • Lobivia • Mammillaria • Maranta • Miltonia • Mimosa • Monstera • Myrtillocactus • Notocactus • Odontoglossum • Opuntia • Oreocereus • Oxalis • Pachyphytum • Pachystachys • Parodia • Passiflora • Peperomia • Pereskia • Philodendron • Phlebodium • Pilea • Piper • Rebutia • Rechsteineria • Rhipsalidopsis • Rhipsalis • Rhoeo • Sedum • Setcreasea • Siderasis • Sinningia • Smithiantha • Stromanthe • Syngonium • Tillandsia • Tradescantia • Trichocereus • Vriesea • Yucca • Zebrina • Zygocactus

Central and South America are the treasure chests from which so many of our house plants have been collected. It is the tropical rain forests of the New World and not the jungles of Africa which have yielded the popular climbers and trailers such as Tradescantia, Zebrina, Philodendron, Monstera and Syngonium. Before the colonisers came to move plants around the world it was only in this region where Columnea and Peperomia clung on to the trees and Anthurium, Caladium, Aphelandra and the Marantas clothed the forest floor.

Not all the plants which have been domesticated came from the tropical forests. Some, like Poinsettia, have drier regions as their native home and one giant group, the Cacti, occur mainly in the deserts of southern U.S.A. and Mexico. Not all Cacti grow in arid regions — Epiphyllum lives and flowers in the hot and humid areas of tropical America and the West Indies.

The Cacti are not the only major plant group we owe to the Americas, for the New World is also the ancestral home of the Bromeliads (pages 51 and 130) we grow indoors. In nature most of them are epiphytes, clinging on to trees and rocks.

North America has been a relatively poor hunting ground for the collectors. Some Cacti (e.g Ferocactus), some Bromeliads (e.g Guzmania), Tolmiea, Selaginella, Stenotaphrum and a few Ferns represent the meagre haul.

Tillandsia growing on Swamp Cypress in sub-tropical America

Africa

NORTH AFRICA

Aeonium • Chamaerops • Chrysanthemum frutescens • Cineraria • Cyperus papyrus • Cytisus • Davallia • Dracaena draco • Hedera • Narcissus • Phoenix

CENTRAL AFRICA & MADAGASCAR

Central Africa: Asplenium • Begonia • Calathea • Celosia • Clerodendrum • Coffea • Dracaena • Exacum • Ficus lyrata • Gardenia • Gloriosa • Impatiens • Kalanchoe • Pentas • Plectranthus • Saintpaulia • Thunbergia

Madagascar: Bryophyllum • Catharanthus • Chrysalidocarpus • Cyperus • Dracaena marginata • Euphorbia milii • Hypoestes • Kalanchoe • Nicodemia • Stephanotis

SOUTHERN AFRICA

Agapanthus • Aloe • Amaryllis • Asparagus • Begonia • Bryophyllum • Ceropegia • Chlorophytum • Clivia • Cotyledon • Crassula • Cyperus • Cyrtomium • Erica • Euphorbia • Faucaria • Gasteria • Haemanthus • Haworthia • Kleinia • Lachenalia • Lithops • Nerine • Pelargonium • Plumbago • Rhoicissus • Rochea • Sansevieria • Selaginella • Senecio • Sparmannia • Stapelia • Strelitzia • Streptocarpus • Vallota • Veltheimia • Zantedischia

The vast forests and open grasslands of Central Africa have yielded surprisingly few house plants, and yet without this small group there would be a large gap in our displays. The ancestor of the African Violet was found in N.E. Tanzania at the end of the 19th century, Busy Lizzie came originally from the same country and many Dracaenas have Tropical Africa as their native home.

Southern Africa has given us a vast array of plants for the home, ranging from the dazzling Strelitzia to the lowly Lithops, from the ever-popular Sansevieria, Pelargonium and Chlorophytum to the uncommon Stapelia and Haemanthus. The range of house plants from the area of Africa below the Tropic of Capricorn is immense, but the types gathered from the drier regions have one outstanding feature in common — succulent foliage.

North Africa has yielded few indoor plants, but the tiny Canary Islands have given us Hedera canariensis, Dracaena draco, Chrysanthemum frutescens, Cineraria, Cytisus canariensis and Phoenix canariensis.

An island off the other coast of Africa (Socotra Is.) gave us both Exacum and one of the parents of the Begonia Hiemalis hybrids. Even more spectacular is the list of plants collected from Madagascar — the Bryophyllums, the Crown of Thorns, the Polka Dot Plant and Flaming Katy.

Ericas at Salmonsdam, Cape Province

Asia

Acorus (China/Japan) • Aeschynanthus • Aglaonema • Ardisia (China/Japan) • Aspidistra (Japan) • Asplenium • Aucuba • Azalea (China/Japan) • Begonia rex (India) • Camellia (China/Japan) • Carex (Japan) • Caryota • Celosia • Chrysanthemum (China/Japan) • Cissus discolor • Citrus • Clerodendrum • Cleyera • Codiaeum • Coelogyne • Coleus • Cordyline • Crossandra (India) • Cycas (Japan) • Cyclamen • Cyrtomium (China/Japan) • Davallia • Dracaena • Duchesnea • Euonymus • Fatsia (Japan) • Ficus • Gardenia (China) • Gloriosa • Gynura • Hedera • Heptapleurum • Hibiscus (China/Japan) • Hoya • Hydrangea (Japan) • Impatiens hawkeri • Ixora (India) • Jasminum • Nerium • Ophiopogon (Japan) • Pellionia • Pilea cadierei • Pittosporum (China/Japan) • Plectranthus (India) • Podocarpus (Japan) • Polyscias • Primula (China) • Pteris • Radermachera (China) • Rhapis (China) • Rhododendron (China/Japan) • Rohdea (China/Japan) • Rosa chinensis • Scindapsus • Sedum (China/Japan) • Tetrastigma • Thunbergia (India) • Trachycarpus (China)

It is not surprising that Asia should have provided so many varied plants — within that vast expanse of land are some of the coldest, warmest, wettest and driest spots on earth.

Asia has been a source of indoor plants for centuries. Oranges were one of the first exotic fruits to be grown outdoors and wintered indoors in Europe, and this began in the 16th century. Ficus pumila and F. benjamina were introduced into Britain in the 18th century, and in the 19th century came the Aspidistra, Palms and Rubber Plants for the Victorian villa.

The story still goes on. Heptapleurum, Dracaena marginata tricolor and the Impatiens New Guinea Hybrids were introduced to our homes in the 1970s. Radermachera is a plant of the 80s, and there is undoubtedly more to come from the flora of Asia.

Each major region of Asia has made its own special contribution. From India came the ancestor of all the Begonia rex hybrids and the original specimens of Ficus elastica. China and Japan are the native homes of the Chrysanthemum and the Azalea, the robust Aspidistra and the temperamental Gardenia. So many flowering plants came to us from this part of the world, including the Primulas and the Miniature Rose. Coleus came from Java and so did Gynura, but most of the plants collected from Asia have no respect for national boundaries and grow wild in many countries.

Ficus retusa (Chinese Banyan) at home in S.E. Asia — note the aerial roots which become secondary trunks

Oceania

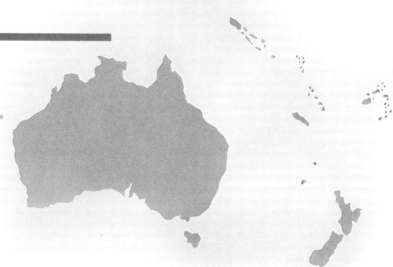

PACIFIC ISLANDS

Acalypha wilkesiana • Asplenium nidus • Breynia • Cocos •
Codiaeum • Davallia • Dizygotheca • Hemigraphis •
Pandanus • Pellionia • Pisonia • Platycerium • Polyscias •
Pseuderanthemum • Scindapsus

AUSTRALIA, NEW ZEALAND & DEPENDENCIES

Acacia • Adiantum hispidulum •
Araucaria heterophylla (Norfolk Islands) •
Asplenium • Callistemon • Cissus •
Cordyline • Dicksonia • Eucalyptus •
Ficus benjamina • Fuchsia • Grevillea •
Howea (Lord Howe Island) •
Hoya carnosa • Nertera •
Pellaea rotundifolia • Pisonia •
Platycerium • Plectranthus •
Pteris • Schefflera

Oceania consists of Australia, New Zealand and the vast number of islands which make up Melanesia, Polynesia and Micronesia. As most schoolchildren know it was Captain (actually Lieutenant) Cook who discovered Australia. Less well known is the fact that he was accompanied by Joseph Banks, one of the most distinguished naturalists of his day. The site of the landing in 1770 was called Botanists Bay in honour of Banks — later changed to Botany Bay despite Banks' disappointment in the plant life.

In Australia and New Zealand today there are house plant displays to match any in the world, but nearly all the varieties come from elsewhere. If all the native-born types were removed from the windowsills of the world the effect would be noticeable but not really serious. Two popular plants would go — Cissus antarctica and Schefflera actinophylla.

The situation would be more serious if we lost the South Sea Island plants. The Howea Palm and the Norfolk Island Pine came from islands between Australia and New Zealand — from the Pacific Islands the Bird's Nest Fern and Dizygotheca were collected and the popular Devil's Ivy (Scindapsus aureus) was collected.

Thus the Oceanic group of indoor plants are an interesting collection, with colourful and welcome ones such as Callistemon, Hoya and Acalypha. But the size of the group does not begin to compare with the American, Asian and African collections.

Cordyline australis in flower in its S. Hemisphere home

CHAPTER 6
FLOWERING HOUSE PLANTS

Flowers play an important role in the display of indoor plants. As the outdoor garden seems to come alive when the flower buds open in spring, so the indoor display takes on a new look when plants in bloom are added.

Flowering house plants are grown primarily for their floral effect, although a few (Ardisia, Duchesnea, Citrus etc.) are grown for their display of fruits. The choice seems almost limitless — for flower size you can grow a spectacular Bird of Paradise with 6 in. blooms or even a Stapelia gigantea with flowers the size of a dinner plate; at the other end of the scale you can pick Heliotrope, with its tiny blossoms clustered together in order to be seen.

Take your choice of flowering season — Pink Jasmine and Kalanchoe in winter, Spathiphyllum and Anthurium in spring, Hibiscus and Campanula in summer or Aphelandra and Oleander in autumn. In some cases the flowering season is fleeting but with Busy Lizzie, African Violet, Brunfelsia and Beloperone it is possible with care to have flowers nearly all year round. You can even take your choice of fragrance, ranging from the strong, heady perfumes of Heliotrope, Oleander, Gardenia and Jasmine to the unpleasant stench of the Carrion Flower.

The flowering house plants come in many sizes, shapes and smells but with each of them there comes a time when it is no longer in flower. In most cases the plant is not particularly attractive at this stage, and is perhaps best grown in a Pot Group or Indoor Garden. Some varieties, however, have leaves which are so striking that they are worth growing for their foliage alone; good examples are Aphelandra, the Bromeliads, the Fancy-leaved Geraniums, Sanchezia and Sparmannia.

There are few general rules on cultivation — the plants range from the extremely difficult Acalypha to the cast-iron Beloperone, so look through the following A-Z guide for the specific needs of your plant. You will find that flowering house plants nearly always need more light than foliage ones.

ABUTILON

The Spotted Flowering Maple is grown primarily for its attractive foliage (page 43), but the other species are cultivated for their blooms. The flowers are generally pendent bells borne on slender stalks — the leaves are arrow-shaped or lobed, the stems firm and upright or weak and trailing.

Abutilon is not a difficult plant to grow despite its exotic appearance. It will benefit from being stood outdoors in summer and in winter the plant should be cut back to half its size.

SECRETS OF SUCCESS

Temperature: Average warmth; keep cool in winter (50°–60°F).
Light: Choose a partially shady spot.
Water: Water liberally from spring to late autumn. Water sparingly in winter.
Air Humidity: Mist leaves occasionally.
Repotting: Repot, every year, in spring.
Propagation: Stem cuttings or seeds in spring.

Abutilon megapotamicum

TYPES

A. megapotamicum is a trailing plant suitable for hanging baskets, but tied to supports this evergreen will grow 4 ft high. It has arrow-shaped leaves which are about 3 in. long, and between spring and autumn the flowers appear. These lantern-like blooms are about 2 in. in length, hanging down from wiry stems and giving the plant its alternative common name — Weeping Chinese Lantern. The variety **variegata** has yellow-splashed leaves.

A. hybridum is quite different — it forms a spreading tree about 5 ft high and makes a fine specimen plant if you have plenty of space. The sycamore-like leaves are about 3 in. across and the edges are sometimes white or cream. The flowers are 2 in. long and the colour depends on the variety. There are several to choose from — **Boule de Neige** (white), **Fireball** (red), **'Souvenir de Bonn'** (pink) and **Golden Fleece** (yellow) are examples of the wide range available.

Abutilon hybridum Michael

ACACIA

Several Acacias are suitable for growing indoors but they have never been popular. They are all trees or shrubs with either feathery leaves or spiny false leaves known as phylloclades. In early spring the characteristic yellow flowers appear — small powder-puffs more popular in flower arrangements than in house plant collections. Cut back straggly or unwanted growth once flowering has finished. Kangaroo Thorn is a robust plant which is trouble-free provided you keep it in an unheated, well-lit spot in winter and take care not to overwater. If you can, place the pot outside once summer arrives and bring it back indoors in autumn.

Acacia dealbata

spiny leaf 1 in. long

ball-like flower-head ½ in. across

ACACIA ARMATA
Kangaroo Thorn

SECRETS OF SUCCESS

Temperature: Average warmth; keep cool in winter (minimum temperature 40°F).
Light: Provide as much light as possible.
Water: Water moderately from spring to autumn; sparingly in winter.
Air Humidity: Misting not necessary.
Repotting: Repot every 2–3 years after flowering.
Propagation: Stem cuttings in summer. Use rooting hormone.

TYPES

Acacias are useful shrubs where space is not a problem, but they have never been popular. **A. armata** is the best known, reaching 3–4 ft and covered with dark green 'leaves' (really modified leaf stalks). The fluffy flower-heads are scented. The ferny-leaved **A. dealbata** is more attractive but is even larger, and is sold by the florist as 'Mimosa'. Both species need fresh air — stand the pot outdoors in summer.

ACALYPHA

Acalypha hispida

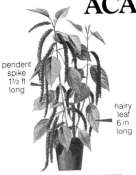

pendent spike 1½ ft long

hairy leaf 6 in. long

ACALYPHA HISPIDA
Chenille Plant
(Red-hot Catstail)

Red-hot Catstail is an apt name for the most popular Acalypha — the brightly-coloured flower spikes hang like long tassels from the stems. Unfortunately this attractive plant is more suited to the greenhouse than to the living room as it requires constantly moist air. In a dry atmosphere leaf fall will occur and red spider mite will flourish. Prune old plants in the spring and remove dead tassels. Take cuttings each year; root them in a warm place and flowering can be expected when the plants are about one year old.

SECRETS OF SUCCESS

Temperature: Keep the shrub warm; minimum 60°F at night.

Light: Slight shade is best — avoid sun in spring and summer.

Water: Keep the compost moist at all times.

Air Humidity: Surround pot with damp peat and mist leaves frequently.

Repotting: Repot every year in spring.

Propagation: Stem cuttings in spring. Use rooting hormone and bottom heat.

TYPES

A tall shrub reaching 6 ft or more, grown for its tassels of tiny red flowers which appear amongst the leaves. **Alba** is an unusual white variety.

AGAPANTHUS

Agapanthus orientalis alba

ball-like flower-head 3–8 in. across

strap-like leaf 1 ft long

AGAPANTHUS AFRICANUS
Blue African Lily

You will need space and a sunny position for the attractive Blue African Lily. Large round heads of blue tubular flowers are borne on tall stalks which appear in succession throughout the summer from the rosette of long strap-like leaves. There is no difficulty in growing this showy plant as long as you can move it to a cold but frost-free room in winter. There it will need very little water until spring, when it should be brought back to its well-lit spot and started into growth by watering and feeding. Frequent watering will be necessary during the flowering season. Do not repot frequently as this plant blooms best when it is pot-bound.

SECRETS OF SUCCESS

Temperature: Average warmth; keep cool in winter (night temperature 40°–45°F).

Light: Choose sunniest spot available.

Water: Keep compost moist at all times during the growing season; give very little water in winter.

Air Humidity: Misting is not necessary.

Repotting: Not required until division takes place.

Propagation: Divide plants in spring every 4–5 years.

TYPES

A. africanus bears its blooms on 2 ft flower-stalks. Plant in a tub or large pot. **A. orientalis** is larger and will need even more space.

ALLAMANDA

tubular flower 3 in. across

leaf 4 in. long

ALLAMANDA CATHARTICA
Golden Trumpet

TYPES

A. cathartica is truly a beauty with flaring yellow trumpets. Two varieties are available — **grandiflora** (compact, pale yellow flowers) and **hendersonii** (red buds, golden flowers).

A spectacular climbing plant which would undoubtedly be much more popular if it had a more robust constitution. The leaves are glossy and the large blooms appear all summer long. Its demand for warmth and a humid atmosphere plus plenty of sunlight means that it is a plant for the conservatory rather than the living room, and in the right home it will reach 12 ft or more. Cut back to half its size at the beginning of the year.

SECRETS OF SUCCESS

Temperature: Keep the plant warm; minimum 60°F in winter.

Light: Some direct sun is essential.

Water: Water moderately from spring to autumn; sparingly in winter.

Air Humidity: Surround pot with damp peat and mist frequently.

Repotting: Repot every year in spring.

Propagation: Stem cuttings in spring. Use rooting hormone and bottom heat.

Allamanda cathartica grandiflora

AESCHYNANTHUS

The best way to display the trailing stems of Aeschynanthus is in a hanging basket. It is not easy to grow under ordinary room conditions. Misting is essential in spring and summer, and in winter the plant must be allowed to rest with a temperature of about 60°F and infrequent watering. Keep it in a well-lit spot and cut back the stems immediately after flowering if pruning is necessary. The most popular variety has a characteristic flower form and a descriptive common name — the Lipstick Vine.

SECRETS OF SUCCESS

Temperature: Average warmth; not less than 55°F.

Light: Bright light or slight shade; avoid direct sunshine.

Water: Water regularly from spring to autumn; sparingly in winter. Use tepid water.

Air Humidity: Mist the leaves frequently, especially in hot weather.

Repotting: Repot every 2–3 years in spring.

Propagation: Stem cuttings in spring or summer. Use rooting hormone and bottom heat.

TYPES

The general popular name for Aeschynanthus species is Basket Vine. Unfortunately they are not easy to grow under ordinary room conditions — a feature shared with the closely-related Columnea. The two can be confused — a rough-and-ready way of distinguishing between them is to look at the flower. The upper lobes on the Columnea bloom fuse and form a prominent downturned hood — the lobes of Aeschynanthus form a much less prominent hood. **A. speciosus** is readily available and is also the most colourful — 2–3 ft stems bearing 3 in. long flowers which stand erect, darkening from yellow bases to red mouths. **A. lobbianus** is a smaller plant, its red flowers arising from brown 'lipstick cases'. **A. hildebrandii** is sold in winter — a small creeping plant with red flowers. **A. marmoratus** is grown for its foliage (mottled above and red below) rather than the flowers.

leaf 1½ in. long — waxy and edged with purple

tubular 2 in. long red flower — brown calyx below, borne at stem tip

stems 1½ ft long

AESCHYNANTHUS LOBBIANUS
Lipstick Vine

Aeschynanthus speciosus

ANTHURIUM

The exotic flowers of Anthurium have a distinct air of luxury — large waxy 'palettes' each with a coloured 'tail' at its centre. The flowering season extends over many months and each bloom lasts for many weeks. Unfortunately Anthuriums are not easy to grow, but A. scherzerianum (Flamingo Flower) is reasonably tolerant of ordinary room conditions. The leaves are spear-shaped, the tail is coiled and the flowers appear from spring to midsummer. The much larger A. andreanum is more difficult to grow.

SECRETS OF SUCCESS

Temperature: Average warmth; minimum temperature 60°F in winter.

Light: Bright in winter; protect from summer sun.

Water: Give a little water every few days to keep the compost moist at all times but never waterlogged. Use soft, tepid water.

Air Humidity: Mist leaves very frequently.

Repotting: Repot, when necessary, in spring.

Propagation: Divide plants at repotting time.

Anthurium scherzerianum

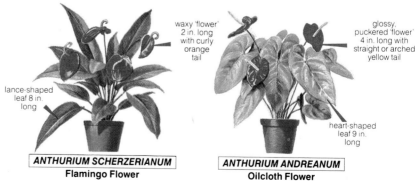

waxy 'flower' 2 in. long with curly orange tail

lance-shaped leaf 8 in. long

ANTHURIUM SCHERZERIANUM
Flamingo Flower

glossy, puckered 'flower' 4 in. long with straight or arched yellow tail

heart-shaped leaf 9 in. long

ANTHURIUM ANDREANUM
Oilcloth Flower

TYPES

There are 2 species — the one to choose for the living room rather than the conservatory is **A. scherzerianum**, which grows about 1 ft high with red or orange flowers. **A. andreanum** reaches 2–3 ft — the blooms are white, pink, orange or red.

APHELANDRA

The Zebra Plant has been a favourite house plant for generations. It is a double-purpose plant — all year round its large leaves with silvery veins provide an attractive feature, and then for about 6 weeks in autumn it is crowned by a golden cone. It is not easy to keep an Aphelandra under ordinary room conditions for more than a few months. The fate of nearly all of them is to become leggy and leafless. The way to avoid this is to feed regularly, never allow the compost to dry out, mist regularly and keep warm in winter. Remove dead blooms after flowering.

SECRETS OF SUCCESS

Temperature: Average warmth; minimum temperature 55°F in winter.

Light: Brightly lit spot away from direct sun in summer.

Water: Keep compost moist at all times but never waterlogged. Reduce watering in winter. Use soft, tepid water.

Air Humidity: Mist leaves frequently.

Repotting: Repot every year in spring.

Propagation: Stem cuttings in spring. Rooting hormone and warmth are necessary.

SPECIAL PROBLEMS

LOSS OF LEAVES
Cause: Most likely reason is dryness at the roots; even a short period of drying out can cause serious leaf loss. Cold air is another common cause of defoliation. Other possibilities are too much sun or draughts.

BROWN LEAF TIPS
Cause: Air humidity too low. Surround the pot with moist peat; mist leaves regularly.

Aphelandra squarrosa louisae

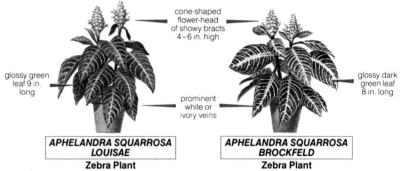

cone-shaped flower-head of showy bracts 4–6 in. high

glossy green leaf 9 in. long

prominent white or ivory veins

glossy dark green leaf 8 in. long

APHELANDRA SQUARROSA LOUISAE
Zebra Plant

APHELANDRA SQUARROSA BROCKFELD
Zebra Plant

TYPES

The flower is made up of bracts which are nearly always yellow or golden, but there is a scarlet type — **A. aurantica**. The most popular Zebra Plant is **A. squarrosa** and the common variety is the golden **louisae** (1–1½ ft). Other varieties are the compact **Dania** and **Brockfeld**. **Fritz Prinsler** is grown for its stunning leaves.

ARDISIA

The glossy leathery leaves make this slow-growing shrub an attractive foliage plant, but its main feature is the presence of red berries at Christmas. These berries follow the tiny flowers which appear in summer and they stay on the plant for many months. The Coral Berry should be kept cool in winter and away from draughts at all times. Never let the compost dry out and prune back the shoots in early spring. Not many house plant suppliers offer Ardisia as it is so slow to grow.

Ardisia crenata

fragrant flowers followed by red berries

stem 3 ft high

ARDISIA CRENATA
Coral Berry

SECRETS OF SUCCESS

Temperature: Average warmth; minimum temperature 45°F in winter.

Light: Brightly lit spot away from direct sun.

Water: Keep compost moist at all times. Reduce watering in winter.

Air Humidity: Mist leaves frequently with tepid water.

Repotting: Repot, when necessary, in spring.

Propagation: Stem cuttings in spring or summer. Sow seeds in early spring.

TYPE

A. crenata is a handsome tree, sometimes sold as **A. crispa**. The leaves are oval and leathery and the flowers are white or pale pink. Stand outdoors in summer — cut back when the display of berries is over.

BEGONIA

Flowering begonias are many and varied and identification is often difficult. There are a few basic points which can help you through the maze. The showiest blooms are generally borne by the tuberous begonias and some fibrous-rooted ones which become dormant after flowering (see page 168). These are all flowering pot plants, grown for temporary display and then discarded or kept for replanting to provide fresh blooms next season.

The flowering begonias which are shown here are the evergreen ones — less spectacular in bloom, perhaps, but with the advantage of keeping their leaves all year round. To succeed with these begonias you have to avoid hot dry days, really cold nights, too much water and too much sun.

Temperature: Average warmth; not less than 55°F.

Light: A bright spot away from direct sunlight. A few hours of morning or evening sun in winter are beneficial.

Water: The compost should be kept moist from spring to autumn; allow surface to dry out slightly between waterings. Water sparingly in winter.

Air Humidity: Moist air needed — surround pots with damp peat. Mist surrounding air, but never wet the leaves.

Repotting: Repot, when necessary, in spring.

Propagation: Stem cuttings root very easily — take cuttings from a branch low down on the plant. Seed can be sown at 70°F.

SPECIAL PROBLEMS

Diseases are a menace. See page 245.

TYPES

● CANE-STEMMED TYPES

waxy flower ½ in. across

glossy, red-margined leaf 5 in. long

underside red

BEGONIA COCCINEA
Angel Wing Begonia

white-spotted leaf 5 in. long

pink flower ½ in. across

BEGONIA LUCERNA

glossy leaf 5 in. long

olive green blotched with white

BEGONIA ARGENTEO-GUTTATA
Trout Begonia

The Cane-stemmed Begonias are the giants of the group, reaching 6 ft or more if left unpruned. However, it is usually a good idea to pinch them back in spring to induce bushiness. Use a heavy clay pot to prevent the plant from toppling over and stake the tall, bamboo-like stems. The flower trusses are pendulous and the most popular species is **B. lucerna** — tall-growing and often sold under its full name **B. Corallina de Lucerna**. Flowers appear all year round and the truss bears 30–60 flowers. **B. coccinea** is more compact and summer-flowering — **B. argenteo-guttata** is bushy and not often seen.

● TRAILING TYPES

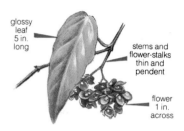

glossy leaf 5 in. long

stems and flower-stalks thin and pendent

flower 1 in. across

BEGONIA GLAUCOPHYLLA
(BEGONIA LIMMINGHEIANA)
Shrimp Begonia

B. glaucophylla (often sold as **B. limmingheiana**) is grown in hanging baskets when winter flowers are required and the much more popular Basket Begonias (page 168) are at rest. The leaves are much less lopsided than other large-leaved begonias and the blooms are rose-red.

Begonia coccinea

Begonia lucerna

Begonia glaucophylla

BEGONIA TYPES continued

• BUSHY TYPES

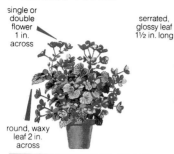

single or double flower 1 in. across

round, waxy leaf 2 in. across

BEGONIA SEMPERFLORENS
Wax Begonia

serrated, glossy leaf 1½ in. long

plant 3 ft high

pink or red flower 1 in. across

BEGONIA FUCHSIOIDES
Fuchsia Begonia

plant 2 ft high

pale pink flower ½ in. across

hairy leaf 8 in. long

underside red

BEGONIA HAAGEANA
Elephant Ear Begonia

deep pink flower ½ in. across

lobed, serrated leaf 3 in. long

green blotched with red

BEGONIA SERRATIPETALA
Pink Spot Begonia

Begonia fuchsioides

By far the most popular of the bushy evergreen begonias is the Wax Begonia — **B. semperflorens.** The plant is a leafy rounded bush 6–12 in. high and is the easiest flowering begonia to grow. Choosing which variety to buy is much more difficult — there are hybrids with leaves ranging from greenish-yellow to deepest red, and there is a wide range of flower types in white, pink, orange and red. The Wax Begonia blooms at any time of the year.

The other types of bushy begonia are much less common. **B. haageana** is the only reasonably easy one — the flowers appear in summer amid the very large leaves. **B. fuchsioides** is attractive but difficult — the drooping clusters of flowers which appear during the winter months give it a Fuchsia-like appearance. **B. serratipetala** is easy to identify — the arching stems bear leaves which are deeply notched — the flowers open in summer. **B. metallica** is another type which is easy to recognise — the dark green leaves have deeply sunken purplish veins. Red or white flowers are borne in summer or autumn.

Begonia metallica

---

curved flower-head 4 in. long

oval leaf 2 in. long

BELOPERONE GUTTATA
Shrimp Plant

TYPE

B. guttata is the only species grown. Both stems and leaves are downy, and each flower-head is made up of overlapping colourful bracts through which the tubular white flowers protrude.

BELOPERONE

An easy to grow shrubby plant which bears salmon-coloured, prawn-shaped flower-heads at the end of arching stems. The blooms appear nearly all year round, and the simple requirements are warm days, cool nights and a sunny windowsill.
When young, remove some of the first flowers to make sure that a vigorous bush is formed. Cut the plant back to half size each spring to maintain bushiness, and remember to feed regularly.

SECRETS OF SUCCESS

Temperature: Average warmth; keep at 50°–55°F in winter.

Light: Some direct sun is essential.

Water: Water liberally from spring to late autumn. Water sparingly in winter.

Air Humidity: Mist occasionally.

Repotting: Repot, when necessary, in spring.

Propagation: Stem cuttings root easily.

Beloperone guttata

BOUGAINVILLEA

pink or purple flower 1 in. across

leaf narrow and smooth

stems woody and spiny

BOUGAINVILLEA GLABRA

Paper Flower

A showy climbing plant with brightly coloured, papery bracts. It is difficult to grow under ordinary room conditions. A well-grown plant brought indoors will bloom profusely in spring and summer on the windowsill, after which you have the challenge of trying to make it bloom next season. Prune in autumn and reduce watering. Keep the plant cool throughout the winter and then increase temperature and watering once spring arrives.

SECRETS OF SUCCESS

Temperature: Warm in summer; cool (45°–50°F) in winter.

Light: Choose sunniest spot available.

Water: Keep compost moist in spring and summer; almost dry in winter.

Air Humidity: Mist if room is heated.

Repotting: Repot, when necessary, in spring.

Propagation: Stem cuttings in summer. Rooting hormone and bottom heat are necessary.

Bougainvillea buttiana Mrs Butt

TYPES

The basic species is **B. glabra**, but its hybrids are more popular. Top of the list is the large-leaved, large-flowered **B. buttiana Mrs Butt** (rose-crimson).

BOUVARDIA

Bouvardia domestica Mary

Bouvardia is well worth growing for the fragrant flowers that appear from midsummer to early winter. The white, pink or red tubular blooms are borne in large clusters above the pointed leaves. The main requirement is for a brightly-lit spot which is cool in winter. Pinch out the tips of young plants to promote bushy growth and cut back the stems once flowering is over. With proper care the shrub will grow about 2 ft high, but even in expert hands it will deteriorate after a few years.

SECRETS OF SUCCESS

Temperature: Average warmth; not less than 50°F in winter.

Light: As much light as possible, but shade from hot summer sun.

Water: Water liberally from spring until flowering stops, then keep the compost fairly dry until spring.

Air Humidity: Mist leaves regularly.

Repotting: Repot, when necessary, in spring.

Propagation: Stem cuttings in spring. Use rooting hormone.

tubular flower ¾ in. across

oval leaf 2 in. long

BOUVARDIA DOMESTICA

Bouvardia

TYPES

B. domestica is unfortunately hard to find. There are several named varieties — **Mary** (white and pink), **President Cleveland** (red) and **Bridesmaid** (double, pink) are examples.

BRUNFELSIA

fragrant, white-eyed flower 2 in. across

leathery leaf 3 in. long

BRUNFELSIA CALYCINA

Yesterday, Today and Tomorrow

A slow-growing evergreen shrub with an unusual common name — Yesterday, Today and Tomorrow. It describes the changing flower colours — yesterday's purple, today's pale violet and tomorrow's white. Brunfelsia can be easy to grow or very difficult, depending on whether you can put it in a room where there will be no sudden and drastic changes in temperature. With care the shrub will grow 2 ft tall, and can be kept compact by light pruning.

SECRETS OF SUCCESS

Temperature: Average warmth; not less than 50°F in winter.

Light: Semi-shade in summer; a well-lit spot in winter with a little direct sunlight.

Water: Water freely from spring to autumn. Water sparingly in winter.

Air Humidity: Mist leaves in summer.

Repotting: Repot, when necessary, in spring.

Propagation: Stem cuttings in summer. Rooting hormone and bottom heat are necessary.

TYPE

B. calycina is an evergreen which bears clusters of flowers. These blooms are borne nearly all year round, with just a short winter break. Place the pot outdoors occasionally during the day in summer.

Brunfelsia calycina

BROMELIADS

Some Bromeliads are grown for the beauty of the foliage (pages 51–54) — shown here are the ones which are admired for the beauty of their flowers. A few belong in both camps — the two most popular Bromeliads (Aechmea fasciata and Vriesea splendens) are grown for both their attractive foliage and the bold flower-heads.

The usual pattern is a rosette of leathery, strap-like leaves and a flower-head which arises on a stalk from the cup-like centre of the rosette. It may take several years before the flowering stage is reached, but the display may last for several months. Once the flower-head fades the rosette of leaves starts to die and is replaced by the offsets at the base.

In most cases the display is due to the presence of colourful bracts — the true flowers are small and short-lived. The 2 exceptions are the Coral Berry grown for its red fruits, and the Pineapple grown for the small fruits it bears under greenhouse conditions. Getting Bromeliads to flower is generally difficult — the small and grassy Billbergia nutans readily produces its arching flower-heads under ordinary room conditions, but the large-leaved Bromeliads require patience, skill and warm surroundings. If all else fails you can try the American technique of placing the pot in a sealed bag with an apple for 4 days.

SECRETS OF SUCCESS
See page 51.

TYPES

deep orange bract 2 in. long — droops to reveal yellow-tipped flowers

arching, saw-edged leaf 1½ ft long

AECHMEA CHANTINII
Amazonian Zebra Plant

flower-head 6 in. long — pink-red bracts and small blue flowers

arching, saw-edged leaf 2 ft long

AECHMEA FASCIATA
Urn Plant

fruit aromatic but not edible

leaves stiff and spiny

stalk 2–3 ft high

ANANAS COMOSUS VARIEGATUS
Ivory Pineapple

The Common Pineapple **(A. comosus)** and its yellow-striped form **variegatus** will produce pink flowers on mature plants. These are followed by small pink fruits if the plants have been kept under warm and humid conditions.

Aechmea fasciata

purple flowers; red berries

underside purple

AECHMEA FULGENS DISCOLOR
Coral Berry

The Aechmeas are typical Bromeliads with leathery, arching leaves and a distinct central 'vase'. **A. fasciata (A. rhodocyanea)** is by far the most popular, but there are others. **A. chantinii** has colourful leaves as well as showy flowers and **A. caudata** has branching heads of yellow flowers. **A. fulgens discolor** is grown for its berry display which remains on the plant for several months.

Ananas comosus variegatus

flattened flower-head 9–12 in. long

pink bracts and white-throated blue flowers

grass-like leaf 1 ft long

TILLANDSIA LINDENII
Blue-flowered Torch

The two most popular Tillandsias have grassy leaves like the well-known Billbergias, but their flowers are quite different. **T. lindenii** is illustrated — **T. cyanea** has a green and more compact flower-head with flowers which are all-blue.

drooping flower-head — bracts 3 in. long

grass-like leaf 1 ft long — reddish in good light

BILLBERGIA NUTANS
Queen's Tears

B. nutans is the best-known Billbergia and is by far the easiest Bromeliad to grow — young plants flower quite readily. **B. windii** is larger — the flower-stalks are 18 in. long and the foliage is grey-green. Billbergia can withstand winter temperatures as low as 35°–40°F.

arching, smooth-edged leaf 1–1½ ft long

flower-head up to 2 ft long — bracts bright red

VRIESEA SPLENDENS
Flaming Sword

The Vrieseas are typical Bromeliads with **V. splendens (V. speciosa)** as the best-known species. There are a number of others available, such as the giant **V. regina** and compact ones like **V. minor** and **V. psittacina. V. carinata** has all-green leaves and yellow-tipped bracts.

bright red or orange bract 1½ in. long — central cluster of small white flowers

arching, smooth-edged leaf 4 in. long

GUZMANIA LINGULATA MINOR
Scarlet Star

The best known Guzmania is the compact **G. lingulata minor.** There is a wide variety of flower forms — strap-like red or orange bracts like **Amaranth, Grand Prix** and **minor**, 'flaming swords' such as **bertenonia** and yellow-tipped flowers like **Marlebeca.**

Billbergia windii

Vriesea carinata

CALLIANDRA

Calliandra inaequilatera

The Powderpuff Plant is popular in the U.S. but is rarely grown in Britain. The leaves are made up of a large number of segments and the ball-like flowers are made up entirely of stamens. It blooms in winter and the 'powderpuffs' last for 6–8 weeks. It should be better known, but it needs light, warmth and moist air which means that it is more suited to the conservatory than the living room. In time a bushy tree is formed — keep it pruned to 2–3 ft by trimming in spring.

SECRETS OF SUCCESS

Temperature: Warm; not less than 60°F in winter.

Light: As much light as possible, but shade from hot summer sun.

Water: Keep moist at all times; reduce watering in winter.

Air Humidity: Mist leaves frequently.

Repotting: Repot, when necessary, in early spring.

Propagation: Stem cuttings in spring. Rooting hormone and bottom heat are necessary.

ball-like flower-head 3 in. across

leaflet 2 in. long

CALLIANDRA INAEQUILATERA
Powderpuff Plant

TYPES

C. inaequilatera has bright red flowers and dark green foliage which is divided into large leaflets. A better choice is the hardier **C. tweedyi** — the flowers are smaller and the leaves are feathery.

CALLISTEMON

Callistemon citrinus

The flowering spikes look like bottle brushes. It is an excellent choice if you want a 'novelty' plant, and it is also a good choice if you want an easy-to-grow plant which blooms in summer. It does not mind dry air; all it needs is a sunny spot, cool conditions in winter and a good soaking in spring and summer when the compost begins to dry out. Prune in early spring and stand the pot outdoors in summer.

SECRETS OF SUCCESS

Temperature: Average warmth; not less than 45°F in winter.

Light: As much light as possible, but shade from hot summer sun.

Water: Water liberally from spring to late autumn. Water sparingly in winter.

Air Humidity: Misting is not necessary.

Repotting: Repot, when necessary, in spring.

Propagation: Stem cuttings in spring. Rooting hormone and warmth are necessary. Sow seed in spring.

erect spike 3 in. long
narrow leaf 3 in. long

CALLISTEMON CITRINUS
Bottlebrush Plant

TYPE

C. citrinus will reach about 3 ft high and in summer the cylindrical flower-spikes appear — no petals, just yellow-tipped red stamens. Leaves bronzy when young.

CAMELLIA

single or double flower 3–5 in. across
glossy leaf 4 in. long

CAMELLIA JAPONICA
Camellia

It is a waste of time and money to try to grow this temperamental shrub if the conditions are not right. The room must be cool and airy. Buds appear in profusion in early spring, but they will rapidly drop if the plant is moved or if there is a sudden change in temperature or soil moisture. Stand the pot outdoors once flowering has finished and bring it indoors in autumn.

SECRETS OF SUCCESS

Temperature: Cool; room temperature should be in the 45°–60°F range.

Light: Bright light is necessary, but avoid direct sun in summer.

Water: Keep compost moist at all times but never waterlogged. Use soft water.

Air Humidity: Mist leaves frequently.

Repotting: Repot in spring — do not repot unless root bound.

Propagation: Stem cuttings in summer. Rooting hormone and warmth are necessary.

TYPES

C. japonica is the basic species. Well-known varieties include **Adolphe Audusson** (red, semi-double), **Alba Simplex** (white, single) and **Pink Perfection** (pink, double).

Camellia japonica Florentine

CAMPANULA

Campanula isophylla alba

The Italian Bellflower is an old favourite, grown for generations before the house plant boom began. It remains one of the best of all summer-flowering trailing plants, its long grey-green stems bearing a profusion of star-shaped flowers throughout the summer. Bright and cool conditions are necessary and after flowering the stems should be cut back. Keep the plant fairly dry and at about 45°–50°F during the winter rest period.

SECRETS OF SUCCESS

Temperature: Cool or average warmth; not less than 45°F in winter.

Light: Brightly lit spot, but shade from direct sun in summer.

Water: Keep compost moist at all times; reduce watering in winter.

Air Humidity: Mist the leaves occasionally.

Repotting: Repot every year in spring.

Propagation: Stem cuttings or sow seeds in spring.

star-shaped flower 1½ in. wide
grey-green hairy stems 1 ft long

CAMPANULA ISOPHYLLA
Italian Bellflower

TYPES

The popular Campanula is **C. isophylla** (blue). An excellent and easy-to-grow trailer or climber — the varieties **alba** (white) and **mayi** (pale purple) are available. Dead-head to prolong display.

CITRUS

There is an obvious fascination in having an orange or lemon tree at home, but if you want it to bear fruit a pip-raised plant will not do — see below. You will have to buy a variety selected for indoor cultivation — the Calamondin Orange produces white fragrant flowers and small bitter oranges nearly all year round. The requirements are good drainage, careful watering, ample feeding, full sun, summer spent outdoors and cool conditions in winter.

SECRETS OF SUCCESS

Temperature: Average warmth; not less than 50°F in winter.
Light: Choose the sunniest spot available.
Water: Water moderately all year round.
Air Humidity: Mist occasionally.
Repotting: Repot, when necessary, in spring.
Propagation: Stem cuttings in spring; rooting hormone and warmth are necessary.

leathery leaf 3 in. long

white fragrant flowers followed by small fruit — flowers and fruit appear all year round

CITRUS MITIS
Calamondin Orange

TYPES

You can raise plants by sowing orange, lemon or lime pips but they cannot be expected to flower and fruit. The trouble is that most types of Citrus will not fruit until they are too large for an ordinary room. There are a few dwarfs which can be relied upon to form oranges or lemons indoors, but you will have to provide good conditions and even then you cannot expect to match the quality of shop-bought fruits. **Citrus mitis** is the most popular species — a 4 ft bush which bears small (1–1½ in. diameter) bitter oranges whilst the plant is still quite small. Other indoor types include the Sweet Orange (**C. sinensis** — 4 ft, spiny, 2½ in. fruits under greenhouse conditions), Lemon (**C. limon** — the dwarf varieties are **meyeri** and the large-fruited **Ponderosa**) and Seville Orange (**C. aurantium** — 3 ft spiny tree).

Citrus limon

COLUMNEA

Columnea is one of the most colourful of all the hanging basket plants which bloom in winter or early spring. Success is not easy — it depends on maintaining sufficient moisture around the leaves; constant misting is usually the only answer. Another requirement is careful winter watering plus cool (less than 60°F) winter nights. Cut back stems as soon as flowering has finished. There are many varieties which with proper care will bear abundant yellow, orange or red tubular flowers year after year.

SECRETS OF SUCCESS

Temperature: Average warmth; not less than 50°F in winter.
Light: Bright light, away from direct sunlight.
Water: Keep compost moist at all times during growing season. Water sparingly in winter.
Air Humidity: Mist leaves frequently.
Repotting: Repot every 2 years in late spring.
Propagation: Stem cuttings taken after flowering. Rooting hormone and warmth are necessary.

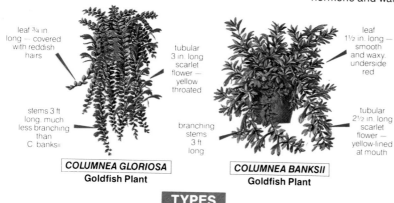

leaf ¾ in. long — covered with reddish hairs

tubular 3 in. long scarlet flower — yellow throated

stems 3 ft long, much less branching than C. banksii

COLUMNEA GLORIOSA
Goldfish Plant

branching stems 3 ft long

leaf 1½ in. long — smooth and waxy, underside red

tubular 2½ in. long scarlet flower — yellow-lined at mouth

COLUMNEA BANKSII
Goldfish Plant

Columnea microphylla

TYPES

The usual flower colour is red with a yellow throat, but other shades are available for the collector — e.g the golden **Columnea affinis**. Unless you are skilled choose one of the easier ones — the hybrid **C. Stavanger** (3 ft stems, smooth leaves, 3 in. long yellow-throated, red flowers) or **C. banksii**. The hairy-leaved ones are harder to grow. **C. gloriosa** is an old favourite — others include **C. microphylla** (4 ft stems, tiny leaves, small C. gloriosa-like blooms) and **C. hirta** (creeping stems, red flowers in spring).

CLERODENDRUM

inflated flower 1 in. long — white with red tip

leaf 5 in. long

CLERODENDRUM THOMSONIAE
Glory Bower

TYPE

C. thomsoniae has long, weak stems — pinch out tips for room display. Allow stems to trail or to twine around an upright support. The leaves have a quilted look.

The Glory Bower is usually regarded as a greenhouse plant, its tall climbing stems reaching 8 ft or more. By pruning in winter, however, it can be trained as a compact bush or hanging basket plant. The flowers appear in summer among the dark green heart-shaped leaves. In summer it requires high air humidity, good light and warmth — in winter it must be given a rest with infrequent watering and cool conditions (55°–60°F). Some leaves will fall during this winter rest period.

SECRETS OF SUCCESS

Temperature: Warm or average warmth; keep cool in winter. Minimum temperature 55°F.

Light: Brightly lit spot away from direct sunlight.

Water: Keep compost moist at all times throughout spring and summer; water very sparingly in winter.

Air Humidity: Mist leaves frequently.

Repotting: Repot every year in spring.

Propagation: Stem cuttings in spring.

Clerodendrum thomsoniae

CLIANTHUS

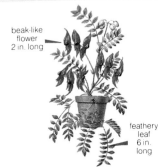

beak-like flower 2 in. long

feathery leaf 6 in. long

CLIANTHUS FORMOSUS
Glory Pea

TYPES

Two types are grown — both are rarities. They are **C. formosus** (2 ft, late spring-summer flowers) and **C. puniceus** (10 ft climber, late spring flowers).

Lobster Claw is one of the common names given to Clianthus — an apt description of the large claw-like red flowers which are borne in clusters in late spring or summer. Prune and train the stems once flowering is over and in summer provide adequate ventilation. The low-growing C. formosus is short-lived and is best treated as an annual; the tall-growing C. puniceus (Parrot Bill) can be kept as a room plant but is best grown in the conservatory.

SECRETS OF SUCCESS

Temperature: Average warmth; keep cool (50°–55°F) in winter.

Light: Keep in full sun.

Water: Water liberally from spring to autumn; let compost dry out slightly between waterings. Water sparingly in winter.

Air Humidity: Mist leaves occasionally on hot days.

Repotting: Repot, when necessary, in spring.

Propagation: Sow seeds in warm conditions in spring. Take Parrot Bill stem cuttings in summer.

Clianthus formosus

CLIVIA

Clivia miniata

An old favourite with an undeserved reputation for being easy to grow; but it will fail to bloom year after year if it is left in a heated room in winter or if the watering rules are not followed. In fact, it has special needs. It needs space. It needs winter rest — an unheated room, no fertilizer and just enough water to prevent wilting. And it needs to be undisturbed — don't move the pot when in bud or flower and don't repot unless the plant is pushing out of the container.

SECRETS OF SUCCESS

Temperature: Cool or average warmth; keep cool (40°–50°F) in winter.

Light: Bright light; avoid direct sun in summer.

Water: Water moderately from spring to autumn. Water sparingly from late autumn to early spring until flower-stalk is 4–6 in. high.

Air Humidity: Sponge leaves occasionally.

Repotting: Repot after flowering when necessary.

Propagation: Divide at repotting time.

bell-shaped flower 3 in. across

strap-like leaf 1½ ft long

CLIVIA MINIATA
Kaffir Lily

TYPE

C. miniata bears clusters of 10–20 flowers in early spring on top of a tall stalk. Orange is the usual colour, but there are red, yellow and cream varieties.

fragrant lily-like flower 6 in. across

sword-like leaf 3 ft long

CRINUM POWELLII
Swamp Lily

TYPES

C. powellii has pink drooping flowers and pale green leaves. There are several hybrids with white, pink or red blooms. **C. bulbispermum** (flowers white inside, deep pink outside) is one of the parents of C. powellii.

CRINUM

Everything about Crinum is extraordinarily large — the 6 in. bulb, the 3 ft tall flower-stalk and the magnificent 7 in. long trumpets which appear during late summer. You will need patience if you begin by planting a bulb — it will take several years before flowering starts, but the wait is worthwhile. The floral display lasts for 4 – 5 weeks, after which it needs to rest in a cool room or greenhouse. Good light is essential all year round.

SECRETS OF SUCCESS

Temperature: Average warmth; keep at 50° – 55°F in winter.
Light: Bright light with some direct sun.
Water: Water thoroughly when the compost begins to dry out from spring until flowering stops. Water sparingly in winter.
Air Humidity: Sponge leaves occasionally.
Repotting: Repot every 3 – 4 years in spring.
Propagation: Detach offsets from mature plants and pot up in summer.

Crinum powellii

CROSSANDRA

The Firecracker Flower is a small slow-growing plant with two special advantages. It starts to flower when seedlings are only a few months old and the flowering season lasts from spring to autumn. The tubular orange flowers are borne on top of green flowering spikes. The shiny leaves make this an attractive plant all year round. The distinct disadvantage of the Firecracker Flower is its need for moist air — it will probably not survive unless it is frequently misted and surrounded by other plants. Remove dead flowers to prolong the flowering season.

SECRETS OF SUCCESS

Temperature: Average warmth; not less than 55°F in winter.
Light: Bright light; avoid direct sun in summer.
Water: Keep compost moist at all times; reduce watering in winter.
Air Humidity: Mist leaves frequently. If possible surround pot with damp peat.
Repotting: Repot in spring. Only repot if it is necessary.
Propagation: Stem cuttings in summer; rooting hormone and warmth are necessary. Sow seeds in spring.

Crossandra undulifolia

tubular flower 1½ in. across

glossy leaf 3 in. long

CROSSANDRA UNDULIFOLIA
Firecracker Flower

TYPES

C. undulifolia (sometimes sold as **C. infundibuliformis**) grows about 1 – 2 ft high. The blooms appear on top of short flower-stalks borne at the stem tips. The variety **Mona Wallhed** is reputed to be the best type.

CUPHEA

A pretty plant, rather than a spectacular one. It can be used to add colour and variety to a mixed display, but the Cigar Plant is not bold enough to serve as a specimen plant. It grows quickly, reaching its adult height of 12 in. in a single season. Cigar-shaped flowers are borne in profusion among the narrow leaves. Overwinter the plant in a cool room and water sparingly. Cut back the stems in early spring — for maximum display raise new plants every year as old plants become leggy and unattractive.

SECRETS OF SUCCESS

Temperature: Average warmth; not less than 45°F in winter.
Light: A well-lit spot; some direct sunlight is beneficial.
Water: Keep moist at all times; reduce watering in winter.
Air Humidity: Misting is not necessary.
Repotting: Repot in spring. Only repot if it is necessary.
Propagation: Stem cuttings in spring or summer. Sow seeds in spring.

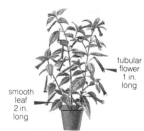

tubular flower 1 in. long

smooth leaf 2 in. long

CUPHEA IGNEA
Cigar Plant

TYPE

C. ignea is a 1 ft high bush which produces flowers from spring to late autumn. Red tubes with white and purple mouths. With a little imagination, a tiny cigar with ash at the tip.

Cuphea ignea

DATURA

Just one look at the magnificent 10 in. long flaring trumpets in the photograph and you may be tempted to rush off and buy a Datura. Before you do, remember that these exotic plants need space and care, and all parts are poisonous. They are tub plants, spending part of the summer outdoors and the whole of the winter in a cool, wel-lit place. After flowering the stems are pruned back to encourage fresh growth for next season's flowers.

oval leaf 9 in. long

tubular flower 8–10 in. long

DATURA CANDIDA
Angel's Trumpet

TYPES

Two species are occasionally sold as house plants — **D. candida** and **D. suaveolens**. Both bear pendulous, sweet-smelling white flowers in summer — D. candida is the better choice.

SECRETS OF SUCCESS

Temperature: Average warmth; keep cool (40°–45°F) in winter.

Light: A well-lit spot; some direct sunlight is beneficial.

Water: Water regularly from spring to autumn; sparingly in winter.

Air Humidity: Mist leaves occasionally.

Repotting: Repot, when necessary, in spring.

Propagation: Stem cuttings in spring; rooting hormone and warmth are necessary.

Datura suaveolens

DIPLADENIA

Large petunia-like flowers appear in summer on the twining stems. Dipladenia can be grown as a climber, reaching 10 ft or more, or it can be pruned back severely once flowering is finished in order to maintain it as a bush. The pink blossoms will appear on a plant while it is still small, and the glossy leaves make it attractive all year round. But it has never become popular because of its need for high air humidity and warm surroundings, especially in spring.

SECRETS OF SUCCESS

Temperature: Warm; not less than 55°F in winter.

Light: Bright light or semi-shade; not direct sun.

Water: Water regularly from spring to autumn; sparingly in winter.

Air Humidity: Mist regularly, especially when in bud or flower.

Repotting: Repot every year in spring.

Propagation: Stem cuttings in spring; rooting hormone and warmth are necessary.

Dipladenia sanderi rosea

leaf 2 in. long

twining woody stems

trumpet-shaped flower 3 in. across

DIPLADENIA SANDERI ROSEA

TYPES

D. sanderi rosea is a tall climber grown for its yellow-throated, pink flowers. **Dipladenia (Mandevilla) splendens** is similar, but is larger-leaved with pink-throated flowers.

DUCHESNEA

There has been a rapid increase in the popularity of hanging plants in recent years. Some excellent trailers, however, still remain rarities and the Indian Strawberry is a good example. It is a vigorous grower, quite hardy and easy to care for — it will quite happily spend the winter in an unheated room. In summer the flowers appear and these are followed by small strawberry-like fruits. These are edible, but unfortunately they are completely tasteless. True strawberries can be grown indoors (see page 218).

strawberry-like fruits ¾ in. across

branching runners

DUCHESNEA INDICA
(FRAGARIA INDICA)
Indian Strawberry

TYPE

D. indica bears trailing runners and the bright yellow flowers are present throughout the summer months. It will not flower if it is kept in a semi-shady spot. Stand the pot outdoors occasionally in summer.

SECRETS OF SUCCESS

Temperature: Cool or average warmth; keep cool but frost-free in winter.

Light: Bright light; not direct sun.

Water: Keep compost moist at all times; water sparingly in winter.

Air Humidity: Mist leaves occasionally.

Repotting: Repot every year in spring.

Propagation: Divide when repotting; layer runners in spring.

Duchesnea indica

EPISCIA

Episcia is an attractive trailing plant which has never enjoyed the popularity of its well-known relative, the African Violet. Because it requires high air humidity it is often difficult to grow as an isolated specimen plant or in a hanging basket, but it makes an excellent ground cover between taller plants. There are two types — the Flame Violet and the delicate Lace Flower. Both bloom throughout the summer and the runners root in surrounding compost, forming plantlets for propagation. Shorten stems after flowering.

SECRETS OF SUCCESS

Temperature: Average warmth; not less than 55°F in winter.
Light: Bright light, away from direct sunlight in summer.
Water: Keep compost moist at all times during growing season. Reduce watering in winter.
Air Humidity: Mist frequently. Surround pot with damp peat.
Repotting: Repot every year in spring.
Propagation: Layer runners in spring or summer (see page 234).

Episcia cupreata

tubular flower ¾ in. across — orange-red with yellow eye

surface dark green or coppery — veins silver or pale green

leaf 2–4 in. long, covered with rough hairs

EPISCIA CUPREATA
Flame Violet

tubular flower 1½ in. across — white with feathered edges

surface green and velvety — veins purple or brown

leaf 1–2 in. long, covered with downy hairs

EPISCIA DIANTHIFLORA
Lace Flower

TYPES

Episcia is grown for its attractive foliage and pretty, if rather small, flowers. The two most popular species are shown above — **E. cupreata** and **E. dianthiflora**. E. cupreata has produced many hybrids and sports — **Amazon, Metallica, Acajou, Cleopatra** and **Harlequin** are examples. **E. reptans** is not easy to distinguish from some of these varieties — it has the same pale veining (usually pale green against a dark green background) and the surface is heavily wrinkled. On the other hand **E. lilacina** is easy to recognise — the flowers have lilac lobes and a yellow throat.

EUPHORBIA

The Crown of Thorns is an old favourite, but it still remains an excellent and undemanding choice for a sunny window. It does not need misting, will withstand some neglect and does not have to be moved to an unheated room in winter. Leaves may drop in winter but new leaf buds will appear within a month or two. Scarlet Plume is much less common and its growth habit is quite different. Long arching branches bear willow-like leaves, and in winter the flower-heads appear. Keep cool and rather dry for a month or two after flowering.

SECRETS OF SUCCESS

Temperature: Average warmth; not less than 55°F in winter.
Light: As much light as possible, but shade from summer sun.
Water: Water moderately from spring to autumn; sparingly in winter. Let soil surface dry between waterings.
Air Humidity: Mist E. fulgens occasionally in spring and summer.
Repotting: Repot every 2 years in spring.
Propagation: Stem cuttings in spring or summer. Let milky sap dry before placing in compost.

Euphorbia milii

grooved stems covered with sharp thorns

leaf 2 in. long

EUPHORBIA MILII
Crown of Thorns

yellow-centred 'flower' ½ in. across

narrow leaf 4 in. long

EUPHORBIA FULGENS
Scarlet Plume

TYPES

The most popular Euphorbia is **E. milii** (sometimes sold as **E. splendens**). Its 3 ft stems bear tiny flowers which are surrounded by showy bracts — red is the usual flower-head colour but both salmon and yellow types are available. The length of the flowering season depends on the light intensity. E. milii is normally in bloom from early spring to midsummer, but in a brightly-lit spot it can flower almost all year round. The sap is poisonous.

E. fulgens is not often seen and is more difficult to care for. The stems are arched and thornless — quite unlike those of E. milii, but the flower-heads have the same structure. Coloured bracts surround tiny true flowers — the colour is orange or white with a yellow eye.

EUCHARIS

Eucharis grandiflora

At first it seems strange that this bulbous plant should be missing from the house plant bestseller lists. The flowers are fragrant and attractive, and with care it can be made to bloom twice a year. The problem is that the Amazon Lily does not like cold nights — a minimum temperature of 60°F is required, even in midwinter. If you start with a bulb rather than a potted specimen, plant in spring or autumn and keep warm until growth starts. Water sparingly at this stage.

SECRETS OF SUCCESS

Temperature: Average warmth; not less than 60°F in winter.

Light: Bright light or semi-shade; not direct sun.

Water: Water liberally from spring to autumn; moderately in winter.

Air Humidity: Sponge leaves occasionally.

Repotting: Repot every 3–4 years in spring.

Propagation: Detach offsets from mature plants in summer.

fragrant flower 3 in. across

oval leaf 8 in. long

EUCHARIS GRANDIFLORA
Amazon Lily

TYPE

E. grandiflora flowers in late summer, and again a few months later if conditions are favourable. Each bloom looks like a narcissus with a spiky trumpet, and 3–6 are borne on a 2 ft stalk.

FELICIA

Felicia amelloides

Felicia is worth looking for if you like out-of-the-ordinary plants. Few will recognise it, yet this undemanding mini-shrub will produce a floral display almost the whole year round if you follow the Secrets of Success. F. amelloides should be pinched back regularly to keep the plant bushy, but be careful not to cut off stems bearing buds. Avoid the two pet hates of Felicia — low light intensity and dry soil.

SECRETS OF SUCCESS

Temperature: Average warmth; not less than 50°F in winter.

Light: Brightly lit spot, but shade from hot summer sun.

Water: Keep the compost moist at all times.

Air Humidity: Mist leaves occasionally.

Repotting: Repot, when necessary, in spring.

Propagation: Stem cuttings in spring or sow seeds in summer.

daisy-like flower 1 in. across

oval leaf ½ in. long

FELICIA AMELLOIDES
Blue Daisy

TYPE

F. amelloides is a perennial — keep it about 1 ft high by pruning the growing tips. Midsummer is the main flowering season — blue daisies with yellow centres which open only in sunlight.

GARDENIA

Gardenia jasminoides

In spring the large flowers appear and the surrounding air is filled with fragrance. For the rest of the year it is an attractive foliage plant. Sadly it is more often a disappointment than a delight, because Gardenia is extremely temperamental. For flower buds to form a night temperature of 60°–65°F is required, and the day temperature should be about 10°F higher. An even temperature and careful watering are needed to prevent the buds dropping off.

SECRETS OF SUCCESS

Temperature: Average warmth; not less than 60°F in winter.

Light: Bright light is essential, but avoid direct midday sun in summer.

Water: Keep moist at all times; reduce watering in winter. Use soft, tepid water.

Air Humidity: Mist leaves frequently.

Repotting: Repot every 2–3 years in spring.

Propagation: Stem cuttings in spring. Rooting hormone and warmth are necessary.

glossy leaf 4 in. long

fragrant flower 3 in. across

GARDENIA JASMINOIDES
Gardenia

TYPE

The blooms of **G. jasminoides** are semi-double or double and the petals are waxy. The plant grows about 1½ ft high and several varieties are available. Flower colour is white or cream.

HAEMANTHUS

Haemanthus katharinae

The Blood Lilies are spectacular plants — a stout stalk bears the giant ball-like flower above the few large leaves at the base. The species of Haemanthus differ in more than flower colour and size — the one you choose may be either evergreen or devoid of leaves for part of the year, and it may or may not produce offsets at the base. The starting point in all cases is generally a fully-grown bulb — plant one per pot with the tip above the compost.

SECRETS OF SUCCESS

Temperature: Average warmth; not less than 50°F in winter.
Light: Bright light with some direct sun.
Water: Keep compost moist at all times; water sparingly in winter.
Air Humidity: Sponge leaves occasionally.
Repotting: Repot every 4–5 years in spring.
Propagation: Detach offsets and pot up in summer. Sow seeds in spring.

ball-like flower-head 8 in. across

wavy leaf 1 ft long

HAEMANTHUS KATHARINAE
Blood Lily

TYPES

H. katharinae is the most popular evergreen species. The globe of red tubular flowers appears in summer — offsets are not produced. The flower-head of **H. albiflos** is white and much smaller — offsets are formed.

HELIOTROPIUM

fragrant flower-head 4–6 in. across

deeply-veined leaf 3 in. long

HELIOTROPIUM HYBRIDUM
Heliotrope

TYPE

H. hybridum is an excellent but little-used shrub for indoor decoration — the large heads of tiny flowers will perfume a room throughout the summer months.

Heliotrope is a good choice if you are looking for an easy-to-grow flowering plant with a strong fragrance. Purple, blue and white varieties are available. The leaves are dull green and prominently veined, and the plant can be trained as a standard (see page 177 for instructions). Heliotrope can be kept for years as a house plant but the ability to produce attractive flower-heads rapidly deteriorates with age, so raise new cuttings each year.

SECRETS OF SUCCESS

Temperature: Cool or average warmth; keep at 40°–50°F in winter.
Light: As much light as possible, but shade from hot summer sun.
Water: Keep moist at all times; reduce watering in winter.
Air Humidity: Mist occasionally.
Repotting: Repot every year in spring.
Propagation: Stem cuttings in summer; use rooting hormone. Sow seeds in spring.

Heliotropium hybridum Mrs Lowther

HYPOCYRTA

Hypocyrta glabra

The Clog Plant produces large numbers of orange flowers which look like tiny goldfish. When not in bloom it is an attractive foliage plant with shiny, dark green succulent leaves. It is used for planting in mixed arrangements, bottle gardens and hanging baskets. In the growing season the main needs of the Clog Plant are careful watering and frequent misting; in winter place the plant in a cool, sunlit spot and cut the stems back to encourage flowering growth next spring.

SECRETS OF SUCCESS

Temperature: Average warmth; not less than 50°F in winter.
Light: Bright or light shade; some direct sun in winter.
Water: Water moderately from spring to autumn; sparingly in winter.
Air Humidity: Mist leaves regularly.
Repotting: Repot every 2 years in spring.
Propagation: Stem cuttings in spring or summer.

pouch-like flower 1 in. long

glossy leaf 1½ in. long

HYPOCYRTA GLABRA
Clog Plant

TYPES

H. glabra needs moist air and so is not a popular plant. The branches are erect or gracefully arching, and the orange blooms (mid-summer) are waxy. **H. nummularia** is a trailing relative.

HIBISCUS

Hibiscus is becoming increasingly popular as a specimen plant for the sunny windowsill. Its large papery flowers last for only a day or two, but with proper care there will be a continuous succession of blooms from spring to autumn. A Hibiscus bush can live for 20 years or more, and may be kept small by regular pruning. In a large tub it will reach 5–6 ft and can also be trained as a standard (see page 177). Prune back stems in late winter to induce bushiness.

Hibiscus rosa-sinensis Holiday

prominent central column

double or single flower 4–5 in. across

saw-edged leaf 3 in. long

HIBISCUS ROSA-SINENSIS
Rose of China

TYPES

H. rosa-sinensis has numerous named varieties in white, yellow, orange, pink and red. The variety **cooperi** has variegated foliage. **H. schizopetalus** stems require support — its petals are frilly edged, tubular and pendent.

SECRETS OF SUCCESS

Temperature: Average warmth; not less than 55°F in winter.
Light: As much light as possible, but shade from hot sun.
Water: Keep moist at all times; reduce watering in winter.
Air Humidity: Mist leaves occasionally.
Repotting: Repot every year in spring.
Propagation: Stem cuttings in late spring.

SPECIAL PROBLEMS

BUD DROP
Cause: Dry compost is the usual reason. Other causes are underfeeding or a sudden change in temperature or location.

CURLING OF LEAVES
Cause: Air too dry. Mist leaves in spring and summer.

LOSS OF LEAVES
Cause: Dry compost is the usual reason. Other possibilities are draughts and overwatering.

INSECTS
Aphid and red spider mite can be a problem; see page 244.

HOYA

The Wax Plant (H. carnosa) is an easy-to-grow flowering climber. Its vigorous twining stems can reach 15 ft or more, and they must be trained on wires, trellis work or on a moss stick. New stems are bare; the leaves which later appear are fleshy and green, or green-and-cream on the Variegated Wax Plant. The fragrant flower-heads appear between late spring and early autumn. The Miniature Wax Plant needs more heat and humidity but less light; it is best planted in a hanging basket. There are several 'do nots' for growing Hoyas — do not disturb the plant once buds appear, do not remove the dead flowers and do not repot until it is unavoidable.

SECRETS OF SUCCESS

Temperature: Average warmth; keep at 50° – 55°F in winter.
Light: Bright light; some direct sun is beneficial.
Water: Water liberally from spring to autumn; sparingly in winter.
Air Humidity: Mist regularly, but not when plant is in bloom.
Repotting: Repot only when necessary in spring.
Propagation: Stem cuttings, using mature shoots, in spring.

single flower

non-glossy leaf 1 in. long

fragrant white flower with reddish-purple centre — approximately 10 per cluster

glossy leaf 3 in. long

fragrant pale pink flower with red centre — approximately 20 per cluster

single flower

HOYA BELLA
Miniature Wax Plant

HOYA CARNOSA VARIEGATA
Variegated Wax Plant

TYPES

Hoya bella

The Hoyas are climbers or trailers with fleshy leaves and clusters of waxy, star-shaped flowers. **H. carnosa** is the basic species. Several varieties are available, including **variegata** (cream-edged leaves), **exotica** (yellow-centred leaves) and **Krimson Princess** (red-coloured young foliage). **H. australis** is quite similar, but its leaves are almost round. **H. bella** is a trailer and is much more difficult to grow under room conditions than the popular H. carnosa. **H. multiflora** is another species which is commercially available — pale yellow flowers are its claim to fame.

IMPATIENS

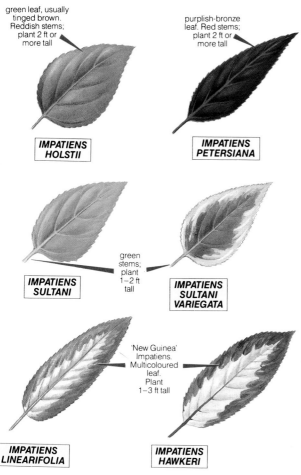

green leaf, usually tinged brown. Reddish stems; plant 2 ft or more tall

IMPATIENS HOLSTII

purplish-bronze leaf. Red stems; plant 2 ft or more tall

IMPATIENS PETERSIANA

IMPATIENS SULTANI

green stems; plant 1–2 ft tall

IMPATIENS SULTANI VARIEGATA

'New Guinea' Impatiens. Multicoloured leaf. Plant 1–3 ft tall

IMPATIENS LINEARIFOLIA

IMPATIENS HAWKERI

There is a Busy Lizzie in about one quarter of Britain's households. Some of these plants have been bought, but many more have been raised at home from cuttings which root very easily at any time of the year. It has been extremely popular for generations because, with proper care, it will bear its flowers almost all year round.

Breeders and plant hunters have introduced many new varieties in recent years. Most of the Busy Lizzies sold today are small, compact hybrids with flowers in white, orange, pink, purple or red. Even more exciting are the 'New Guinea' types with multicoloured leaves.

Busy Lizzies are not difficult to grow but they do need regular care. Pinch out the tips of young plants several times to ensure bushy plants — prune mature plants each spring. The stems are succulent and brittle — tall plants may require staking. Feed regularly during the growing season and provide ventilation on hot days. Above all, remember to water frequently in summer.

SECRETS OF SUCCESS

Temperature: Average warmth; not less than 55°F in winter. Keep at 60°F or more to ensure flowering during winter.

Light: Bright light is necessary, but avoid direct sunlight in summer. A few hours of sun are necessary in winter if the plant is to continue flowering.

Water: Keep the compost moist at all times — daily watering may be necessary in summer. Reduce water in winter.

Air Humidity: Mist leaves occasionally, but avoid open blooms.

Repotting: Pot must be filled with roots before the plant will flower freely. Repot, only when necessary, in spring.

Propagation: Stem cuttings root readily at any time of the year. Sow seeds in spring.

SPECIAL PROBLEMS

LOSS OF LEAVES
Cause: Usual reason for sudden leaf fall is prolonged exposure to low temperatures. Irregular watering and severe insect attack are other common causes.

LEAVES WILTED
Cause: Underwatering. Wilting can occur the day after watering in summer. Frequent watering is the only answer — do not keep the plant standing in a saucer of water.

POOR FLOWERING
Cause: Many possibilities — the five most common causes are too little light, too little food, too much food, too cold or repotting too early.

INSECTS
Red spider mite is a menace in hot, dry weather; leaves become bronzed and mottled. Both aphid and whitefly can be a serious nuisance, disfiguring and weakening the plant. See Chapter 15 for methods of insect control.

SPINDLY GROWTH
Cause: Too much warmth coupled with too little light will certainly produce this condition, but some older varieties soon become lanky with age even when well grown. Choose a modern compact hybrid; take cuttings and discard old plants.

NO FLOWERS
Cause: Repotting is the usual reason why a mature plant fails to flower. Busy Lizzie must be kept somewhat pot-bound.

ROTTING STEMS
Cause: This is always caused by overwatering, especially in cool, shady conditions. Always reduce watering in winter; water very sparingly if plant is kept below 60°F.

LOSS OF FLOWERS
Cause: Too little light is the usual reason. Other possibilities are dry air, dry compost or red spider mite attack.

IMPATIENS TYPES

flat-faced flower 1–2 in. across — long spur at rear

stems brittle and succulent, 1–3 ft long

leaf 3 in. long

IMPATIENS WALLERANA
Busy Lizzie
(Patient Lucy)

single plain flower

single candystripe flower

double plain flower

Impatiens has long been grown on both sides of the Atlantic. Known as Busy Lizzie in Britain and Patient Lucy in the U.S., this plant bears flowers almost non-stop from January to December when cared for properly. Until fairly recently it was the species which were grown. There was (and still is) much confusion over their names — **I. holstii** and **I. sultani** have green leaves, **I. petersiana** is the red-leaved one and all are occasionally grouped together as **I. wallerana.** The common characteristics are a somewhat straggly growth habit, and flowers (usually red) which are no more than 2 in. in diameter.

Nowadays it is much more usual to grow the Impatiens Hybrids which have one or more of the species mentioned above as parents. These varieties are compact (½–1 ft) and the flower colour range has been extended to include white, orange, purple, pink, red and bicolours. Many can be bought as seed and raised at home.

Impatiens Hybrids:
Imp (9 in.) single, plain flowers — mixed colours.
Novette (6 in.) single, plain flowers — mixed colours.
Rosette (6 in.) semi-double and double, plain flowers — mixed colours.
Zig-Zag (9 in.) single, candystripe flowers — white plus orange or red.
Blitz (6 in.) single, plain flowers — mixed colours, very free-flowering.
Grand Prix (9 in.) single, plain flowers — mixed colours, large blooms.

The latest introductions are the Impatiens New Guinea Hybrids evolved from **I. hawkeri** or **I. linearifolia.** The plants are 1–3 ft tall and the leaves are highly decorative. Flowers are often large.

Impatiens New Guinea Hybrids:
Fanfare leaves yellow/green — flowers pink.
Aflame leaves yellow/green/red — flowers pink.
Red Magic leaves bronzy — flowers red.
Arabesque leaves yellow/green/red — flowers pink.

Impatiens sultani variegata

Impatiens Zig-Zag

Impatiens Fanfare

Impatiens petersiana

IXORA

Ixora coccinea

Flame of the Woods is a 3–4 ft shrub with glossy leathery leaves. From late spring to autumn it bears large clusters of tubular flowers. This is definitely not a plant for the novice — leaves drop if it is exposed to cool air for even a short time; flower buds drop if it is moved from one spot to another. Humid air is essential. After flowering in summer keep rather dry for a month, then resume normal watering to bring back into flower.

SECRETS OF SUCCESS

Temperature: Warm or average warmth; not less than 60°F in winter.

Light: Bright light; avoid direct sun in summer.

Water: Keep compost moist at all times; reduce watering in winter. Use soft water.

Air Humidity: Mist leaves regularly.

Repotting: Repot, when necessary, in spring.

Propagation: Difficult. Stem cuttings in spring; rooting hormone and warmth are needed.

flower-head 4 in. across

tubular flower ½ in. across

glossy, leathery leaf 3–4 in. long

IXORA COCCINEA
Flame of the Woods

TYPE

I. coccinea is a difficult shrub — with care the large flower-heads in white, yellow, salmon, pink or red will last throughout the summer months.

JACOBINIA

plume-like flower-head 5 in. long

coarse leaf 6 in. long

JACOBINIA CARNEA

King's Crown

TYPES

J. carnea flowers in late summer, each pink pompon bearing numerous 2 in. tubular flowers. **J. pauciflora** bears yellow-tipped scarlet flowers in winter.

When seen in bloom the King's Crown seems a most desirable house plant. Unfortunately the flowering period in late summer is short. This bushy plant can reach 4 ft or more, but old plants are unattractive. For this reason 1- or 2 year-old plants are grown for display. Cut plants back after flowering; during winter keep the pot in a well lit, fairly warm spot. In summer both air and compost must be kept constantly moist.

SECRETS OF SUCCESS

Temperature: Average warmth; not less than 55°F in winter.

Light: Bright indirect light in summer; some direct sun in winter.

Water: Keep compost moist at all times; reduce watering in winter.

Air Humidity: Mist leaves frequently in summer.

Repotting: Repot every 2–3 years in spring.

Propagation: Stem cuttings in spring; rooting hormone and warmth are needed.

Jacobinia carnea

JATROPHA

Jatropha podagrica

Jatropha belongs in the textbooks rather than the garden centre, which is perhaps a shame. It is a remarkable oddity — the tall bottle stem remains bare throughout the winter, and then in early spring the flower-stalks appear with a crown of small red blooms. Later the long-stalked leaves appear — a conversation piece rather than a thing of beauty. Few plants are easier to grow — hardly any watering is required and it has no special needs.

SECRETS OF SUCCESS

Temperature: Average warmth; not less than 50°F in winter.

Light: Bright light; avoid hot summer sun.

Water: Water sparingly from spring to summer, hardly at all in winter.

Air Humidity: Misting is not necessary.

Repotting: Repot, when necessary, in spring.

Propagation: Sow seeds in spring.

lobed leaf 1 ft across

flower-head 2 in. across

JATROPHA PODAGRICA

TYPE

Only one species is grown — **J. podagrica.** The flower-stalk is about 2 ft tall and the flowers are coral red. Available in some countries but very rare in Britain.

JASMINUM

The easiest to grow is the Pink Jasmine, the pink buds open into clusters of starry white flowers with a delightful fragrance. This plant is a vigorous climber which must be cut back after flowering. Not all Jasmines are white and fragrant — the Primrose Jasmine produces yellow flowers which have no fragrance. The basic rules for success with Jasmines are to keep the plant cool in winter, stand it outdoors in summer, give it plenty of light and never let it dry out.

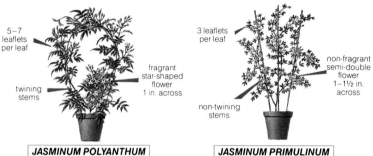

5–7 leaflets per leaf
fragrant star-shaped flower 1 in. across
twining stems

JASMINUM POLYANTHUM
Pink Jasmine

3 leaflets per leaf
non-fragrant semi-double flower 1–1½ in. across
non-twining stems

JASMINUM PRIMULINUM
Primrose Jasmine

Jasminum officinale

TYPES

The favourite one is **J. polyanthum,** with pink buds which open in winter. **J. officinale grandiflora** (White Jasmine) is similar in appearance — twining stems, much-divided leaves and long-tubed white and fragrant flowers. There are, however, important differences — the flowers appear in summer or autumn and do not have a rosy tinge on the reverse. Also, the blooms do not appear until the plant is mature. **J. primulinum (J. mesnyi)** is the odd one out — the flowers are yellow with 6 or more petals and fragrance is absent. There are just 3 leaflets per leaf and the stems are not twining — they must be tied to the supports.

KALANCHOE

Kalanchoe blossfeldiana is a popular Christmas-flowering gift plant. Under natural conditions this easy-to-grow succulent blooms in early spring, but by reducing its light supply growers are able to induce it to bloom in mid winter. The leaves turn reddish in sunlight and the large flower-heads last for many weeks. After flowering prune the tops and place the pot on a shady windowsill. Keep the compost nearly dry for a month then put in a well-lit spot and water normally.

tubular flower ¼ in. across
plant 1 ft high
fleshy leaf 2 in. long
flower-head of 20–50 blooms

KALANCHOE BLOSSFELDIANA
Flaming Katy

TYPES

By far the most popular Kalanchoe is **K. blossfeldiana** — a bushy plant which can be bought in flower at any time of the year. It is most frequently bought as a Christmas gift plant and the basic colour is red, but these days you can buy hybrids in white, yellow, orange and lilac, bearing large heads on 18 in. high plants. At the other end of the scale the miniatures are becoming popular — these compact plants grow about 6 in. high and bear glowing red flowers. Varieties include **Tom Thumb** and **Compact Lilliput** — **Vulcan** can be bought as seed as well as a pot-grown plant. The plants are usually thrown away, but with care can be kept to produce a repeat display.

Kalanchoe blossfeldiana Vesuvius

KOHLERIA

Kohleria eriantha Success

Kohleria is closely related to the better-known Smithiantha (page 199) but unlike its more popular cousin does not lose its leaves in winter. Plant the rhizomes about ½ in. below the compost surface and keep fairly dry until growth appears. The velvety plants produce tubular flowers which are orange or red with yellow-speckled mouths. The blooming period is usually spring or summer, but flowers can appear almost all year round.

SECRETS OF SUCCESS

Temperature: Average warmth; not less than 55°F in winter.

Light: Bright light; protect from hot summer sun.

Water: Water moderately from spring to autumn; sparingly in winter.

Air Humidity: Mist frequently around the plant but do not wet leaves.

Repotting: Repot every year in spring.

Propagation: Divide plants at repotting time.

tubular flower 1–2 in. long

red-edged leaf 3 in. long

KOHLERIA ERIANTHA

TYPES

Hybrids of **K. eriantha** and other species are chosen for cultivation indoors — the average height is 1–1½ ft. The favourite variety is **K. Rongo** — red flower with white-veined mouth.

LANTANA

flower-head 1–2 in. across

rough leaf 2 in. long

LANTANA CAMARA
Yellow Sage

TYPE

L. camara is the only species grown as a house plant. It is usually kept trimmed to 1–2 ft — both leaves and blooms are pungent and the flowering season lasts from spring to late summer.

When not in bloom this shrub is unimpressive with coarse wrinkled leaves and prickly stems. However, in summer it is eye-catching — the globular flower-heads change colour from pale yellow to red as the tiny flowers mature. The main requirements are for full sun and adequate water in summer. Keep watch for whitefly, which find Lantana particularly attractive. Cut back the stems after flowering and raise new plants every 2 or 3 years.

SECRETS OF SUCCESS

Temperature: Average warmth; not less than 55°F in winter.

Light: Give as much light as possible, but shade from summer noonday sun.

Water: Water regularly from spring to autumn; sparingly in winter.

Air Humidity: Mist leaves occasionally.

Repotting: Repot, when necessary, in spring.

Propagation: Sow seeds in spring; stem cuttings at any time of the year.

Lantana camara

LIRIOPE

Liriope muscari

The Blue Lily Turf can be mistaken for its close relative Ophiopogon (page 85) or a giant Grape Hyacinth (page 184). It is not a popular plant in most European countries although it is colourful and easy to grow. The violet ball-like flowers clothe the flower-stalk during late summer and early autumn — they are followed by black berries. There are no special needs, but good light is essential for flowering and leaf-tips turn brown in draughts or dry air.

SECRETS OF SUCCESS

Temperature: Average warmth; not less than 45°F in winter.

Light: Brightly lit spot away from direct sun.

Water: Keep compost moist at all times.

Air Humidity: Mist leaves occasionally.

Repotting: Repot every 3–4 years in spring.

Propagation: Divide plants at repotting time.

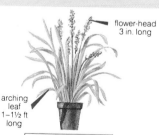

flower-head 3 in. long

arching leaf 1–1½ ft long

LIRIOPE MUSCARI
Blue Lily Turf

TYPES

L. muscari produces a 1 ft flowering spike and boldly veined leaves. The popular type is **variegata** with yellow-striped leaves and lilac flowers. A white-flowered variety is available.

MANETTIA

tubular flower ¾ in. long

oval leaf 2 in. long

twining stems

MANETTIA INFLATA
Firecracker Plant

The Firecracker Plant should be more popular. The thin twining stems will quickly cover a wire support or trellis, or they can be left to trail from a hanging basket. The tubular yellow-tipped flowers sometimes almost cover the dark green, pointed leaves. Pinch out the tips occasionally to stop the plant becoming straggly. In winter Manettia needs a period of rest — keep it at 50°–60°F.

TYPE

M. inflata (sometimes sold as **M. bicolor**) is the only species grown as a house plant. In good light it will bloom for most of the year — the flowers are small but plentiful.

SECRETS OF SUCCESS

Temperature: Average warmth; not less than 50°F in winter.

Light: Bright light; some direct sun is essential.

Water: Keep compost moist at all times; reduce watering in winter.

Air Humidity: Mist leaves regularly.

Repotting: Repot every year in spring.

Propagation: Stem cuttings in summer; use rooting hormone.

Manettia inflata

MEDINILLA

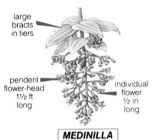

large bracts in tiers

pendent flower-head 1½ ft long

individual flower ½ in. long

MEDINILLA MAGNIFICA
Rose Grape

The pride of any collection, but almost certainly not for you unless there is a warm greenhouse or conservatory. This tropical 4 ft shrub needs space and skill. The long leathery leaves are borne in pairs and in late spring the magnificent flower-heads appear. Temperature must be carefully controlled and the air must be kept constantly moist — in the house you would need a plant window (see page 34).

TYPE

M. magnifica is the only species grown. The oval leaves are shiny and prominently veined, the stems are winged and somewhat hairy, and the flowers as spectacular as anything to be seen indoors.

SECRETS OF SUCCESS

Temperature: Warm; 65°–75°F in summer and 60°–65°F in winter.

Light: Brightly lit spot screened from direct sun.

Water: Water moderately from spring to autumn; sparingly in winter.

Air Humidity: Mist frequently; stand pot on a pebble tray (page 27).

Repotting: Repot every 1–2 years in spring.

Propagation: Very difficult. Stem cuttings in spring. Rooting hormone and warmth are necessary.

Medinilla magnifica

MYRTUS

oval leaf 2 in. long

fragrant flower ¾ in. across

MYRTUS COMMUNIS
Myrtle

Myrtle has been grown as a decorative plant for thousands of years and yet it is still a rarity in Britain. This surprising situation is not due to difficulty of cultivation nor to lack of beauty. It is easy to care for in a well-lit unheated room and it is attractive all year round. The small oval leaves are shiny and aromatic; the white flowers appear in large numbers in summer. In autumn the purple berries appear. The shrub will grow about 2 ft tall if left untrimmed and can be stood outdoors during the summer months.

SECRETS OF SUCCESS

Temperature: Cool or average warmth; not less than 40°F in winter.

Light: Bright with some direct sunlight, but protect from midday summer sun.

Water: Water regularly from spring to autumn; sparingly in winter. Use soft water.

Air Humidity: Mist leaves frequently.

Repotting: Repot, when necessary, in spring.

Propagation: Stem cuttings in summer.

TYPES

M. communis bears bowl-shaped blooms, each with a prominent central boss of golden stamens. Where space is limited choose the small-leaved variety **microphylla.** Myrtus is ideal for indoor topiary.

Myrtus communis

MUSA

The Victorians gave pride of place to the Banana Plant in their conservatories and hothouses, but only recently has there been a revival of interest. Few other leaves give such a tropical look to a plant collection, but this plant is much more suited to the greenhouse than the living room. Even under glass you have to choose the variety with care, as described below. The prime requirements are good light, plenty of water and protection from cool nights.

SECRETS OF SUCCESS

Temperature: Warm; not less than 60°F in winter.
Light: Bright light with some direct sun.
Water: Keep compost very moist at all times.
Air Humidity: Mist leaves frequently.
Repotting: Repot, when necessary, in spring or summer.
Propagation: Not practical in the home.

yellow flowers within red bracts

velvety reddish fruits

leaf 2 ft long

MUSA VELUTINA

TYPES

The Common Banana (**Musa paradisiaca**) and many other species and varieties are far too large to grow. Perhaps the best one for growing in a large tub is **M. acuminata** — the Canary Island or Dwarf Banana. It grows about 6 ft high and its tubular flowers are followed by typical bananas . . . if you have been able to provide the light, warmth and high humidity required. Bananas are best regarded as decorative rather than productive plants indoors. **M. velutina** grows about 4 ft high — the yellow flowers are followed by attractive but inedible fruit. Even smaller is **M. coccinea**, the Flowering Banana. The plant grows 3 ft high and the ornamental bananas are only 2 in. long.

Musa coccinea

> *Many people, I know, have an idea that there are insurmountable difficulties and great expenses to be encountered in growing plants in-doors; but these hindrances only exist in fancy, and it is surprising to find how easily and how cheaply, after a little practice, a lady can keep her hours supplied with a good display of flowers. Many well-sounding and plausible reasons are given, I know, against making such attempts; — the badness of air, the want of light, of space, or of time, too much smoke, and too great expenses. But although these are great hindrances they do not make the thing impossible.*

E.A. Maling
A Handbook for Ladies on In-door Plants, Flowers for Ornaments and Song-birds (1867)

Nerium oleander La Aitana

NERIUM

Oleander needs a large room or conservatory. The fragrant blooms appear in summer and are borne in clusters above the willow-like foliage. The wood and sap are poisonous. Oleander is not an easy plant to care for when it is large — the pot or tub must be moved to an unheated room in winter and it benefits from a summer vacation in the garden. In autumn cut back the stems which have flowered.

SECRETS OF SUCCESS

Temperature: Average warmth; not less than 45°F in winter.
Light: Choose sunniest spot available.
Water: Water liberally in spring and summer; sparingly in winter. Use tepid water.
Air Humidity: Do not mist leaves.
Repotting: Repot, when necessary, in spring.
Propagation: Stem cuttings in spring or summer.

fragrant flower 2 in. across

NERIUM OLEANDER
Oleander

willow-like leaf 6–8 in. long

TYPE

N. oleander may look compact in the garden centre, but remember that it will grow into a spreading shrub about 6 ft tall. White, pink, red and yellow varieties are available.

ORCHIDS

It is possible to grow Orchids in your living room, but only a tiny fraction of the 100,000 known types are suitable. Choose from the 'house plant' group illustrated on the next page and buy a well-grown plant. Each type has its own special needs, but there are a number of general rules for Orchids.

You can't just place the plant anywhere. Miniature varieties can be grown in a terrarium (see page 34) but the usual home for a potted Orchid is on a pebble tray (see page 27). Place this tray on a windowsill which is close to a radiator. The window may need a blind or screen to provide protection from strong direct sunlight. Turn the pot occasionally and move the tray away from the window on frosty nights.

House plant Orchids cannot tolerate hot, stuffy conditions so good ventilation is required even in winter — don't be afraid to stand the pot outdoors on warm, sunny days. Indoors, however, you must avoid cold draughts which can be fatal.

Feed during the summer months. Orchids appreciate being pot-bound but after a few years repotting and division may be necessary. You will require a special orchid compost.

SECRETS OF SUCCESS

Temperature: Individual types vary, but the general rule is a day temperature of about 70°F in summer, 60°F in winter and a drop at night of 10°F. Cool nights are important.

Light: Good light, shaded from hot sun. Orchids need 10–15 hours of light each day — in winter supplement daylight with artificial light.

Water: Keep the compost moist, reduce watering in winter. Use tepid, soft water. With Cattleya and Miltonia let surface dry between waterings.

Air Humidity: Moist atmosphere essential. Mist leaves occasionally.

Repotting: Do not worry if a few roots grow outside the pot. Repot only when growth begins to suffer.

Propagation: Divide plants at repotting time. Leave at least 3 shoots on each division. Stake each newly potted plant.

SPECIAL PROBLEMS

BROWN SPOTS ON LEAVES
Cause: If the spots are hard and dry, the plant has been scorched by the sun. Provide shade; there is no need to remove the spots. If the spots are soft, then a fungus disease is present and the affected parts should be removed immediately.

HORIZONTAL OR DROOPING GROWTH
Cause: Lack of light is the common reason; Orchids need good illumination. If the growth is limp and the light is good then incorrect watering may be the cause of loss of vigour.

MOULD ON LEAVES
Cause: Mildew may develop if the leaves are thoroughly misted under cool conditions and the water does not quickly evaporate.

NO FLOWERS
Cause: When growth is unhealthy any incorrect cultural condition can be the reason. If growth appears healthy then insufficient light is the probable cause.

TYPES

The old idea that Orchids are only for skilled growers with a greenhouse or conservatory is not true. Several types will grow quite happily under ordinary room conditions — provided you remember that each type has its own special needs.

In general, Orchids need bright light and high humidity. To ensure moist air the plants should be kept in a glass case (terrarium) or the pot should be placed in a tray of wet pebbles. All need a special orchid compost and some will need a period of rest (almost dry compost) for part of the year — some also need constant warmth. So choose with care and seek advice from either a book, catalogue or an expert. If you follow the rules the 'easy' ones (**Cymbidium, Coelogyne, Odontoglossum, Paphiopedilum, Vuylstekeara**, etc) can be grown in the living room. Flowers of some popular house plant Orchids are shown here — others include **Dendrobium, Oncidium, Lycaste, Pleione** and **Vanda**.

CATTLEYA
Corsage Orchid

Waxy, beautiful flowers 4–6 in. across. A terrarium plant as it needs high humidity and a fairly constant temperature.

CYMBIDIUM

The miniature Cymbidium hybrids are the most popular house plant Orchids. Waxy flower 1½ in. across — succeeds under ordinary room conditions.

flower has 3 sepals and 3 petals. Lowest petal is the lip — this is always different from the others

most Orchids have a thickened stem-base — the pseudobulb. Shapes vary — oval, cylindrical or globular

COELOGYNE

Fragrant flower 2–4 in. across. **C. cristata** (illustrated above) is the easy one. Winter rest needed.

MILTONIA
Pansy Orchid

Velvety, pansy-like flower 2–4 in. across. Not easy under room conditions — dislikes temperature changes.

ODONTOGLOSSUM
Tiger Orchid

O. grande (flower 6 in. across) is the popular one shown here — not difficult if good light, high humidity and winter rest are provided.

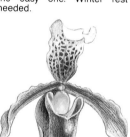

PAPHIOPEDILUM
Slipper Orchid

Many hybrids available — sometimes listed as **Cypripedium**. Prominently-pouched flower 2–4 in. across — suitable for room cultivation.

PHALAENOPSIS
Moth Orchid

Flat-faced flower 2 in. across — numerous blooms borne on arching stalks. Quite fussy — needs steady temperature and high humidity.

VUYLSTEKEARA

Popular man-made hybrid. Flower about 4 in. across — has the same requirements as Odontoglossum, one of its parents.

Cymbidium Rievaulx Hamsey

Paphiopedilum Hybriden

Phalaenopsis Happy Rose

golden
flower-head
5 in. long

oval
leaf 4 in
long

**PACHYSTACHYS
LUTEA**
Lollipop Plant

TYPE

P. lutea grows about 1½ ft high, with flower-heads made up of golden bracts and white blooms peeping through. The leaves are prominently veined.

PACHYSTACHYS

The Lollipop Plant was relatively unknown not many years ago but it is now often seen on display, with its cone-shaped flower-heads above the oval leaves. The main appeal is the long flowering season — from late spring until autumn if the plant is liberally watered and fed regularly. Leaf fall is a sign of dryness at the roots. This shrubby plant can get out of hand if it is not pruned in the spring. The stem tips which are removed can be used as cuttings.

SECRETS OF SUCCESS

Temperature: Average warmth; not less than 55°F in winter.

Light: Brightly lit spot away from direct sun in summer.

Water: Water liberally from spring to late autumn; sparingly in winter.

Air Humidity: Mist leaves in summer.

Repotting: Repot every year in spring.

Propagation: Stem cuttings in spring or summer.

Pachystachys lutea

Passiflora caerulea

PASSIFLORA

The Passiflora flower has an intricate structure — despite the delicacy of the flower there is nothing delicate about the plant. It is a rampant climber which will outgrow its welcome if it is not cut back hard each spring. The stems bear deeply-lobed leaves, tendrils and short-lived flowers all summer long. The Passion Flower is hardy enough to be grown outdoors in sheltered districts and so it requires cool conditions indoors in winter. In summer it can be stood outdoors.

SECRETS OF SUCCESS

Temperature: Average warmth; keep at 40°–50°F in winter.

Light: Choose sunniest spot available.

Water: Keep compost moist at all times; may need daily watering in summer. Reduce watering in winter.

Air Humidity: Mist leaves occasionally.

Repotting: Repot every year in spring.

Propagation: Stem cuttings in summer. Sow seeds in spring.

ornate
flower
3 in.
across

hand-like
leaf 4 in.
across

**PASSIFLORA
CAERULEA**
Passion Flower

TYPES

There are several Passifloras, including the Granadilla (**P. quadrangularis**) which bears large yellow fruit, but only **P. caerulea** is grown as a house plant. Several named varieties are available.

Pittosporum tobira

PITTOSPORUM

Pittosporum is popular with American interior decorators who require a glossy-leaved tree which will grow under rather poor conditions. In Britain and some other European countries it has never found favour. There are a few problems — the creamy flowers with a fragrance reminiscent of orange blossom only appear under good light conditions, and cool winter quarters are needed.

SECRETS OF SUCCESS

Temperature: Average warmth; keep at 40°–50°F in winter.

Light: Brightly lit spot away from direct sun in summer.

Water: Water thoroughly when compost begins to dry out. Water sparingly in winter.

Air Humidity: Mist leaves occasionally.

Repotting: Repot, when necessary, in spring.

Propagation: Stem cuttings in spring; use rooting hormone.

fragrant
flower ½ in.
across

leathery
leaf
4 in.
long

**PITTOSPORUM
TOBIRA**
Mock Orange

TYPES

P. tobira is a flat-topped tree with dark leaves — in spring the branches are topped with clusters of tubular star-faced flowers. **Variegatum** leaves have white blotches.

Pentas lanceolata

PENTAS

The Egyptian Star Cluster is not a plant you are likely to find in your local garden shop, but it is well worth growing in a sunny window if you can obtain a rooted cutting. The growth becomes straggly if you fail to pinch out the stem tips regularly. Keep the plant about 18 in. high. The flowers may appear at any time of the year — winter is the most usual. Pentas is easy to grow; keep the plant at about 60°F in winter.

SECRETS OF SUCCESS

Temperature: Average warmth; not less than 50°F in winter.

Light: Bright light with some direct sun.

Water: Keep compost moist at all times; reduce watering in winter.

Air Humidity: Mist leaves occasionally.

Repotting: Repot every year in spring.

Propagation: Stem cuttings in spring; use rooting hormone.

flower-head 3–4 in. across

hairy leaf 2–3 in. long

PENTAS LANCEOLATA
Egyptian Star Cluster

TYPES

P. lanceolata (sometimes sold as **P. carnea**) is the basic species. The flower-head is composed of numerous tubular starry flowers — there are named varieties in white, pink, red and mauve.

PLUMBAGO

Clusters of sky blue flowers appearing throughout summer and autumn make the Cape Leadwort an oustanding house plant when trained around a window. This vigorous and rambling climber can be kept as a specimen plant on a sunny windowsill by regular pruning. The secret of success is to keep it cool throughout the winter and early spring. If it gets too cool the leaves may fall but new foliage will appear. The stems soon become straggly — prune during the dormant season.

SECRETS OF SUCCESS

Temperature: Cool or average warmth; not less than 45°F in winter.

Light: Bright light with some direct sun.

Water: Keep compost moist at all times; water sparingly in winter.

Air Humidity: Mist occasionally.

Repotting: Repot, when necessary, in spring.

Propagation: Stem cuttings in autumn. Sow seeds in spring.

star-faced tubular flower 1 in. across

leaf 2 in. long — underside grey

PLUMBAGO AURICULATA
(PLUMBAGO CAPENSIS)
Cape Leadwort

TYPES

Grow **P. auriculata** as a trailer or tie it to supports as a climber — the stems will reach 3–4 ft. Cut back old shoots in early spring. A white variety (**alba**) can be bought.

Plumbago auriculata

Boys & Girls

African Violets are sometimes described as boy- or girl-types, but this has nothing to do with the sex of the flowers. The first African Violet hybrid to be raised and offered for sale in the U.S. was *Blue Boy* — a cross between Saintpaulia ionantha and S. confusa by Armacost and Royston in 1927. The leaves of this plant were all-green, but a sport or mutation occurred. The leaves of the sport had a pale-coloured blotch at the base — not particularly attractive but quite definitely different. The new plant was duly called *Blue Girl*, and as a result all-green African Violets are now called boy-types, and those with foliage bearing a basal pale blotch are referred to as girl-types.

Some years later another sport appeared — the leaves were splashed all over with creamy-white markings. This was one of the early variegated African Violets, and was appropriately called *Blue Boy in the Snow.*

BOY-TYPE AFRICAN VIOLET

GIRL-TYPE AFRICAN VIOLET

PELARGONIUM (GERANIUM)

It is not surprising that the Pelargonium is one of the world's favourite house plants. It is easy to grow and propagate, it has a long flowering period and the clusters of blooms are large and colourful.

By far the most popular type is the Common or Zonal Pelargonium. It will bloom almost all year round if kept on a sunny windowsill at 55°F or more. Keep the compost rather dry — overwatering is the main enemy of Pelargoniums.

The Regal Pelargonium is the glamorous member of the family. Unfortunately it has a shorter flowering season and it is not as easy to grow. Overwinter at 45° – 50°F.

The Trailing Pelargonium is becoming increasingly popular. Its long brittle stems bear long-stalked flower clusters throughout summer and autumn if the plant is kept in a sunny spot.

There are a few general rules for all Pelargoniums. Pinch back young plants to induce bushiness. Do not repot until it is essential. Provide plenty of fresh air and not much humidity. Remove dead flowers and prune in early spring (Regal Pelargonium in autumn).

YELLOWING OF LOWER LEAVES
Cause: If the leaves remain firm or are crisp with scorched edges then underwatering is the reason. If the leaves wilt or rot then overwatering is the cause. In both cases leaf fall may occur.

REDDENING OF LEAF EDGES
Cause: Temperature too low. Move pot away from window on frosty nights.

BLACKENING OF STEM BASE
Cause: Black leg disease. Destroy infected plant; in future use sterile compost and avoid overwatering.

SPINDLY GROWTH: LOSS OF LOWER LEAVES
Cause: Too little light; Pelargoniums will not grow in shade.

WATER-SOAKED CORKY PATCHES ON LEAVES
Cause: Oedema disease, associated with over-moist conditions. Non-infectious — reduce watering.

GREY MOULD ON LEAVES
Cause: Botrytis, associated with over-wet conditions. Infectious — remove diseased leaves, spray with a systemic fungicide, improve ventilation and reduce watering.

NO FLOWERS ON REGAL PELARGONIUM
Cause: If the plant is healthy the likely reason is too much heat in winter.

INSECTS
Whitefly, aphid and vine weevil can be troublesome; see page 244.

SECRETS OF SUCCESS

Temperature: Average warmth with cool nights; not less than 45°F in winter (50°F for Trailing Pelargonium).

Light: Provide as much light as possible. Direct sunlight is essential.

Water: Water thoroughly, then leave until compost is moderately dry. Avoid overwatering. Reduce watering frequency in winter, compost should be barely moist if plant is not in bloom.

Air Humidity: Do not mist the leaves.

Repotting: Repot, when necessary, in spring.

Propagation: Stem cuttings in summer. Do not use a rooting hormone and do not cover. Sow seed in spring.

TYPES

● **TRAILING PELARGONIUMS**

Pelargonium peltatum roulettii

fleshy leaf 2–3 in. across

straggling stems 1–3 ft long

star-shaped flower ½–1½ in. across — single or double

PELARGONIUM PELTATUM
Trailing Pelargonium
(Ivy-leaved Geranium)

The Ivy-leaved Geranium is widely used in hanging baskets. The flowers are available in a range of colours — **Madame Margot** (white), **Charles Turner** (pink), **Apricot Queen** (salmon), **La France** (lilac) and **Madame Crousse** (red). Some varieties are grown for their decorative foliage as well as their flowers — e.g **L'Elégante** (white-edged leaves) and **Sussex Lace** (creamy-veined leaves).

Pelargonium peltatum La France

● ZONAL PELARGONIUMS

The Zonal (or Common) Pelargonium is the type you are most likely to see. These bushy plants are usually 1–2 ft high, but some varieties can reach 4 ft or more. With care the flowering season can last nearly all year round — all they need is sun and rather dry compost.

brittle, thick stems

rounded leaf 3–4 in. across. Most varieties have a horseshoe marking or 'zone'

PELARGONIUM HORTORUM
(PELARGONIUM ZONALE)

flower ½–1½ in. across. Single, semi-double and double are the usual forms. Colours — white, pink, orange, red and purple

SINGLE

DOUBLE

STELLAR

CACTUS

Marechal MacMahon   Distinction   Mrs Pollock   Mrs Henry Cox

Pelargonium Paul Crampel

Standard varieties: Height 1–2 ft.
Propagate from cuttings taken in late summer.

P. **Paul Crampel** Bright red, single
P. **King of Denmark** Rose, semi-double
P. **Gustave Emich** Bright red, double
P. **Jane Campbell** Orange, single
P. **Queen of the Whites** White, single
P. **Vera Dillon** Purple, single
P. **Hermione** White, double
P. **Festiva Maxima** Purple, double
P. **Distinction** Red, single
P. **Mrs Pollock** Vermilion, single
P. **Mrs Henry Cox** Rose, single
P. **Gazelle** Pink, stellar

Irenes: Vigorous and free flowering. Flowers semi-double — flower-heads larger than Standard varieties.

P. **Springtime** Salmon-pink
P. **Modesty** White
P. **Surprise** Pink
P. **Electra** Red with blue overtones
P. **Fire Brand** Red

F₁ Hybrids raised from seed:
Can be bought as seeds or bedding plants.

P. **Cherie** Salmon-pink
P. **Ringo** Red
P. **Mustang** Red
P. **Bright Eyes** White-eyed red
P. **Sprinter** Red
P. **Carefree Mixed** Various colours

Deacons: Compact. Flower-heads small but very numerous.

P. **Deacon Fireball** Bright red, double
P. **Mandarin** Orange, double
P. **Deacon Bonanza** Bright pink, double

Rosebuds: Small flowers, centre petals remaining unopened like miniature rosebuds.

P. **Red Rambler** Red
P. **Appleblossom** Rosebud pink
P. **Rosebud Supreme** Red

Cactus: Petals narrow and twisted.

P. **Fire Dragon** Red
P. **Noel** White

Miniatures and dwarfs: Height 9 in. or less.

P. **Red Black Vesuvius** Red
P. **Fantasia** White
P. **Pixie** Salmon
P. **Video** Various colours

● REGAL PELARGONIUMS

The Regal (or Martha Washington) Pelargoniums have more eye-catching blooms than the ordinary Zonal types — each flower is larger, frillier and more colourful. But there are drawbacks — there are fewer blooms and there is a limited flowering season (early spring to midsummer).

Pelargonium Carisbrooke

brittle, thin stems

scalloped leaf with serrated edge 3 in. across

flower 1½–2½ in. across. Petals are usually frilled, with splashes or lines of a second colour. Prominent eye often present. Colours — white, pink, orange, red and purple

PELARGONIUM DOMESTICUM
(PELARGONIUM GRANDIFLORUM)

Height 1–2 ft. Propagate from cuttings taken in late summer.

P. **Easter Greetings** Rose with brown blotches
P. **Aztec** White with pink blotches
P. **Lavender Grand Slam** Lavender with purple blotches
P. **Grandma Fischer** Orange with brown blotches
P. **Snowbank** White, frilled
P. **Geronimo** Red, frilled

P. **Applause** Pink, frilled
P. **Gay Nineties** White with purple blotches
P. **Elsie Hickman** Vermilion, pink and white
P. **Georgia Peach** Peach, frilled
P. **Carisbrooke** Rose-pink
P. **Sue Jarrett** Salmon-pink with maroon blotches
P. **Swabian Maid** Carmine-rose

ROCHEA

The proper name of the flowering succulent sold as 'Crassula' is Rochea coccinea. The stems are clothed with ranks of leathery triangular leaves and at their tips the showy clusters of flowers appear. Rochea needs standard succulent treatment — plenty of light and water in summer and a period outdoors in sunny weather. Good ventilation is important and let it rest with cool conditions and drier compost in winter. Cut back stems after they have flowered.

Rochea coccinea

SECRETS OF SUCCESS

Temperature: Cool or average warmth; not less than 45°F in winter.

Light: Brightly lit spot with some direct sunshine.

Water: Water thoroughly when the compost begins to dry out. Water sparingly in winter.

Air Humidity: Misting is not necessary.

Repotting: Repot, when necessary, in spring.

Propagation: Stem cuttings in spring or summer. Allow cuttings to dry for 2–3 days before inserting in compost.

leathery leaf 1 in. long

fragrant flower 1 in. long

ROCHEA COCCINEA
Crassula

TYPES

R. coccinea is usually bought in flower. It is a neat plant, 1–1½ ft high, with clusters of red tubular flowers. The varieties are more popular — **alba** (white) and **bicolor** (red and white).

RUELLIA

You would expect a plant with the appeal of the Monkey Plant to be more popular. The velvety leaves are tinged with purple and veined in silver, the flowers are 2 in. long flared trumpets. The stems droop gracefully, making it suitable for hanging baskets. The problem is its constitution — Ruellia needs an atmosphere which is warm and moist. This calls for standing the pot on a pebble tray and misting daily in summer.

trumpet-shaped flower 1½ in. across

oval leaf 3 in. long

purple underside

RUELLIA MAKOYANA
Monkey Plant

TYPES

R. makoyana produces weak stems about 2 ft long — leave to trail or tie to a support. Pinch out tips to induce bushiness. **R. macrantha** is a larger plant with plain green leaves.

SECRETS OF SUCCESS

Temperature: Warm or average warmth; not less than 55°F in winter.

Light: Brightly lit spot away from direct sun in summer.

Water: Keep compost very moist when growing and flowering. Reduce watering after flowering.

Air Humidity: Use pebble tray; mist leaves frequently.

Repotting: Repot, when necessary, in spring.

Propagation: Stem cuttings in summer. Rooting hormone and warmth are necessary.

Ruellia macrantha

SANCHEZIA

This striking greenhouse shrub can be grown as a house plant if its requirement for high air humidity is met; stand the pot on a pebble tray (page 27) and mist the leaves frequently. The yellow flowers are borne in upright clusters above the foliage. These blooms are attractive, but the large leaves, up to 12 in. long, provide the main display with their yellow or ivory veins. Prune each spring.

Sanchezia nobilis

SECRETS OF SUCCESS

Temperature: Average warmth; not less than 55°F in winter.

Light: Brightly lit spot away from direct sun in summer.

Water: Keep compost moist at all times; reduce watering in winter.

Air Humidity: Use pebble tray; mist leaves frequently.

Repotting: Repot every year in spring.

Propagation: Stem cuttings in summer; rooting hormone and warmth are necessary.

tubular flower 2 in. long

prominently-veined leaf 1 ft long

SANCHEZIA NOBILIS

TYPE

S. nobilis (S. speciosa) is a larger but much less popular relative of the Zebra Plant (page 126). The bush grows about 3 ft high and the flowers appear in early summer.

SAINTPAULIA

It is only 60 years since the first African Violet was sold as a house plant, but in that time it has become a world-wide favourite. Its main attraction is the ability to flower at almost any time of the year and its compact size means it can fit on a narrow windowsill.

The original African Violet was notoriously difficult to grow, but modern varieties are much more robust and freer flowering. A beginner cannot expect to match the expert in keeping the plant in bloom continually for 10 months or more, but there should be no difficulty in producing several flushes each year.

There are five basic needs — steady warmth, careful watering, good light, high air humidity and regular feeding. Note these few extra tips from the experts: Keep the leaves off the windowpane. Remove dead flowers and damaged leaves immediately — do not leave a stalk. Remove side shoots on older plants as they develop. Keep the plant moderately root-bound. Use a plastic pot when repotting is essential.

SECRETS OF SUCCESS

Temperature: Average warmth; not less than 60°F in winter. Avoid cold draughts and sudden changes in temperature.

Light: Bright light — ideally an east or south window in winter, and a west window in summer. Always protect from strong sunlight. For winter blooming provide some artificial light at night. To grow entirely by artificial light use two 40 W fluorescent tubes about 12 in. above the plants for 14 hours each day.

Water: Keep compost moist; wait until the surface is dry before watering. Use tepid water. Push the spout below the foliage. Use immersion method occasionally.

Air Humidity: High humidity is essential. Surround the pot with damp peat or place on a pebble tray (see page 27). Mist with care — tepid water, plant not in flower, very fine spray and keep misted plant away from sunshine.

Repotting: Repot, when necessary, in spring.

Propagation: Leaf cuttings or sow seeds in spring.

SPECIAL PROBLEMS

STRAW-COLOURED PATCHES ON LEAVES
Cause: Too much direct sun in summer. Leaf edges may turn yellow and holes may develop.

BROWN SPOTS ON LEAVES
Cause: Cold water has been used for watering. Always use tepid water.

YELLOWING LEAVES
Cause: There are several possible reasons. Dry air is a frequent cause, so is too much sun and incorrect watering. Overfeeding can result in yellowing; make sure you follow the instructions.

PALE GREEN LEAVES WITH LONG STALKS; LEAF EDGES CURLED
Cause: The plant has been chilled. The minimum temperature should be 60°F, although it will survive short periods at 50° – 60°F if the compost is fairly dry. Move pots away from the window on frosty nights.

LIMP LEAVES; CENTRE CROWN ROTTEN
Cause: Crown rot disease, caused by overwatering and wide fluctuations in temperature. This is a difficult disease to control and it is infectious; the best plan is to remove and destroy the plant as soon as possible.

NO FLOWERS
Cause: There are many possible reasons. The most likely cause is insufficient light, especially in winter. Other possibilities are dry air, cold air, too frequent repotting and failure to remove side shoots. Moving the pot to a new location can cause the plant to cease blooming for some time.

MOULDY LEAVES & FLOWERS
Cause: Botrytis or powdery mildew disease. Stop misting the leaves. Pick off and destroy diseased parts. Spray the plant with systemic fungicide; use tepid water and keep out of sun until the spray deposit has dried.

INSECTS
Whitefly, mealy bug and cyclamen mite can be troublesome. See page 244.

TYPES

● TRAILING TYPES

The trailing types are officially described as African Violets with a main stem which divides into a multicrown plant, and has leaves which are more widely spaced than the foliage of standard varieties. In popular language the trailers have long drooping stems which often form small plants at their tips. All are hybrids — the most important parent is **S. magungensis**. The flowers borne by Trailing African Violets are usually smaller than those produced by the Standard African Violets — the plants may be miniature or standard-sized. Several varieties are available from specialist growers:

violet-like flower 1 in. across

rounded leaf 2 in. across

SAINTPAULIA HYBRID
Trailing African Violet

Star Trail Star-shaped flowers — blue with white edge. Miniature-sized plant.
Jet Trail Double flowers — wisteria blue. Miniature-sized plant — semi-trailing habit.
Trail Along Double flowers — bright pink. Miniature-sized plant.
Snowy Trail Double flowers — white. Miniature-sized plant.
Breezy Blue Double flowers — bright blue. Standard-sized plant.
Sweetheart Trail Double flowers — bicolour pink. Standard-sized plant.

Saintpaulia Breezy Blue

SAINTPAULIA TYPES continued

● STANDARD & MINIATURE TYPES

violet-like flower usually 1–1½ in. across. White, blue, pink red and purple — bicolours available

fleshy foliage with velvety surface

round or heart-shaped leaf usually 2–4 in. across

SAINTPAULIA HYBRID
African Violet

There are thousands of varieties with a bewildering assortment of flower forms and colours. The parentage of these hybrids is complex, with **S. ionantha** and **S. confusa** as the original species. These early Saintpaulias were discovered in East Africa in 1892 — its offspring were first shown in Germany in 1893 and in Britain in 1894. The first commercial plants were raised in Germany, and it was seeds from Germany and England which started the U.S. interest in the 1920s. The first commercial hybrid **(Blue Boy)** was offered in 1927 — the next fundamental breakthrough was in the 1960s when the semi-doubles, the star-shaped flowers and the frilly-edged petals were introduced. The search goes on for the yellow, the orange and the highly scented.

Several important strains have appeared over the years. The **Rhapsodie** strain contains varieties which dominated the British and Continental scene for years — upright plants with an abundance of flowers. **Rococo** varieties are girl-type plants with double flowers — the **Ballet** strain with fringed petals has long been popular in the U.S. The latest arrival is the **Chimera** strain with large, boldly-striped petals.

Size refers to a single crown of a full-grown plant

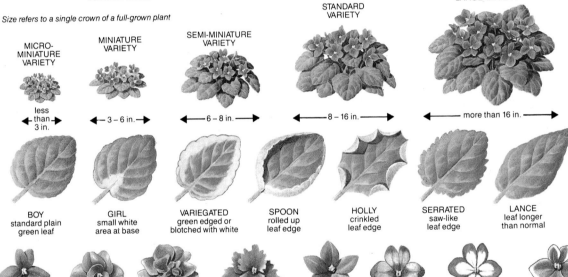

MICRO-MINIATURE VARIETY — less than 3 in.

MINIATURE VARIETY — 3 – 6 in.

SEMI-MINIATURE VARIETY — 6 – 8 in.

STANDARD VARIETY — 8 – 16 in.

LARGE VARIETY — more than 16 in.

BOY standard plain green leaf

GIRL small white area at base

VARIEGATED green edged or blotched with white

SPOON rolled up leaf edge

HOLLY crinkled leaf edge

SERRATED saw-like leaf edge

LANCE leaf longer than normal

SINGLE top 2 petals smaller than bottom 3 — the standard type

SEMI-DOUBLE more than 5 petals — yellow centre still visible

DOUBLE at least 10 petals — yellow centre covered

FRILLED petal edges wavy. *Ruffled* means slightly wavy — *Fringed* means very wavy

STAR 5 equal-sized and evenly-spaced petals

BICOLOUR 2 or more shades of the same colour

MULTICOLOUR 2 or more different colours — *Fantasy* when splashed, speckled or striped

GENEVA white (rarely pink or green) edge to petals

PINKS: Becky Semi-double flowers — fringed pink. **Classic Pink** Double flowers — bicolour pink. **Lisa** Single flowers — frilled pink. **Rococo Pink** Double flowers — pink. **Rhapsodie Gisela** Single flowers — clear pink.

REDS: Helene Double flowers — deep red. **Amigo** Star-shaped flowers — deep red. **Mark** Double flowers — fringed deep red. **Andrew Ian** Double flowers — deep fuchsia. **Emily** Semi-double flowers — bicolour magenta. **Silver Milestone** Semi-double flowers — geneva magenta.

CORALS: Fluted Coral Double flowers — deeply ruffled dark coral. **Coral Crest** Star-shaped flowers — coral.

BLUES & PURPLES: Wonderland Large semi-double flowers — ruffled light blue. **Wisteria** Double flowers — lavender blue. **Tessa** Single flowers — frilled purple. **Blue Ice** Single flowers — light blue. **Delft Imperial** Double flowers — fringed mid blue with occasional white edge. **Lady Diana** Single/semi-double flowers — bicolour lavender. **Carefree** Double flowers — light lavender.

WHITES: Aca's Snowbird Double flowers — white. **Arctic Mist** Double flowers — white. **White Kathleen** Single flowers — white. **Lily White** Double flowers — white. **Snow Ballet** Double flowers — white.

MULTICOLOURS: Fancy Pants Single flowers — frilled red and white. **Candy Dandy** Double flowers — red and white. **Ms Pretty** Single flowers — fringed pink and white. **Dandy Dancer** Double flowers — ruffled purple and white. **Kiwi Dazzler** Single flowers — fringed chimera red with white stripes.

VARIEGATED LEAVES: Crimson Frost Double flowers — fringed fuchsia with white edge. **Blue Storm** Semi-double flowers — geneva blue. **Just Beautiful** Double flowers — geneva light pink.

SEMI-MINIATURES: Irish Angel Double flowers — light blue with green edge. **Dora Baker** Double flowers — pink. **Window Lace** Double flowers — bicolour pink.

MINIATURES: Midget Valentine Single flowers — red. **Tiny Rose** Double flowers — rose pink. **Davy Crockett** Star-shaped flowers — light blue. **Edith's Toy** Star-shaped flowers — pink.

MICRO-MINIATURES: Novelty plants which can be grown in a wine glass. **Twinkle** Star-shaped flowers — pink. **Pip Squeek** Single bell-like flowers — light pink. **Blue Imp** Star-shaped flowers — blue.

Saintpaulia Silver Milestone

Saintpaulia Blue Storm

Saintpaulia Kiwi Dazzler

Saintpaulia Diana Blue

Saintpaulia Rhapsodie Gisela

Saintpaulia Rhapsodie No. 3

Saintpaulia Rococo Pink

Saintpaulia Fancy Pants

Saintpaulia Pip Squeek

serrated leaf ½ in. across

4-petalled flower 1 in. across

SCHIZOCENTRON ELEGANS
Spanish Shawl

SCHIZOCENTRON

Schizocentron is a mat-forming creeping plant which can be used in a hanging basket. The small, dark green leaves are rather plain — it is the display of rose-purple flowers during early summer which makes Spanish Shawl worth growing. These silky flowers are borne in large numbers at the tips of the stems. It is an uncommon plant and the experts can't agree on whether it is difficult or not. Spanish Shawl does prefer moist air, but it seems to grow quite happily under room conditions.

Schizocentron elegans

TYPE

S. elegans has creeping reddish stems which root at the nodes. Under suitable conditions the flowers may almost cover the foliage — each bloom has a central boss of purple stamens. Trim back after flowering.

SECRETS OF SUCCESS

Temperature: Average warmth; not less than 50°F in winter.
Light: Brightly lit spot away from direct sun.
Water: Keep compost moist at all times.
Air Humidity: Mist leaves regularly.
Repotting: Repot every year after flowering.
Propagation: Stem cuttings in spring or summer.

Sparmannia africana

SPARMANNIA

The House Lime is a useful plant for the larger room, where its pale downy leaves make a pleasant contrast to the dark leathery foliage of Philodendron or Ficus. It grows quickly and may need repotting more than once a year. Keep growth in check by pinching out the stem tips of young plants and by cutting back the stems after flowering. Sparmannia blooms in early spring if it has been kept in direct sunlight during winter.

SECRETS OF SUCCESS

Temperature: Average warmth; not less than 45°F in winter.
Light: Brightly lit spot away from direct sun in summer.
Water: Keep compost moist at all times; may require daily watering in summer. Water more sparingly in winter.
Air Humidity: Mist leaves occasionally in summer.
Repotting: Repot every year in spring.
Propagation: Stem cuttings root easily in spring or summer; use rooting hormone.

golden-centred flower 1½ in. across

downy leaf 9 in. long

SPARMANNIA AFRICANA
House Lime

TYPE

S. africana is tree-like, quickly growing several feet high. The flowers appear in long-stalked clusters. Prune after blooming has finished — repeat flowering may occur.

arum-like flower 3 in. long

lance-shaped leaf 6 in. long

SPATHIPHYLLUM WALLISII
Peace Lily

SPATHIPHYLLUM

The Peace Lily is a good choice if it can be kept out of direct sunlight in a room which is reasonably warm in winter. There must be no cold draughts and the pot should be surrounded by moist peat or stood on a pebble tray (page 27). The glossy leaves grow directly out of the compost; in spring and sometimes again in autumn the flowers appear. These arum lily-like blooms, borne on long stalks are long lasting. Wash the leaves occasionally and feed regularly.

Spathiphyllum wallisii

TYPES

There are two types — the popular **S. wallisii** which grows about 1 ft high, and the less hardy but much larger **S. Mauna Loa**. The flowers change from white to pale green with age.

SECRETS OF SUCCESS

Temperature: Warm or average warmth; not less than 55°F in winter.
Light: Semi-shade in summer; bright light in winter. Strong sunlight will damage the leaves.
Water: Keep the compost moist at all times; reduce watering in winter.
Air Humidity: Mist leaves very frequently.
Repotting: Repot every year in spring.
Propagation: Divide plants at repotting time.

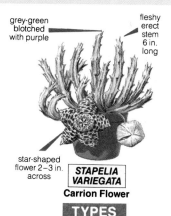

grey-green blotched with purple

fleshy erect stem 6 in. long

star-shaped flower 2–3 in. across

STAPELIA VARIEGATA
Carrion Flower

TYPES

S. variegata bears uniquely-patterned blooms at the base of the succulent stems during the summer. For the really keen there is the odourless **S. gigantea** (blooms 10–12 in. across).

STAPELIA

The smell of the blooms of the Carrion Flower has been described as 'disagreeable', 'offensive', and 'disgusting'. It is therefore not surprising that these flowering succulents have never been popular, although some types produce flowers which have little or no smell. All Stapelias have spectacular flowers. By far the most popular type is S. variegata. Unfortunately it is one of the strong-smelling species and it may be necessary to stand the pot outdoors when in flower.

SECRETS OF SUCCESS

Temperature: Average warmth; not less than 50°F in winter.

Light: As much light as possible, but shade from hot summer sun.

Water: Water moderately, then leave until the compost surface is dry. Water sparingly in winter.

Air Humidity: No need to mist leaves.

Repotting: Repot, when necessary, in spring.

Propagation: See Propagation of Succulents, page 104.

Stapelia variegata

Stephanotis floribunda

STEPHANOTIS

Stephanotis is usually associated with bridal bouquets, but can also be grown as a free-flowering house plant. Its vigorous climbing stems must be trained on a support and should be cut back once flowering has finished. The Wax Flower is a beautiful but difficult plant — it hates sudden changes in temperature, needs constant cool conditions in winter and is particularly attractive to scale and mealy bug. Do not turn or move the pot when the plant is in flower.

SECRETS OF SUCCESS

Temperature: Average warmth; keep at 55°–60°F in winter.

Light: Brightly lit spot, away from direct sun in summer.

Water: Keep compost moist at all times; water sparingly in winter.

Air Humidity: Mist leaves occasionally.

Repotting: Repot every 2 years in spring.

Propagation: Stem cuttings in summer; rooting hormone and warmth are necessary.

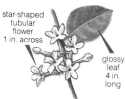

star-shaped tubular flower 1 in. across

glossy leaf 4 in. long

STEPHANOTIS FLORIBUNDA
Wax Flower
(Madagascar Jasmine)

TYPE

The stems of **S. floribunda** can reach 10 ft or more, but is usually sold twined around a wire hoop. The heavily-scented waxy flowers appear throughout the summer months.

---

multicoloured flower 6 in. across

paddle-shaped leaf 1 ft long on 1–2 ft leaf-stalk

STRELITZIA REGINAE
Bird of Paradise

TYPE

S. reginae is the species grown indoors. The long-stalked leaves arise from the roots and not a stem — the flowers usually appear in spring, but sometimes occur earlier or later. Do not repot mature plants.

STRELITZIA

Surely the most spectacular of all the flowers which can be grown in the home. The vivid flowers last for several weeks on top of tall stalks, surrounded by large leaves. It needs patience (new plants take 4–6 years before flowering starts) and space (mature plants in a 10 in. pot grow 3–4 ft high). But it is surprisingly easy to grow if it can be kept well-lit and cool in winter.

SECRETS OF SUCCESS

Temperature: Average warmth; keep at 55°–60°F in winter.

Light: As much light as possible, but shade from hot summer sun.

Water: Water thoroughly, then leave until surface is dry. Water sparingly in winter.

Air Humidity: Mist occasionally.

Repotting: Repot young plants every year in spring.

Propagation: Divide when repotting.

Strelitzia reginae

Streptocarpus Constant Nymph

STREPTOCARPUS

Many colourful hybrids have appeared in recent years, but the old favourite Constant Nymph still remains the most popular Streptocarpus. When growing conditions are satisfactory a succession of blooms appear above the rosette of coarse, stemless leaves throughout the summer, but the Cape Primrose can be temperamental. It needs a shallow pot, moist air, bright light and freedom from draughts and cold air in winter. Remove flowers as they fade.

SECRETS OF SUCCESS

Temperature: Average warmth; not less than 55°F in winter.

Light: Brightly lit spot away from direct sun in summer.

Water: Water freely, then leave until the compost surface is dry. Reduce watering in winter.

Air Humidity: Mist occasionally, but do not wet the leaves.

Repotting: Repot every year in spring.

Propagation: Divide plants at repotting time. Seeds may be sown in spring.

trumpet-shaped flower 2 in. across

strap-shaped leaf 8–12 in. long

STREPTOCARPUS HYBRIDA
Cape Primrose

TYPES

Many hybrids are available with large flowers in white, blue, purple, pink and red with prominently-veined throats. **S. Constant Nymph** blooms are lilac with violet veins on the petals.

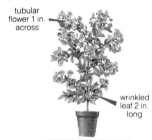

tubular flower 1 in. across

wrinkled leaf 2 in. long

STREPTOSOLEN JAMESONII
Marmalade Bush

TYPE

S. jamesonii will grow 4–6 ft high if left unpruned. The branches are weak and arching, and the best way to grow this rambling shrub in a conservatory is to train it against a wall.

STREPTOSOLEN

You will have to search for Streptosolen. Its main feature is the large clusters of marmalade-coloured flowers borne at the tip of each branch in spring or summer. The stems require some form of support — you can stake the main stem and train it as a standard (page 177). Streptosolen becomes leggy with age, especially if the compost is not kept constantly moist during the growing season. A well-lit spot is essential, especially in winter, and fresh air is needed in summer.

SECRETS OF SUCCESS

Temperature: Average warmth; not less than 50°F in winter.

Light: Bright light, away from direct sun in summer.

Water: Keep compost moist at all times.

Air Humidity: Mist leaves occasionally.

Repotting: Repot after flowering only when necessary.

Propagation: Stem cuttings in spring or summer.

Streptosolen jamesonii

bell-like flower 3 in. across

sword-like leaf 1 ft long

VALLOTA SPECIOSA
Scarborough Lily

TYPES

V. speciosa is an excellent plant for a sunny windowsill. The leaves are evergreen and the red flowers are borne at the top of 1–2 ft flower-stalks. White and salmon varieties are available.

VALLOTA

In spring plant the bulb firmly in a 5 in. pot; leave the top half of the bulb uncovered. Vallota is an easy plant to care for — keep it cool during winter, remove dead flowers and leaves, and let the compost dry out slightly between waterings. In late summer clusters of trumpet-shaped flowers appear. Don't repot until the clump of bulbs becomes overcrowded. Pot up each large bulb separately; flowering size bulbs are 1½ in. across.

SECRETS OF SUCCESS

Temperature: Average warmth; keep at 50°–55°F in winter.

Light: Bright light with some direct sun.

Water: Water thoroughly when the compost begins to dry out. Water sparingly in winter.

Air Humidity: Sponge leaves occasionally.

Repotting: Repot every 3–4 years in spring.

Propagation: Divide plants at repotting time, or detach offsets from mature plants and pot up in summer.

Vallota speciosa

CHAPTER 7

THE COLLECTORS OF INDOOR PLANTS

The first recorded plant collectors were the soldiers in the army of Thothmes III, Pharaoh of Egypt, 3500 years ago. In his Temple at Karnak these soldiers are shown bringing back 300 plants as booty from the campaign in Syria.

Over the centuries many travellers have collected unusual plants from overseas and brought or sent them back to their native countries. There were soldiers, such as the Crusaders, and also merchants, missionaries, sailors, naval surgeons, explorers and so on. These part-time collectors picked up their specimens whilst they were involved in some other profession — the day of the full-time collector did not dawn until the start of the 18th century.

These early part-time collectors provided the first house plants for temperate Europe — plants which needed protection from frost during the winter. As noted in Chapter 3 Italian sea captains brought back exotic flowering plants from Asia in the early years of the 15th century. Pineapples were sent to Europe from the New World during the 16th century, and other Bromeliads soon followed. Unknown collectors had brought Orange, Lemon and Pomegranate to Northern Europe during the same century, and in the 17th century the prototype of the professional plant collector appeared — John Tradescant the Elder. As Gardener to Charles I he travelled overseas to collect plants, but he obtained many of his exotics from agents in Paris, Constantinople etc. The end of the 17th century saw the arrival of the greenhouse in Europe and a keen interest in growing plants from tropical regions. "There is a vast number of East and West Indian seeds come over this year" wrote Sir Hans Sloane in 1684. An early collector, Herr Fagel, sent hundreds of new plants from the Indian sub-continent to be grown in the Hampton Court Orangery. These public displays of greenhouse plants helped to start the active quest for new varieties in the 1700s.

The 18th century saw the appearance of a new breed — the professional plant collector financed by a botanical garden, rich patron or learned society — in later years nurseries became important sponsors for such expeditions. An example of the early professional collector was James Harlow, sent by Sir Arthur Rawdon to the West Indies to collect new plants for his Irish garden.

These pioneers were to be followed by a long line of professional plant collectors, but the age of the amateur was not over. It has continued until this day — it began with missionary/botanists such as the Reverend John Banister who collected in North America in the 17th century. Then came the physicians such as Thunberg, and Government Officials like Von Saint Paul-Illaire who discovered the African Violet named after him. In the 18th century the most important amateur collectors were the missionaries — the most notable example was the French priest Père Nicholas d'Incarville. Between 1740 and 1757 he sent many thousands of seeds from the East to the two great European centres for raising and cultivating new plants — le Jardin des Plantes in Paris and the Apothecaries' Garden in Chelsea.

Le Jardin des Plantes in 1845. Collectors had been sending seeds and plants there for centuries — there were over 4000 types growing in 1665

*Sir Joseph Banks (1743–1820) Botanist,
plant collector and patron*

At the time d'Incarville was starting his plant collecting marathon in China one of the immortals of botany was born — Joseph Banks. At 23 Banks was off on his first plant hunting expedition. The destination was Newfoundland — this was followed by his voyage with Cook to Australia and with Dr Solander to Iceland. But Banks' great contribution was not as a collector — it was as a director of the efforts of others.

In 1772 George III purchased Kew House and so Kew became a royal garden. Banks was Botanical Adviser to the King, and thus he became virtual dictator of the botanical garden. Kew's reputation was growing — it was already taking over from Chelsea as the collection house for plants and seeds from overseas, and in 1772 Banks sent out the first of the Kew Collectors — Francis Masson.

Masson was born in Aberdeen in 1741. Trained as a gardener at Kew, he was despatched to the Cape of Good Hope. This visit and later expeditions yielded about 400 new species, including Stapelias, Ixias, Gazanias, Chincherinchees and Ericas. In 1778–1779 he collected in the Canaries, Tenerife and the West Indies — perhaps the most notable find was the Senecio species from which the present-day Cineraria was evolved. Masson never stopped collecting — he died still searching in North America in 1805.

Perhaps the most surprising name amongst the people who collected plants for Kew was William Bligh. As every film-goer knows, he was the Captain of the *Bounty* and was set adrift by Mr Christian after the famous mutiny.

*Rear-Admiral William Bligh (1754–1817)
Captain of the first sea-borne plant transporter*

Less well know is the fact that the *Bounty* was the first floating plant carrier — it had been sent by Banks to transport Breadfruit plants from Tahiti to the West Indies to provide food for the slaves. His second trip as a Rear-admiral in command of the *Providence* was more successful. The Breadfruit was duly delivered to Kew and in 1793 Bligh brought back Maidenhair Ferns, Philodendron scandens, Peperomia magnoliaefolia and several hundred new species to Kew.

The Kew Collectors organised by Banks continued to search for plants. Caley sent back Cissus antarctica and the Staghorn Fern from Australasia — from the same region of the world Austin and Smith sent back the Norfolk Island Pine in 1793. Allan Cunningham (1791–1839) collected in Brazil, Australia, and New Zealand — James Bowie accompanied Cunningham to South America and then went to South Africa, from where he despatched many of our now-popular Succulents to Kew.

Then it was all over. With the death of Banks in 1820 Kew declined and it was more than 20 years after his death before a collector was again sent out from Kew.

The Horticultural Society of London took over as the new patron. The German Karl Theodor Hartweg (1812–1871) was sent by them to Central and South America in 1836. During the next seven years he sent back many Cacti and Orchids, plus one of the parents of the modern-day Fuchsia hybrids.

From the beginning, of course, there were collectors from other European countries who preceded, succeeded and very occasionally actually bumped into the British collectors. The Dutch East India Company was founded in 1602 and throughout the century remained a powerful force in South Africa and the East Indies. Plants were collected and sent back to Holland — we know that Pelargoniums, Aloes etc from the Cape were being grown in Europe at the start of the 18th century. Carl Pehr Thunberg (1743–1828) was a Swedish doctor in Japan and was permitted to send out plants from this forbidden country. The collection sent by Phillip Franz von Siebold to Europe between 1823 and 1830 was even more important — as an eye surgeon in the employ of the Dutch East India Company he was allowed to roam in Japan whilst it was still closed to the West.

All of the collectors mentioned so far faced a common problem. Living plant specimens had to be transported back to Europe by sea, and the chance of survival was slim — perhaps 1 in 1000 from Australia. Plants were placed within slatted boxes on the deck. Here they had to withstand wide variations in temperature, irregular watering and shortage of light. They had also to face salt from the sea spray, jettisoning overboard when fresh water was short and the gnawing teeth of rats. So until a better method of transport came along the only reliable method of transporting plants was in the form of seeds or bulbs.

A better method did come along — the Wardian Case. In 1843 the Horticultural Society of London sent Robert Fortune to China and he took 18 Wardian Cases with him. As a result he was able to send thousands of Tea Plant seedlings from Shanghai to the Himalayas and so found the Indian tea industry. Plants sent by Fortune to Europe include many Primulas, Azaleas and Chrysanthemums.

At the start of the Wardian Case era a new breed of plant hunter appeared in Britain — the Veitch Collectors. The Royal Exotic Nurseries in Chelsea developed under James Veitch (1815–1869) into the greatest indoor plant nursery of the Victorian era. Between 1840 and 1905 they sent out 22 plant hunters to scour the tropical and sub-tropical region of the world — the 19th century hunger for new conservatory plants had to be fed.

The first of the Veitch Collectors were the Lobb brothers. William was sent out first — in 1840 he sailed for S. America and spent the next 8 years in Brazil and Chile, sending back Sinningia, Begonias, Calatheas and the Monkey Puzzle

The Wardian Case

The hobby of London physician Dr Nathaniel Bagshaw Ward was collecting butterflies. In 1829 he placed a chrysalis in damp soil at the bottom of a wide-mouthed glass jar and sealed the top. He observed the emergence of the moth, but was much more interested in the grass and fern seedlings which appeared. The fern was Dryopteris felix-mas, and Ward knew that it would not survive for long in the smoke-filled air outside the jar. Yet the plants continued to grow in the sealed jar for 4 years without the addition of water, and it occurred to the doctor that he had discovered the way to transport plants by sea.

In 1833 he placed ferns in the damp soil at the bottom of 2 miniature sealed greenhouses (Wardian Cases) and shipped them to Sydney. They travelled safely, and the cases were then filled with native Australian plants for the return journey. These plants arrived back "in the most healthy and vigorous condition". The round trip had taken 8 months, and no water had been added to the soil. Ward published his findings in 1842 and plant collectors around the world quickly put them to use.

Tree. His younger brother Thomas was despatched to Asia in 1843. He visited many countries — Java, India, Burma, Borneo, the Philippines, Malaysia etc, and he sent back to the nursery an extensive collection of plants such as Orchids, Scindapsus, Hoya and Aeschynanthus.

Richard Pearce was another of the early Veitch Collectors. In 1859 he began collecting in S. America, and his important contributions include the parents of the modern Tuberous Begonia and Hippeastrum hybrids. One of the most outstanding of this band of plant collectors was John Gould Veitch, one of the sons of the proprietor of the nursery. He was the first collector to work in Japan when it opened its doors to foreigners. From 1860 until his premature death in 1870 at the age of 31 he collected a vast number of well-known house plants — Pandanus, Dizygotheca, Codiaeums, Aglaonemas and Dracaenas from Japan, Australasia and the Pacific Islands.

There is not enough space to list all the Veitch Collectors — we can pick out the remaining notable ones, such as Charles Maries (China and Japan from 1877) and Gustave Wallis who found Spathiphyllum wallisii (S. America from 1872). Charles Curtis worked for them in Malaysia in the 1880s, and most famous of all was 'Chinese' Wilson who collected for Veitch from 1899 to 1905. Wilson marked the end of an era, an era of 19th century plant hunters who enriched our homes and gardens. He is one of the immortals, but his contribution to the world of house plants was small.

Hunters or Collectors?

The romantic figure of the botanist cutting his way through the dense jungle to discover a new plant really did exist, and continues to do so. John Tradescant was finding plants and fighting off pirates in 1621 — Dr Graf was trekking through remote Brazilian rain forests in the middle of the 20th century.

These people were the plant hunters. Ordinary plant collectors were perhaps less romantic, but no less important to our story. Many house plants were first brought to our shores from gardens in their native home rather than from the wilderness. Coleus, Azalea indica, many Chrysanthemums etc came to us this way. The Creeping Fig and Rubber Tree came from the Calcutta Botanic Gardens — other overseas botanic garden species now grown as house plants include Scindapsus aureus and Begonia masoniana. These plant collectors searched nurseries, gardens and botanical collections rather than jungles and mountains, but their contribution has been a rich one.

With the arrival of the 20th century both the cultivation and search for house plants went into decline for many years, but there are still notable contributions. In the 1970s the parents of the New Guinea Hybrids of Impatiens were collected — in the 1980s Hans Rood brought Radermachera from Taiwan to Holland. From the United States there is Dr Alfred Byrd Graf — President of the Exotic Nurseries of Roehrs Company. He has scoured jungles and mountains in the footsteps of earlier plant hunters and has introduced hundreds of new varieties.

Thomas Rochford III (1904–   )
Nurseryman, collector and pioneer
of the post-war British house plant revival

The Rochford Nursery was the 20th century equivalent in Britain of the Veitch Royal Exotic Nurseries in Victorian times. It was Thomas Rochford III (1904–   ) who led the modern revival of house plants in the U.K. and was responsible for the introduction of many varieties to Britain, including Heptapleurum arboricola and Dracaena marginata tricolor which he collected from Japan during the 1970s.

It is obvious that this century will not yield a crop of romantic names like 'Chinese' Wilson, Robert Fortune, J. G. Veitch and the Lobb brothers. This is the age of the hybridist rather than the discoverer. Still, there is a plant in some isolated tropical place waiting for the old-style hunter to bring it back to cooler shores and give us an exciting new house plant for the 1990s.

CHAPTER 8
FLOWERING POT PLANTS

Don't choose a flowering pot plant if you want something which will permanently adorn your living room. Unlike the flowering house plants members of this group can only be temporary residents, and once the flowers fade their display days are over. This lack of permanence is, of course, a disadvantage but it has its own attraction. Like the days of a short and exciting holiday, they must be enjoyed *now*.

An important group of flowering pot plants, sometimes known as 'florist' or 'gift' plants, have an essential part to play in the indoor plant scene. During the dark winter months they provide a welcome splash of colour when garden flowers are absent and cut flowers are expensive.

The Azalea, Poinsettia, Cyclamen, Solanum and Chrysanthemum, bought in bud or full flower, are found in countless homes as the first flowers to welcome in the New Year.

The second important group are the Garden Bulbs, providing an ever-popular spring display. The remaining flowering pot plants are a mixed bag — quick-growing climbers such as Gloriosa and Thunbergia, shrubs like Cytisus and Punica, and scores of pretty annuals like Browallia, Exacum and many garden favourites. Also included are a number of indoor (non-hardy) bulbs.

With practically all of them, after a few weeks or perhaps months, the flowers will fade and the leaves will fall. This is not your fault, because it is a basic feature of the group. Of course, flower fading and leaf fall should not take place in a matter of days — this would indicate that you were doing something wrong. As a general rule flowering pot plants need bright, cool conditions and moist compost — warm air is the biggest enemy of all.

However skilful you are, flowering will come to an end and the A-Z guide will tell you what to do with each plant. Many have to be thrown away, but some can be made to provide another display next season. As the following pages reveal, millions of flowering pot plants are needlessly thrown away every year.

ACHIMENES

Each Achimenes bloom is short-lived, but the flowering season extends from early summer to mid autumn. The stems are weak and wiry, making this plant an excellent subject for a hanging basket. If you want to grow it as a bushy plant then pinch out the tips of young shoots and provide support for tall stems. Proper care is quite easy — just keep the plant reasonably warm and make sure that the compost does not dry out.

Temperature: Average warmth; not less than 55°F during the growing season.
Light: Bright light away from summer sun.
Water: Keep the compost moist at all times during the growing season with tepid water.
Air Humidity: Mist occasionally around the plant with tepid water. Do not wet leaves.
Care After Flowering: Stop watering once flowering has finished. Store rhizomes in dry peat in a frost-free room. Plant in compost (½ – 1 in. deep) in early spring.
Propagation: Separate rhizomes at planting time.

stems 6–12 in. high

leaf 1–1½ in. across — heart-shaped, serrated and velvety

trumpet-like flared flower

ACHIMENES HYBRIDA
Cupid's Bower
(Hot Water Plant)

TYPES

Achimenes erecta (a trailer despite its name) produces 18 in. long reddish stems and red blooms — **A. longiflora** is a bigger plant, growing 2 ft high when staked and with 3 in. long leaves. Its flowers are purple. These species are not easy to find — at your local shop you will be offered one of the many types of **A. hybrida**. These compact plants are available in many colours — red, pink, purple, blue, white and yellow, and are much used in hanging baskets. Named types include **Rose** and **Little Beauty** (pink), **Purple King** and **Paul Arnold** (purple), **Valse Bleu** (blue) and **Ambroise Verschaffelt** (white, veined purple).

Achimenes hybrida English Waltz

AZALEA

Countless Azaleas are bought every year at Christmas time to provide decoration during the holiday season and into the New Year. By far the more usual type is the Indian Azalea. When buying a plant pick one with a few open flowers and a mass of buds. Without correct care the flowers wilt and the leaves drop in a week or two. The secret of keeping a plant in bloom for many weeks and capable of coming back into flower the following year is to keep it wet (not just moist), distinctly cool and brightly lit. Remove faded flowers promptly.

Temperature: Cool; 50°–60°F is ideal.
Light: Brightly lit spot away from direct sunlight.
Water: Keep the compost wet at all times, using soft water.
Air Humidity: Mist leaves daily during flowering season.
Care After Flowering: Move to a cool but frost-free room; continue watering. Place pot in a shady spot in the garden once the danger of frost is past — keep fed, watered and sprayed until early autumn. Bring into a cool room; when flowers open move into display area.

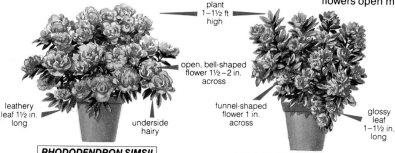

plant 1–1½ ft high

open, bell-shaped flower 1½–2 in. across

funnel-shaped flower 1 in. across

leathery leaf 1½ in. long

underside hairy

glossy leaf 1–1½ in. long

RHODODENDRON SIMSII
(AZALEA INDICA)
Azalea
(Indian Azalea)

RHODODENDRON OBTUSUM
Japanese Azalea
(Kurume Azalea)

TYPES

The variety range of **R. simsii** covers single and double blooms in white, red, pink and orange. The Japanese Azalea **R. obtusum** is much less popular. The blooms are smaller and less numerous, but it has the distinct advantage of thriving as a garden shrub if planted out when flowering is over.

Rhododendron obtusum Coral Bells

BEGONIA

● TUBEROUS TYPES

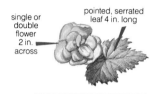

pointed, serrated leaf 6–9 in. long

single or double flower 3–5 in. across

BEGONIA TUBERHYBRIDA

brittle leaf 4 in. across

stems and flower-stalks thin and pendent

flower 2–3 in. across

BEGONIA TUBERHYBRIDA PENDULA
Basket Begonia

single or double flower 2 in. across

pointed, serrated leaf 4 in. long

BEGONIA MULTIFLORA

There are many begonias which can be used as part of the permanent collection of plants in the home — see pages 48 and 127. There are also begonias which are used as temporary residents to provide a splash of winter colour or summer display, and the three groups of pot plant types are shown here.

The most spectacular ones are the Tuberous Begonias, which bloom in summer and autumn. Included here are the pendulous Basket Begonias. All of them can be raised by planting tubers in spring in boxes of moist peat. Keep at 60°–70°F and when shoots are a couple of inches high transplant into 5 in. pots. Repot later into 8 in. pots. At the end of the flowering season withhold water, cut off shoots, lift tubers and store in peat.

The second group are the Lorraine or Cheimantha Hybrids, which are old favourites as they bloom around Christmas. The third group, the Hiemalis Hybrids, have been greatly improved in recent years. They can be bought in flower at any season and will last for months with proper care.

● LORRAINE TYPES

white or pink flower 1 in. across

glossy, round leaf 3 in. across

green stems

BEGONIA CHEIMANTHA
Lorraine Begonia

● HIEMALIS TYPES

flower 2 in. across

glossy, round leaf 3 in. across

red stems

BEGONIA FIREGLOW

SECRETS OF SUCCESS

Temperature: Average warmth; not less than 55°F in winter. Avoid temperatures above 70°F.

Light: A bright spot away from direct sunlight. A few hours of winter sun are beneficial.

Water: Water freely when plant is in flower, but do not keep compost constantly soggy.

Air Humidity: Moist air needed — surround pots with damp peat and mist air around plant.

Care After Flowering: Tuberous Begonias — see above. Other types are usually discarded; otherwise cut back and keep cool with little water. Increase water in spring. New shoots can be used as cuttings.

SPECIAL PROBLEMS

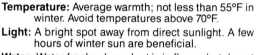

BROWN BLOTCHES, TURNING GREY & MOULDY
Cause: Botrytis. Move away from other Begonias, cut off diseased parts and spray with a systemic fungicide. Avoid low light and over-damp conditions. Improve ventilation.

INSECTS
Keep watch for aphid and red spider mite.

YELLOWING LEAVES
Cause: Too little light; too little or too much water. Look for other symptoms.

LOSS OF LEAVES
Cause: There are a number of possible causes and you must look for other symptoms. There is not enough light if the stems are thin and leggy; too much heat if leaves are dry and curled; and too much water if leaves are wilted and rotten.

LEAVES WITH BROWN TIPS
Cause: Air humidity too low. Follow rules in Secrets of Success.

PALE, ROTTING LEAVES
Cause: Overwatering. Follow rules in Secrets of Success.

WHITE POWDERY SPOTS
Cause: Powdery mildew. Move away from other Begonias, cut off diseased leaves and spray with a systemic fungicide. Avoid over-damp conditions and low temperatures. Improve ventilation.

FLOWER BUDS DROP
Cause: Dry air or underwatering.

PLANT COLLAPSE
Cause: Several possible reasons — stem rot disease due to overwatering, root knot eelworm (look for swollen bumps on roots) or vine weevil (look for tunnels in tubers). Read Chapter 15.

BEGONIA TYPES

The most popular Tuberous Begonias are the **B. tuberhybrida** hybrids — single, semi-double and double in a wide range of colours and colour combinations. The 1 ft tall fleshy-stemmed plants bear large and showy male flowers and smaller female ones. **B. multiflora** flowers are similar in shape, but they are more numerous and smaller. The Basket Begonias are varieties of **B. tuberhybrida pendula** — the flowers are single or semi-double in white, yellow, pink, orange and red. The non-tuberous Begonias are raised from seed or bought in pots. The Lorraine Hybrids (e.g **Gloire de Lorraine**) have **B. cheimantha** as a parent — they are old favourites for winter flowering. In recent years the Rieger-Elatior strain of Hiemalis Hybrids have taken over as the most popular bushy Begonias. Named varieties include **Fireglow, Schwabenland** and **Heidi** (red), and **Elfe** (pink).

Begonia tuberhybrida Judy Langdon

Begonia tuberhybrida pendula Bridal Cascade

Begonia Heidi

BROWALLIA

Browallia major

The Bush Violet is usually bought in flower, but it can be easily raised from seed. Sow in early spring for summer flowers or delay sowing until summer for winter flowering. Pinch out the growing tips occasionally to promote bushiness. With proper care the flowering period will last for many weeks — keep the pot in a cool room where it will receive some direct sunlight. Feed regularly and pick off the flowers as they fade.

SECRETS OF SUCCESS

Temperature: Cool; 50°–60°F is ideal during the flowering season.

Light: Bright light with some direct sun.

Water: Keep the compost moist at all times.

Air Humidity: Mist leaves occasionally.

Care After Flowering: Plant should be discarded.

Propagation: Sow seeds in spring or summer.

star-shaped tubular flower 2 in. across

drooping leaf 2 in. long

BROWALLIA SPECIOSA
Bush Violet

TYPES

B. speciosa bears violet flowers with white throats. The stems are weak — stake to maintain bushy shape. Varieties **major** (large, blue-violet) and **alba** (white) are available.

CALCEOLARIA

pouch-like flower 1–2 in. across

hairy leaf 4–6 in. across

CALCEOLARIA HERBEOHYBRIDA
Slipper Flower

The Slipper Flower is a springtime favourite. The soft leaves are large and hairy and the flowers are curious and colourful. They are pouch-shaped in yellow, orange, red or white with dark-coloured spots or blotches. The plant is bought in flower (propagation is a skilled job best left to the nurseryman) and should last about a month if kept in a cool spot which is brightly lit. Provide moist conditions — stand the pot on a pebble tray or surround with moist peat. Keep away from draughts, keep water off the leaves and flowers when watering and keep careful watch for aphids.

SECRETS OF SUCCESS

Temperature: Cool; 50°–60°F is ideal.

Light: Bright light away from direct sunlight.

Water: Keep compost moist at all times.

Air Humidity: Mist occasionally around the plant — take care not to wet leaves or flowers.

Care After Flowering: Plant should be discarded.

Propagation: Difficult; sow seeds in summer in a cool greenhouse for flowering next year.

CAPSICUM

One of the popular names of this plant is Christmas Pepper, as large quantities are sold in December to provide traditional colour during the festive season. The plants should remain attractive for 2 or 3 months with care. Some direct sunlight is essential, and the compost must never be allowed to dry out. Hot dry air will cause the fruit to fall, and attacks of aphid and red spider mite are likely.

SECRETS OF SUCCESS

Temperature: Cool or average warmth; not less than 55°F.

Light: Brightly lit spot with morning or afternoon sun.

Water: Keep the compost moist at all times. Water occasionally by the immersion method (see page 227).

Air Humidity: Mist the leaves frequently.

Care After Flowering: Plant should be discarded.

Propagation: Difficult; sow seeds in early spring.

TYPES

There are many varieties of **C. annuum** but these are rarely named in the shops. A few bear ball-like fruits, but the popular types bear erect cone-like peppers. These may be 1 in. **(Christmas Greeting)** or 2 in. **(Fiesta)** and the usual pattern is for them to change from green to yellow and finally red. There are variations — some varieties bear purple fruits (**Variegated Flash** is an example) and some are in full colour in summer — making the common name rather meaningless. These Christmas Peppers have been bred from Chilli Peppers and Cayenne Peppers, so the ornamental fruits are edible . . . but fiery and best avoided.

white, star-shaped flowers followed by fruit

oval leaf 4 in. long

upright fruits darkening with age

CAPSICUM ANNUUM
Christmas Pepper

Capsicum annuum Red Missile

❝ It is but recently that the beauty of leaves has been fully recognised, and the passion that has arisen for collecting and cultivating fine foliaged plants is one of the newest, but it is not at all likely to be transient. We do now and then hear that Ferns are less cared for than formerly, and perhaps we shall soon be told that Begonias, Caladiums, Palms, Cycads and Yuccas have had their day. Nevertheless, we do not anticipate that a single plant figured in this work will be less interesting fifty years hence than now . . . **❞**

Shirley Hibberd
New and Rare Beautiful-Leaved Plants (1869)

CELOSIA

There are two distinct types of this showy pot plant. Celosia plumosa has feathery plumes; C. cristata has a curious velvety 'cockscomb'. Celosia is sometimes sold for bedding outdoors, but it can be kept in full flower for many weeks indoors. Some direct sunlight during the day is essential, and regular feeding is necessary. It needs cool, airy conditions to prolong the flowering season. The usual height is 1½–2 ft. Celosia can be raised from seed, but it is usually more satisfactory to buy nursery-grown plants.

conical flower-head 6–9 in. long

lance-shaped leaf 4 in. long

CELOSIA PLUMOSA
Plume Flower

TYPES

C. plumosa bears its red or yellow plumes in summer — dwarfs (8–12 in.) such as **Golden Plume** and **Kewpie** are available. **C. cristata** has a yellow, orange or red convoluted flower-head.

SECRETS OF SUCCESS

Temperature: Cool; 50°–60°F is ideal.

Light: As much light as possible, but shade from hot summer sun.

Water: Keep compost moist at all times.

Air Humidity: Mist leaves occasionally.

Care After Flowering: Plant should be discarded.

Propagation: Sow seeds in spring at 60°–65°F.

Celosia cristata

CHRYSANTHEMUM

Decorative varieties of Chrysanthemum have been popular as greenhouse plants for many years, and the multitude of varieties are listed in gardening books and catalogues. More recently the Pot Chrysanthemum has become a favourite pot plant. The nurseryman uses chemicals to dwarf its growth and keeps it in the dark for part of the day to make it bloom on a set date. By this means Pot Chrysanthemums, less than 1 ft high but large-flowered in every colour but blue, are offered for sale in bloom throughout the year. If you choose your plant carefully and look after it properly then it should stay in bloom for 6–8 weeks. In the shop there should be a few open blooms and a mass of buds which are showing colour. At home place the pot in a cool room on a windowsill where it will get some early morning or evening sunlight.

By comparison the other Chrysanthemum types are almost rarities. The Marguerites, with daisy-like flowers and fern-like foilage, are summer-flowering. The Charm Chrysanthemums are rather similar in shape but the flowers are much smaller and more numerous. The Cascade Chrysanthemums are extremely graceful, their pendent stems covered with hundreds of tiny blooms.

single flower 2–3 in. across

plant 1–1½ ft high

grey-green ferny leaf 2–4 in. long

CHRYSANTHEMUM FRUTESCENS
Marguerite

single or double flower 2–4 in. across

plant 1 ft high

dark green lobed leaf 3–5 in. long

CHRYSANTHEMUM MORIFOLIUM
Pot Chrysanthemum

plant 1–2 ft high

single flower 1 in. across

CHRYSANTHEMUM MORIFOLIUM CHARM
Charm Chrysanthemum

small leaves almost hidden by flowers

daisy-like flower 1–1½ in. across

CHRYSANTHEMUM MORIFOLIUM CASCADE
Cascade Chrysanthemum

SECRETS OF SUCCESS

Temperature: Cool; 50°–60°F is ideal.

Light: Bright light is essential, but Pot Chrysanthemums must be shaded from midday sun.

Water: Keep the compost moist at all times. It may be necessary to water several times each week.

Air Humidity: Mist the leaves occasionally.

Care After Flowering: Most plants are discarded, but Pot Chrysanthemums can be planted out in the garden where, if they survive, they will revert to their natural growth habit.

Propagation: Raising Pot Chrysanthemums is for the professional. Marguerites — take stem cuttings in early summer. Cascade and Charm Chrysanthemums — sow seeds in spring.

SPECIAL PROBLEMS

WILTED LEAVES
Cause: Underwatering is the most likely reason. Even a short period of dryness will lead to wilting and this generally causes the lower leaves to fall.

SHORT FLOWERING PERIOD
Cause: The plant is too warm. Temperatures of 70°–75°F result in the flowers rapidly opening and then wilting.

FLOWER BUDS FAIL TO OPEN
Cause: Two major reasons cause buds not to open. The buds may have been all-green when the plant was purchased or the plant was not placed in a bright enough spot.

INSECTS
Aphid and red spider mite can be a problem; see Chapter 15.

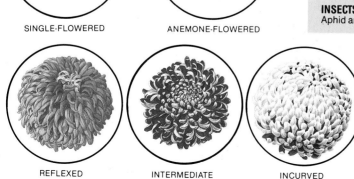

SINGLE-FLOWERED

ANEMONE-FLOWERED

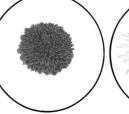

REFLEXED

INTERMEDIATE

INCURVED

POMPON

SPIDERY-FLOWERED

Chrysanthemum morifolium Princess Anne

CHRYSANTHEMUM TYPES

Unlike the ordinary types of **C. morifolium** which are grown in the greenhouse, the **Pot Chrysanthemum** is usually bought by colour and not by variety name. The **Charm Chrysanthemum** is a variety of C. morifolium which produces its single flowers so abundantly in summer and autumn that the foliage may be almost entirely covered. White, orange, yellow, pink and red strains are available. You will have to raise your own plants from seed — the same course of action is necessary for obtaining specimens of **Cascade Chrysanthemums.** The trailing stems can be trained into decorative shapes on wire frames — a mass of flowers cover the stems in late summer and autumn. The baby of the house plant Chrysanthemums is the **Mini-Mum** (single flowers, 6–8 in. high).

Marguerites (**C. frutescens**) are generally summer flowering. The central disc of each flower is yellow — the surrounding petals may be white, yellow or pink.

Chrysanthemum morifolium Charm Pink

CATHARANTHUS

You will probably have to raise this uncommon house plant from seed if you want to see what it looks like — few nurserymen offer it for sale. Seed sown in late winter will produce plants which start to flower in late spring and stay in bloom until the autumn. The periwinkle-like flowers form at the stem tips and may cover much of the shiny foliage. Catharanthus is an easy plant to grow, but it is not worth trying to overwinter it, so treat as a flowering pot plant.

Catharanthus roseus

star-shaped flower 1–1½ in. across
oval leaf 2 in. long

CATHARANTHUS ROSEUS
(VINCA ROSEA)
Madagascar Periwinkle

SECRETS OF SUCCESS

Temperature: Average warmth; not less than 50°F.

Light: Bright light with some sun.

Water: Keep the compost moist at all times.

Air Humidity: Mist leaves occasionally.

Care After Flowering: Plant should be discarded.

Propagation: Sow seeds in late winter or early spring.

TYPES

C. roseus bears lavender or rose-pink flowers with a darker-coloured throat. The plant is compact and bushy and the leaves have a pale midrib. White varieties are available.

COSTUS

The place for Costus is a greenhouse, conservatory or plant window — it will quickly deteriorate in the darker and drier conditions of the living room. The leaves are large and in some species attractively marked — they spiral around the reddish stem. The flat, bright orange flowers appear in late spring — colourful but short-lived. Costus has a resting period in winter when most or all of the leaves die — cut back and new growth will appear. Moist air and direct sunlight are essential.

ragged-petalled flower 2 in. across

glossy leaf 5 in. long

COSTUS IGNEUS
Spiral Ginger

TYPES

The species to grow is **C. igneus** — 1½ ft tall and the most popular Spiral Ginger. The other species are large and spreading. Examples are **C. speciosus** (6 ft) and **C. lucanusianus** (5 ft).

SECRETS OF SUCCESS

Temperature: Warm or average warmth; not less than 55°F in winter.

Light: As much light as possible, but shade from midday summer sun.

Water: Keep the compost very moist during growing season.

Air Humidity: Stand pot on a pebble tray or surround with damp peat.

Repotting: Repot, when necessary, in spring.

Propagation: Divide plants at repotting time.

Costus igneus

daisy-like
flower 1–3 in.
across

plant
¾–2½ ft
tall

heart-shaped
leaf up to
8 in. across

underside
usually
purple

SENECIO CRUENTUS
(SENECIO HYBRIDUS)
Cineraria

CINERARIA

A well-grown Cineraria (proper name Senecio cruentus) is always a welcome gift. Masses of daisy-like flowers cover the soft, heart-shaped leaves and the colour range is impressive — white, blue, purple, pink and red varieties are available. The showiest strain is the Grandiflora group — large-flowered plants about 18 in. high. The tallest Cinerarias are varieties belonging to the Stellata group, reaching a height of 2 ft or more with small, star-shaped flowers. At the other end of the scale is the Nana group, small and compact, with masses of brightly-coloured flowers.

Buy plants with some open flowers and masses of unopened buds. They should last for 4 – 6 weeks. Unfortunately Cineraria can be a disappointing plant and will collapse in a week or two in a hot room or if it is not watered properly.

SPECIAL PROBLEMS

YELLOWING, WILTED FOLIAGE
Cause: Cold draughts are the usual culprit, although wilting is the first sign of underwatering. A wilted plant may recover if watered and moved to a draught-free spot, but the flowering period is bound to be shortened.

SHORT FLOWERING PERIOD
Cause: Too much warmth; temperature above 60°F speeds up flower death. Too much sun and too little water can also bring flowering to a premature end.

SUDDEN PLANT COLLAPSE
Cause: Waterlogging due to overwatering or poor drainage.

INSECTS
Both aphid and whitefly can be a nuisance. See Chapter 15.

SECRETS OF SUCCESS

Temperature: Cool; 45° – 55°F is ideal.

Light: Bright light away from direct sunlight.

Water: Keep the compost moist at all times with tepid water. Take care not to overwater.

Air Humidity: Stand pot on a pebble tray (see page 27) or surround with damp peat. Occasionally mist air around the plant.

Care After Flowering: Plant should be discarded.

Propagation: Not easy; sow seeds in midsummer in a cool greenhouse.

TYPES

There are scores of **S. cruentus** hybrids, varying in height, colour and flower form. The usual flower form is the typical daisy pattern — a central boss of stamens and a ring of wide or narrow petals. In the Grandiflora group the petals generally have an inner white ring and with a typical Cineraria the flower-head measures about 9 in. across. Double-flowered types in which the central disc is hidden by petals are available, but they are not popular.

The growth form is a leafy bush — large and rounded in the Grandifloras (which occasionally needs staking) or small and compact with the Multiflora Nana group. The exception is the Stellata group — the stems are branched and spreading. Cinerarias are bought between late winter and mid spring — after brightening the home for several weeks they are thrown away.

GRANDIFLORA
bloom 2–3 in.
plant 1½–2 ft

DOUBLE
bloom 2 in.
plant 1–2 ft

Exhibition Mixed (grandiflora strain. Height 1½ ft)
Spring Glory (multiflora nana strain. Height 9 in.)
Gaytime (multiflora nana strain. Height 10 in.)
Triumph (multiflora nana strain. Height 1 ft)
Gubler's Mixed (double strain. Height 1½ ft)
Mixed Star (double strain. Height 2 ft)

MULTIFLORA NANA
bloom 1–2 in.
plant ¾–1¼ ft

STELLATA
bloom 1–1½ in.
plant 2–2½ ft

Senecio cruentus Exhibition Mixed

Senecio cruentus Spring Glory

Senecio cruentus Gubler's Mixed

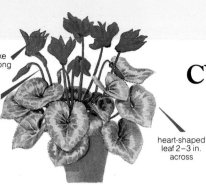

shuttlecock-like
flower 1–2 in. long

slender
flower-stalk
9–12 in. tall

heart-shaped
leaf 2–3 in.
across

CYCLAMEN PERSICUM
Cyclamen

CYCLAMEN

The charm of Cyclamen is obvious — compact growth, beautiful swept-back flowers on long stalks and decorative foliage which is patterned in silver and green. The blooms are in bright colours or pastel shades, large and eye-catching or small and perfumed.

Most Cyclamens are unfortunately consigned to the dustbin after a few weeks. With care they will bloom indoors for several months and then can be kept to provide another display next winter. First of all, try to buy a plant in autumn and not mid winter, and choose one with plenty of unopened buds. Then put it in a suitable home; a north-facing windowsill is ideal. The spot must be cool and away from direct sunlight; a warm room means a short life for a Cyclamen.

SPECIAL PROBLEMS

YELLOWING FOLIAGE, CROWN FIRM & HEALTHY
Cause: Hot, dry air is the usual reason; Cyclamen dislikes temperatures above 60°F. Other possible causes are underwatering and direct sunlight.

PLANT COLLAPSE, CROWN SOFT & ROTTEN
Cause: Overwatering, especially from above. Never let water stand on the fleshy crown.

SHORT FLOWERING PERIOD
Cause: There are many possible reasons — too much warmth, incorrect watering and dry air are common causes. Feed regularly during the growing and flowering season.

TWISTED, STUNTED LEAVES
Cause: Cyclamen mite; see page 244 for details.

GREY MOULD ON LEAVES & CROWN
Cause: Botrytis; spray with carbendazim. Remove dead flowers and leaves promptly. Twist and pull; do not cut.

SECRETS OF SUCCESS

Temperature: Cool; 50°–60°F is ideal.

Light: Bright light away from direct sunlight.

Water: Keep the compost moist at all times. Employ the immersion method (see page 227), using soft, tepid water.

Air Humidity: Stand pot on a pebble tray (see page 27) or surround with damp peat. Occasionally mist air around the plant.

Care After Flowering: Reduce watering and stop feeding. Place pot on its side in a cool spot and keep it dry until midsummer. Then repot using fresh compost, burying the tuber to half its depth. Stand the pot in a cool, well-lit spot; water to keep the compost moist.

Propagation: Sow seeds in late summer at 60°–70°F. It will take 15–18 months to flower.

TYPES

The wild **C. persicum** of the Middle East has narrow, pink petals — the hybrids which first began to appear about 100 years ago are sometimes listed as **C. persicum giganteum**. These plants have wide petals which may be frilled and are available in many colours — white, pink, red, purple and salmon. Fragrant varieties are available and the foliage is usually edged, marbled or lined in white. This leaf patterning is sometimes bold enough to rival the flowers in display value.

Cyclamens are bought in vast numbers between autumn and early spring. You can save the tubers for planting in summer but it is usually better to buy fresh ones. You can also raise Cyclamen from seed, but germination is slow and erratic and you will have to wait about 1½ years for the plants to bloom.

Once there were only standard-sized hybrids but now there are also dwarfs with pretty scented flowers on stalks which are only a few inches high.

Standard varieties: Height 9–12 in.
 Triumph strain. Large and abundant flowers. Attractive leaves.
 Rex strain. Compact plants. Leaves boldly marbled in silver — the best for foliage display.
 Ruffled strain. Fringed petals in pink, red and mauve.
 Decora strain. Noted for pastel shades (salmon, lavender, etc) and attractive foliage.
 Grandia strain. Large flowers with frilled and wavy petals.
 Firmament strain. Noted for early flowering.
 Fuzzy-Wuzzy strain. Bearded petals.
 Other standard varieties include **Cardinal** (red), **Cattleya** (lavender), **Pannevis** strain and the bicoloured **Victoria**.

Dwarf varieties: Height 7 in. or less
 Puppet strain. Scented flowers.
 Kaori strain. Scented flowers with distinct eye. Attractive foliage.
 Symphony strain. Scented flowers. Reputed to withstand central heating.
 Other dwarf varieties include **Mini-Sirius**, **Mini-Dresden** strain and **Mirabel** strain.

Cyclamen persicum Decora

Cyclamen persicum Suttons Puppet

CYTISUS

Two types of Cytisus are commonly called Genista and are sold for indoor cultivation — C. canariensis and the more attractive C. racemosus. These shrubs are included in this section because, unlike true house plants, they must spend their summers outdoors. They are stood out after the shoots which have borne flowers are cut back. In early autumn the plants are brought back indoors and kept in a cool but frost-free room. In mid winter they are moved to a bright, warmer spot and watered more freely to promote growth and flowering.

pea-like flower ¾ in. long

silky leaflet ½ in. long

CYTISUS RACEMOSUS
Genista

TYPES

Cytisus outdoors is called Broom — indoors it is Genista. Long sprays of fragrant yellow flowers appear in spring at the end of arching branches. Choose **C. racemosus** rather than **C. canariensis**.

SECRETS OF SUCCESS

Temperature: Cool; not less than 40°F in winter.

Light: Well-lit during flowering season; light shade in winter.

Water: Water liberally during flowering season; sparingly in winter.

Air Humidity: Mist frequently during flowering season.

Repotting: Repot, when necessary, after flowering.

Propagation: Stem cuttings in summer; use rooting hormone.

Cytisus racemosus

DAHLIA

Pot Dahlias are much less popular than Pot Chrysanthemums. They are beginning to appear at garden centres and a wide variety of flower forms and colours are available. These plants are natural miniatures — they are not artificially dwarfed like their chrysanthemum counterparts. One advantage is that they can be raised from seed. Treat like Pot Chrysanthemums — keep well-lit, well-watered and in a cool place.

SECRETS OF SUCCESS

Temperature: Cool, 50°–60°F is ideal.

Light: Bright light is essential, but shade from midday sun.

Water: Keep the compost moist at all times.

Air Humidity: Mist the leaves occasionally.

Care After Flowering: Plant should be discarded.

Propagation: Sow seeds in spring.

Dahlia Figaro

single or double flower 2 in. across

oval leaflet 2 in. long

DAHLIA VARIABILIS
Pot Dahlia

TYPES

The Pot Dahlias are hybrids of **D. variabilis**. They grow about 1 ft high and you will find them listed as Bedding Dahlias in the seed catalogues. Varieties include **Figaro**, **Rigoletto**, **Redskin** and **Dahl-Face**.

DIANTHUS

fragrant flower 1½ in. across

You may occasionally find pots of Dianthus for sale in the house plant section of a garden centre. You will not, however, find them in the textbooks — neither the Annual Pink nor the Annual Carnation are accepted as pot plants. They do need cool conditions and are not always long-lasting, but they are easily raised from seed and the white, pink or red frilly-edged blooms are attractive. Give them a well-lit spot and do not let the compost dry out. Provide fresh air on hot days.

grass-like leaf 2 in. long

DIANTHUS CHINENSIS
Annual Pink

TYPES

The Annual (Indian) Pinks are hybrids of **D. chinensis** — look for **Baby Doll**, **Snowflake** or **Telstar**. The Annual Carnations (hybrids of **D. caryophyllus**) have blooms which are larger and double.

SECRETS OF SUCCESS

Temperature: Cool; 50°–60°F is ideal.

Light: Bright light is essential, but shade from midday sun.

Water: Keep the compost moist at all times.

Air Humidity: Mist the leaves occasionally.

Care After Flowering: Plant should be discarded.

Propagation: Sow seeds in spring.

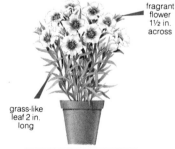

Dianthus caryophyllus

ERICA

The Ericas are small shrubby plants which are bought in flower during the winter months. Their tiny leaves and masses of bell-shaped flowers are attractive, but these plants will give disappointing results in a centrally heated room. In hot, dry air the leaves drop very rapidly, so only choose an Erica for winter decoration if you can provide a cool and well-lit spot. Pay careful attention to watering — never use hard water and make sure that the compost is never allowed to dry out. There are two popular varieties to choose from — E. gracilis bears tiny globular pink or pale purple flowers, E. hyemalis bears larger tubular flowers which are pink with white tips.

SECRETS OF SUCCESS

Temperature: Cool; must be kept at 40°–55°F when in flower.
Light: Bright light; some direct sun is beneficial.
Water: Keep the compost moist at all times; frequent watering may be necessary. Use soft water.
Air Humidity: Mist leaves frequently.
Care After Flowering: Plant is usually discarded. To keep for a second year, trim back shoots after flowering and stand pot outdoors during summer.
Propagation: Not easy. Stem cuttings in late summer; use rooting hormone.

Erica canaliculata

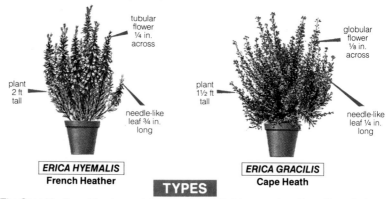

tubular flower ¼ in. across
plant 2 ft tall
needle-like leaf ¾ in. long

ERICA HYEMALIS
French Heather

globular flower ⅛ in. across
plant 1½ ft tall
needle-like leaf ¼ in. long

ERICA GRACILIS
Cape Heath

TYPES

The Cape Heath and its close relatives are bought in bloom and are then discarded once the flowering period is over. There are needle-like leaves and masses of small flowers — **E. gracilis** is more popular than the larger-flowering **E. hyemalis.** The Christmas Heather (**E. canaliculata**) bears tiny white blooms with black centres. There is a midsummer-flowering heather — the white or mauve **E. ventricosa** (2 ft).

Handle-with-Care Plants

Within the indoor plant kingdom there are very few plants which call for caution. Only one (Nerium oleander) can lead to serious trouble — the wood should never be burnt or thrown on a fire as the smoke is highly toxic. The sap of Dieffenbachia can be distinctly unpleasant if allowed to come in contact with the mouth or throat, but the effect is not permanent.

Spines can be a problem — keep sharp-leaved Bromeliads, Pandanus and Cacti well away from inquisitive little fingers and well out of the line of traffic. Finally there are the allergies — some people are allergic to the leaves of Primula obconica and to the pollen of Exacum and Poinsettia.

EXACUM

fragrant gold-centred flower ½ in. across
shiny leaf 1 in long

EXACUM AFFINE
Arabian Violet

TYPE

Raise **E. affine** from seed or buy as a pot plant. An easy to care for plant but it does dislike draughts. Remove dead flowers regularly to prolong display.

Exacum is a small plant, a few inches high when offered for sale. Its flowers, pale purple with a yellow centre, are also small, but this plant still has several points in its favour. The blooms are abundant and fragrant, and the flowering season extends from midsummer to late autumn. Keep the plants reasonably cool and in good light. To ensure the maximum flowering period, pick a plant which is mainly in bud and not in full flower.

SECRETS OF SUCCESS

Temperature: Cool or average warmth; keep at 50°–70°F.
Light: Bright light; protect from hot summer sun.
Water: Keep compost moist at all times.
Air Humidity: Mist leaves frequently.
Care After Flowering: Plant should be discarded.
Propagation: Sow seeds in late summer.

Exacum affine Starlight Fragrance

FUCHSIA

plant 1–3 ft high

flower 1½–3 in. long

slightly serrated leaf 1–2 in. long

FUCHSIA HYBRIDA

Fuchsias occur in a wide range of colours, shapes and sizes. There are hundreds of named varieties of F. hybrida, with the familiar bell-shaped flowers hanging from the stems. These blooms may be single, semi-double or double, with colour combinations of white, pink, red or purple. A collection of these hybrids can provide blooms from spring to autumn, and some experts regard the Fuchsia as the most satisfactory of all flowering house plants.

Unfortunately nearly all of the plants bought for home decoration or as gifts are consigned to the dustbin once flowering stops and the leaves begin to fall. It is, however, quite easy to overwinter the plant in a cool room. The leaves will fall but growth begins again in the spring and with proper care the plant can be kept for many years. Flowers are borne on new growth, so cut back the stems in early spring just before growth begins.

Regular training and pruning are necessary to keep the plant free-flowering and shapely. With young plants pinch out the stem tips to promote bushy growth, and with flowering plants remove dead blooms to induce bud formation.

SECRETS OF SUCCESS

Temperature: Cool or average warmth; plant may suffer if temperature exceeds 70°F. Keep at 50°–60°F in winter.

Light: Bright light away from direct sunshine.

Water: Keep the compost moist at all times from spring to autumn. Water sparingly in winter.

Air Humidity: Mist leaves occasionally during the growing season.

Repotting: Repot every year in spring.

Propagation: Stem cuttings in spring or summer. Use rooting hormone.

BUSH   TRAILER   STANDARD

SPECIAL PROBLEMS

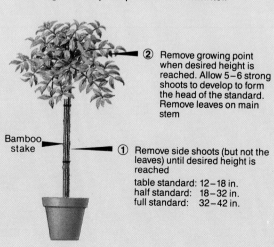

HOW TO MAKE A FLOWERING STANDARD
Choose a vigorous upright variety. Use a rooted cutting and keep the plant well-lit in winter.

② Remove growing point when desired height is reached. Allow 5–6 strong shoots to develop to form the head of the standard. Remove leaves on main stem

Bamboo stake

① Remove side shoots (but not the leaves) until desired height is reached

table standard: 12–18 in.
half standard: 18–32 in.
full standard: 32–42 in.

LOSS OF LEAVES
Cause: Hot dry atmosphere is the usual reason for general leaf fall; mist leaves occasionally and stand the plant outdoors in hot weather. The common causes of the progressive loss of lower leaves are underwatering and lack of light.

FLOWER BUDS DROP
Cause: Poor watering (too much or too little) is the common cause. Other possibilities are too little light, too much heat and moving or turning the pot.

POOR FLOWERING
Cause: Many factors can shorten the flowering period. Keeping the plant moist and warm in winter will certainly have this effect; so will too little food or water and too little light.

BROWN SPOTS WITH YELLOW MARGINS ON LEAVES
Cause: Leaf spot disease, encouraged by over-watering in cold weather.

INSECTS
Both red spider mite and whitefly can be serious in hot and dry conditions— see page 244.

FUCHSIA TYPES

F. hybrida is deservedly a popular house plant. There are hundreds of named hybrids — in nearly all cases the colour is derived from both the showy sepals and petals, which may or may not be the same colour. These are the familiar Fuchsia flowers — single, semi-double or double bells on soft-stemmed bushes. To induce bushiness, pinch out the tip after 3 sets of leaves have formed. When each of the resulting side shoots has developed 3 sets of leaves, repeat the pinching-out operation. Remove dead flowers to promote bud formation.

In addition to the familiar hooped-skirt types, there are the Clustered Hybrids or Honeysuckle Fuchsias, generally derived from **F. triphylla**. Here the colour of the bloom comes from the sepals — the petals are either insignificant or absent.

Fuchsias are usually grown as bushes, although the trailing types are widely used in hanging baskets. Examples of Trailing Fuchsias include **Marinka** (red), **Golden Marinka** (red, variegated foliage), **Red Ribbons** (white and red) and **Pink Galore** (pink).

It is possible to train a vigorous upright variety as a standard (see page 177), but this will take several seasons and is more suited to the conservatory than to the living room.

Fuchsia hybrida Golden Marinka

SINGLE HYBRIDS	SEMI-DOUBLE HYBRIDS	DOUBLE HYBRIDS	CLUSTERED HYBRIDS

Winston Churchill (pink sepals, purple petals)	**Snowcap** (red sepals, white petals)	**Dollar Princess** (red sepals, lilac petals)	**Gartenmeister Bonstedt** (salmon-orange sepals)
Citation (pink sepals, white petals)	**Tennessee Waltz** (pink sepals, lilac petals)	**Fascination** (pink sepals, pink petals)	**Swanley Yellow** (orange sepals)
Bon Accord (white sepals, lilac petals)	**Texas Longhorn** (red sepals, white petals)	**Midge** (rose sepals, pink petals)	**Leverkusen** (red sepals)
Checkerboard (red and white sepals, red petals)	**Whirlaway** (white sepals, white petals)	**Alice Hoffman** (red sepals, white petals)	**Thalia** (deep pink sepals)
Brutus (red sepals, purple petals)	**Satellite** (red sepals, white petals)	**Brigadoon** (red sepals, purple petals)	**Traudchen Bonstedt** (pale salmon sepals)

Fuchsia Winston Churchill

Fuchsia Texas Longhorn

Fuchsia Traudchen Bonstedt

GARDEN ANNUALS

TYPES

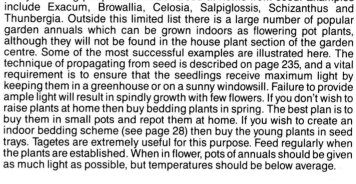

Many flowering pot plants can be raised at home from seed. Examples include Exacum, Browallia, Celosia, Salpiglossis, Schizanthus and Thunbergia. Outside this limited list there is a large number of popular garden annuals which can be grown indoors as flowering pot plants, although they will not be found in the house plant section of the garden centre. Some of the most successful examples are illustrated here. The technique of propagating from seed is described on page 235, and a vital requirement is to ensure that the seedlings receive maximum light by keeping them in a greenhouse or on a sunny windowsill. Failure to provide ample light will result in spindly growth with few flowers. If you don't wish to raise plants at home then buy bedding plants in spring. The best plan is to buy them in small pots and repot them at home. If you wish to create an indoor bedding scheme (see page 28) then buy the young plants in seed trays. Tagetes are extremely useful for this purpose. Feed regularly when the plants are established. When in flower, pots of annuals should be given as much light as possible, but temperatures should be below average.

AGERATUM HOUSTONIANUM
Ageratum

Height 8 in. In flower all summer. Pick a compact blue (**Blue Mink** or **Blue Blazer**). Or choose **Summer Snow** (white) and **Fairy Pink** (rose).

ANTIRRHINUM MAJUS
Snapdragon

Height 9 in. In flower all summer. Choose one of the dwarf varieties — **Magic Carpet, Floral Carpet** or **Tom Thumb.** Pinch out tip when 3 in. high.

CALENDULA OFFICINALIS
Pot Marigold

Height 1–2 ft. In flower all summer. Colours range from pale cream to deep orange. The best compact variety is the 1 ft **Fiesta Gitana.**

CENTAUREA CYANUS
Cornflower

Height 1 ft. In flower all summer. Choose a dwarf variety such as **Polka Dot** or **Jubilee Gem.** The grassy leaves are grey-green.

CLARKIA ELEGANS
Clarkia

Height 1½ ft. In flower all summer (spring if sown in autumn). Available in white, pink, red and purple. **C. pulchella** (1 ft) is a daintier species.

CONVOLVULUS TRICOLOR
Dwarf Morning Glory

Height 9 in. In flower all summer. Bright-coloured trumpets on bushy plants — sow the compact **Blue Flash** or **Rainbow Flash.** Remove dead flowers.

GODETIA GRANDIFLORA
Godetia

Height 9 in.–1½ ft. In flower all summer (spring if sown in autumn). Choose a short, bushy variety such as **Sybíl Sherwood** or **Kelvedon Glory.**

IBERIS UMBELLATA
Candytuft

Height 9 in. In flower late winter if sown in summer. **Fairy Mixture** will give a variety of white, pink and red fragrant flowers.

IPOMOEA TRICOLOR
Morning Glory

Height 6 ft. In flower all summer. Each large trumpet-shaped flower lasts only a day — choose **Heavenly Blue** (white-eyed bloom) or **Flying Saucers** (blue and white stripes).

LATHYRUS ODORATUS
Sweet Pea

Height 1 ft. In flower all summer. Grow a dwarf variety — no support will be needed. **Bijou, Little Sweethearts** and **Patio** are examples.

LINUM GRANDIFLORUM
Flax

Height 1 ft. In flower midsummer. The best one to choose is Scarlet Flax (**L. grandiflorum rubrum**). For white flowers grow **album.**

LOBELIA ERINUS
Lobelia

Height 4–8 in. In flower all summer. The deep blue variety is **Mrs Clibran Improved** — for hanging baskets grow **Sapphire** or **Cascade Mixed.**

MATTHIOLA INCANA
Stock

Height 1–2 ft. In flower winter–spring if sown in summer. For a long flowering season sow both **Brompton** and **Ten Week** strains. Excellent for fragrance.

MESEMBRYANTHEMUM CRINIFLORUM
Livingstone Daisy

Height 4–6 in. In flower all summer. Usually sold as a multicoloured mixture — **M. Lunette** is all yellow. A windowsill plant — direct sunlight is necessary.

MYOSOTIS ALPESTRIS
Forget-me-not

Height 6 in.–1 ft. In flower spring if sown in summer and kept outdoors until frosts arrive. Compact varieties are best — **Ultramarine** (deep blue) or **Carmine King** (pink).

NEMESIA STRUMOSA
Nemesia

Height 9 in. In flower midsummer (winter if sown in midsummer). Sow **Carnival** or **Sparklers** mixture. Grow numerous plants in a large container for a bold multicoloured display.

NICOTIANA HYBRIDA
Tobacco Plant

Height 9 in.–1½ ft. In flower all summer. Buy a day-flowering compact hybrid, such as **Tinkerbelle, Nicki Mixed, Red Devil** or **Domino Mixed.**

GARDEN ANNUAL TYPES continued

PETUNIA HYBRIDA	***PHLOX DRUMMONDII***	***SALVIA SPLENDENS***	***TAGETES ERECTA***	***TAGETES PATULA***

Petunia

Height 6 in. –1½ ft. In flower all summer. Catalogues offer a wide range of single and double varieties in a large and varied assortment of colours and patterns.

Annual Phlox

Height 6–9 in. In flower all summer. Pick from the **nana compacta** group — examples include **Twinkle, Beauty Mixed** and **Dwarf Petticoat.**

Salvia

Height 9 in. –1 ft. In flower all summer. Choose a compact variety such as **Blaze of Fire** or **Scarlet Pygmy** (red). **Dress Parade Mixed** provides various colours.

African Marigold

Height 1–2 ft. In flower all summer. Grow one of the dwarf varieties which rarely exceed 1½ ft — **Gay Ladies, Inca Yellow, Space Age Mixed**, etc.

French Marigold

Height 6–9 in. In flower all summer. All sorts of blends of yellow, orange, red and mahogany in single and double blooms are listed in catalogues.

TROPAEOLUM MAJUS	***VERBENA HYBRIDA***	***VIOLA TRICOLOR***	***VIOLA HYBRIDA***	***ZINNIA ELEGANS***

Nasturtium

Height 6 in. –1 ft. In flower all summer. The **Gleam** hybrids are the most popular choice, especially for hanging baskets. Dwarfs (6 in.) are also available.

Verbena

Height 6 in. –1 ft. In flower midsummer. Pick one of the compact varieties — **Sparkle, Springtime** and **Dwarf Compact Mixed** are all good choices.

Pansy

Height 6–9 in. In flower spring, summer or autumn, depending on variety and date of sowing. For the largest flowers, choose one of the **Swiss Giants. Floral Dance** is winter flowering.

Viola

Height 6–9 in. In flower spring, summer or autumn, depending on date of sowing. Plants remain in bloom for 2–3 months. Various colours, such as **Blue Heaven** and **Yellow Bedder.**

Zinnia

Height 6 in. –1½ ft. Select a low-growing strain, not one of the 2½ ft giants. Good ones include **Thumbelina, Pulchino, Peter Pan** and **Lilliput.**

Calendula officinalis

Lobelia erinus

Petunia hybrida

Phlox drummondii

Tagetes erecta

Tropaeolum majus

GARDEN BULBS

Many of the popular bulbs which flower in the garden during the spring months can be grown indoors. For many people, helping to plant up a bowl of Tulips or Hyacinths was their first introduction to the world of indoor gardening. There are two basic growing techniques — the large bulbs are nearly always 'forced' so that they will bloom well ahead of their garden counterparts. This forcing technique involves keeping them cold and dark to make the roots grow and then providing more light and warmth for leaf and flower development. Hyacinths are the most reliable — Tulips the least satisfactory. The second growing technique is used for small bulbs and is simpler than forcing. The pots are placed outdoors after planting and then simply brought indoors when the flower buds have formed and are ready to open. In this case flowering will only be a few days ahead of similar bulbs in the garden.

SECRETS OF SUCCESS

● **FORCING TECHNIQUE**
   for Hyacinths, Tulips & Narcissi

Planting: Choose varieties which are recommended for indoor cultivation and make sure that the bulbs are good-sized, disease-free and firm. Bulb fibre is sometimes used as the growing medium, but if you intend to save the bulbs for garden use after blooming then choose Seed and Cutting Compost. Place a layer of moist compost in the bottom of the bowl and set the bulbs on it. They should be close together but must not touch each other nor the sides of the bowl. Never force bulbs downwards into compost. Fill up with more compost, pressing it firmly but not too tightly around the bulbs. When finished the tips should be above the surface and there should be about ½ in. between the top of the compost and the rim of the bowl.

Care After Planting: The bulbs need a 'plunging' period of complete darkness and a temperature of about 40°F. The best spot is in the garden covering the bowl with about 4 in. of peat. Failing this, place the container in a black polythene bag and stand it in a shed, cellar or garage. Any warmth at this stage will lead to failure. The plunging period lasts for about 6 – 10 weeks. Check occasionally to make sure that the compost is still moist.

Care During Growth: When the shoots are about 1 – 2 in. high move the bowl into a cool room indoors — 50°F is the ideal temperature. Place in a shady spot at first, then move near to the window after a few days. The leaves will now develop and in a few weeks the flower buds will appear. Now is the time to move the bowl to the chosen site for flowering. This spot should be bright but not sunny, free from draughts, away from a radiator or heater and fairly cool — 60° – 70°F is the ideal. Keep the compost moist at all times. Turn the bowl occasionally so that growth will be even and provide some support for tall-flowering types. Feed with a liquid fertilizer.

Care After Flowering: Cut off flowers, not flower stalks. Continue watering and feeding until leaves have withered. Remove bulbs and allow to dry, then remove dead foliage and store in a cool dry place. These bulbs will not provide a second display indoors; plant in the garden in autumn.

● **NON-FORCING TECHNIQUE**
   for other bulbs

Planting: It is essential to choose a container with adequate drainage holes. Place a layer of crocks at the bottom and add a layer of Seed and Cutting Compost. Plant the bulbs closely together and add more compost. The tips of the bulbs should be completely covered.

Care After Planting: Place the pot in the garden.

Care During Growth: When the plants are fully grown and flower buds are present bring the pot indoors to the site chosen for flowering. Treat in the same way as Forced Bulbs.

Care After Flowering: Treat in the same way as Forced Bulbs.

HOW TO MAKE BULBS BLOOM AT CHRISTMAS

It is quite simple to raise Hyacinths, Narcissi and Tulips which will be in bloom on Christmas Day, but it is not a matter of planting the bulbs earlier than the recommended time. The essential step is to buy bulbs which have been specially prepared for early flowering. These bulbs are more expensive than ordinary garden types and they must be planted as soon as possible after purchase. September is the usual time for planting, and the technique described for Forced Bulbs should be followed. Bring the pots indoors when the shoots are 1 in. high; this should not be later than the first day of December. After flowering the bulbs can be stored for planting outdoors in autumn.

SPECIAL PROBLEMS

YELLOW LEAVES
Cause: Draughts are the usual reason. Other possible causes are incorrect watering and keeping the bowl in a spot with insufficient light.

STUNTED GROWTH
Cause: The usual reason is that the bowl has not been kept in the dark for the required period — the shoots should be an inch or two high before being exposed to light. Another cause is dry compost.

BUDS FAIL TO OPEN
Cause: Water is the problem here. Erratic watering can cause buds to die without opening; so can wetting the buds by watering carelessly.

NO FLOWERS AT ALL
Cause: There are several possible reasons. The trouble may start at planting time by using undersized bulbs. Keeping the bowl too warm or bringing it too quickly into bright sunlight will have this effect. Dry compost will also inhibit flowering.

ERRATIC FLOWERING
Cause: The most likely reason is that the bulbs were either different in size or vigour. If the bulbs were evenly matched then the probable cause was failure to turn the bowl occasionally.

DEFORMED FLOWERS
Cause: A clear symptom of keeping the bowl too warm during the plunging period. At this first stage the temperature should be about 40°F — do not keep the pot in a stuffy cupboard or sunny room even if unheated.

LONG, LIMP LEAVES
Cause: A clear sign of keeping the bowl in the dark for too long. Another possibility is too little light at flowering time.

ROTTING FLOWERS
Cause: Overwatering is the problem. A bowl without drainage holes kept under cool conditions can easily become waterlogged — take care. Remove excess water by carefully tipping the bowl.

GARDEN BULB TYPES

Pots of Narcissi and Daffodils continue to be the heralds of spring in countless households. Nearly all types can be grown indoors, but the 5 groups described below are generally considered to be the most reliable. The name 'Daffodil' is used when the large central tube ('trumpet') is at least as long as one of the petals — all the rest of the plants are called Narcissi. Some of the large-flowered types are quite suitable for indoor cultivation, but perhaps the best group of all are the Tazettas which produce bunches of flowers on each stem at Christmas or early in the New Year.

Plant: August-October
In flower: January-April (Tazettas: December-January)

NARCISSUS HYBRIDA	*NARCISSUS HYBRIDA*	*NARCISSUS HYBRIDA*	*NARCISSUS CYCLAMINEUS*	*NARCISSUS TAZETTA*
Daffodil	**Single Narcissus**	**Double Narcissus**	**Cyclamineus Narcissus**	**Tazetta Narcissus**
12–20 in. tall One flower per stem — central trumpet surrounded by shorter petals.	12–24 in. tall One flower per stem — central cup surrounded by longer petals.	12–18 in. tall More than one ring of petals — cup and petals indistinguishable.	6–12 in. tall Drooping flowers with long trumpets and strongly reflexed petals.	12–18 in. tall Several flowers per stem — central cup surrounded by longer petals.
Examples:	Examples:	Examples:	Examples:	Examples:
King Alfred (yellow)	**Carlton** (yellow)	**White Lion** (white and yellow)	**Peeping Tom** (yellow)	**Soleil d'Or** (yellow)
Spellbinder (white and yellow)	**Verona** (white)	**Golden Ducat** (yellow)	**Tête-a-Tête** (yellow)	**Paperwhite** (white)
Mount Hood (creamy white)	**La Riante** (white and orange)	**Texas** (yellow and orange)	**February Gold** (yellow)	**Geranium** (white and orange)
Dutch Master (yellow)	**Passionale** (white and pink)	**Irene Copeland** (white and yellow)	**Dove Wings** (cream and yellow)	**Cragford** (white and orange)

Narcissus Dutch Master

Narcissus Golden Ducat

Narcissus Paperwhite

Crocus chrysanthus Cream Beauty

flower 3–4 in. long

flower 4–5 in. long

CROCUS CHRYSANTHUS	*CROCUS VERNUS*
Crocus	Crocus

Crocus corms are planted in the autumn for flowering in early spring. The varieties of **C. chrysanthus** are often yellow (**Cream Beauty, E. A. Bowles, Goldilocks,** etc), but pale blues and mauves also occur, often with a golden base — **Blue Pearl, Princess Beatrix,** and so on. Flowering time is January-February — the varieties of **C. vernus** bloom a few weeks later, the flowers are larger, and blues and whites predominate. Popular types include **Vanguard** (silvery-lilac), **Kathleen Parlow** (white) and **Pickwick** (mauve, striped purple).

Crocus vernus Vanguard

GARDEN BULB TYPES continued

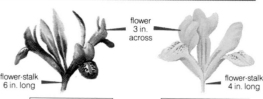

flower 3 in. across

flower-stalk 6 in. long

IRIS RETICULATA

flower-stalk 4 in. long

IRIS DANFORDIAE

Iris reticulata

Iris danfordiae

Dwarf Irises are excellent for growing indoors, producing large blooms in January and February. They have never gained the popularity of crocuses, hyacinths, etc, but there are at least 3 species which are well worth cultivating in the house. Plant the bulbs in September and provide plenty of light once the leaves have appeared above the compost. Choose from **Iris histrioides major** (deep blue, white centres), **I. reticulata** (purple, yellow centres — fragrant) and **I. danfordiae** (yellow — fragrant).

Scilla tubergeniana

strap-like leaf

pendent flower ½ in. long

SCILLA SIBERICA
Bluebell

urn-shaped flower ¼ in. long

strap-like leaf

MUSCARI ARMENIACUM
Grape Hyacinth

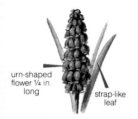

Muscari armeniacum

Some garden species can be grown indoors — plant in September-October for blooming in January-March. **S. tubergeniana** (3 in.) is the earliest species — **S. siberica** (6 in.) is the popular one. There are tender types (**S. adlamii, S. violacea**) which can be kept indoors for years.

Often seen outdoors but rarely recommended in house plant books. It is still a good choice — plant in September for January-March flowers. The usual species is **M. armeniacum** (8 in., blue flowers with white rims) — for sky blue flowers pick **M. botryoides** (6 in.).

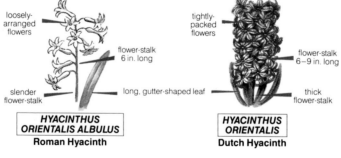

loosely-arranged flowers

flower-stalk 6 in. long

slender flower-stalk

long, gutter-shaped leaf

HYACINTHUS ORIENTALIS ALBULUS
Roman Hyacinth

tightly-packed flowers

flower-stalk 6–9 in. long

thick flower-stalk

HYACINTHUS ORIENTALIS
Dutch Hyacinth

Hyacinthus orientalis Amsterdam

The Dutch or Common Hyacinth is the most popular of all indoor bulbs. The leafless flower-stalks bear 30 or more crowded bell-like flowers with a fragrance that can fill a room. Each bulb bears a single stalk and the waxy 1–2 in. long blooms last for 2–3 weeks. Bulbs specially prepared for Christmas blooming should be planted in September — bulbs for January-March flowering are planted in October. There are scores of varieties — the range of colours is demonstrated by **L'Innocence** (white), **Yellow Hammer** (yellow), **Lady Derby** (pink), **Jan Bos** (red), **Ostara** (blue) and **Amethyst** (violet). Roman Hyacinths differ in a number of ways — 2 or 3 stalks are produced by each bulb and the flowers are smaller and less tightly packed. The flower-stalks are thinner and the colour range is restricted to white, pink and blue. Plant in August-September for December-January flowering. A third group, the Multiflora Hyacinths, bear several flower-stalks per bulb.

Galanthus Neil Frazer

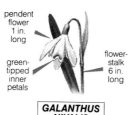

pendent flower 1 in. long

green-tipped inner petals

flower-stalk 6 in. long

GALANTHUS NIVALIS
Snowdrop

Planting time is September — flowering time is January. The one you are most likely to see is the Common Snowdrop (**G. nivalis**). The best variety is **S. Arnott** (9 in.) — for double flowers choose **flore pleno.** The tallest Snowdrop is **G. elwesii** (10 in.).

star-shaped flower 1 in. across

flower-stalk 6 in. long

CHIONODOXA LUCILIAE
Glory of the Snow

The popular Chionodoxa is **C. luciliae** — 10 white-centred, blue starry flowers appear on each slender stalk in late winter. **C. sardensis** has all-blue flowers, and the largest blooms (1½ in. across) are borne by **C. gigantea.** Plant the bulbs in September for February flowers.

Chionodoxa sardensis

Convallaria majalis

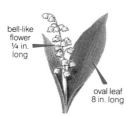

bell-like flower ¼ in. long

oval leaf 8 in. long

CONVALLARIA MAJALIS
Lily of the Valley

The dainty white bells and heavy fragrance are well known. For Christmas flowers you will have to buy specially prepared crowns ('pips') and plant a month before. Alternatively, lift crowns from outdoor plants and pot up in October for blooming in February.

star-shaped flower 1 in. across

flower-stalk 3 in. long

ERANTHIS HYEMALIS
Winter Aconite

Many of the bulbs in this section are instantly recognisable by the average gardener, but not this one. The bright yellow flowers have a frilly, leafy collar — plant in September for flowering in January alongside the Snowdrops. For 2 in. flowers grow **E. tubergenii**.

Eranthis tubergenii

Gladiolus primulinus Robin

trumpet-shaped flower 3 in. across

flower-stalk 2 ft long

GLADIOLUS COLUMBINE

Gladioli are not usually thought of as indoor bulbs, and the large-flowering types are not suitable. Choose one of the Primulinus or the Miniature Hybrids, such as **Columbine** or **Bo Peep**, or pick a low-growing species such as **G. colvillii** (1–2 ft).

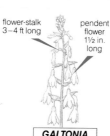

flower-stalk 3–4 ft long

pendent flower 1½ in. long

GALTONIA CANDICANS
Summer Hyacinth

This imposing plant is in marked contrast to the many dainty dwarfs in this section. Bulbs are planted in large pots in September and each flower-stalk bears 20 or more white bells in May-June. The strap-like leaves are 2 ft long.

Galtonia candicans

GARDEN BULB TYPES continued

The most satisfactory Tulips to grow indoors are the compact hybrids classed as Single Earlies (one ring of petals) and Double Earlies (several rings of petals). Some Species Tulips are also excellent for indoor use — both **T. kaufmanniana** and **T. greigii** include suitable varieties. The tall-growing tulips which are so colourful outdoors in May are much less useful for growing in bowls or pots. The best ones to choose are the strong-stemmed Darwin and Lily-flowered hybrids.

Plant: September-October (early September for bulbs prepared for Xmas flowering)

In flower: January-April

TULIPA HYBRIDA	*TULIPA HYBRIDA*	*TULIPA HYBRIDA*	*TULIPA HYBRIDA*	*TULIPA KAUFMANNIANA*	*TULIPA GREIGII*
Single Early Tulip	**Double Early Tulip**	**Darwin Tulip**	**Lily-flowered Tulip**	**Species Tulip**	**Species Tulip**
9–16 in. tall Blooms rather small — open flat when mature.	9–16 in. tall Long-lasting — petals sometimes frilled.	24–30 in. tall Very large flowers opening in April.	20–24 in. tall Long flowers with pointed reflexed petals.	6–10 in. tall The Water Lily Tulip — the pointed petals opening flat in sunlight.	8–12 in. tall Later than T. kaufmanniana — leaves are streaked or mottled with brown.
Examples:	Examples:	Examples:	Examples:	Examples:	Examples:
Brilliant Star (red)	**Peach Blossom** (rosy-pink)	**Apeldoorn** (red)	**West Point** (yellow)	**The First** (white and red)	**Red Riding Hood** (red)
Princess Margaret (pink)	**Orange Nassau** (orange)	**Striped Apeldoorn** (yellow and red)	**China Pink** (pink)	**Stresa** (red and yellow)	**Plaisir** (cream and red)
Keizerskroon (yellow and red)	**Scarlet Cardinal** (red)	**Sunkist** (gold)	**Aladdin** (red and yellow)		

Tulipa Brilliant Star

Tulipa Peach Blossom

Tulipa greigii Plaisir

GERBERA JAMESONII

Barbeton Daisy

daisy-like flower 2 in. across

deeply-lobed leaf 6 in. long

GERBERA

Gerbera jamesonii has been grown as a flowering pot plant for many years. The flowers are available in many striking colours and both single and double forms can be obtained. The trouble with the species is the height of the flower-stalks — these can reach 2 ft and give the plant a lanky appearance. A compact strain (**G. jamesonii Happipot**) with 10–12 in. flower-stalks has recently appeared. Home-sown seeds unfortunately produce some tall-stemmed plants — the variety **Parade** is more uniform.

SECRETS OF SUCCESS

Temperature: Average warmth; 50°–70°F when flowering.

Light: Brightly lit spot with some direct sun.

Water: Keep the compost moist at all times.

Air Humidity: Mist leaves occasionally.

Care After Flowering: Discard or place in a greenhouse.

Propagation: Sow seeds in spring.

upturned
bell-shaped
flower 3 in.
across

oval,
velvety leaf
9 in. long

SINNINGIA SPECIOSA
Gloxinia

GLOXINIA

Gloxinias (proper name Sinningia speciosa) are usually bought in flower during summer. Choose a plant with plenty of unopened buds and with proper care it should continue to bloom for 2 months or more. Tubers for potting up are available in spring; for details of planting see Secrets of Success. The bell-shaped velvety blooms are 3 in. or more in diameter; white, pink, red and purple varieties can be purchased. Gloxinia, unlike so many gift plants, can be kept for growing again next season but it is not a particularly easy plant for the novice. It needs moist air, freedom from draughts, regular feeding and careful watering.

SECRETS OF SUCCESS

Temperature: Average warmth; not less than 60°F.

Light: Bright light away from direct sunlight.

Water: Keep the compost moist at all times. Use tepid water; keep off leaves and flowers.

Air Humidity: Stand pot on a pebble tray (see page 27) or surround with damp peat. Occasionally mist the air around the plant.

Care After Flowering: Reduce watering and stop feeding. Allow to dry out completely when leaves turn yellow; store pot at about 50°F. Repot tuber in fresh compost in spring; plant hollow side up with top of tuber level with compost surface. Keep warm and rather dry until leaves appear, then treat as above.

Propagation: Sow seeds in spring or take leaf cuttings in early summer.

Sinningia speciosa Gregor Mendel

TYPES

The petal edges of **S. speciosa** are either plain or ruffled. Multi-lobed (double) varieties are available.

Gregor Mendel (double, red with white edge)
Emperor Frederick (single, red with white edge)
Duchess of York (single, violet with white edge)
Mont Blanc (single, white)
Red Tiger (single, white with red spots)

SPECIAL PROBLEMS

CURLED LEAVES WITH BROWN TIPS
Cause: Hot, dry air is the usual reason. During flowering it is essential to increase the humidity around the plant.

PLANT COLLAPSE, TUBER SOFT & ROTTEN
Cause: Waterlogging due to overwatering or poor drainage. Another possible cause is the use of cold instead of tepid water.

PALE ELONGATED LEAVES WITH BROWN EDGES
Cause: Not enough light. Gloxinia needs protection from hot summer sun but it will not tolerate dark places.

FLOWER BUDS FAIL TO OPEN
Cause: Several possibilities — most usual reasons are dry air and cold draughts.

Gloriosa superba

GLORIOSA

The Glory Lily bears large lily-like flowers in midsummer. The spear-shaped leaves bear tendrils at their tips, and some form of support must be provided. At flowering time keep warm and well-lit. Gloriosa is either bought in flower or raised at home from a tuber. Plant the tuber upright in a 6 in. pot in spring with the tip about 1 in. below the surface. Water sparingly at first, then more freely as the stems start to grow.

SECRETS OF SUCCESS

Temperature: Warm or average warmth; not less than 60°F in the growing season.

Light: Brightly lit spot, but shade from hot summer sun.

Water: Water liberally during the growing season.

Air Humidity: Mist leaves occasionally.

Care After Flowering: Reduce and then stop watering. Store tuber in its pot at 50°–55°F. Repot in spring.

Propagation: Remove and plant offsets at repotting time.

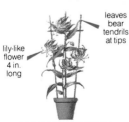

leaves
bear
tendrils
at tips

lily-like
flower
4 in.
long

**GLORIOSA
ROTHSCHILDIANA**
Glory Lily

TYPES

G. rothschildiana is a spectacular climber reaching 4 ft or more. Swept-back petals are red with a yellow base — **G. superba** is similar but petals change from green to orange and finally to red.

INDOOR BULBS

A large number of the plants that are grown indoors produce 'bulbs' which can be used for propagation. Some produce true bulbs (see page 247 for definitions) and others form rhizomes, tubers and corms.

Some of these bulb-forming plants (Clivia, Eucharis, Vallota etc) keep their leaves all year round and are therefore Flowering House Plants — see Chapter 6 for details. Most of the flowering bulbs, however, lose their leaves during the dormant period, which means that they are Flowering Pot Plants — left on display until flowering is over and then removed.

These temporary-display bulbs are divided into two basic groups. First of all there are the frost-hardy ones which are happy outdoors but need special treatment for blooming indoors. They must be subjected to cold conditions during the rooting stage and are only placed in the living room, hall etc when the flower buds have formed. These are the *Garden Bulbs* (see page 181).

The other group are the *Indoor Bulbs*. These plants cannot tolerate frost and are never placed outdoors in winter. They are left in the pot when the foliage dies down — the compost is kept almost dry until growth starts again. This is the way to treat the true bulbs and most corms, tubers and rhizomes. A few (Achimenes, Tuberous Begonia and Canna) are stored in slightly moist peat during the dormant period and then potted up prior to the start of the growing season.

The list of Indoor Bulbs is an impressive one, and can provide colour all year round. Some of the important ones are described individually in this section — see table on the left. The remainder are illustrated and described here. For the really keen there are also Lycoris aurea (Golden Spider Lily), Sprekelia formosissima (Jacobean Lily) and Habranthus robustus.

OTHER INDOOR BULBS

TYPES

Hippeastrum Safari

Hippeastrum Apple Blossom

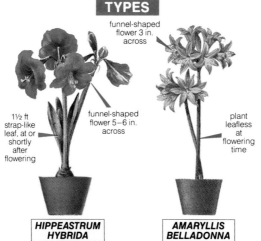

funnel-shaped flower 3 in. across

1½ ft strap-like leaf, at or shortly after flowering

funnel-shaped flower 5–6 in. across

plant leafless at flowering time

HIPPEASTRUM HYBRIDA
Amaryllis

AMARYLLIS BELLADONNA
Belladonna Lily

Amaryllis belladonna alba

Hippeastrum Ludwig's Dazzler

These 2 plants are often confused — both are large bulbs which produce clusters of trumpet-like flowers on thick stalks. The Belladonna Lily, however, is not often seen — the popular 'Amaryllis' offered for sale in autumn is really a Hippeastrum hybrid. These hybrids are orange, purple, white, pink or red — sometimes edged or striped in other shades. **H. hybrida** has hollow stalks and there are 3–6 flowers per cluster. **A. belladonna** has solid stalks and 6–12 flowers per cluster. Hippeastrum blooms in winter or spring (Amaryllis — autumn).

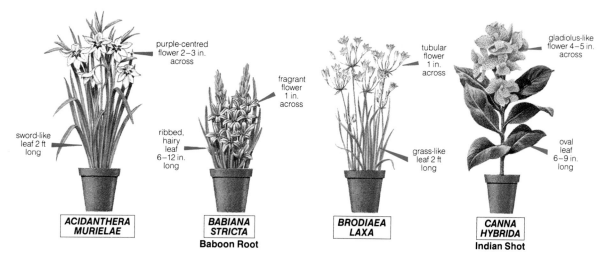

purple-centred flower 2–3 in. across	
sword-like leaf 2 ft long	
ribbed, hairy leaf 6–12 in. long	
fragrant flower 1 in. across	
tubular flower 1 in. across	
grass-like leaf 2 ft long	
gladiolus-like flower 4–5 in. across	
oval leaf 6–9 in. long	

ACIDANTHERA MURIELAE

BABIANA STRICTA
Baboon Root

BRODIAEA LAXA

CANNA HYBRIDA
Indian Shot

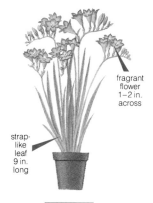

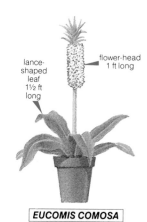

fragrant flower 1–2 in. across

strap-like leaf 9 in. long

FREESIA HYBRIDA

lance-shaped leaf 1½ ft long

flower-head 1 ft long

EUCOMIS COMOSA
Pineapple Lily

Acidanthera murielae is a gladiolus-like plant, bearing sweetly-scented blooms in late summer or autumn. Plant the corms in late winter. **Babiana stricta** is also related to the gladiolus but it is a much smaller plant — the flower-stalks grow 6–12 in. high. Plant in autumn for spring flowers — hybrids with white, yellow, red, blue or purple blooms are available.

Brodiaea is an uncommon bulb for people who prefer delicate blooms to big showy ones. **B. laxa** bears white or blue blooms in large clusters — it flowers in spring, unlike **B. coronaria** which blooms in summer. **B. ida-maia** is quite different — the flowers are pendent, red and edged with green. **Canna hybrida** plants are big, bold and colourful. The large flowers are borne on a 2–4 ft stalk, and specialist growers can offer a bewildering array of varieties — white, yellow, pink and red; plain, striped and spotted. There is also a choice of leaf colour — standard green, dark green and bronzy-purple.

The funnel-shaped flowers of **Freesia hybrida** grow on one side of the 1–1½ ft long wiry stems — all varieties are sweet-smelling and you can choose from white, yellow, blue, lilac, orange, pink and red. Plants can be raised from seeds or corms.

Eucomis comosa needs lots of space. The long leaves form a large rosette and the cylindrical spike of small flowers bears a leafy crown. **E. bicolor** (purplish-green flowers, purple-spotted stalk) is smaller.

Acidanthera murielae

Canna hybrida J B van der Schoot

Freesia hybrida Marie Louise

INDOOR BULB TYPES continued

fragrant flower 4 in. across

strap-like leaf 1 ft long

HYMENOCALLIS FESTALIS
Spider Lily

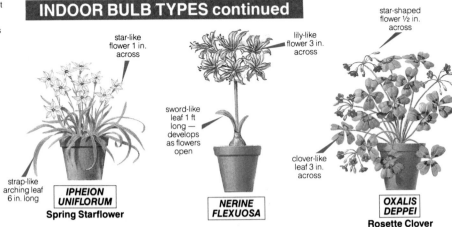

star-like flower 1 in. across

strap-like arching leaf 6 in. long

IPHEION UNIFLORUM
Spring Starflower

lily-like flower 3 in. across

sword-like leaf 1 ft long — develops as flowers open

NERINE FLEXUOSA

star-shaped flower ½ in. across

clover-like leaf 3 in. across

OXALIS DEPPEI
Rosette Clover

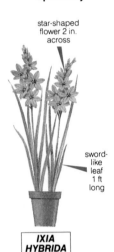

star-shaped flower 2 in. across

sword-like leaf 1 ft long

IXIA HYBRIDA
African Corn Lily

Hymenocallis festalis is cultivated for its attractive sweet-smelling blooms which appear in late spring or summer. These flowers look like daffodils with long and narrow petals, borne on 2 ft stalks above the arching leaves. The foliage of H. festalis dies down in winter. **Ipheion uniflorum** is a low-growing plant, its starry blooms appearing on top of the 6 in. stems in spring. Use your nose for identification — the blue or white flowers have a pleasant smell, but the crushed leaves have the pungent odour of garlic.

Nerine flexuosa is an uncommon plant — a cluster of wavy-petalled pink or white bells are borne on 2 ft flower-stalks in autumn. **N. sarniensis** is the Guernsey Lily — narrow-petalled white, orange or red flowers tightly clustered crowning the stalks. The leaves appear after flowering. Oxalis has never become a popular plant, despite its shamrock-like appearance. **Oxalis deppei** has red flowers in spring, **O. cernua** (Bermuda Buttercup) bears yellow blooms and **O. bowiei** is pale purple. The leaves close at night, and so do the flowers of some species. Buy Oxalis plants in bloom or raise your own from bulbs.

The strap-like leaves of **Ornithogalum thyrsoides** arise from the bulb, followed by a 1½ ft stalk crowned with about 20 starry flowers in late spring. A close relative (**O. caudatum**) has a 3 ft stalk which bears up to 100 green-striped blooms. **Ixia hybrida** is known for its gaily-coloured flowers, but is much less popular than Freesia. You can identify Ixia from its 6-petalled dark-centred flowers borne on upright wiry stalks. Many varieties are available — flowers appear in early summer.

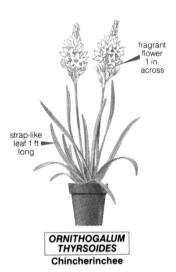

fragrant flower 1 in. across

strap-like leaf 1 ft long

ORNITHOGALUM THYRSOIDES
Chincherinchee

Ipheion uniflorum Wisley Blue

Nerine sarniensis

Hymenocallis festalis

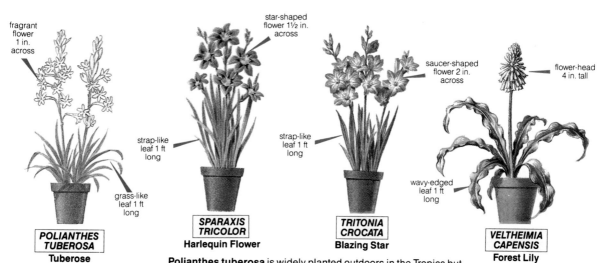

fragrant
flower
1 in.
across

star-shaped
flower 1½ in.
across

saucer-shaped
flower 2 in.
across

flower-head
4 in. tall

strap-like
leaf 1 ft
long

strap-like
leaf 1 ft
long

grass-like
leaf 1 ft
long

wavy-edged
leaf 1 ft
long

**POLIANTHES
TUBEROSA**
Tuberose

**SPARAXIS
TRICOLOR**
Harlequin Flower

**TRITONIA
CROCATA**
Blazing Star

**VELTHEIMIA
CAPENSIS**
Forest Lily

trumpet-shaped
flower 6–9 in.
long

arrow-shaped
leaf 1½ ft
long

**ZANTEDESCHIA
AETHIOPICA**
Calla Lily

Polianthes tuberosa is widely planted outdoors in the Tropics but is not often seen as a pot plant in Europe. The bulb-like rhizomes are planted in spring to bloom in winter. The leaves are narrow and the flowering spike can reach 2–3 ft. The flowers are white and waxy. A mixture of **Sparaxis tricolor** hybrids will produce a riot of colour in late spring when the flowers open above the dense foliage. Many (but not all) types have a black-edged yellow throat. Plant the corms in autumn.

Like its relatives Ixia and Sparaxis, **Tritonia crocata** produces a fan of narrow leaves. In summer the floral display appears on wiry stalks — varieties in white, glowing orange, deep pink and several other bright colours are available. Somewhat like the Red Hot Poker of the garden, **Veltheimia capensis** is a good choice for indoors. Plant the large bulb in early autumn and about 3 or 4 months later the 1 ft flower-stalk arises from the centre of the leaf rosette. This stalk bears about 60 small but long-lasting bell-like flowers.

Calla Lily is one of the real beauties of the indoor plant world. **Zantedeschia aethiopica** bears its upturned white trumpets on 3 ft stalks in early spring — other species include **Z. rehmannii** (pink) and **Z. elliottiana** (yellow), plus many hybrids in various colours. The Zephyr Lily is a much smaller and more dainty plant — **Zephyranthes grandiflora** produces 6 in. flower-stalks in early summer, each bearing a crocus-like bloom which soon opens out into a pink star. **Z. candida** (white) is even smaller, but there are several large-flowering hybrids.

crocus-like
flower 3 in.
across

strap-like
leaf 5 in.
long

**ZEPHYRANTHES
GRANDIFLORA**
Zephyr Lily

Veltheimia capensis

Zantedeschia aethiopica

Zephyranthes grandiflora

HYDRANGEA

Hydrangeas are usually bought in flower during spring or summer. With care the blooms will last for about 6 weeks and the plants can be kept to provide displays in future years. The heads are so large that they may need staking. The two vital needs at the flowering stage are cool conditions and compost which is never allowed to dry out — this may mean watering every day. After flowering cut back the stems to half their height.

SECRETS OF SUCCESS

Temperature: Cool; not less than 45°F in winter.

Light: Bright light away from direct sunlight.

Water: Keep the compost moist at all times from spring to autumn. Use rainwater if tap water is hard.

Air Humidity: Mist leaves occasionally.

Care After Flowering: Repot and continue to water and feed; stand pot outdoors during summer if possible. Overwinter in a cold but frost-free room. Water sparingly. In mid winter move to a warmer, brighter room and increase watering.

Propagation: Not practical in the home.

globular flower-head 6–8 in. across

oval, saw-edged leaf 4–6 in. long

HYDRANGEA MACROPHYLLA

Hydrangea (Hortensia)

TYPES

White, pink and blue varieties of **H. macrophylla** are available — pink varieties can be 'blued' by adding a proprietary blueing compound to the compost before the flowers open.

Hydrangea macrophylla

LACHENALIA

Cape Cowslip is an attractive plant, providing a host of pendent, tubular flowers in winter. Despite its novel appearance, Lachenalia has never been popular, which is probably due to its inability to live in a heated room. In late summer plant 6–8 bulbs in a 6 in. pot with the tips of the bulbs just below the surface. Keep in a cool bright room, water once and then leave until shoots appear. At this stage start to water and feed regularly.

SECRETS OF SUCCESS

Temperature: Cool; not less than 40°F in winter.

Light: Bright light with some direct sun.

Water: Keep the compost moist at all times during the flowering season.

Air Humidity: Mist leaves occasionally.

Care After Flowering: Continue watering for several weeks, then reduce and stop. Keep dry; repot in autumn.

Propagation: Remove and plant offsets at repotting time.

Lachenalia tricolor

pendent flower 1 in. long

spotted leaf 9 in. long

LACHENALIA ALOIDES

Cape Cowslip

TYPES

The blooms of **L. aloides** are yellow tinged with green and red. They are borne on 1 ft stalks which bear brown or purple blotches. The variety **lutea** has all-yellow flowers.

NERTERA

The berries follow the tiny flowers which appear in early summer. Provide plenty of water, fresh air and strong light during the growing season. The Bead Plant is classed as a temporary pot plant because nearly all of them are discarded once the display of berries is finished. With care, however, this plant can be kept for several years.

SECRETS OF SUCCESS

Temperature: Cool; not less than 40°F in winter.

Light: Bright light with some direct sun.

Water: Keep compost moist at all times; water sparingly in winter.

Air Humidity: Mist occasionally.

Care After Flowering: Keep cool and rather dry during winter; increase watering when new growth appears. Place outdoors from late spring until the berries have appeared. Bring indoors for display.

Propagation: Divide plants in spring before placing outdoors.

creeping stems with tiny leaves. Glassy orange berries cover surface in autumn

NERTERA DEPRESSA

Bead Plant

TYPE

The mat of creeping stems and ¼ in. leaves of **N. depressa** might be mistaken for Helxine at first glance, but it is immediately recognisable once the pea-sized berries appear.

Nertera depressa

LILIUM

The most popular Lilium species for growing indoors is the Easter Lily. The tall stems grow 3 ft high and the white 6 in. long trumpet-shaped blooms are heavily scented. The main requirements are space and cold nights. In the U.S. millions are forced by nurserymen for sale in bloom at Easter; in Britain it is an unusual summer-flowering plant grown at home from a bulb. Make sure that the bulb is plump and not shrivelled. In autumn plant it in a 6 in. pot immediately after purchase, covering the tip with 1½ – 2 in. of compost. Keep cold, dark and moist. When shoots appear move to a brightly lit spot.

SECRETS OF SUCCESS

Temperature: Cool; not less than 35°F. Night temperature should not exceed 50°F during the growing season.

Light: Bright light away from direct sunlight.

Water: Keep compost moist at all times during the growing season.

Air Humidity: Mist leaves occasionally.

Care After Flowering: Reduce watering as leaves turn yellow and stems die down. Keep the compost just moist and repot bulb in autumn. Unfortunately growth will be less vigorous and the flowers smaller than on plants raised from newly-purchased bulbs.

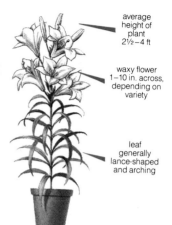

average height of plant 2½ – 4 ft

waxy flower 1 – 10 in. across, depending on variety

leaf generally lance-shaped and arching

TYPES

BOWL SHAPED
The petals flare open to produce a wide bowl. The flowers are usually large.

L. auratum (Golden-rayed Lily) Height 4 – 5 ft. Flowers 8 – 10 in. across. White with yellow stripes and brown spots. Fragrant. Flowering period late summer.

L. speciosum (Japanese Lily) Height 3 – 4 ft. Flowers 3 – 5 in. across. White with red markings. Fragrant. Flowering period summer. Half hardy — grow indoors.
   Grand Commander — the best variety, petals deep red with paler edges.

L. Empress of China Height 3 – 4 ft. Flowers 8 in. across. White with dark red spots. Fragrant. Flowering period summer. Half hardy — grow indoors.

TRUMPET SHAPED
The petals are grouped together for part of the length of the flower to produce a basal tube.

L. longiflorum (Easter Lily) Height 3 ft. Flowers 5 in. across. White. Fragrant. Flowering period summer. Half hardy — grow indoors.
   Mount Everest — giant (6 ft) variety with large flowers.

L. regale (Regal Lily) Height 4 ft. Flowers 5 in. across. White with yellow throat. Fragrant. Flowering period summer.
   Royal Gold — all-yellow.

L. Mid-Century Hybrids Height 2 – 4 ft. Flowers 4 – 5 in. across. Yellow, orange or red — all spotted. Flowering period early summer.
   Enchantment — orange-red, very popular   **Brandywine** — apricot
   Destiny — lemon-yellow   **Prosperity** — pale yellow
   Cinnabar — maroon-red   **Connecticut King** — gold
   Paprika — crimson   **Chinook** — orange
   Sterling Silver — cream   **Tabasco** — dark red

L. Golden Splendor Height 4 ft. Flowers 6 in. across. Gold; maroon-striped on reverse. Flowering period summer.

TURK'S-CAP SHAPED
The petals are rolled and swept back. The flowers are usually small.

L. pumilum Height 1 – 2 ft. Flowers 2 in. across. Red. Flowering period early summer.

L. Fiesta Hybrids Height 3 – 4 ft. Flowers 3 in. across. Various colours. Flowering period summer.

L. Citronella Height 3 ft. Flowers 3 in. across. Yellow with black dots. Flowering period summer.

Lilium longiflorum

Lilium Destiny

POINSETTIA

red, pink
or white
flower-head
1 ft across

lobed
leaf
5 in.
long

**EUPHORBIA
PULCHERRIMA**
Poinsettia

The symbol of Christmas outdoors is the Holly with its bright red berries. Indoors it is now the Poinsettia (proper name Euphorbia pulcherrima) with its large, scarlet flower-heads. This was not always so — in the early 1960s it was a tall-growing shrub which was distinctly difficult to keep in leaf or flower in the average home. Two things have changed — modern varieties are bushier, more attractive and much less delicate; in addition modern chemicals are used to keep the plants small. The result is that the Poinsettia of today is compact (1 – 1½ ft high) and the flowers (which are really coloured bracts) should last for 2–6 months. Red remains the favourite colour, but white and pink varieties are available. When buying a plant look at the true flowers (yellow and tiny in the centre of the flower-head); they should be unopened for maximum flower life. Also the plant should not have been stood outdoors or in an icy shop. Once in your living room put it in a well-lit spot away from draughts and keep it reasonably warm. Surround the pot with moist peat if you can and avoid overwatering.

HOW TO MAKE A POINSETTIA BLOOM AGAIN NEXT CHRISTMAS

When the leaves have fallen cut back the stems to leave stumps 4 in. high. The compost should be kept almost dry and the pot placed in a mild, shady position. In early May water and repot the plant, removing some of the old compost. Continue watering and shoots will soon appear. Feed regularly and remove some of the new growth to leave 4–5 strong new stems. The prunings can be used as cuttings.

From the end of September careful light control is essential. Cover with a black polythene bag from early evening and remove next morning so that the plant is kept in total darkness for 14 hours. Continue daily for 8 weeks, then treat normally. Your Poinsettia will again be in bloom at Christmas time, but it will be taller than the plant you bought.

SECRETS OF SUCCESS

Temperature: Average warmth; not less than 55°–60°F during the flowering season.

Light: Maximum light during winter; protect from hot summer sun if plant is to be kept for next Christmas.

Water: Water thoroughly; wait until the compost is moderately dry before watering again. Water immediately if leaves begin to wilt. Water more liberally in summer.

Air Humidity: Mist leaves frequently during the flowering season.

Care After Flowering: Plant should be discarded, but if you like a challenge it can be kept and will bloom again next Christmas. The lighting will have to be very carefully controlled in autumn — see detailed instructions on this page.

Propagation: Stem cuttings in early summer. Use rooting hormone.

SPECIAL PROBLEMS

LOSS OF FLOWER-HEADS; LEAF MARGINS YELLOW OR BROWN
Cause: The usual reason is dry air in a warm room. Poinsettia needs moist air — mist leaves frequently.

INSECTS
Red spider mite and mealy bug are the main pests; see Chapter 15.

LOSS OF LEAVES FOLLOWING WILTING
Cause: Overwatering is the likely culprit; the surface of the compost must be dry before water is applied. Of course, failure to water when the compost around the roots is dry will also cause leaves to wilt and fall.

LOSS OF LEAVES WITHOUT WILTING
Cause: If the temperature is too low or if the plant has been subjected to hot or freezing draughts then the leaves will suddenly fall. Another cause of leaf fall is poor light.

PRIMULA

The Primula group contains some of the best of all winter- and spring-flowering pot plants. The plants bear large numbers of flowers, clustered in the centre of the leaf rosette (the stalkless varieties) or on long, erect flower stems (the stalked varieties).

The Primroses and Primulas which grow in the garden make pretty pot plants — the blooms are large and colourful and after flowering they can be planted in the garden.

It is usually the tender species which are grown indoors. The flowers are smaller and are borne on stalks. The Fairy Primrose is the daintiest, the Chinese Primrose has frilly leaves and flowers, and the Poison Primrose is the one not to touch if you have sensitive skin.

Do not plant too deeply — the crown should be just above the compost surface. Keep your plant well-lit, free from draughts, away from heat and protected from direct sun. Remove dead flowers and feed regularly.

Temperature: Cool; keep at 55°–60°F during the flowering season.

Light: Maximum light, but protect from direct sunlight.

Water: Keep compost moist at all times during flowering season.

Air Humidity: Mist leaves occasionally. Place on a pebble tray (see page 27) if conditions are rather warm.

Care After Flowering: Plant P. acaulis in the garden; other types are generally discarded. P. obconica and P. sinensis can be kept — repot and provide cool airy conditions in light shade throughout summer. Water very sparingly; in autumn remove yellowed leaves and resume normal watering.

Propagation: Sow seeds in midsummer.

TYPES

● TENDER TYPES

yellow-eyed flower ½ in. across

flower-stalk 1½ ft long

oval, toothed leaf

PRIMULA MALACOIDES
Fairy Primrose

green-eyed flower 1–1½ in. across

flower-stalk 1 ft long

heart-shaped, coarse leaf

PRIMULA OBCONICA
Poison Primrose

frilly flower 1–1½ in. across

flower-stalk 1 ft long

lobed, toothed leaf

PRIMULA SINENSIS
Chinese Primrose

fragrant flower ¾ in. across

flower-stalk 1 ft long

powdery, toothed leaf

PRIMULA KEWENSIS

Primulas bear large numbers of flowers during the winter months. Two garden types are grown indoors to brighten up the winter windowsill — the Common Primrose (**P. vulgaris** or **P. acaulis**) with its large flowers in white, yellow, red or blue clustered in a rosette of leaves, and the Polyanthus (**P. variabilis**) with its bright and often bicoloured flowers clustered on stout 1 ft stalks.

P. malacoides is the most popular of the tender types which are grown as temporary pot plants. The fragrant, small flowers in white, pink, purple or red are arranged in tiers on slender stalks. The flowers of **P. obconica** are large, fragrant and available in a wide range of colours, but the leaves can cause a rash on sensitive skins. The yellow-eyed **P. sinensis** is available in white, pink, red, orange and purple — the popular varieties have red, frilly-edged petals. **P. kewensis** is unmistakable — it is the only yellow-flowering tender Primula.

● GARDEN TYPES

showy flower 1–1½ in. across

flower-stalk 3 in. long

oblong, wrinkled leaf

PRIMULA ACAULIS
Common Primrose

Primula malacoides

Primula obconica

Primula kewensis

PUNICA

Punica granatum nana

The ordinary Pomegranate is not suitable for the living room but the Dwarf Pomegranate makes an excellent pot plant for a sunny window. The flowers may be followed by bright orange fruit, but these miniature pomegranates will not ripen. In spring cut back any unwanted growth. In summer the pot can be stood outdoors and in winter a cool but frost-free spot is required. During the dormant period the leaves will drop.

SECRETS OF SUCCESS

Temperature: Average warmth; not less than 40°F in winter.

Light: Bright light; some direct sun is essential.

Water: Water liberally from spring to autumn; very sparingly in winter.

Air Humidity: Mist leaves occasionally in summer.

Repotting: Repot, when necessary, in spring.

Propagation: Stem cuttings in summer; rooting hormone and warmth are necessary.

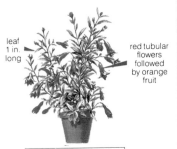

leaf 1 in. long

red tubular flowers followed by orange fruit

PUNICA GRANATUM NANA

Dwarf Pomegranate

TYPE

P. granatum nana grows about 3 ft high. The leaves are glossy and bright scarlet flowers appear in summer. Ball-like fruit develop ... if you are lucky.

RECHSTEINERIA

Rechsteineria cardinalis

The Cardinal Flower is closely related to Gloxinia, and the treatment required is very similar. The shape of the flowers, however, is completely different — R. cardinalis bears tubular blooms quite unlike the open bells of Gloxinia. The bright red blooms appear in summer — removing stems which bear faded blooms will prolong the flowering season. Plants are bought in flower in late spring but you can raise them by planting tubers in winter.

SECRETS OF SUCCESS

Temperature: Average warmth; not less than 60°F.

Light: Bright light; protect from summer sun.

Water: Keep the compost moist at all times. Use tepid water and keep it off the leaves and flowers.

Air Humidity: Mist around plants frequently.

Care After Flowering: Water sparingly; stop when leaves turn yellow. Keep at 50°–60°F. Repot tubers in early spring.

Propagation: Take stem cuttings in early summer.

tubular flower 2 in. long

velvety leaf 4 in. long

RECHSTEINERIA CARDINALIS
(GESNERIA CARDINALIS)

Cardinal Flower

TYPES

The hooded, bright red blooms of **R. cardinalis** are borne horizontally at the top of the 1 ft stems. **R. leucotricha** (Brazilian Edelweiss) has woolly silvery-grey leaves and pink flowers.

SALPIGLOSSIS

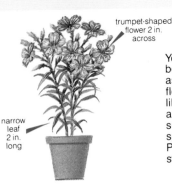

trumpet-shaped flower 2 in. across

narrow leaf 2 in. long

SALPIGLOSSIS SINUATA

Painted Tongue

TYPE

The 1–2 ft stems of **S. sinuata** bear large velvety blooms in a wide range of colours, the petals dark veined and regularly arranged to form a 5-pointed star.

You will not find Salpiglossis in many house plant books, but it is an outstanding pot plant. When grown as a garden annual the beauty of the individual flowers is often lost; indoors the yellow, orange, red or lilac flowers provide an eye-catching display. Plants are raised from seed — sow in early spring for summer flowering or sow in autumn for an early spring display. Transfer each seedling to a 5 in. pot. Provide cool, well lit and airy conditions; stake the tall stems.

SECRETS OF SUCCESS

Temperature: Cool or average warmth; keep at 50°–65°F.

Light: Bright light with some direct sun.

Water: Keep compost moist at all times.

Air Humidity: Mist leaves occasionally.

Care After Flowering: Plant should be discarded.

Propagation: Sow seeds in spring or autumn.

Salpiglossis hybrids

ROSA

It may seem surprising that roses are found in nearly all gardens but very few homes possess an indoor rose. This cannot be due to a lack of appeal — Miniature Roses bear lovely ½ – 1½ in. blooms which are similar to their larger outdoor relatives. There is fragrance, a wide array of colours and a variety of shapes including bushes (6 – 12 in. high), climbers and standards. The reason for the lack of popularity is their inability to flourish in the average room, but with care they can be grown successfully, providing blooms from early spring to late summer. The secret is to treat it as an outdoor plant which is brought indoors for flowering. Outdoors it needs little care — keep pests and diseases at bay and prune in winter. Indoors it needs abundant light, cool airy conditions, high humidity and plenty of water. Remove faded blooms to prolong the flowering season.

SECRETS OF SUCCESS

Temperature: Average warmth; keep at 50° – 70°F during the growing season.

Light: Maximum light; a sunny windowsill is ideal. In the short-day months extra light will be needed; place the pot near a fluorescent lamp at night.

Water: Water liberally when indoors. Allow to dry out slightly between waterings.

Air Humidity: Stand pot on a pebble tray (see page 27) if the room is warm. Mist leaves frequently.

Care After Flowering: Repot in autumn and transfer outdoors; bury the pot in soil if you can. Bring indoors in mid winter and remove top half of stems — move into an unheated spot for a week or two before placing it in a heated room.

Propagation: Take stem cuttings in early spring; use rooting hormone.

flowers
single,
semi-double
or double

plant
6 – 12 in.
high

flower
½ – 1½ in.
across

ROSA CHINENSIS MINIMA
Miniature Rose
(Fairy Rose)

TYPES

You will have no difficulty at all in recognising a Miniature Rose in bloom. It looks just like an ordinary garden variety scaled down to size — the same leaves, the same wide range of colours and flower-shapes, the same range of fragrance. With such properties and with our traditional love of the rose you would expect these hybrids of **R. chinensis minima (R. roulettii)** to be popular, but they are not. People have tried them as pot plants and have been disappointed. The secret is to choose a variety listed as 12 in. tall or less, pick a plant grown from a cutting or micro-cutting rather than a grafted rose, and treat as an indoor/outdoor plant as described above.

Baby Darling (double, orange and pink, no fragrance, 12 in.)

Judy Fischer (double, pink, no fragrance, 9 in.)

Yellow Doll (double, pale yellow, fragrant, 10 in.)

Starina (double, vermilion, fragrant, 10 in.)

New Penny (double, coppery-pink, no fragrance, 9 in.)

Cinderella (double, silvery-pink, slight fragrance, 10 in.)

Scarlet Gem (double, bright red, no fragrance, 10 in.)

SINGLE
less than
8 petals

SEMI-DOUBLE
8 – 20
petals

DOUBLE
more than
20 petals

Rosa Baby Darling

Rosa Judy Fischer

Rosa Yellow Doll

SCHIZANTHUS

Schizanthus hybrida

Poor Man's Orchid is an apt name for this plant; exotic multicoloured blooms can be obtained for the price of a packet of seed. Sowings are made in spring for late summer flowering or in autumn for blooming in spring. Pinch out the tips of young plants to induce bushiness. Move seedlings into larger pots as required; final pot size should be 5 in. for dwarf varieties, 7 in. for taller types. Keep the plants cool, well lit and provide fresh air on warm days.

orchid-like flower 1 in. across

ferny leaf 2 in. long

SCHIZANTHUS HYBRIDA
Poor Man's Orchid

SECRETS OF SUCCESS

Temperature: Cool or average warmth; keep at 50°–65°F.

Light: Bright light with some direct sun.

Water: Keep compost moist at all times.

Air Humidity: Mist leaves occasionally.

Care After Flowering: Plant should be discarded.

Propagation: Sow seeds in spring or autumn.

TYPES

S. hybrida bears unevenly lobed and yellow-eyed flowers. Choose a compact variety (10–15 in.) such as **Hit Parade, Star Parade** or **Dwarf Bouquet**.

> *I have always found that, with the aid of a manservant, who, although perfectly ignorant of gardening and plants, was always ready to work where I was directing, and the still more frequent assistance of a female domestic, I could get through all the labour of managing my indoor plants. The lady must obtain a man who does not know too much, not a gardener, but a man who will fetch and carry, wash, sweep and clean, attend to what he is told, and not act on his own opinion.*

"A Lady"

Every Lady's Guide to her own Greenhouse, Hothouse and Conservatory (1851)

SOLANUM

Solanum plants bear tiny flowers in summer and these are followed in autumn by green berries which change colour as winter approaches. The Winter Cherry is a familiar sight at Christmas. The orange or red berries among the dark green leaves provide a festive touch, and if this small shrubby plant is placed on a sunny windowsill in a cool room then the berries will last for months. A closely related species, Jerusalem Cherry (S. pseudocapsicum) bears larger berries. A word of warning — these fruits can be poisonous. The Winter Cherry should last till February — early leaf fall usually means overwatering; dropping berries indicate too little light or hot, dry air.

SECRETS OF SUCCESS

Temperature: Cool; keep at 50°–60°F during winter.

Light: Bright light with some direct sun.

Water: Keep the compost moist at all times.

Air Humidity: Mist leaves frequently.

Care After Flowering: Prune back stems to half their length in late winter. Keep the compost almost dry until spring, then repot. Stand the pot outdoors during the summer months; spray the plants when in flower. Bring back indoors in autumn.

Propagation: Sow seeds or take stem cuttings in spring.

TYPES

leaf 2 in. long with wavy edges

star-shaped flowers followed by roundish-oval berries

downy stems

SOLANUM CAPSICASTRUM
Winter Cherry

S. capsicastrum is sold in vast quantities every Christmas from supermarkets, garden centres and market stalls. The dark green leaves are narrowly oval and the white flowers form berries which are about ½ in. in diameter when mature. The plants are usually bought when the fruits have changed from green to orange-red and these will remain on the plants for months if kept in a cool place. There are several varieties, such as **Cherry Ripe** (bright red berries) and **variegatum** (cream-splashed leaves). The Jerusalem Cherry (**S. pseudocapsicum**) is also popular, especially in the U.S., and is quite similar. If you look closely, however, you will see that the stems are smooth. Also the berries are larger, the leaves shorter and the colours generally brighter. The species is quite tall (1½ – 2½ ft) but 1 ft dwarf varieties (**nanum, Tom Thumb,** etc) are the favourite types.

Solanum pseudocapsicum

SMITHIANTHA

Temple Bells, the popular name given to Smithiantha hybrids, describes the pendent bell-like flowers which appear on long stalks in autumn above the mottled velvety leaves. Smithiantha is not an easy plant to grow in the average room; it needs the warm humid conditions associated with the greenhouse or conservatory. It is raised from rhizomes planted on their sides in potting compost in late winter; they should be ½ in. below the surface and you will need about three rhizomes for a 4 in. pot.

Smithiantha hybrida

pendent flower 2 in. long

mottled leaf 4 in. long

SMITHIANTHA HYBRIDA
Temple Bells

SECRETS OF SUCCESS

Temperature: Warm or average warmth; not less than 60°F.

Light: Brightly lit spot away from direct sun.

Water: Keep the compost moist at all times.

Air Humidity: Mist frequently around the plant but do not wet the leaves.

Care After Flowering: Stop watering and leave rhizome to overwinter in the pot. Repot in late winter.

Propagation: Divide rhizomes at repotting time.

TYPES

S. zebrina is a tall-growing plant — it is better to choose one of the varieties of **S. hybrida** (12 – 15 in.). The flowers are a blend of yellow, orange and/or pink.

THUNBERGIA

Black-eyed Susan is one of the best pot plants to choose for covering a large area quickly and for providing summer colour. A few seeds sown in early spring will produce enough plants to clothe a screen or trellis with twining stems several feet long. When grown as a climber some form of support is essential; it can also be grown as a trailing plant in a hanging basket. Pinch out tips of young plants. Remove faded flowers before they produce seed.

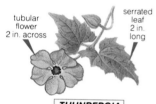

tubular flower 2 in. across

serrated leaf 2 in. long

THUNBERGIA ALATA
Black-eyed Susan

TYPE

Sow seeds or buy a plant of **T. alata** in spring. Throughout the summer the brown-throated flowers appear, with petals of white, yellow or orange depending upon the variety.

Thunbergia alata

SECRETS OF SUCCESS

Temperature: Average warmth.

Light: Bright light with some direct sun.

Water: Keep the compost moist at all times.

Air Humidity: Mist leaves occasionally, especially in hot weather.

Care After Flowering: Plant should be discarded.

Propagation: Sow seeds in early spring.

TORENIA

This summer-flowering annual is raised from seed sown in early spring. Its growth habit is rather lanky — pinch out the tips to induce bushiness and provide some means of support when it is fully grown. The flowers are quite unmistakable. The face of each bloom is violet with a dark purple lower lip and a distinctive yellow blotch. There are no special needs — keep it in a well-lit spot, water regularly and avoid draughts. Dead-head regularly.

tubular flower 1 in. across

serrated leaf 2 in. long

TORENIA FOURNIERI
Wishbone Flower

TYPES

T. fournieri is the usual type — compact bush 10 – 12 in. when staked — can be left unstaked in hanging baskets. Two varieties are available — **alba** (all-white) and **grandiflora** (larger and freer-flowering).

SECRETS OF SUCCESS

Temperature: Average warmth; Keep at 55° – 70°F.

Light: Bright light away from direct sun.

Water: Keep compost moist at all times.

Care After Flowering: Plant should be discarded.

Propagation: Sow seeds in spring.

Torenia fournieri

CHAPTER 9

THE NAMING OF INDOOR PLANTS

NAMING HOUSE PLANTS

Latin name Botanical name 'Proper' name Scientific name	Common name Popular name English name
Hedera helix	= *Common Ivy*

Name of genus:
This is equivalent
to a surname

Name of species:
This is equivalent
to a Christian name

Only one type of plant can have this name. Once the full latin name has been used on a page, a nearby reference is abbreviated.
For example: H. helix

A species such as H. helix may have several closely-related varieties. The variety name is usually in latin.
For example: H. helix cristata
                           H. helix scutifolia

If the variety originated in cultivation and not in the wild then it is called a cultivar (short for "cultivated variety"). The cultivar name is usually not in latin.
For example: H. helix Chicago
                           H. helix Little Eva

One genus or several genera which have a basically similar floral pattern make up a family. Hedera, Fatsia, Dizygotheca and Schefflera all belong to the Araliaceae or Ivy family.

A number of different plants can have the same common name. For example, both Zebrina pendula and Tradescantia fluminensis are popularly known as "Wandering Jew". On the other hand a single species may have more than one common name — Impatiens wallerana is "Busy Lizzie" in Britain and "Patient Lucy" in the U.S. For these reasons it is usually better to refer to plants by their latin names.

The Ancient Greek philosopher Theophrastus began it all with a list of about 450 plants. That was over 2000 years ago, but it was not until 1753 when Linnaeus published his masterpiece *Species Plantarum* that plant naming was put on to a scientific and orderly footing.

It was Linnaeus who founded the binomial naming system outlined above, and each genus has a different name. There are two main types of generic name, and the most popular one is the *descriptive* name. This is usually a Greek word which has been latinised. The description may be an unusual part of the plant, the plant's appearance, its resemblance to another plant, its practical use and so on. The second major type is the *commemorative* name — a latinised version of a person's name which was considered worthy of posterity. Linnaeus was Swedish, so it is perhaps not surprising that many Swedish scientists have been immortalised in house plant names, such as Billbergia, Bromeliad, Browallia, Sparmannia, Tillandsia etc. Botanists from many other countries have given their names to house plants, and so have patrons, soldiers, garden curators, noblemen and so on. One of the surprises is that very few discoverers and collectors have been remembered in this way — Allamanda and Saintpaulia are exceptions.

Descriptions and proper names are the major sources of plant names, but the list does not end there. The *native* name has sometimes been retained (Kalanchoe, Ananas, Yucca etc) and the old *Classical* name may have been kept, as in the case of Amaryllis and Euphorbia.

Every plant name tells a story, but we are not always sure of the story. The origin of a few generic names, such as Rhoeo and Setcreasea, remains a mystery and others are a matter of dispute. Polyscias is a good example. We know it is Greek in origin, but some authorities believe it means 'shade-loving' and others claim the proper meaning is 'much-divided'.

ABUTILON Arabic — 'mallow-like'. Flowers have a mallow-like appearance.

ACACIA Greek — 'I sharpen'. Sharp spines on the stems are a common feature.

ACALYPHA Greek — 'nettle'. Leaves have a nettle-like shape.

ACHIMENES Greek — 'tender'. Plant cannot withstand frost.

ADIANTUM Greek — 'dry'. Leaves are not wetted by rain.

AECHMEA Greek — 'a point'. The bracts in the flower-head are spear-like.

AEONIUM Greek — 'eternal'. The foliage is evergreen.

AESCHYNANTHUS Greek — 'shameful flower'. The flowers in some species do not fully appear — see page 125.

AGAVE Greek — 'admirable'. The flower-heads are imposing.

AGLAONEMA Greek — 'bright thread'. The stamens are eye-catching.

ALLAMANDA Named after Dr. Allamand, 18th century Swiss botanist who discovered the plant.

ALOE Greek — 'bitter'. The sap is bitter — used in folk medicine.

AMARYLLIS Classical name — a shepherdess in Greek mythology.

ANANAS American Indian name for the plant.

ANTHURIUM Greek — 'tailed flower'. An apt description of the flower — see page 125.

APHELANDRA Greek — 'simple male'. Anthers are one-celled.

ARAUCARIA Name of Indian tribe in Chile in whose territory the plant was first collected.

ARDISIA Greek — 'spear head'. The anthers are pointed.

ASPARAGUS Greek — 'to rip'. Some species have stems with sharp spines.

ASPIDISTRA Greek — 'small round shield'. The stigma has a shield-like shape.

ASPLENIUM Greek — 'not the spleen'. The plant was used in folk medicine for liver complaints.

AUCUBA Japanese name for the plant.

AZALEA Greek — 'dry'. An odd origin for this moisture-loving plant. The name was first given to a N. European plant which thrives in dry conditions.

BEGONIA Named after Michael Begon, 18th century Governor of French Canada. He was the patron of Charles Plumier, the discoverer of the plant.

BELOPERONE Greek — 'buckled arrow'. Fanciful description of the shape of the stamen filament.

BILLBERGIA Named after J. G. Billberg, 19th century Swedish botanist.

BOUGAINVILLEA Named after Antoine de Bougainville, 18th century French explorer who led the expedition which discovered the plant.

BOUVARDIA Named after Charles Bouvard, 17th century French physician and Curator of the Jardin de Roi, Paris.

BROMELIADS Named after Olof Bromel, 17th century Swedish botanist.

BROWALLIA Named after Johan Browall, 18th century Swedish botanist — sometime friend and sometime enemy of Linnaeus.

BRUNFELSIA Named after Otto Brunfels, 16th century German monk and botanical author.

BRYOPHYLLUM Greek — 'sprouting leaf'. Small plantlets appear on the leaves — see page 106.

CACTUS Ancient Greek name for a spiny plant — certainly not a true Cactus as this family is native to the Americas.

CALATHEA Greek — 'basket'. The plant was used by American Indians for basket-making.

CALLISIA Greek — 'beautiful lily'. An inappropriate name as the flowers are inconspicuous.

CAMELLIA Named after Georg Joseph Kamel, 17th century Moravian priest and botanist.

CAMPANULA Latin — 'little bell'. The flowers are bell-shaped.

CAPSICUM Greek — 'I bite'. An appropriate name for the genus which contains Cayenne and Chilli Pepper.

CAREX Ancient Latin name for the plant.

CELOSIA Greek — 'burning'. The flowers are bright yellow or red.

CEROPEGIA Greek — 'wax fountain'. The long pendent stems bear waxy flowers.

CHAMAEDOREA Greek — 'low-growing gift'. The fruits of this palm are easily reached.

CHAMAEROPS Greek — 'low bush'. Some species are low-growing.

CHLOROPHYTUM Greek — 'green plant'. No one knows why this plant was chosen to bear the basic name for foliage plants.

CHRYSANTHEMUM Greek — 'golden flower'. The basic types have bright yellow blooms.

CISSUS Greek — 'Ivy'. An apt name for this climbing vine.

CLERODENDRUM Greek — 'fateful tree'. The plant was used in folk medicine.

CLEYERA Named after Andreas Cleyer, 17th century Dutch botanist.

CLIVIA Named after Lady Charlotte Clive, Duchess of Northumberland. The bulb was first induced to flower on her estate.

CODIAEUM Moluccan name for the plant.

COLEUS Greek — 'sheath'. The stamens are enclosed.

COLUMNEA Named after Fabio Colonna, 17th century Italian botanist and illustrator.

CORDYLINE Greek — 'club'. The roots bear club-like tubers.

CRASSULA Latin — 'solid'. The foliage is thick and succulent.

CRINUM Greek — 'Lily'. Flowers are lily-like.

CROCUS Ancient Greek name for Saffron.

CROSSANDRA Greek — 'male fringe'. The anthers are frilled.

CRYPTANTHUS Greek — 'hidden flower'. The true flowers are hidden within the bracts of the flower-head.

CUPHEA Greek — 'curved'. The base of the fruit is curved.

CYCAS Greek — 'Palm'. Despite the origin of the name, this plant is not a true palm — see page 88.

CYCLAMEN Greek — 'circular'. The corms are round in shape.

DATURA Ancient Indian name for the plant.

DIEFFENBACHIA Named after Josef Dieffenbach, 19th century Austrian head gardener at Schönbrunn Palace, Vienna.

DRACAENA Greek — 'female dragon'. When the stem of the Dragon Tree is cut, the milky sap turns into resinous 'dragon's blood'.

DUCHESNEA Named after Antoine Duchesne, 18th century French horticulturist who wrote a book on strawberries.

ECHEVERIA Named after Athanosio Echeverria Godoy, 18th century Mexican botanical illustrator.

EPIPHYLLUM Greek — 'upon leaf'. The flowers are borne on leaf-like stems, once thought to be true stems.

EPISCIA Greek — 'shade'. The natural habitat of this plant is beneath the leafy canopy of jungle trees.

EUPHORBIA Thought to be named after Euphorbus, physician to the King of Mauretania and the discoverer of the plant's medicinal properties.

EXACUM Greek — 'I drive out'. The plant was used as a poison antidote in ancient times.

FATSHEDERA Combination of the names of the 2 parents — Fatsia and Hedera.

FATSIA Japanese name for the plant.

FICUS Latin name for the Common Fig.

FITTONIA Named after Elizabeth and Sarah Mary Fitton, 19th century English horticultural authors.

FUCHSIA Named after Leonhart Fuchs, 16th century German physician and botanist.

GARDENIA Named after Alexander Garden, 18th century American naturalist.

GLORIOSA Latin — 'glorious'. Flowers are impressive.

GLOXINIA Named after Benjamin Peter Gloxin, 18th century German botanical author.

GREVILLEA Named after Charles Francis Greville, 18th century English naturalist and one of the founders of the Horticultural Society of London.

GUZMANIA Named after Anastasio Guzman, 18th century Spanish naturalist.

GYNURA Greek — 'female tail'. The stigmas are long.

HAWORTHIA Named after Adrian Hardy Haworth, 19th century English naturalist and authority on succulents.

HEDERA Latin name for the plant.

HIBISCUS Greek name for the plant.

HIPPEASTRUM Greek — 'horse rider'. Fanciful description of the shape of the flower.

HOWEA Named after the Lord Howe Islands situated east of Australia, the only native home of this palm.

HOYA Named after Thomas Hoy, 18th century English head gardener to the Duke of Northumberland.

HYPOCYRTA Greek — 'curved beneath'. The flower has a basal pouch.

IMPATIENS Latin — 'impatient'. Ripe seed pods burst and eject seeds when touched.

IRESINE Greek — 'wool'. Some species have woolly flowers.

IXORA Classical name — Ancient Egyptian (or Sanskrit) god.

JACARANDA Brazilian name for the plant.

JASMINUM Arabic name for the plant.

KALANCHOE Chinese name for the plant.

KENTIA Capital of the Lord Howe Islands, the home of the Howea (Kentia) Palm.

KOHLERIA Named after Michael Kohler, 19th century Swiss scientist.

LACHENALIA Named after Werner de la Chenal, 18th century Swiss botanist.

LILIUM Latin name for the plant.

LIRIOPE Classical name — mother of Narcissus.

LITHOPS Greek — 'stone-like'. Appropriate name for these pebble-like succulents.

MARANTA Named after Bartolommeo Maranti, 16th century Italian physician and botanist.

MONSTERA Latin — 'monstrous'. An obscure name, which probably refers to the large and deeply divided leaves.

MUSA Classical name — physician to the Roman Emperor Augustus.

NEOREGELIA Named after E. A. von Regel, 19th century Curator of the Botanical Gardens at St. Petersburg, Russia.

NEPHROLEPIS Greek — 'kidney-like scale'. The spore cases on the leaves are kidney-shaped.

NERINE Classical name — the Nereids were the daughters of Zeus.

ORCHID Greek — 'a testicle'. Swollen pseudo-bulbs appear at the base of some species.

OXALIS Greek — 'sour'. The leaves have an acid taste.

PACHYSTACHYS Greek — 'thick spike'. The flower-head is densely clothed with bracts.

PANDANUS Malay name for the plant.

PASSIFLORA Latin — 'Passion flower'. Named by early South American missionaries who saw symbols of the Passion within the flower.

PELARGONIUM Greek — 'stork'. The seed pod has a stork-like beak.

PELLAEA Greek — 'dark'. The leaf stems are black.

PELLIONIA Named after Alphonse Pellion, 19th century French sailor.

PEPEROMIA Greek — 'pepper-like'. The plant resembles Piper, the Pepper Plant.

PHILODENDRON Greek — 'tree lover'. An apt name for this climber which attaches itself to trees in its natural habitat.

PHOENIX Greek name for the plant.

PILEA Latin — 'cap'. The calyx is cap-shaped.

PLATYCERIUM Greek — 'broad horn'. The fronds are antler-shaped.

PLECTRANTHUS Greek — 'spurred flower'. The flowers of some species are spurred.

PODOCARPUS Greek — 'foot fruit'. The fruits are borne on fleshy stalks.

POLYSCIAS Greek — 'many canopied'. The flower-head is divided into many parts.

PRIMULA Latin — 'first'. Some species flower early in the year.

PTERIS Greek — 'wing'. A fanciful description of the shape of the fronds.

RECHSTEINERIA Named after Rechsteiner, 19th century Swiss clergyman and botanist.

RHODODENDRON Greek — 'rose-coloured tree'. The name was probably first applied to Oleander, which bears rose-coloured flowers.

RHOEO Origin unknown.

RHOICISSUS Greek — 'Sumach-like Ivy'. An odd name for this plain-leaved vine.

ROCHEA Named after Daniel de la Roche, 18th century Swiss physician.

SAINTPAULIA Named after Baron Walter von Saint Paul-Illaire, 19th century District Officer in German East Africa who discovered the plant.

SANSEVIERIA Named after Prince of Sanseviero, 18th century Italian patron of horticulture.

SCHEFFLERA Named after J. C. Scheffler, 19th century German botanist.

SCHLUMBERGERA Named after Frederick Schlumberger, 19th century Belgian horticulturist.

SCINDAPSUS Greek name for a similar plant.

SEDUM Latin — 'hold'. The plant holds on to stones, roofs etc.

SENECIO Latin — 'old man'. The fruits of some species have a hoary coating.

SETCREASEA Origin unknown.

SINNINGIA Named after Wilhelm Sinning, 19th century Curator of the Botanical Gardens at Bonn, Germany.

SMITHIANTHA Named after Matilda Smith, 19 – 20th century English botanical illustrator.

SOLANUM Latin name for the plant.

SPARMANNIA Named after Andreas Sparmann, 18th century Swedish botanist who sailed with Captain Cook.

SPATHIPHYLLUM Greek — 'blade leaf'. The flower spathe is blade-like.

STEPHANOTIS Greek — 'eared corn'. The stamen crowns bear ear-like appendages.

STRELITZIA Named after Queen Charlotte von Mecklenburg-Strelitz, wife of George III and patron of botany in the 18th century.

STREPTOCARPUS Greek — 'twisted fruit'. The long seed pods are twisted.

SYNGONIUM Greek — 'joined reproductive organs'. The ovaries are united.

TETRASTIGMA Greek — 'four stigmas'. The stigmas are divided into 4 parts.

THUNBERGIA Named after Carl Pehr Thunberg, 18th century Swedish botanist/physician.

TILLANDSIA Named after Elias Tillands, 17th century Swedish biologist.

TRADESCANTIA Named after John Tradescant, 17th century gardener to Charles I.

VRIESEA Named after Willem Hendrik de Vriese, 19th century Dutch botanist.

YUCCA American Indian name for Cassava (not Yucca).

ZEBRINA Portuguese — 'zebra'. The leaves are prominently striped.

CHAPTER 10

CACTI

Cacti are perhaps the most popular and least understood of all house plants. Their popularity is easy to appreciate when you remember that hardly any other indoor living thing can be expected to put up with so much neglect and yet outlive its owner.

There are scores of millions of cactus plants in the homes of this country, yet in most cases they are kept as semi-alive, green ornaments which hardly alter throughout their stay. This lack of active growth is due to a misunderstanding of their needs. After all, in the popular view they enjoy neglect, only flower once every seven years and come from deserts where they exist on a staple diet of sand, drought and year-round heat.

The truth is that too much fine sand may actually kill them and summer drought will put them to sleep. For proper development and

regular flowering they need winter temperatures which will make you shiver, and in summer many prefer fresh air outdoors to overheated stuffy rooms. Given proper treatment, as outlined in the Secrets of Success on the next page, your dusty desert cactus will come alive and, depending on the variety, may flower as regularly as the daffodils in the spring.

The cacti are a vast and varied family of plants, but every variety has a few features in common. All cacti (except Pereskia and young Opuntia) are leafless. On the stems you will find a number of areoles (woolly or bristly cushions). In most cases you will find outgrowths from these areoles — there may be spines, needles, long hairs or short hooks.

The cactus family is divided into two groups — the desert cacti and the forest cacti. The original home and the cultural needs of these two groups are different, as outlined below:

DESERT CACTI	**FOREST CACTI**
Natural home is the warm semi-desert regions of America. Despite the name of the group very few can exist in sand alone.	Natural home is the forest regions of tropical America, where they grow as epiphytes on trees.
Nearly all cacti belong to this group and there are hundreds to choose from. Most types are easily propagated from cuttings.	Only a few varieties are commercially available, and most of them can be recognised by their trailing habit and their flattened leaf-like stems.
Need very little or no water between mid autumn and early spring.	May need some water and feeding during winter months.
Require as much sunshine as possible, especially for flowering. Suitable for south-facing windowsills.	Require some shade during hottest months of the year. Suitable for north- and east-facing windowsills.

DESERT CACTI

HOW TO MAKE A DESERT CACTUS BLOOM

Although some cacti, especially the ones illustrated, will bloom when the plant is still quite young, there are others, such as Opuntia and Cereus, which will not bloom under ordinary conditions.

About half the cactus varieties can be expected to bloom indoors by the time they are three or four years old. They will continue to bloom each year, and although spring is the usual flowering season even a modest collection can be selected to provide a few blooms all year round.

The secret lies in the fact that most cacti will only flower on new growth. This calls for summer care and winter 'neglect' as described in Secrets of Success. Another point to remember is that flowering is stimulated when the plant is slightly pot-bound.

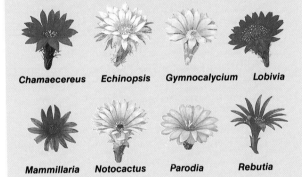

Chamaecereus	**Echinopsis**	**Gymnocalycium**	**Lobivia**
Mammillaria	**Notocactus**	**Parodia**	**Rebutia**

SECRETS OF SUCCESS

Temperature: Average warmth from spring to autumn. Keep cool in winter; 50°–55°F is ideal but no harm will occur at 40°F. Windowsill plants should be brought into the room at night if the weather is very cold and there is no artificial heat. The hairy cacti (Cephalocereus senilis and Espostoa lanata) need a minimum of 60°F in winter.

Light: Choose the sunniest spot available, especially in winter. In the greenhouse some shading may be necessary in the hottest months.

Water: Increase watering in spring, and in the late spring-late summer period treat as an ordinary house plant by watering thoroughly when the compost begins to dry out. Use tepid water. In late summer give less water and after mid autumn keep almost dry — just enough water to prevent shrivelling.

Air Humidity: Do not mist in summer (exception — Cleistocactus). The main requirement is for fresh air; open windows on hot summer days.

Repotting: Repot annually when young; after that only repot when essential. Transfer in spring into a pot which is only slightly larger than the previous one.

Propagation: Cuttings of most varieties root easily. Take stem cuttings or offsets in spring or summer. It is vital to let the cuttings dry for a few days (large cuttings for 1–2 weeks) before inserting in peat-based compost. Another propagation method is seed sowing — germination temperature 70°–80°F.

SPECIAL PROBLEMS

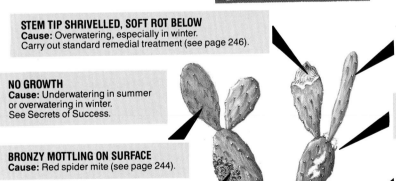

STEM TIP SHRIVELLED, SOFT ROT BELOW
Cause: Overwatering, especially in winter. Carry out standard remedial treatment (see page 246).

NO GROWTH
Cause: Underwatering in summer or overwatering in winter. See Secrets of Success.

BRONZY MOTTLING ON SURFACE
Cause: Red spider mite (see page 244).

CORKY PATCHES ON SURFACE
Cause: Localised damage due to insects, physical injury or sudden chilling. Another possible reason is underwatering in summer.

BROWN SOFT PATCHES
Cause: Stem rot disease — well-grown plants are rarely attacked. Cut out infected tissue and water compost with carbendazim. Improve growing conditions.

STEM ELONGATED & MISSHAPEN
Cause: Too much warmth in winter or too little light in summer. Refer to Secrets of Success; turn pots occasionally to ensure even growth.

PATCHES OF WHITE WOOL ON SURFACE
Cause: Mealy bug (see page 244).

BROWN HARD SHELLS ON SURFACE
Cause: Scale insect (see page 244).

ROT AT BASE FOLLOWED BY STEM COLLAPSE
Cause: Basal rot disease, due to overwet conditions in winter. Use upper stem for propagation. Next time avoid overwatering in winter, and cover compost surface with a layer of stone chippings.

DESERT CACTUS TYPES

slender green stems and brown spines. Pink tubular flowers

APOROCACTUS FLAGELLIFORMIS
Rat's Tail Cactus

globular white-flaked stem with prominent ribs and curved spines

ASTROPHYTUM CAPRICORNE
Goat's Horn Cactus

finger-like stems and white spines

CHAMAECEREUS SILVESTRII
Peanut Cactus

grey-green columnar stem covered with long silvery hairs

CEPHALOCEREUS SENILIS
Old Man Cactus

columnar stem with prominent ribs and brown spines

CEREUS PERUVIANUS
Column Cactus

Aporocactus flagelliformis is a popular and easy cactus — the ½ in. wide stems grow several inches each year and the 3 in. long flowers appear in spring. Good for hanging baskets, but remember that the ⅛ in. spines are sharp. **A. mallisonii (Heliaporus smithii)** is similar but the stems are thicker, the spines longer and the flowers larger.

Astrophytum begins life as a ribbed ball but becomes cylindrical with age. Yellow daisy-like flowers are produced in summer on mature plants, which grow 6–12 in. tall depending on the species. **Astrophytum capricorne** has curved spines, **A. ornatum** (Star Cactus) bears long straight spines and **A. myriostigma** (Bishop's Cap) has no spines at all.

Chamaecereus silvestrii is an old favourite — it spreads rapidly, the 3 in. long stems readily producing red flowers in early summer. If you think that cacti never bloom, grow this one.

On the other hand **Cephalocereus senilis** will never flower indoors. It is grown for its columnar stem which reaches about 1 ft and is completely covered by 5 in. long hairs.

Cereus peruvianus is the pride of many a collection — the stem reaching 2–3 ft in time and bearing 6 in. long flowers in summer. **C. jamacaru** is quite similar, but the spines are yellow and the white, night-opening flowers are even longer. **C. peruvianus monstrosus** is a slow-growing grotesque mutant.

distorted branched stems with irregular ribs

CEREUS PERUVIANUS MONSTROSUS
Rock Cactus

Aporocactus flagelliformis

Cereus jamacaru

Astrophytum ornatum

DESERT CACTUS TYPES continued

globular, wavy-ribbed stem and long spines

ECHINOFOSSULOCACTUS ZACATECASENSIS
Brain Cactus

globular ribbed stem and sharp yellow spines

ECHINOCACTUS GRUSONII
Barrel Cactus

small, globular dark green stem and small spines

ECHINOCEREUS KNIPPELIANUS

columnar stem with numerous ribs and small comb-like spines

ECHINOCEREUS PECTINATUS
Hedgehog Cactus

slender many-ribbed columnar stem covered with fine white bristles

CLEISTOCACTUS STRAUSSII
Silver Torch Cactus

columnar stem covered with silky white hairs

ESPOSTOA LANATA
Snowball Cactus

The convoluted ribs of Echinofossulocactus are almost as complex as its name — fortunately the ball-like Brain Cactus is usually sold as Stenocactus. There are several species — **E. multicostatus, E. hastatus, E. zacatecasensis** etc, and the usual form is a 6 in. globe with 1 in. spines.

Echinocactus is a slow-growing ball — it will take 10 years or more to reach a diameter of 9 in. **E. grusonii** is the common one — there is a golden crown of woolly hairs at the top and prominent spines along the ribs. It will not flower indoors — for deep pink flowers grow **E. horizonthalonius**.

There are many species of Echinocereus and some confusion over their names. The column-like one covered with spines is either **E. pectinatus** or the very similar **E. rigidissimus**. Height is about 10 in. and the pink flowers are scented. The much smaller **E. knippelianus** is more ball-like and less spiny. **E. salm-dyckianus** produces bright orange flowers.

The Cleistocacti are slow-growing, tall and densely covered with spines. Flowering does not begin until the plants are many years old, and the tubular flowers only partly open. **C. straussii** is the favourite species, reaching 4 ft or more after several decades. The wool and spines are white, giving the plant a silvery appearance.

Espostoa, like Cephalocereus, is a densely hairy species — the main difference is the presence of sharp spines on Espostoa. **E. lanata** is the only one you are likely to find — a 1–2 ft column which does not bloom indoors. **E. melanostele** is white at first, but later the hairs turn black.

Echinocactus horizonthalonius

Echinocereus salm-dyckianus

Espostoa melanostele

globular
or short
columnar stem and
short spines

globular or
columnar stem
and long spines

grey-green globular
stem with prominent
ribs and large red
hooked spines

brightly-coloured
stem grafted
on to another
cactus stock

ECHINOPSIS RHODOTRICHA
Sea Urchin Cactus

FEROCACTUS LATISPINUS
Fish Hook Cactus

ECHINOPSIS EYRIESII
Sea Urchin Cactus

GYMNOCALYCIUM MIHANOVICHII FRIEDRICHII
Hibotan Cactus

columnar stem
and dense
cover of
yellow spines

HAAGEOCEREUS CHOSICENSIS

There is nothing special about the ball-like or oval stems of Echinopsis — the notable feature is the outstanding floral display which appears each summer. **E. eyriesii** is the popular one, bearing ¼ in. brown spines on prominent ribs — the 6 in. long flowers are scented. The large Sea Urchin Cactus is **E. rhodotricha** which bears 1 in. spines and scentless flowers.

Ferocactus is a fearsome plant — barrel-shaped and armed with stout spines. The red bristles of **F. latispinus** are hooked — hence the common name. This cactus rarely blooms indoors — for orange flowers in summer grow **F. acanthodes**.

Gymnocalycium is the Chin Cactus, and most species and varieties are rather ordinary. The small globular bodies are green, ribbed and spined, but there is one group which are entirely red or yellow. These strains of **G. mihanovichii friedrichii** are the Hibotan or Red Cap Cacti — their brightly-coloured stems lack chlorophyll and so are grafted on to a green cactus.

Most of the cacti in this chapter are reasonably common, but Haageocereus appears in few shops and even fewer textbooks. The basic species is **H. chosicensis** — a broadly columnar cactus with the green surface hidden by bristle-like spines.

Hamatocactus setispinus is a close relative of Ferocactus — there are prominent ribs and large hooked spines. The ribs, however, are curved and notched, and the yellow blooms are readily produced each summer.

globular or
short columnar
stem. Flowers
followed by
red fruits

HAMATOCACTUS SETISPINUS
Strawberry Cactus

Echinopsis rhodotricha

Ferocactus acanthodes

Gymnocalycium mihanovichii friedrichii

DESERT CACTUS TYPES continued

globular stem with many ribs and pale brown spines

LOBIVIA AUREA

Golden Lily Cactus

columnar stem with many ribs and yellow spreading spines

LOBIVIA FAMATIMENSIS

Sunset Cactus

globular stem with hooked spines and dense white hairs

MAMMILLARIA BOCASANA

Powder Puff Cactus

short columnar stem with prominent tubercles and hooked spines

MAMMILLARIA WILDII

columnar stem with prominent ribs. Closely-packed areoles form white line

LEMAIREOCEREUS MARGINATUS

Organ Pipe Cactus

Lobivia is a good cactus for the beginner — it remains compact (3–6 in. high) and readily produces red or yellow blooms. Several species are available — the oval **L. famatimensis** is covered with flat yellow bristles and bears large golden flowers. Both **L. aurea** and **L. hertrichiana** are ball-shaped with prominent ribs and the summer blooms measure several inches in diameter.

Any large collection of cacti will contain several Mammillaria species and varieties. Their popularity is based on the compact growth habit and their free-flowering nature even when quite young — many bear attractive fruits once the small flowers have faded. One of the recognition features is the presence of tubercles in place of ribs, each tubercle bearing spines at the apex. The favourite species is **M. bocasana** — a cluster-forming silvery plant which bears a ring of small white blooms around the stem in spring. The oval-shaped **M. wildii** is quite similar — **M. rhodantha** and **M. hahniana** bear pink flowers.

In contrast to Lobivia and Mammillaria, Lemaireocereus is not easy to grow and often succumbs to disease. It is one of the much-branched cacti seen in Western films, growing 20 ft or more, but in the home **L. marginatus** is usually a single column with dense white wool along the ribs to tell you that it is not a Cereus (page 205).

Myrtillocactus geometrizans is an unusual type, with stems which branch and turn blue with age. **Heliocereus speciosus** (Sun Cactus) is another odd one — its green stems branch at the base and trail downwards. Bright red flowers appear in early summer.

branched columnar stem with prominent ribs and long spines

MYRTILLOCACTUS GEOMETRIZANS

Blue Myrtle Cactus

Lobivia hertrichiana

Mammillaria hahniana

Heliocereus speciosus

oval pads with long yellow spines

oval pads with tufts of golden bristles

globular stem with yellow bristly spines

globular stem with red hooked spines

OPUNTIA MICRODASYS
Bunny Ears

PARODIA CHRYSACANTHION

PARODIA SANGUINIFLORA
Tom Thumb Cactus

OPUNTIA BERGERIANA

columnar stem with yellow spines. Flat top slopes towards sun

NOTOCACTUS LENINGHAUSII
Golden Ball Cactus

Opuntias come in all sizes, ranging from prostrate plants no taller than a mouse to towering trees as high as an elephant. The most popular ones bear flattened pads and are the Prickly Pears of tropical regions, although they rarely fruit indoors. The favourite Opuntia is **O. microdasys** which grows about 1 ft tall and bears groups of tiny hooked barbs known as glochids. In the variety **albinospina** they are white — in **O. rufida** (Red Bunny Ears) they are brown. Many different Opuntias are available as house plants — grow the long-spined **O. bergeriana** if you want flowers, **O. brasiliensis** if you want a tall, tree-like plant or choose **O. cylindrica** if you want a column-like Opuntia which your friends won't be able to recognise.

Like Mammillarias, the Parodias are small, ball-like cacti which are tubercled rather than ribbed and which bear flowers from an early age. Unlike Mammillarias, they are usually solitary plants which do not readily form a large number of offsets at the base. The red-flowering one is **P. sanguiniflora** — the yellow-flowering types are **P. aureispina** (Golden Tom Thumb Cactus) which bears hooked spines and **P. chrysacanthion** which has bristle-like spines.

Notocactus has the common name Ball Cactus because the globular shape is not lost, although some species change to an oval form with age. **N. ottonis** is a typical Notocactus — spherical, fiercely spined and bearing 3 in. wide yellow flowers on plants which are only a few years old. **N. apricus** is another yellow-flowering ball-like type, but **N. leninghausii** is grown for its columnar stem rather than its blooms.

globular stem with spreading red spines

NOTOCACTUS OTTONIS
Ball Cactus

Opuntia rufida

Parodia aureispina

Notocactus leninghausii

DESERT CACTUS TYPES continued

columnar stem with yellow spines and long white hairs

globular stems and short white spines

finger-like stems and tiny spines

columnar stem with large areoles and long yellow spines

OREOCEREUS CELSIANUS
Old Man of the Andes

REBUTIA MINISCULA
Mexican Sunball

REBUTIA PYGMAEA

TRICHOCEREUS CANDICANS
Torch Cactus

semi-evergreen shrub with spiny stems and green leaves

semi-evergreen shrub with spiny stems and leaves red on underside

Oreocereus celsianus is an oval cactus bearing white hairs and a woolly top — the common name of this plant from the S. American mountains seems quite appropriate. With age the yellow spines turn red, branches arise from the base and red flowers appear. **O. trollii** is a less common species which is smaller and bears fewer ribs.

Rebutia is a popular cactus because it is small and starts to flower while still quite young. It is similar to Mammillaria in many ways — the globular stems are covered with tubercles rather than ribs and offsets are readily produced at the base. The bright funnel-shaped flowers, however, are borne close to the base rather than as a ring around the top as occurs with so many Mammillarias. **R. miniscula** is the favourite one — 2 in. balls bearing orange or pink flowers in early summer. The variety **grandiflora** bears large red blooms — **violaciflora** produces mauve ones. The baby is **R. pygmaea** (less than 1 in. high) and the giants are **R. kupperiana** and **R. senilis** (3–4 in. high).

Trichocereus is the Torch Cactus, grown for its columnar stems and huge white flowers which are borne on mature plants. **T. candicans** branches freely and grows about 3 ft tall — the more popular **T. spachianus** forms an impressive bristly column reaching 5 ft or more.

The odd man out — Pereskia bears thin spiny stems and true leaves. The flowers look like wild roses — hence the common name. **P. aculeata** is the common one, growing to 6 ft — the golden-leaved **P. godseffiana** is attractive but hard to find.

PERESKIA ACULEATA
Rose Cactus

PERESKIA GODSEFFIANA
Rose Cactus

Oreocereus celsianus

Rebutia senilis

Pereskia aculeata

FOREST CACTI

In their natural home the Forest Cacti are attached to trees in woodlands and jungles, and so it is not surprising that they are so different in form and requirements from the spine-covered Desert Cacti. There is an exception — the Rat's Tail Cactus (Aporocactus flagelliformis) grows on trees in its ancestral home in the mountains of Mexico, but it looks like and should be treated like a Desert Cactus (see page 205).

The typical Forest Cactus has leaf-like stems and a trailing growth habit, making it suitable for hanging baskets. A few, such as Rhipsalis, are grown for their stem form but their main attraction is their flowers. The most spectacular group are the Epiphyllums, with their fragrant saucer-size blooms.

Unfortunately the Forest Cacti can be shy bloomers, and there are rules to follow if you want a good display every year. Provide a cool and dry resting period, never move a plant once buds appear and allow stems to harden outdoors during summer. There are also specific needs for each type, as illustrated on page 212.

SECRETS OF SUCCESS

Temperature: Ideal temperature range is 55°–70°F. During resting period keep at 50°–55°F (see page 212).

Light: Choose a well-lit spot, shaded from direct sunlight for most varieties. Epiphyllum thrives on an east-facing windowsill.

Water: Increase watering when resting period is over and buds begin to form. Treat as an ordinary house plant when flowers appear and during active growth — water liberally when compost begins to dry out. Use rain water if tap water is very hard.

Air Humidity: Mist the leaves frequently.

Repotting: Repot annually shortly after flowering has finished. Epiphyllum is an exception — flowering is encouraged by pot-bound conditions so do not repot annually.

Propagation: Cuttings of most varieties root easily. Take stem cuttings in summer, using a terminal 'leaf' pad or stem tip. Allow cutting to dry for a few days before inserting in peat-based compost.

FOREST CACTUS TYPES

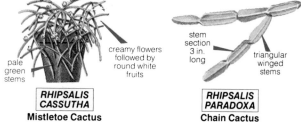

pale green stems

creamy flowers followed by round white fruits

RHIPSALIS CASSUTHA
Mistletoe Cactus

stem section 3 in. long

triangular winged stems

RHIPSALIS PARADOXA
Chain Cactus

Rhipsalis burchellii

In its natural habitat **R. cassutha** hangs from trees — indoors its long, branching stems trail over the rim of the pot. Small flowers are produced in summer and the fruits which appear later have a mistletoe-like appearance.

The long stems of **R. paradoxa** are narrowed at intervals, giving a branched chain effect. A suitable plant for a hanging basket — white flowers appear in summer. Another hanging basket Rhipsalis is **R. houlletiana** (leaf-like branches, white flowers).

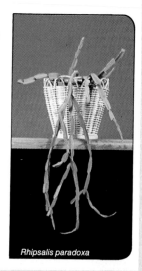

Rhipsalis paradoxa

FOREST CACTUS TYPES continued

flower 1 in. across with 2 tiers of swept-back petals

stems made up of distinctly tooth-edged segments

stems made up of scalloped-edged segments

flower 1½ in. across — open bell of sharply-pointed petals

ZYGOCACTUS TRUNCATUS
(SCHLUMBERGERA TRUNCATA)
Christmas Cactus

RHIPSALIDOPSIS GAERTNERI
(SCHLUMBERGERA GAERTNERI)
Easter Cactus

Rhipsalidopsis gaertneri Electra

Both the popular Christmas and the Easter Cactus have branching and arching stems composed of leaf-like flattened segments which are 1½ – 2 in. long. The margins are the key to identification — the segments of **Zygocactus truncatus** bear pointed projections whereas those of **Rhipsalidopsis gaertneri** and the smaller **R. rosea** are shallowly scalloped. Plants are usually bought in bud and many varieties are available. Z. truncatus varieties bloom between mid November and late January — white, pink, red or purple. R. gaertneri varieties range from pink to dark red and bloom in April or May. These shop-bought specimens usually produce a large number of blooms, but in unskilled hands never flower again. The reason is that these forest cacti need both a resting period (when water and warmth are decreased) and a spell outdoors in order to produce next year's flower buds.

	Christmas Cactus	Easter Cactus	Epiphyllum
JAN	FLOWERING PERIOD	RESTING PERIOD	RESTING PERIOD Keep cool (maximum temperature 50°F). Water infrequently
FEB	RESTING PERIOD Keep cool. Water infrequently	PRE-FLOWERING PERIOD Keep dryish and cool until flower buds form. Then increase water and temperature	
MAR			PRE-FLOWERING PERIOD Keep dryish and cool until flower buds form. Then increase water and temperature
APR	Treat normally; water thoroughly when compost begins to dry out	FLOWERING PERIOD Water normally. Maintain a minimum temperature of 60°F	
MAY			FLOWERING PERIOD Water normally. Maintain a minimum temperature of 60°F
JUN			
JULY	OUTDOORS Place in a shady spot; protect from slugs	OUTDOORS Place in a shady spot; protect from slugs	OUTDOORS Place in a shady spot; protect from slugs
AUG			
SEPT			
OCT	PRE-FLOWERING PERIOD Keep dryish and cool until flower buds form. Then increase water and temperature	RESTING PERIOD Keep cool (55°F). The soil ball should be moist, but do not overwater	Treat normally; water thoroughly when compost starts to dry out
NOV	FLOWERING PERIOD Water normally. Maintain a minimum temperature of 55°F		
DEC			RESTING PERIOD

notched stem 2 ft long

funnel-shaped flower 4 – 6 in. across

EPIPHYLLUM ACKERMANII
Orchid Cactus

The Epiphyllums are untidy plants, the strap-shaped stems sprawling outwards unless staked when in flower. This lack of an attractive growth habit is more than made up for by the flowers — flaring, multi-petalled trumpets which can be as large as a saucer. Nearly all the commercial varieties are hybrids of **E. ackermanii** — day-flowering plants which are available in a wide range of shades. The white, night-flowering Epiphyllums are hybrids of **E. cooperi** — the 5 in. flowers are very fragrant.

This cactus is closely related to the Easter and Christmas Cacti and like them will bloom every year with proper treatment. The range of colours is illustrated by **London Glory** (red), **Gloria** (orange), **Little Sister** (white), **Midnight** (purple), **Reward** (yellow), **Padre** (pink) . . . but no blue.

Epiphyllum Sabra

CHAPTER 11

MISCELLANEOUS INDOOR PLANTS

The indoor plants described in this book are separated into four major groups, each containing hundreds of varieties. There are the Foliage House Plant and the Flowering House Plant groups — included here are the types which spend their lives on display all year round in the home. The Flowering Pot Plant group contains the temporary residents, and the Cactus group includes the members of this quite distinct family of plants.

This classification is wholly artificial and has no natural basis. It is solely for the benefit of the reader. It tells you whether a plant is grown for its leaves (stems in the case of Cacti) or for its flowers — in the case of flowering plants it indicates whether the variety is likely to be a permanent member of the family or just a temporary visitor.

Like all artificial classification systems, there are some individuals which cannot be neatly pigeon-holed into any of the groups. These left-overs are gathered together and described here — the Miscellaneous Indoor Plants.

Some have a distinctly odd life-style which excludes them from the major groups. The Living Stones are grown for the odd shape of their stems, the Insect Eaters are purchased for their carnivorous nature, and the Air Plants are kept for their ability to live without watering.

Not all the Miscellaneous Indoor Plant group have odd habits. The Food Plants are ordinary types which usually have little intrinsic beauty but are grown for the fruit or leaves they produce in the kitchen. Bonsai, too, are plants without in-built peculiarities but have been miniaturised into pot plants and are grown for the beauty of their shape rather than for their foliage or flowers.

Lastly there are the Fun Plants which are the types we associate with children on wet days during school holidays. Growing Mustard & Cress and Garden Bulbs in bowls are described elsewhere — in the Fun Plants section on page 220 are the types of indoor plants which can be raised from pips, fruit, stones and plant tops. The popular examples are included but others can be tried — Mango, Peach, Horse Chestnut and Pomegranate.

AIR PLANTS

These are the Grey Tillandsias, which differ from their normal green relatives (see page 131) by bearing absorbent furry scales on their foliage. These scales take up water from humid air, and obtain nutrients from air-borne dust — they literally live on air! The commonest species is Tillandsia usneoides — the familiar Spanish Moss which hangs from trees in the warmer regions of America. Until recently they were virtually unknown as house plants in Britain, but you can now find several species for sale at large garden centres. These plants are stuck on coral, shells, driftwood, etc — they are not planted in compost. Four popular Air Plants are shown below — others include T. aeranthos, T. butzii, T. plumosa and T. bulbosa. The leaves around the flowers may change colour and provide a long-lasting bright display, but the blooms themselves last for only a few days.

Tillandsia ionantha forms a compact rosette of arching silvery leaves. It grows only a couple of inches high, and the inner foliage turns red when the stalkless violet flowers appear.

Tillandsia caput-medusae is perhaps the most popular of all the Air Plants. Thick and twisted leaves arise from a bulbous base. The red bracts and blue flowers are very showy.

Tillandsia juncea is a long-leaved species — rush-like foliage spreads outwards and a single flower-stalk bears the terminal blooms well above the heart of the plant.

Tillandsia argentea is a silvery species — the short leaves spread untidily outwards as the plant develops. The flower-stalk also bends and twists, bearing blue or red flowers.

BONSAI

The sight of a mature but miniature-sized tree growing in a small pot has a special fascination. It seems to be the ideal house plant, but be warned — it is not. Bonsai can have a spell indoors for four or five days at a time — place the pot in a well-lit spot and mist the leaves daily. For the rest of the time it must be kept in the garden or on a patio, to be admired through the window and provided with some protection against wind and rain.

A large number of hardy trees and shrubs can be used, but types with large leaves are not usually suitable. Conifers are favourite subjects — non-conifers include Maple, Birch, Willow, Azalea, Camellia, Hawthorn, Mountain Ash and Wisteria. It is not just a matter of keeping the plant in a pot to cramp the roots — according to the official definition a bonsai is ''a tree encouraged to conform in all aspects with ordinary trees, except for its miniature size. The technique . . . consists of keeping the tree confined to its pot by pinching out the top growth and pruning the roots to strike a balance between the foliage above and the roots below, and at the same time to develop a satisfactory shape.''

All of this skilful pruning and training account for the high price of bonsai. The work doesn't stop when you take it home — daily watering will be necessary in summer.

Acer palmatum

Chamaecyparis pisifera

Juniperus chinensis

Pyracantha angustifolia

● BONSAI continued

Sageretia theezans

INDOOR BONSAI

Indoor Bonsai is a relatively new idea which has not come from Japan. The centre of interest appears to be Germany but the concept is now spreading to other countries.

The basic difference from standard Bonsai is the use of non-hardy trees. This means that the plants cannot be kept outdoors during the winter months — they are kept on a pebble tray (see page 27) in the living room or hall for all to enjoy — the ideal spot is bright but away from direct sunlight, away from draughts and well away from radiators and fires.

During the indoor period water with rainwater or tepid tap water — mist the leaves occasionally with tepid water. In summer treat the plants in the usual Bonsai way — leave them outdoors and bring inside for only a few days at a time.

Trees and shrubs which have been successfully grown in this way include Olea europaea (Olive), Pistacia terebinthus (Pistachio), Punica granatum (Pomegranate), Jasminum primulinum (Primrose Jasmine), Carmona microphylla (Fukien Tea) and Sageretia theezans.

Bonsai Styles

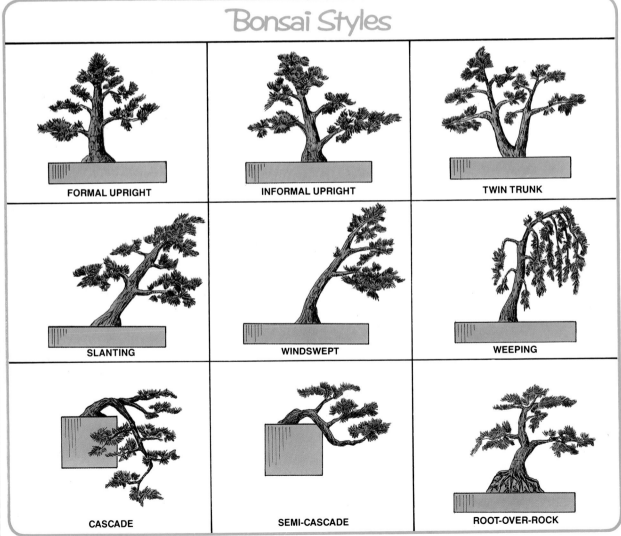

FORMAL UPRIGHT

INFORMAL UPRIGHT

TWIN TRUNK

SLANTING

WINDSWEPT

WEEPING

CASCADE

SEMI-CASCADE

ROOT-OVER-ROCK

FOOD PLANTS

House plants are not usually regarded as a source of food for the kitchen, but a surprisingly large number of culinary types can be grown.

Mustard and cress of course, but in addition a number of other leaf vegetables and herbs can be raised — see page 219. Fruit is possible, but don't expect too much. Some textbooks paint far too rosy a picture of the living room as a growing area for fresh fruit for the table. In the average room pineapples rarely ripen, oranges remain small and bitter, pomegranates fall off the plant shortly after the fruits have formed and ripe bananas remain just a dream. Still, a number of other plants will bear edible fruit if grown on a large windowsill and these are described below and overleaf.

The range of vegetables is strictly limited. Lettuce can be grown, but it is not really worthwhile and they do attract insects. Chives are a much better idea, or you can grow Spring Onions from seed. Pots of herbs on the kitchen windowsill in winter are a good idea — it saves the walk to the vegetable garden in mid winter to gather Mint, Sage, Thyme etc.

● FRUITS

Tomato Minibel

Cucumber Fembaby

Aubergine Long Purple

Once the idea of growing the Tomato (**Lycopersicon esculentum**) as a house plant was unthinkable, but the introduction of bushy dwarfs such as **Florida Petit, Minibel** and **Tiny Tim** now make it possible. Follow the standard rules — water daily when necessary, feed regularly, stake if required and tap the stems to aid pollination. Clusters of cherry-sized fruit will be your reward.

Cucumber (**Cucumis sativus**) sounds even less like a house plant, but the F₁ hybrid **Fembaby** has brought this greenhouse crop into the home. The plants grow no more than 3 ft high and are easily trained. The yellow flowers are all-female and each one should produce a cucumber. Stand the pot on a windowsill in a saucer and keep topped up with water. Mist leaves daily.

The Aubergine (**Solanum melongena ovigerum**) makes an excellent windowsill plant, growing about 1 ft high. Pinch out the tips if the stems exceed this height — stake as necessary and mist the leaves regularly. Grow **Easter Egg** for white fruits, **Long Purple** for the standard Eggplant of the supermarket or **Black Enorma** (1 lb. or more) to impress the neighbours.

● FRUITS continued

Peanut

Strawberry

Sweet Pepper

The Peanut or Groundnut (**Arachis hypogaea**) is an annual grown by planting unshelled and unroasted peanuts. The result is a rather plain 1 ft high plant with oval leaflets and short-lived yellow flowers borne just above soil level. Nothing special — but after the flowers have faded there is the extraordinary growth habit of stalks which curve downwards and drive the developing fruits into the compost. Warm conditions are essential.

You can grow ordinary strawberries in tubs or clay strawberry pots indoors, but it is usually better to choose the more compact Alpine Strawberry (**Fragaria vesca sempervirens**). It is easily raised from seed and the small plant (there are no runners) will produce its first fruits about 4 or 5 months after germination. Choose **Alexandria** for the largest berries.

The varieties of **Capsicum annuum** grown indoors are nearly always the small-fruited Christmas Pepper (page 170) used to brighten up the winter windowsill. But there are also the large-fruited Sweet Peppers, which are picked at the green or red stage for cooking. You will need a large well-lit area — they grow 2–3 ft high. Insects love them, which can make them a poor indoor plant. Suitable varieties include **Canape** and **Gypsy.**

Mushroom

Okra

Kumquat

The Mushroom (**Psalliota campestris**) may seem a strange choice for a book on indoor plants, but it is a fruit-bearing plant which is easily grown in an ordinary room and so earns its place here. Buy a Mushroom Tub — they are readily available and everything will have been done for you. No special care is needed — the upper surface or casing is kept moist and the first buttons will appear in 4–6 weeks.

Okra (**Hibiscus esculentus**) has begun to appear in the supermarkets — 4 in. long pods used in soups, stews and curries. Seeds are now sold by large nurseries and it is generally grown in the greenhouse. Although you won't find it in the house plant books you can grow it in a sunny spot indoors. You will need space — the plants grow about 3 ft high, but there are no pests to worry about and the pretty yellow flowers and erect pods provide a conversation piece.

The Kumquat is the one member of the Citrus family which can be relied upon to bear edible fruit under well-lit but ordinary room conditions. **Fortunella margarita** (Nagami Kumquat) bears oval orange fruit which are about 1½ in. long and are eaten whole. The glossy leaves are about 4 in. long — the spring and summer sweetly-scented white flowers are followed by the fruit in autumn.

● LEAVES

Lettuce

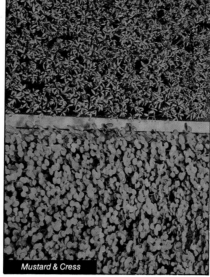
Mustard & Cress

Chives

Growing Lettuce (**Lactuca sativa**) on the windowsill is certainly not a way to save money, nor is it really satisfactory as the plants tend to be leggy. Still, it can be fun if you don't have a garden. Sow a forcing variety such as **Kloek** or **Dandie** — prick out the seedlings into 5 in. pots filled with potting compost. Place on a windowsill and keep the compost moist at all times. The plants will be ready to cut in 2 – 3 months.

The favourite edible indoor plants are, of course, Mustard (**Sinapis alba**) and Cress (**Lepidium sativum**). No description is really necessary for the millions who gained their first horticultural experience with them. Sow Cress seed evenly and thickly on damp kitchen paper in a tray. Sprinkle Mustard seed amongst or alongside the Cress 3 days later — move to a well-lit spot when the leaves start to unfold. Cut when the seedlings are 2 in. high — this will take 10–15 days.

Chives (**Allium schoenoprasum**) will grow happily on a sunny windowsill if the compost is kept moist at all times and the grassy leaves are cut regularly for use in omelettes, potato salad etc. You can start with seed but it is easier to buy a pot from a garden centre or dig up a clump from the garden. With seed-sown Chives trim off the tips of seedlings when they are about 2 in. high — do not let the plants flower.

Parsley

Mint

Basil

Sow Parsley (**Petroselinum crispum**) between spring and midsummer and have patience — it takes a long time to germinate. Pot up the seedlings in ordinary pots or plant in the holes in the sides of a parsley pot. Place the pots on a sunny windowsill and water regularly. Parsley is never really happy indoors — try to stand the pots outdoors on fine days and raise new plants each year to replace the old stock.

There is always a need for a plentiful supply of fresh Mint (**Mentha spicata**) in the kitchen. Many varieties are available. Lift a clump from the garden in autumn or spring and plant in a 5 in. pot, or buy a pot from your local garden shop. Stand the pot in a saucer of water during the summer months — remove the water and keep rather dry in winter. Keep the pot on a windowsill and cut regularly. Repot every spring.

A windowsill in a cool room can be used to grow several varieties of herbs. Grow them in separate pots and the best plan is to buy the pots from your local garden shop rather than trying to raise the plants from seed. Some are annuals — the suitable ones for indoors are Basil (**Ocimum basilicum**) and Sweet Marjoram (**Origanum marjorana**). Others are perennials — the house plant ones are Sage (**Salvia officinalis**) and Thyme (**Thymus vulgaris**).

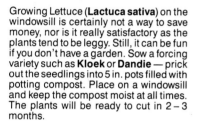

FUN PLANTS

AVOCADO

An Avocado tree (**Persea americana**) can be grown quite easily from the large stone within the fruit — after a few years you will have a large-leaved plant about 3 ft tall — grown from scratch with your own hands. Push the blunt end of the stone into a pot containing a multi-purpose compost — leave the pointed end exposed. Keep warm (65°F) until the leaves appear — keep cool in winter. Repot annually — pinch out tips to encourage bushiness.

CARROT

Growing Carrot (**Daucus carota**) tops is something we usually do with the children on a rainy day, but the plants produced have attractive feathery foliage which can be used in a Pot Group or Indoor Garden. Cut off the top inch from a well-grown Carrot and trim off the outer leaves. Push the cut end into compost in a 5 in. pot and leave just the crown exposed. It will take about a month for the foliage display to fully develop — keep cool and partially shaded.

RESURRECTION PLANT

This one is strictly for fun, and is designed to entertain the children. **Selaginella lepidophylla** is the Resurrection Plant or Rose of Jericho — the leaves are hard and scale like, the flat branches form a rosette which curls up into a ball when the plant is dry. This is the way we buy the Resurrection Plant — when dropped into water the leaves absorb water and the plants open out — once more a flat rosette with emerald green leaves.

DATE PALM

The dates you buy are the fruit of **Phoenix dactylifera**, an attractive Palm with stiff leaves and narrow leaflets. Plant the stone vertically in compost so that the top is about ½ in. below the surface. Keep it warm (70°F) until germination takes place — be patient, you may have to wait for 3 months. Keep the plant fairly cool in winter (50°–55°F) and repot every year. With care the date stone will produce a stately 5 ft tree.

PINEAPPLE

Bromeliads are expensive to buy — you can get one for nothing the next time you buy a Pineapple (**Ananas comosus**). Choose a fruit with a healthy crown of leaves and cut off the top inch of the Pineapple. Pare away the soft flesh so that you are left with a leafy crown attached to a cylindrical fibrous core. Leave this to dry for a couple of days and then plant in seed and cutting compost in a 5 in. pot. See page 51 for cultural details.

LEMON

The pips of citrus fruits germinate quite readily — choose Lemon (**Citrus limon**), Orange (**C. sinensis**) or Grapefruit (**C. paradisi**). Soak the pips overnight and then press each one down to a depth of ½ in. into compost in a 3½ in. pot. Keep in a warm and dark place until the shoots appear, then move to a sunny spot. Your plants will need to spend the summer months outdoors and the winter in a fairly cool room (50°–60°F).

INSECT EATERS

Some plants live in situations where their roots cannot obtain sufficient nutrients, and so they have evolved mechanisms to trap insects and then digest the contents of their bodies. There are three groups of these insectivorous plants — the **Fly Traps** with spiny-edged leaves which are hinged in the middle, the **Sticky-leaved Plants** with hairs which secrete insect-catching fluid, and the **Pitcher Plants** with leaves which are water-filled funnels. These plants are very difficult to grow indoors — water with rainwater, keep the compost constantly moist and the surrounding air humid, and feed very occasionally with tiny bits of meat or dead flies. But even if you follow these rules their life span in the average living room will be quite short. But don't be put off — they will arouse more interest during this limited period than some plants you have had for many years!

Dionaea muscipula

Drosera capensis

Dionaea muscipula (Venus Fly Trap) is the most spectacular Insect Eater in its action but not in appearance. There is a rosette of heart-shaped leaves, each one fringed with teeth and bearing trigger hairs and red glandular hairs on the surface. When touched by an insect the 2 halves immediately close and remain closed for about 2 weeks.

Drosera (Sundew) bears a rosette of leaves covered with red glandular hairs. These hairs secrete the juices which both trap and digest the insects, and 2 species are available. **D. binata** is an Australian Sundew which bears long and deeply-lobed leaves — the American **D. capensis** has undivided leaves. Both grow 6 in. high.

Nepenthes coccinea

Darlingtonia californica

Nepenthes coccinea is one of the lidded Pitcher Plants — insects are attracted by the brightly-coloured pitcher. Once inside this container they drown in the pepsin solution at the base. There are other lidded Pitcher Plants — **Sarracenia drummondii** has pale green tubes streaked with purple.

Darlingtonia californica is a hooded Pitcher Plant. Its snake's-head appearance is responsible for the common name — Cobra Plant. The pale green pitcher will grow to 2 ft or more under ideal conditions — the heavily-veined head and dark forked tongue making this one of the strangest of plants.

LIVING STONES

The Living Stones are interesting rather than beautiful, as they mimic the pebbles which abound in their natural habitat. All are members of the Mesembryanthemum family and each plant consists of a pair of extremely thick leaves. These are fused together to produce a stem-like body with a slit at the top. This slit may be as small as a tiny hole or it may extend right down to ground level, depending upon the species. The sizes of the various types available do not differ very much — the range is a height of ½–2 in. Colours and patterns, however, present a bewildering array and collecting a comprehensive range of Living Stones can be a hobby in itself.

All are extremely slow growing and must be kept dry throughout the winter. Below ground there is a short stem and a long tap root — above ground white, pink or yellow daisy-like flowers appear in autumn, and after many years a clump of 'stones' will fill the pot.

Scores of different Living Stones are available. Nearly all belong to two genera — Lithops and Conophytum, and identification of individual species can be extremely difficult. In some cases leaf colour is affected by the soil type.

1 in. high, olive-green with brown markings

1½ in. high, grey-green with mottled top

1½ in. high, grey with green mottled top

1 in. high, greenish-white

1½ in. high, blue-grey

1 in. high, green with translucent top

| LITHOPS PSEUDOTRUNCATELLA | LITHOPS FULLERI | LITHOPS SALICOLA | ARGYRODERMA TESTICULARE | LAPIDARIA MARGARETAE | CONOPHYTUM FRIEDRICHAE |

The most popular Living Stones are species of Lithops. Three are illustrated above — others which are offered for sale include **L. turbiniformis** (brown, wrinkled), **L. bella** (pale brown with dark markings), **L. lesliei** (brown with green markings) and **L. optica** (grey-green with translucent 'windows' on upper surface). The cleft between the two leaves in Lithops may be shallow or deep, depending on the species, but the cleft between the leaves of Conophytum is reduced to a small fissure through which the flower stalk appears. Several species are available, including **C. bilobum** (grey-green tinged with red) and **C. calculus** (pale green).

Lithops bella

Lithops lesliei

Conophytum pearsonii nana

CHAPTER 12

PLANT CARE

Plants growing in the garden rely to a large extent on the natural elements for their needs. All house plants, however, must depend entirely on you to provide them with their essential requirements. Leave them in deep shade or forget to water them and they will die. Without food they will steadily deteriorate. Virtually all varieties must be kept frost-free and the tender types require a minimum temperature of 60°F. Many plants find the air too dry in heated rooms, and you will have to increase the humidity around them to prevent browning and withering of the foliage. The least important requirement is fresh air, but some varieties demand adequate ventilation. Not all plant care techniques are life-saving exercises — the grooming procedures such as cleaning, training and trimming are designed to make the plant look better.

Light, water, warmth, humidity, food, rest, fresh air, grooming . . . a long list of needs but success calls for neither hard work nor great skill. It is simply a matter of satisfying the particular basic requirements of each plant and not trying to treat all plants in the same way. Remember that excesses can be fatal — too much sun and too much water are common mistakes, and feeding more than the fertilizer manufacturer recommends is foolhardy. Also remember that there is a resting period, usually in winter, when much less water, food and heat are required.

Talk to your plants if you wish, but there is no scientific evidence that it will have any effect at all. What your plants do need is for you to spend a few minutes looking carefully at the leaves, stems and compost. This should be done daily, if possible, during the growing season. You will soon learn to tell when things are wrong. The appearance and feel of the compost will tell you when water is required. The appearance of the foliage will tell you when the water, temperature, light, food or humidity level is wrong. Pick off withered leaves and dead flowers; look for pests and diseases. Some people grow indoor plants for years without ever *really* looking at them or bothering to learn what the leaves have to tell.

Give them the LIGHT they need	pages 224 – 225
Give them the WATER they need	pages 226 – 227
Give them the WARMTH they need	page 228
Give them the HUMIDITY they need	page 229
Give them the FOOD they need	page 230
Give them the REST they need	page 231
Give them the FRESH AIR they need	page 231
Give them the GROOMING they need	pages 232 – 233

Give them the LIGHT they need

Lighting Guide

FULL SUN
Area with as much light as possible, within 2 ft of a south-facing window
Very few house plants can withstand scorching conditions — only the Desert Cacti, Succulents and Pelargonium can be expected to flourish in unshaded continuous sunshine during the summer months. By providing light shade at midday during hot weather a much larger list can be grown — see page 12.

SOME DIRECT SUN
Brightly-lit area, with some sunlight falling on the leaves during the day
Examples are a west-facing or an east-facing windowsill, a spot close to but more than 2 ft away from a south-facing windowsill or on a south-facing windowsill which is partly obstructed. This is the ideal site for many flowering and some foliage house plants — see page 12 for a list of examples.

BRIGHT BUT SUNLESS
Area close to but not in the zone lit by direct sunlight
Many plants grow best when placed in this region which extends for about 5 ft around a window which is sunlit for part of the day. A large sunless windowsill may provide similiar conditions. See page 12 for a list of suitable varieties.

SEMI-SHADE
Moderately-lit area, within 5–8 ft of a sunlit window or close to a sunless window
Very few flowering plants will flourish in this part of the room, but many foliage house plants will grow quite happily here — see page 12 for a list of examples. Most of the Bright but Sunless foliage plants will adapt to these conditions.

SHADE
Poorly-lit area, but bright enough to allow you to read a newspaper during several hours of the day
Few foliage plants will actually flourish here — Aglaonema, Aspidistra and Asplenium are exceptions. Many Semi-Shade plants, however, will adapt and are capable of surviving in the darker conditions. No flowering plants are suitable.

DEEP SHADE
Unsuitable for all indoor plants.

Correct lighting is more than just a matter of giving a plant the brightness it needs; there are two distinct aspects which control growth. The *duration* a plant requires is fairly constant for nearly all types — there must be 12–16 hours of natural light or sufficiently strong artificial illumination in order to maintain active growth. Less light will induce a slowing down in food production, which is why the resting period of foliage plants is not broken by bright days in winter.

The light *intensity* requirement is not constant — it varies enormously from plant to plant. Some types will flourish on a sunny windowsill but quickly deteriorate in a shady corner; others will grow in light shade but cannot survive exposure to sunlight.

The human eye is an extremely poor instrument for measuring light intensity. As you move from a sunny window towards a corner of the room you will pass from Full Sun to Shade in about 8 ft. Walking with your back to the window you may notice little change, yet the light intensity will have dropped by more than 95% over a distance of a few feet.

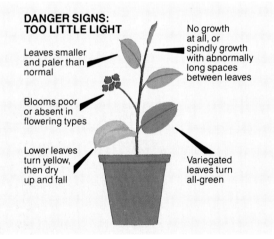

DANGER SIGNS: TOO LITTLE LIGHT
Leaves smaller and paler than normal
No growth at all, or spindly growth with abnormally long spaces between leaves
Blooms poor or absent in flowering types
Lower leaves turn yellow, then dry up and fall
Variegated leaves turn all-green

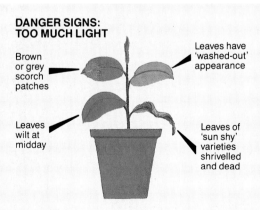

DANGER SIGNS: TOO MUCH LIGHT
Brown or grey scorch patches
Leaves have 'washed-out' appearance
Leaves wilt at midday
Leaves of 'sun shy' varieties shrivelled and dead

Natural light

- White or cream-coloured walls and ceiling improve plant growth by reflecting light in a poorly-lit room. A white background for a plant grown within the room will reduce the tendency for its stem to bend towards the window.

- The leaves and stems of a windowsill plant will bend towards the glass. To prevent lop-sided growth it is necessary to turn the pot occasionally, only make a slight turn each time. Do not turn the pot of a flowering plant when it is in bud.

- A flowering plant will suffer if it is moved from the recommended lighting to a shadier spot. The number and quality of the blooms are strictly controlled by both the duration and intensity of the light. Without adequate lighting the foliage may grow perfectly happily but the floral display is bound to disappoint.

- If possible move plants closer to the window when winter arrives. This will increase both the duration and intensity of the light falling on the leaves.

- Keep the windows clean in winter — removing dust can increase light intensity by up to 10%.

- A plant should not be suddenly moved from a shady spot to a sunny windowsill or the open garden. It should be acclimatised for a few days by moving it to a brighter spot each day.

- A foliage house plant can be suddenly moved from its ideal location to a shadier spot with no ill-effect. It will survive but not flourish — try to move it back to a brighter area for about a week every 1–2 months to allow it to recuperate.

- Practically all plants must be screened from summer sun at midday. New unfolding leaves will suffer most of all if some form of shade is not provided.

Rules for Lighting
Foliage house plants require bright light without direct sunlight; most of them will adapt to semi-shade. Plants with variegated leaves need more light than all-green ones, and flowering plants generally need some direct sunlight. Cacti and Succulents have the highest light requirement of all. There are many exceptions to these rules so consult the A-Z guide for details of specific needs.

Artificial light

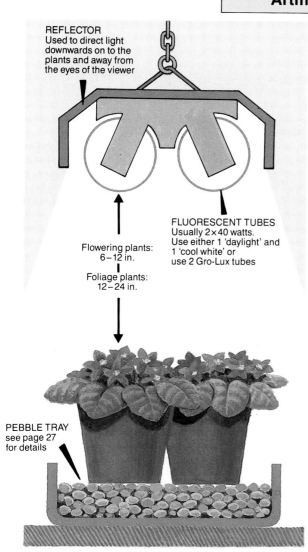

REFLECTOR
Used to direct light downwards on to the plants and away from the eyes of the viewer

FLUORESCENT TUBES
Usually 2 × 40 watts.
Use either 1 'daylight' and 1 'cool white' or use 2 Gro-Lux tubes

Flowering plants: 6–12 in.

Foliage plants: 12–24 in.

PEBBLE TRAY
see page 27 for details

Indoor gardening under lights adds two new dimensions. It means that you can grow flowering and foliage house plants in gloomy or even windowless rooms. It also means that you can supplement the duration and intensity of natural light in winter so that the plants remain in active growth — African Violets can be kept in bloom almost all year round.

Ordinary electric bulbs are not suitable for this purpose — the heat generated would scorch the leaves. Fluorescent lighting is used, usually in the form of long tubes. Many types of suitable units can be bought in countries where artificial-light gardening is popular. In Britain it is more usual to make an installation at home.

The basis of the unit is a tube or series of tubes mounted under a reflector. This arrangement may be permanently fixed above the growing surface or it may be suspended so that it can be raised or lowered as required. The plants should be kept in a pebble tray (see page 27). You will need to provide about 20 watts per sq. ft of growing area — if you use a light meter the reading should be the same as for a shady spot outdoors in summer. Look for danger signs — scorched leaves indicate that the lights are too close; spindly growth and pale leaves indicate that they are not close enough. Change the tubes once a year — do not change all of them at the same time.

The most popular varieties chosen for artificial-light gardening are usually colourful and compact. Examples are Begonia, Bromeliads, Cineraria, Gloxinia, Orchids, Peperomia and Saintpaulia.

Give them the WATER they need

Watering Guide

◀ **DRY IN WINTER Plants**
Desert Cacti and Succulents should be treated as Moist/Dry Plants during the active growth season from spring to autumn. During the winter the compost should be allowed to dry out almost completely.

◀ **MOIST/DRY Plants**
Most foliage house plants belong in this group. The standard recommendation is to water thoroughly and frequently between spring and autumn, and to water sparingly in winter, letting the top ½ in. of compost dry out each time between waterings. This drying out of the surface between waterings is especially important during the resting period from late autumn to mid spring.

◀ **MOIST AT ALL TIMES Plants**
Most flowering plants belong in this group. The compost is kept moist, *but not wet*, at all times. The standard recommendation is to water carefully each time the surface becomes dry, but never frequently enough to keep the compost permanently saturated. There is no rule to tell you which plant belongs in this group — look up individual needs in the A-Z guide.

◀ **WET AT ALL TIMES Plants**
Very few plants belong in this group. Water thoroughly and frequently enough to keep the compost wet, not merely moist. Examples are Acorus, Azalea and Cyperus.

Without water a house plant must die. This may take place in a single day in the case of a seedling in sandy soil, or it may take months if the plant has fleshy leaves. Because of this obvious fact many beginners give daily dribbles of water, they fail to reduce the frequency of watering once winter arrives and they immediately assume that the plant is thirsty whenever leaves wilt or turn yellow. This produces a soggy mass in which practically no house plant can survive. Waterlogging kills by preventing vital air getting to the roots and by encouraging root-rotting diseases. More plants die through overwatering than any other single cause — they are killed by kindness.

Each plant has its own basic need for water — see the chart on the left. Unfortunately the proper frequency of watering is not a constant feature; it depends on the size of plant, the size of pot, the environment and especially the time of year. Because of this your best guide is observation rather than a moisture meter.

Self-watering pots and devices have a role to play in caring for the Moist At All Times group and for plants when you are on holiday, but they have the distinct disadvantage of not reducing the water supply in winter.

Watering troubles

Water runs straight through

Cause: Shrinkage of compost away from the side of the pot

Cure: Immerse the pot to compost level in a bucket or bath of water

Water not absorbed

Cause: Surface caking

Cure: Prick over the surface with a fork or miniature trowel. Then immerse the pot to compost level in a bucket or bath of water

DANGER SIGNS: TOO LITTLE WATER

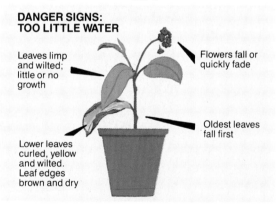

Leaves limp and wilted; little or no growth

Flowers fall or quickly fade

Lower leaves curled, yellow and wilted. Leaf edges brown and dry

Oldest leaves fall first

DANGER SIGNS: TOO MUCH WATER

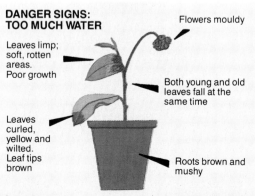

Leaves limp; soft, rotten areas. Poor growth

Flowers mouldy

Leaves curled, yellow and wilted. Leaf tips brown

Both young and old leaves fall at the same time

Roots brown and mushy

The water to use

Tap water is suitable for nearly all plants. Ideally the water should be stood overnight in a bowl to allow it to lose some of its chlorine and to reach room temperature. This standing period is not essential for hardy plants but it is necessary for delicate varieties. If you live in a hard water area a white crust may develop in time on the surface of the compost. This crust is harmless, but hard water can be harmful to lime-hating plants which are permanent residents indoors. For lime-haters which last for only a comparatively short time in our rooms (e.g Azalea, Erica) the use of hard water will not really pose a problem.

The standard source of soft water is rainwater. Collect it by standing a large, clean bowl outdoors; never use rainwater from a stagnant water-butt.

When to water

Tapping the pot is useless; measuring water loss by estimating its weight calls for great skill. The simplest way of discovering when to water remains the best. Look at the surface — weekly in winter, daily if possible in midsummer. If the surface is dry and powdery all over, water if the A-Z guide states that the plant should be moist at all times. With the remaining plants insert your forefinger in the compost to the full depth of your fingernail. If your fingertip remains dry then the pot needs watering. The most important exceptions are the Cacti and Succulents in winter — if the room is cool leave them alone unless there are signs of shrivelling.

Rules for Watering

Roots need air as well as water, which means that the compost should be moist but not saturated. Some plants need a partial drying-out period between waterings, others do not. All will need less water during the resting period. Don't guess your plant's watering requirement — look it up in the A-Z guide.

The way to water

Both the watering can and the immersion methods have their devotees, and both have advantages. The best technique for most plants is to use the quick and easy watering can method as the standard routine and to occasionally water by the immersion method where it is practical.

THE WATERING CAN METHOD

Use a watering can with a long, thin spout. Insert the end of the spout under the leaves and pour the water steadily and gently. During the growing season fill up the space between the surface of the compost and the rim of the pot. In the winter stop as soon as water begins to drain from the bottom of the pot. In either case empty the drip tray after about 30 minutes. Never water in full sun as splashed leaves may be scorched. In winter, water in the morning if the room is unheated. Take great care when watering containers without drainage holes — add a little at a time and pour off any free-standing water immediately. Although an occasional droop of the leaves will do no serious harm to most plants, do not make them beg for water in this way, for when this stage is reached the compost is definitely too dry. The leaves of woody plants, such as Azalea, should never be allowed to wilt.

Plants such as Saintpaulia, Gloxinia and Cyclamen which do not like water on their leaves or crowns can be watered from below. Immerse the pots in water to just below the level of the compost and leave them to soak until the surface glistens. Allow them to drain and then return the pots to their growing quarters.

How often to water

You must never allow watering to become a regular routine whereby the pots are filled up every Sunday. The correct interval will vary greatly — Busy Lizzie may need watering daily in summer, Bishop's Cap may not need watering all winter. The interval between watering for an individual plant also varies with the season and changes in growing conditions.

THE PLANT

Fleshy-leaved plants can tolerate much drier conditions than thin-leaved varieties and a rooted cutting will take up much less water than a mature plant. With any plant, the larger the leaf surface and the more rapidly it is growing the greater will be its need for frequent watering.

THE TIME OF THE YEAR

In winter, growth slows down and may stop; overwatering must be avoided during this resting season. Until new growth starts in the spring, watering one to three times a month is usually sufficient. During the spring and summer, watering willl be necessary one to three times a week.

THE ENVIRONMENT

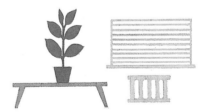

As the temperature and light intensity increase, so does the need for water. Plants in small pots and those which have not been repotted for some time need more frequent watering than those in large containers or ones which have been recently potted on. Plants in clay pots will need watering more often than those in plastic containers; double potted plants (see page 229) will need watering less frequently.

Give them the WARMTH they need

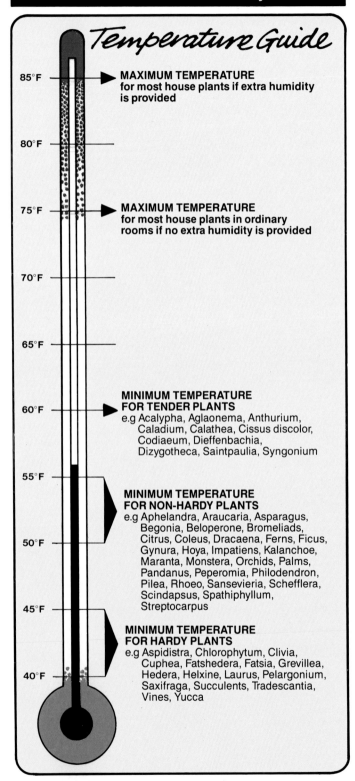

Temperature Guide

MAXIMUM TEMPERATURE
for most house plants if extra humidity is provided

MAXIMUM TEMPERATURE
for most house plants in ordinary rooms if no extra humidity is provided

85°F
80°F
75°F
70°F
65°F
60°F
55°F
50°F
45°F
40°F

MINIMUM TEMPERATURE FOR TENDER PLANTS
e.g Acalypha, Aglaonema, Anthurium, Caladium, Calathea, Cissus discolor, Codiaeum, Dieffenbachia, Dizygotheca, Saintpaulia, Syngonium

MINIMUM TEMPERATURE FOR NON-HARDY PLANTS
e.g Aphelandra, Araucaria, Asparagus, Begonia, Beloperone, Bromeliads, Citrus, Coleus, Dracaena, Ferns, Ficus, Gynura, Hoya, Impatiens, Kalanchoe, Maranta, Monstera, Orchids, Palms, Pandanus, Peperomia, Philodendron, Pilea, Rhoeo, Sansevieria, Schefflera, Scindapsus, Spathiphyllum, Streptocarpus

MINIMUM TEMPERATURE FOR HARDY PLANTS
e.g Aspidistra, Chlorophytum, Clivia, Cuphea, Fatshedera, Fatsia, Grevillea, Hedera, Helxine, Laurus, Pelargonium, Saxifraga, Succulents, Tradescantia, Vines, Yucca

Rule for Warmth
Indoor plants need a fairly constant and moderate temperature during the growing season and a lower temperature during the resting season.

The natural home of most indoor plants lies in the Tropics. In this country they are raised commercially in glasshouses. These two simple facts have given rise to the widespread belief that high temperatures are essential for the proper cultivation of house plants.

The truth is that very few types will grow satisfactorily at temperatures above 75°F under ordinary room conditions. The reason is that the amount of light falling on the leaves and the amount of moisture in the air are far less in a room than outdoors in the Tropics or under glass in Britain, so the need for heat is correspondingly less.

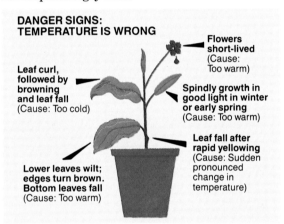

DANGER SIGNS: TEMPERATURE IS WRONG

Flowers short-lived (Cause: Too warm)

Leaf curl, followed by browning and leaf fall (Cause: Too cold)

Spindly growth in good light in winter or early spring (Cause: Too warm)

Leaf fall after rapid yellowing (Cause: Sudden pronounced change in temperature)

Lower leaves wilt; edges turn brown. Bottom leaves fall (Cause: Too warm)

Nearly all indoor plants will flourish if the temperature is kept within the 55°–75°F range — most types will grow quite happily in rooms which are a little too cool for human comfort. There are exceptions to this general rule — many popular flowering pot plants and some foliage house plants need much cooler conditions with a maximum temperature of 60°F in winter. At the other end of the scale the tender varieties require a minimum of 60°F; with warmth- and moisture-loving plants the pots can be stood in a pebble tray (see page 27) on a wide shelf above a radiator.

Most plants are remarkably tolerant and will survive temperatures slightly above or below the preferred range for short periods. The real enemy is temperature fluctuation. As a rule plants appreciate a drop of 5°–10°F at night but a sudden cooling down by 20°F can be damaging or fatal. Try to minimise the winter night drop in temperature by sealing window cracks and moving pots off windowsills in frosty weather. Cacti and Succulents are an exception — in their desert home they are adapted to hot days and cold nights, and so find the fluctuations in the centrally-heated home no problem at all.

Give them the HUMIDITY they need

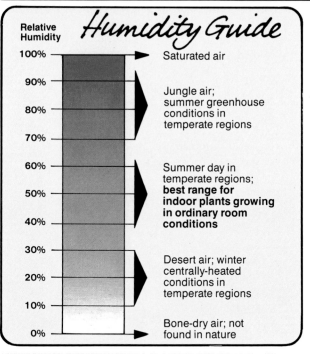

Relative Humidity

Humidity Guide

- 100% — Saturated air
- 90%
- 80% — Jungle air; summer greenhouse conditions in temperate regions
- 70%
- 60% — Summer day in temperate regions; **best range for indoor plants growing in ordinary room conditions**
- 50%
- 40%
- 30% — Desert air; winter centrally-heated conditions in temperate regions
- 20%
- 10%
- 0% — Bone-dry air; not found in nature

Cold air requires only a small amount of water vapour before it becomes saturated, and so on an average winter day the air is moist. When you turn on a radiator to warm up this cold air, its capacity to hold water vapour is greatly increased. As the room becomes comfortable the amount of water vapour in the air is no longer enough to keep it moist. The air becomes "dry"; in technical terms the Relative Humidity has fallen.

Central heating in the depths of winter can produce air with the Relative Humidity of the Sahara Desert. Very few plants actually like such conditions; many foliage plants and most flowering plants will suffer if you don't do something to increase the humidity around the leaves. You can, of course, avoid the problem by finding a moist home for your plants — the kitchen, bathroom or a terrarium, but the living room atmosphere will be dry. You can use a humidifier to increase the moisture content of the whole room, but it is much more usual to use one or more of the techniques below to produce a moist microclimate around the plant whilst the atmosphere in the rest of the room remains as dry as ever.

DANGER SIGNS: TOO LITTLE HUMIDITY

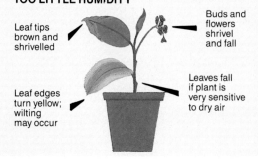

Leaf tips brown and shrivelled

Buds and flowers shrivel and fall

Leaf edges turn yellow; wilting may occur

Leaves fall if plant is very sensitive to dry air

DANGER SIGNS: TOO MUCH HUMIDITY

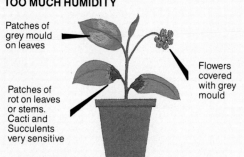

Patches of grey mould on leaves

Patches of rot on leaves or stems. Cacti and Succulents very sensitive

Flowers covered with grey mould

Misting

Use a mister to deposit a coating of small droplets over the leaves. It is best to use tepid water and under cool conditions do this job in the morning so that the foliage will be dry before nightfall. Cover all the plant, not just one side, and do not mist when the foliage is exposed to bright sunlight. Misting does more than provide a temporary increase in humidity; it has a cooling effect on hot sunny days, it discourages red spider mite and it reduces the dust deposit on leaves.

Grouping

Plants grown in Pot Groups and Indoor Gardens have the benefit of increased moisture arising from damp compost and the foliage of surrounding plants. The air trapped between them will have an appreciably higher Relative Humidity than the atmosphere around an isolated plant. The best method of raising the humidity is to use a pebble tray — see page 27. There is a danger of too much humidity when grouping plants together — make sure that there is enough space between them to avoid the onset of Botrytis — see page 245.

Double Potting

Use an outer waterproof container and fill the space between the pot and the container with moist peat. Keep this packing material thoroughly and continually moist so that there will always be a surface layer of moisture to evaporate and raise the Relative Humidity. Double potting does more than raise the humidity; it provides a moisture reservoir below the pot and it insulates the compost inside the pot from sudden changes in temperature.

Rules for Humidity

House plants need less warm air and more moist air than you think; papery leaves generally need more humidity in the air than thick, leathery ones. If your room is centrally heated and you wish to grow more than the dry-air plants listed on page 12, then group the pots together, double-pot specimen plants and mist the foliage as frequently as recommended.

Give them the FOOD they need

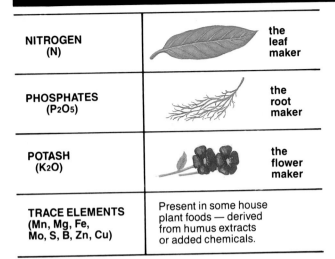

NITROGEN (N)		the leaf maker
PHOSPHATES (P_2O_5)		the root maker
POTASH (K_2O)		the flower maker
TRACE ELEMENTS (Mn, Mg, Fe, Mo, S, B, Zn, Cu)	Present in some house plant foods — derived from humus extracts or added chemicals.	

DANGER SIGNS: TOO LITTLE FERTILIZER

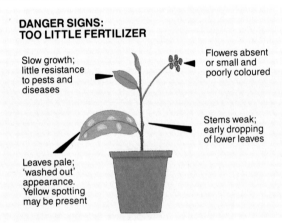

Slow growth; little resistance to pests and diseases

Flowers absent or small and poorly coloured

Stems weak; early dropping of lower leaves

Leaves pale; 'washed out' appearance. Yellow spotting may be present

DANGER SIGNS: TOO MUCH FERTILIZER

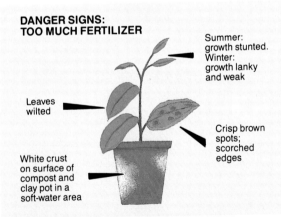

Summer: growth stunted. Winter: growth lanky and weak

Leaves wilted

Crisp brown spots; scorched edges

White crust on surface of compost and clay pot in a soft-water area

Rules for Feeding

If the plant is growing in soil or compost it is advisable not to use a method of feeding which relies on a reservoir of nutrients. There are times when the plant may not need feeding, and when it is necessary, the amount of nutrients needed will depend on the size of the plant and the size of the pot. The most popular method is to feed each time you water when the plant is growing or flowering. Reduce or stop feeding when the plant is resting.

All plants, indoors and out, need an adequate supply of nitrogen, phosphates and potash together with small amounts of trace elements. Only then will they be capable of producing healthy growth with full-sized flowers and leaves.

In the garden it is usual to apply fertilizers to top up the soil's natural resources, but even in their absence the plant can continue to draw on the soil's supply of nutrients by sending out new roots. Indoors the position is quite different. The soil or compost in the pot contains a strictly limited amount of food, and this is continually depleted by the roots of the plant and by leaching through the drainage holes. Once the nutrient supply is exhausted regular feeding when the plant is actively growing must take place. Cacti can survive for a long time without any feeding, but vigorous foliage plants and flowering plants coming into bloom are seriously affected if not fed.

What to feed

House plant foods are nearly always compound fertilizers containing nitrogen, phosphates and potash. By law the label must state the content of each of these elements; if there is no statement for one of them then you can be sure it is missing. Other plant-feeding ingredients, such as humus extracts, trace elements, etc may be present.

INSOLUBLE POWDERS AND GRANULES
Powder and granular fertilizers are widely used in the garden, but they are of limited use indoors. The plant food is deposited on the surface of the compost and it is not readily taken down to the roots where it is required. Furthermore you cannot cut off the supply when the resting period arrives.

PILLS AND STICKS
Pushing a pill or feeding stick into the pot is certainly labour-saving, but there are important disadvantages. The nutrients are concentrated in one spot which does not promote even root development, and you cannot easily cut off the nutrient supply when the resting period arrives.

LIQUID FEEDS
It is generally agreed that the most effective way to feed plants in pots is to use a liquid fertilizer. Watering and feeding are carried out as a single operation, thus saving an extra job and avoiding the danger of overfeeding. The recommended amount is added to the water, and this is used instead of plain water when watering.

When to feed

Potting composts contain enough plant food for about 2 months after repotting. After this time feeding will be necessary, provided the plant is not dormant. The time to feed regularly is during the growing and flowering seasons — spring to autumn for foliage and most flowering plants, and during winter for winter-flowering types. Feeding should be reduced or stopped during the resting period.

Give them the REST they need

Articles on house plant care always trot out the same list of essential needs — light, water, warmth, humidity, fertilizer but one requirement is often omitted — a period of rest.

Nearly all indoor plants need a dormant or resting period during the year, and this generally takes place in winter. Some plants give unmistakable signs that they are at the end of their growing period and even an absolute beginner can tell that the usual maintenance routine will have to change. The top growth of bulbous and tuberous plants (Hyacinth, Cyclamen, Gloxinia, etc) dies down; the leaves of deciduous woody plants (Punica, Poinsettia, etc) drop off. Watering is greatly reduced or stopped altogether as recommended in the A-Z guide. The *dormant period* has arrived.

Evergreen house plants unfortunately give little or no indication that a period of rest is needed. But as midwinter approaches the duration of natural light is too short to support active growth. The *resting period* has arrived. It is essential to reduce the frequency of watering and feeding; cooler conditions may be required. If the plant is kept warmer than recommended and watered as frequently as in spring then it will certainly suffer.

The appearance of new growth in the spring is a sure sign that the resting period is over. Slowly resume normal watering and feeding and repot the plant if necessary. Some plants, such as African Violet and Busy Lizzie seem to have little need of a resting period, but they do benefit from a period of about a month when watering and feeding are reduced below normal.

There is an important exception to the need for a winter rest period. Winter-flowering pot plants must be fed and watered regularly for as long as they are on display indoors.

Give them the FRESH AIR they need

Plants, unlike pets, do not have to be provided with air to enable them to breathe. Green leaves manufacture oxygen, and some plants will grow quite happily in sealed glass containers. Despite this unique property of plants, fresh air is still an important need of some varieties.

A change of air:

- Lowers the temperature in hot weather.
- Lowers the humidity where overcrowded, moist conditions encourage Botrytis.
- Strengthens the stems and increases disease resistance.
- Removes traces of toxic vapours.

Vapours arising from a number of sources commonly found in rooms have been reported as damaging to house plants or their flowers. These include coke and anthracite fires, coke stoves, dirty oil heaters, fresh paint and ripe apples. Plants with thick leathery leaves are the ones most likely to withstand the effect of these fumes. One menace has disappeared — plant-damaging coal gas has been replaced by natural gas. Tobacco smoke is never present in sufficient amount to be harmful.

Fresh air is provided by *ventilation* — which is the opening of either a door *or* a window in the room in which the plant is growing. Provide summer ventilation for the following plants:

Araucaria, Cacti, Fatsia, Impatiens,
Pelargonium, Schizanthus, Succulents, Tolmiea

Guard against *draughts*, which are air currents moving rapidly and directly across the plants. Do not ventilate when the temperature outside is appreciably less than that of the room.

Ventilation is not enough for some plants — they need to be stood outdoors during the summer months. Examples are:

Acacia, Citrus, Cytisus, Euonymus, Forest Cacti,
Jasminum, Laurus, Passiflora, Punica, Yucca

Give them the GROOMING they need

CLEANING

Dust is an enemy in several ways:
- It spoils the appearance of the foliage.
- It blocks the leaf pores so that the plant can no longer breathe properly.
- It forms a light-blocking screen so that the full effect of daylight is lost.
- It may contain plant-damaging chemicals. This is more likely to be a problem in industrial areas than in country districts.

It is therefore necessary to remove dust when it becomes obvious on the foliage. Small plants can be immersed in a bucket of water, but it is more usual to syringe or sponge the leaves with clean water. Wash plants early in the day so that they will be dry before nightfall. When the foliage is very dirty it should be lightly dusted with a soft cloth before washing — failure to do this may result in a strongly adhesive mud when the water dries. Remember to support the leaf in your hand when washing, and it is best to syringe and not sponge young leaves. Cacti, Succulents and plants with hairy leaves should not be sprayed or washed; use a soft brush to remove dust.

POLISHING

Foliage, even when clean, tends to become dull and tired-looking as it ages; the glossy sheen of the new leaf is soon lost. Many plant-polishing materials are available, and you should choose with care. Dilute vinegar, milk and beer are sometimes recommended, but they have virtually no shine-producing properties: Olive oil will certainly produce a shine, but it collects dust and can cause damage.

Buy a product which is specially made for plants — both wipe-on liquids and aerosol sprays are available. Aerosols are simple to apply, but are not suitable for repeat treatments at regular intervals. Leafshine liquids can be safely used on a wide range of smooth-leaved house plants; apply by gently wiping the foliage with a piece of cotton wool impregnated with the liquid.

There are a few rules when polishing. Do not polish young leaves and never press down on the leaf surface. Read the label on proprietary products before use — you will find a list of plants which should not be treated.

Untreated Rubber Plant leaf —
neither washed nor polished

Leaf polished with
a wax-based leafshine product

TRAINING

Training is the support of stems to ensure maximum display. This method of grooming is, of course, essential for climbing plants. It is also necessary for non-climbers with long, weak stems (e.g Fatshedera), heavy flower-heads (e.g Hydrangea) and brittle stems (e.g Impatiens).

Avoid the single cane wherever possible; use a framework of three or four canes. The canes should reach the bottom of the pot. Many other types of support are available — trellises, moss sticks (page 114) and wire hoops for inserting within the pot and climbing frames of wire and wood outside the pot.

Do not tie stems too tightly to the support. Train new growth before it has become long enough to be untidy and difficult to bend. Vines must be trained frequently or the tendrils will tie the stems together. A few untrained shoots hanging down from a climber can sometimes improve its appearance.

PRUNING

Stopping (Pinching out) is the removal of the growing point of a stem. Use finger and thumb or a pair of scissors.

Pruning (Cutting back) involves more extensive cutting out of excessive growth. Use secateurs, scissors or a knife. Whenever possible cut just above a growth bud.

Trimming is the removal of dead leaves, damaged parts and faded flowers.

The main purpose of stopping is to induce branching in many bushy and trailing plants, such as Coleus, Zebrina, Tradescantia and Pilea. The plants should be actively growing and the stem should have at least three leaves. The result is a plant crowded with stems, but with some climbing plants the opposite effect is desired. Here one or more strong main shoots are selected and trained as required, the weak side shoots being cut out cleanly at their junction with the main stems.

Many plants soon get out of hand and deteriorate if not regularly pruned and trimmed. Some climbing plants, such as Ivy and Philodendron scandens, regularly produce stems bearing abnormally small and pale leaves if kept too warm in winter. This growth should be cut back when spring arrives. Always cut out dead and diseased stems, crowded stems and all-green shoots on variegated plants. Cut back over-long branches and old leafless stems. Trimming of dead flowers (dead-heading) will prolong the flowering period of many species.

Prune flowering plants with care — there are no general rules. Some, such as Fuchsia, Pelargonium, and Hydrangea, bear blooms on new growth. Others, such as Hoya, flower on mature wood. Only prune when the Secrets of Success tell you to do so. Never guess with pruning — some plants will fail to bloom if you prune, others will become overgrown and unattractive if you don't.

Plant care at holiday time

Your time for rest and relaxation away from home is a period of strain for the indoor plants which remain behind, but a little preparation before you leave will ensure that they will be unaffected by your absence.

WINTER HOLIDAYS

Leaving plants for a week or two during the winter months should be a minor problem if you can provide them with the minimum temperature they require. On no account should the plants be left on windowsills; if possible put the pots on a table in the centre of the room and water so that the compost is moist.

SUMMER HOLIDAYS

Leaving plants during the summer months is much more of a problem because the plants will be actively growing and their water requirement will be much greater than during the winter months. If your holiday is for more than a week, the most satisfactory solution is to persuade a friend to call in occasionally and look after them. If your friend has little experience make sure that the perils of overwatering are explained.

When a plant babysitter is not available trim off buds and flowers, move the pots out of the sun and water them thoroughly. If you can, surround the pots with damp peat. This procedure will not be enough for a long holiday in midsummer. A number of automatic watering devices are available; capillary matting soaked by a dripping tap in the kitchen sink is an excellent answer to the problem. Individual pots can be stood on wick waterers or they can be slipped into polythene bags, which are then sealed with self-adhesive tape.

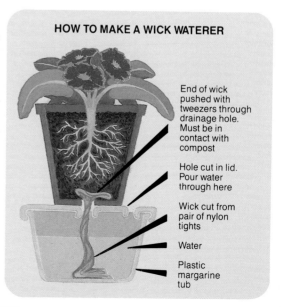

HOW TO MAKE A WICK WATERER

End of wick pushed with tweezers through drainage hole. Must be in contact with compost

Hole cut in lid. Pour water through here

Wick cut from pair of nylon tights

Water

Plastic margarine tub

CHAPTER 13

INCREASING YOUR STOCK

Some indoor plants cannot be raised at home without special equipment — you either have to invest in a thermostatically-controlled propagator or leave it to the nurseryman. But a vast number of different varieties can be propagated quite simply in the kitchen or spare room, and it is strange that there are so many people who grow their own vegetables and paint their own homes and yet are daunted by the idea of raising their own house plants. We now have so many aids which were unknown in grandmother's day — rooting hormone, transparent polythene bags, special composts, rooting bags and so on, yet the Victorians propagated a higher proportion of their own plants than we do.

There are four basic reasons for raising plants at home — to have more plants without having the expense of buying them every time, to replace ageing specimens with vigorous new ones, to have plants which would otherwise be unobtainable and to provide welcome gifts for friends. This final reason is responsible for the term 'friendship plants' given to varieties such as Busy Lizzie and Wandering Jew which are more usually raised at home than bought in a garden shop.

LAYERING

Most climbers and trailers with long, flexible stems can be propagated by layering — the disadvantage of this method is that rooting takes a long time.

Pick a vigorous stem and in spring or early summer pin it down into Seed and Cutting Compost in a small pot, using a hairpin or U-shaped piece of wire. A small nick cut into the underside of the stem will speed up rooting. Several stems arising from the parent plant can be layered at the same time. Once rooting has taken place, fresh growth will appear and the stem can then be cut, thus freeing the new plant.

OFFSETS

Some species produce miniature plants as side shoots from the main stem (e.g Bromeliads, Cacti and Succulents) or as tiny bulbils or bulblets next to the parent bulb (e.g Hippeastrum and Oxalis).

Stem offsets should be cut off as near the main stem as possible — preserve any roots which may be attached. A Bromeliad offset is ready for propagating when it is about a quarter of the size of the parent plant. Pot up each offset in Seed and Cutting Compost and treat as an ordinary cutting — see page 237. Bulb offsets should be separated from the parent bulb and potted up; it will take one or two years before flowering occurs.

PLANTLETS

A few species produce miniature plants at the end of flowering stems (e.g Chlorophytum, Saxifraga sarmentosa and Tolmiea) or on mature leaves (e.g Bryophyllum daigremontianum and Asplenium bulbiferum).

Propagation is easy. If no roots are present on the plantlet, peg it down in moist Seed and Cutting compost — see 'Layering' for details. Sever the plantlet from the parent plant when rooting has taken place. If the plantlet bears roots, it can be propagated by removing it from the parent plant and potting up as a rooted cutting.

DIVISION

A number of house plants form several clumps or daughter rosettes as they develop, and these plants can be easily propagated by division. Examples are Chlorophytum, Cyperus, Maranta, Saintpaulia, Sansevieria and many Ferns.

Knock the plant out of its pot in spring or early summer and carefully pull off one or more segments. Do this by gently removing some compost so as to expose the connection between the clump and the rest of the plant. Break this join by hand or with a sharp knife. Never divide a plant by simply cutting it in two.

Transplant the segments into pots using Seed and Cutting Compost. Trickle compost between the roots and gently firm to prevent air pockets. Water sparingly until new growth appears.

AIR LAYERING

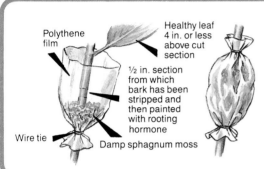

Polythene film

Healthy leaf 4 in. or less above cut section

½ in. section from which bark has been stripped and then painted with rooting hormone

Wire tie

Damp sphagnum moss

When thick-stemmed plants such as Dieffenbachia, Dracaena, Ficus elastica decora or Monstera become leggy due to the loss of their lower leaves, new compact plants can be produced by air layering.

Make the air layer as shown in the illustration; the cut should not be more than 2 ft from the tip of the plant. After a couple of months roots will be seen inside the plastic bag. Sever the stem just below the bottom wire tie, remove the polythene and pot up carefully in Potting Compost. The old plant need not be thrown away; it will produce new shoots on the shortened stem if the compost is kept just moist.

SEED SOWING

Unlike raising plants for the garden, seed sowing is not a popular method of propagating house plants. Nearly all of them require time, skill and heated conditions, but there are special cases where seed sowing is the method to use. Some plants, such as Thunbergia, Exacum and the Garden Annuals have to be raised in this way, and seed sowing allows large numbers of plants such as Coleus to be grown for indoor bedding at very little cost. Lastly, the young (and not-so-young) delight in sowing pips, fruit stones, beans, etc, to produce short-lived foliage plants.

Fill a pot or seed pan with Seed and Cutting Compost; firm lightly with the fingertips or a board and water lightly. Sow seeds thinly — space out each seed if they are large enough to handle. Cover large seeds with a layer of compost; small seeds not at all. Place a polythene bag over the container and secure with a rubber band.

Stand the pot in a shady place at a temperature of 60°–70°F. As soon as the seeds have germinated move the pot to a bright spot, away from direct sunlight. Remove the plastic cover, keep the compost surface moist and turn the pot regularly to avoid lop-sided growth.

As soon as the seedlings are large enough to handle they should be pricked out into small pots filled with Potting Compost.

SPORE SOWING

Ferns produce dust-like spores, not seeds, and it is always a challenge to try to raise fern plants from these spores at home. Collect them in a paper bag from ripe spore-cases which are found on the underside of the fronds. Leave them to dry for a couple of weeks and then spread them very thinly on the surface of moist Seed and Cutting Compost. The compost should be in a plastic pot which has been sterilised by immersion in boiling water. Cover the pot with a sheet of glass after sowing the spores and place it in a shady spot. When the plants are large enough to handle transplant them into small pots.

CUTTINGS

Cuttings are by far the most usual way to raise indoor plants at home. The chance of success depends on the variety — some woody plants are difficult or impossible to propagate without special equipment, whereas several popular plants, such as Tradescantia, Impatiens and Ivy, will root quite readily in a glass of water. Even with easy-to-root cuttings there can be inexplicable failures so always take several cuttings and do not be disappointed if a few of them fail.

Stem Cuttings

Most house plants can be propagated from stem cuttings. Choose a sturdy and healthy non-flowering shoot. Some non-woody plants will root at any time of the year but woody varieties are generally more reliant on active growing conditions so in this latter case always follow the timing specified in the A-Z guide and always use a rooting hormone. As a general rule spring or early summer is the best time for all plants, but late summer is a popular time for striking Fuchsia and Geranium cuttings.

Stem cuttings should be inserted in the compost as soon as they have been prepared, but a Cactus or Succulent cutting should be left to dry for several days before insertion.

With shrubby plants it is preferable to take heel cuttings rather than the stem-tip cuttings illustrated on the right. Pull off a side shoot with a 'heel' (strip of bark from the main stem) attached. Trim any ragged edges and dip the bottom inch in rooting hormone.

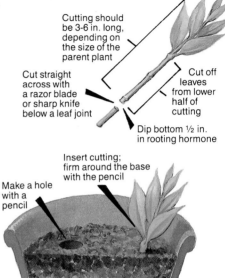

Cutting should be 3-6 in. long, depending on the size of the parent plant

Cut straight across with a razor blade or sharp knife below a leaf joint

Cut off leaves from lower half of cutting

Dip bottom ½ in. in rooting hormone

Insert cutting; firm around the base with the pencil

Make a hole with a pencil

Leaf Cuttings

Some plants do not have stems; the leaves arise directly from the crown of the plant. Obviously stem cuttings are impossible, but leaf cuttings provide an easy way to propagate many of these varieties.

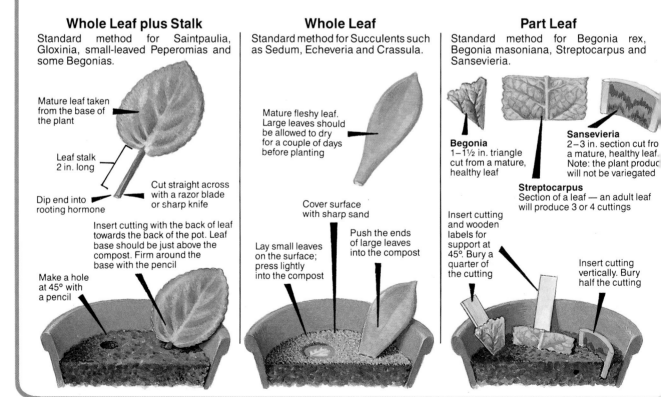

Whole Leaf plus Stalk

Standard method for Saintpaulia, Gloxinia, small-leaved Peperomias and some Begonias.

Mature leaf taken from the base of the plant

Leaf stalk 2 in. long

Dip end into rooting hormone

Cut straight across with a razor blade or sharp knife

Insert cutting with the back of leaf towards the back of the pot. Leaf base should be just above the compost. Firm around the base with the pencil

Make a hole at 45° with a pencil

Whole Leaf

Standard method for Succulents such as Sedum, Echeveria and Crassula.

Mature fleshy leaf. Large leaves should be allowed to dry for a couple of days before planting

Cover surface with sharp sand

Lay small leaves on the surface; press lightly into the compost

Push the ends of large leaves into the compost

Part Leaf

Standard method for Begonia rex, Begonia masoniana, Streptocarpus and Sansevieria.

Begonia
1–1½ in. triangle cut from a mature, healthy leaf

Sansevieria
2–3 in. section cut from a mature, healthy leaf. Note: the plant produc will not be variegated

Streptocarpus
Section of a leaf — an adult leaf will produce 3 or 4 cuttings

Insert cutting and wooden labels for support at 45°. Bury a quarter of the cutting

Insert cutting vertically. Bury half the cutting

Cane Cuttings

A number of important house plants which produce thick and erect stems are propagated by means of cane cuttings. The best time to do this is when one or more stems have lost their lower leaves and are no longer attractive. The bare trunk is cut into several pieces, and each piece is inserted into Seed and Cutting Compost. The cane cuttings can be placed horizontally, as illustrated, or planted upright. If planted upright, make sure you bury the end which was the lower part on the stem. Cane cuttings can be used for Cordyline, Dracaena and Dieffenbachia; ready-to-plant canes ('Ti-Plants') can be bought in gift shops.

Cutting should be 2–3 in. long, bearing at least 1 node. Leaf buds must point upward. Bury lower half in compost.

How to root Cuttings

The problem your cutting has to face is obvious. It will usually be a severed piece of stem or leaf, and it will steadily lose moisture without having any means of replacing the loss. So it is a race against time — roots must form before the cutting dies through lack of moisture within its cells. Keeping the compost wet is certainly not the answer — use one of the rooting methods described below.

The Rooting Bag Method

A recent innovation is the rooting bag, in which Seed and Cutting Compost is tightly packed and sealed in a stout polythene bag. There are two basic advantages compared to the pot method — the covered compost stays moist much longer and weak cuttings are supported by the polythene. The method consists of cutting fourteen slits in the upper surface and inserting a cutting through each slit. If the cuttings wilt after a few hours, the rooting bag is slipped into a large plastic bag which is blown up and the top tied with a wire tie or self-adhesive tape.

The Propagator Method

A propagator is a useful piece of equipment if you intend to raise a large number of house plants. Basically it consists of a firm tray to hold the compost and a transparent cover which bears air vents. A simple unheated model will meet the needs of the average indoor gardener, but if you plan to raise delicate plants which need a propagating temperature of 70°F or more then you will need a heated propagator. This contains a heating element to raise the temperature of the compost and a thermostat to ensure that the temperature stays constant.

The Pot Method

A 5 in. clay or plastic pot will take three to six average-sized cuttings. The rooting medium must be sterile, free-draining, firm enough to hold the cuttings and contain not too much fertilizer. A specially formulated Seed and Cutting Compost is ideal.

Fill the pot with compost and lightly firm to leave a ½ in. watering space at the top. The cuttings should be inserted close to the side of the pot; make sure that they are properly firmed in as an air space around the cut surface is fatal. Some cuttings are inserted vertically and others at 45°; the instructions on the previous page will tell you when the cutting should be put in at an angle. Water in very gently.

Nearly all cuttings will need a humid atmosphere — in dry air large leaves soon shrivel and die, as there is no root system to replace the rapid loss of moisture. Place four canes in the pot and drape a polythene bag over them; secure with a rubber band. There are three important exceptions to this polythene bag technique — do not cover Cactus, Succulent or Geranium cuttings.

Place the pot in light shade or in a bright spot out of direct sunlight. The temperature should be 65°F or more. Pick off any leaves that turn yellow or start to rot.

The great enemy now is impatience — do not keep lifting the cuttings to see if roots are appearing. In a few weeks the tell-tale signs of success should appear — new growth at the tips of stem cuttings, and tiny plantlets at the base of leaf cuttings.

Potting-on time has arrived. Water the compost and then lift out each rooted stem cutting, taking care not to disturb the compost around the roots. Transfer each cutting to a 2½ or 3½ in. pot — fill with Potting Compost. Firm gently and water to settle the compost around the roots. Put the pots back in the same spot for a week or two; then transfer to their permanent quarters.

The technique with leaf cuttings which produce several plantlets is different. When the new plants are large enough to handle, cut away the parent leaf, gently separate and pot on. Make sure that each plantlet has some roots.

CHAPTER 14
POTS AND POTTING

Most of this book is devoted to descriptions of hundreds of different varieties of indoor plants, but not one of them can be grown if it is not planted in a suitable growing medium inside a suitable receptacle. When you buy a plant the nurseryman will have already made a satisfactory choice, but in a year or two it will become pot-bound. The time has come for repotting — you will have to choose a satisfactory pot and the correct compost to house the roots, and you will have to ensure that the plant will settle down successfully in its new home. This chapter will show you how.

GROWING MEDIA

Soil taken straight from the garden is totally unsuitable for filling pots for the cultivation of indoor plants. It may well contain pests and disease organisms which would flourish under the warmer conditions indoors, and its restriction within a pot which is then regularly watered is almost bound to lead to a complete loss of structure. For these reasons indoor plants are grown in special mixtures known as *composts*. In nearly every case multipurpose composts are used, but you can buy special mixes for Orchids, Cacti and lime-hating plants such as Azalea and Cyclamen.

Soil Composts

The basis of soil composts is loam, made from turves stacked grass-downwards until well-rotted. Shortage of supply has meant that good-quality topsoil has been substituted in most cases; poor-quality soil will always produce an unsatisfactory compost. Other organic ingredients are added, and all are either steam- or chemically-sterilised before blending with fertilizer, lime and sand. The introduction of the John Innes Composts has removed the need for a wide array of bewildering mixtures.

Soilless Composts

Because loam is difficult to obtain and its quality is variable, modern composts are based on peat, or peat and sand. These soilless composts have many advantages over soil-based composts. Their quality does not vary and they are lighter and cleaner to handle. Perhaps the most important advantage of all is that the plant to be repotted was almost certainly raised in a peat-based compost, and plants do not like a change in growing medium at repotting time. Most manufacturers of soilless composts produce a single grade which provides an average plant with enough food for a few months. This fertilizer content makes potting compost too rich for sowing seeds or taking cuttings.

Soilless composts can have one or two drawbacks. All-peat composts tend to be difficult to water once they have been allowed to dry out but some contain an additive which makes the peat easy to wet. Lightness can be a disadvantage when a large top-heavy plant is to be potted — use a multi-compost which contains soil and sand as well as peat.

Aggregates

In hydroculture, porous clay aggregates replace compost as anchorage for the roots, and both roots and aggregates are bathed in a dilute fertilizer solution. The system is housed in a special container — the hydropot. These hydropots first appeared in 1976 and can be seen in public buildings where regular maintenance is difficult. They are expensive, but have the advantage of requiring water only once every few weeks. Fertilizer is added through a special filler tube.

The plants grown in hydroculture develop thick, fleshy roots in place of the thin fibrous ones which grow in soil. Some plants succeed better than others. Cacti do surprisingly well, so do Aglaonema, Philodendron, Scindapsus and Spathiphyllum. Repotting can be a problem, and compost-raised plants cannot simply be transferred to a hydropot.

HOW TO RECOGNISE A POT-BOUND PLANT

Most house plants thrive best in pots which appear to the beginner to be too small for the amount of leaf and stem present. It is a mistake to repot into a larger container unless the plant is definitely pot-bound. Check in the A-Z guide — some plants will only flower when in this condition and there are others, such as Bromeliads, which should never need repotting.

Stem and leaf growth very slow even when the plant is fed regularly in spring and summer

Soil dries out quickly, so frequent watering is required

Roots growing through drainage hole

Final check:
Remove the pot in the way described overleaf. If the plant is pot-bound there will be a matted mass of roots on the outside, and not much soil will be visible.

If it is not pot-bound, simply replace the soil ball back into the original pot; no harm will have been done.

REPOTTING

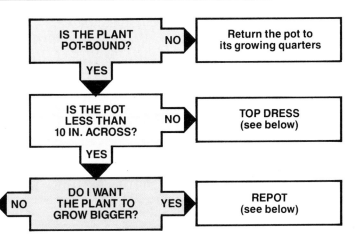

IS THE PLANT POT-BOUND? — NO → **Return the pot to its growing quarters**

YES

IS THE POT LESS THAN 10 IN. ACROSS? — NO → **TOP DRESS (see below)**

YES

NO ← **DO I WANT THE PLANT TO GROW BIGGER?** — YES → **REPOT (see below)**

REPOT (see below) AFTER ROOT PRUNING
At Step 1 choose a clean pot which is the same size as the previous one.

At Step 4 remove about a quarter of the compost in the soil ball together with outer dead roots. Use an old kitchen fork. After repotting trim back some of the top growth of the plant.

SEVEN STEPS TO SUCCESSFUL REPOTTING

The best time is in spring, so that the roots will have plenty of time to become established before the onset of the resting season. Choose a pot which is only slightly larger than the previous one; too large a difference will result in a severe check to growth.

(1) If the pot has been used before, it must be thoroughly scrubbed out. A new clay pot should be soaked in water overnight before use.

(2) If a clay pot is used, cover the drainage hole with 'crocks' (broken pieces of pot or brick). Place a shallow layer of potting compost over the crock layer.

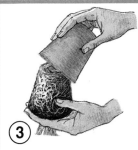

(3) Water the plant. One hour later remove it from the pot by spreading the fingers of the left hand over the soil surface. Invert, and gently knock the rim on the edge of a table. Run a knife around the edge if necessary. Remove the pot with the right hand.

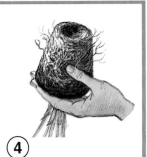

(4) Take away the old crocks. Carefully tease out some of the matted outside roots. Remove any rotten roots but avoid at all costs causing extensive root damage.

(5) Place the plant on top of the compost layer in the new pot and gradually fill around the soil ball with potting compost, which should be slightly damp.

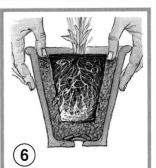

(6) Firm the compost down with the thumbs, adding more until level of the base of the stem is reached. Finally, tap the pot on the table several times to settle the compost.

(7) Water carefully and place in the shade for about a week, misting the leaves daily to avoild wilting. Then place the plant in its growing quarters and treat normally.

TOP DRESSING

For a variety of reasons, especially with large pots and trained specimens, you may not wish or be able to disturb by repotting. In this case the pot should be top dressed every spring by carefully removing the top inch of compost (2 inches for large pots). The removed material is then replaced by fresh potting compost.

POTS

PICKING THE RIGHT POT

Choose a pot with a central drainage hole or several small drainage holes

Pick a colour which is in keeping with the plant and its surroundings

Use a drip tray

The basic pot is made of clay or plastic. Each type has its own group of devotees, but both sorts will support perfectly good plants. Their watering requirements are rather different, so try to keep a plant in one type or the other — repotting from a plastic pot into a clay one will mean that you will have to change your watering routine.

All clay pots have the same earthy terracotta appearance, but plastic pots come in a wide variety of shapes and surfaces. If your room is unheated in winter the insulating properties of foam plastic pots can be a distinct advantage.

Wood, fibreglass and glazed earthenware containers without drainage holes are all available. The choice is up to you, but do remember the basic requirement for good drainage. If holes are not present at the bottom of the receptacle then bore suitable water outlets. It may be impractical to have drainage holes in a large tub for an indoor tree, but a small undrained container is extremely difficult to care for — life for the plant inside it will be a constant struggle against waterlogging.

Clay Pots v Plastic Pots

Advantages:
- Heavy; much less liable to topple over.
- Waterlogging is less likely because of porous nature.
- Traditional 'natural' appearance — no chance of colour clashes.
- Damaging salts are leached away from the compost.

Advantages:
- Lightweight; much less liable to break if dropped.
- Watering is needed less often.
- Decorative and colourful forms available.
- No crocking needed; easy to clean.

Standard Pots

Half Pots
use for Bulbs, Azalea, Bromeliads, Begonia semperflorens and Saintpaulia

Seed Pans

The Standard Pot

Watering Space
This is the recommended distance from the compost level to the top of the pot.

Pot Size	Watering Space
2½ – 5 in.	½ in.
5½ – 7½ in.	¾ in.
8 – 9 in.	1 in.
10 – 12 in.	1½ in.
15 in.	2 in.

Diameter inside rim
This is the size of the pot — a 5 in. pot has a 5 in. diameter inside rim.

Height
The height of the pot is approximately the same as the diameter.

Pot Size
A wide range is available between 1½ and 15 inches. Ideally you should move up only 1 in. every time you repot, but this would call for a large store of pots. You can manage by taking the following steps when repotting, provided you use a good peat-based compost and follow the instructions on page 239. If you wish to stop before the 10 in. stage, root prune before repotting.

For metric sizes see page 248

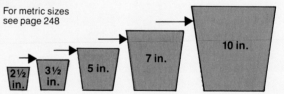

2½ in. / 3½ in. / 5 in. / 7 in. / 10 in.

The Self-Watering Pot

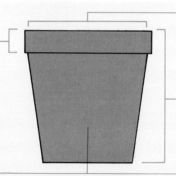

The range of self-watering pots continues to increase, and you can now buy any size from a small plastic container for the windowsill to a floor-standing tub which will house a large indoor garden. They all work on the same two-pot principle — the main container, which houses the compost and plant, draws its water by capillary action from the lower container, or reservoir, which is kept topped up through a filler tube. Liquid feed as well as water is added through this tube.

The self-watering pot can be a boon for areas where watering cannot take place at frequent intervals — weekend cottages, offices, etc. Plants which like to be kept moist at all times grow successfully during the active growing season, but the compost tends to be too wet in winter. For plants which require a period of dryness between waterings, the reservoir should dry out completely for a few days before refilling. Unfortunately, this removes the "automatic" virtue of these containers.

CHAPTER 15
PLANT TROUBLES

It is always disappointing when a cherished specimen suddenly looks sickly, and it is so often the more expensive types which succumb first.

There is not going to be much pleasure in growing indoor plants unless you learn how to avoid plant troubles. Specific pests and diseases are not usually to blame; in most cases the cause of ill-health or death is either too much or too little of one or more of the essential growth factors — light, water, warmth, humidity and food.

To keep your plants in perfect condition, your first task is to choose only those types which can be expected to flourish in the conditions you can provide. Then choose carefully and buy healthy specimens, protect them on their way home and finally provide them with the right conditions. Even so, leaf, stem and flower problems can still occur and you should learn to recognise the cause of problems so that you can take immediate action — pages 242 – 245 will help you. Many troubles can be stopped or cured if tackled quickly enough — delay or the wrong treatment can lead to the death of the plant.

Finally, a word for the beginner. As you will have seen on pages 165 – 199, not all flowering plants dwell permanently indoors. So there is no need to feel you have failed when Poinsettia, Cineraria, Cyclamen and so on die down once their display is over.

Plant collapse

There are scores of possible reasons which can account for the death of an indoor plant. The seven most common fatal factors are:

● **SOIL DRYNESS** No life can survive without water. Many plants can cope with infrequent watering in winter but failure to provide sufficient water during the growing season soon leads to wilting of the leaves and finally to the death of the plant.

● **OVERWATERING** The most usual cause of plant death in winter is overwatering. The leaves of affected plants droop, and the owner thinks that they are short of water. So the plants are thoroughly watered and collapse soon follows.

It is obviously vital not to confuse the symptoms of drought with those of overwatering. Both cause leaves to wilt and sometimes to drop, but too much water results in yellowing of the foliage, whereas dryness is much more likely to cause shrivelling and browning of the leaves. Also waterlogged clay pots are covered with green slime.

● **COLD NIGHTS** The harmful effects of cold nights are heightened if the plants are kept under warm or hot conditions during the day, as it is the sudden fluctuation in temperature rather than cold air which usually causes the damage.

Frost is generally fatal, and plants standing on windowsills are the ones most likely to suffer. Never leave pots between the windows and drawn curtains on a cold night; if frost is expected and the room is unheated then move the plants away from the window.

● **STRONG SUNSHINE** Some plants will quickly succumb if exposed to direct sunlight even if the air temperature is not unusually high. Some flowering plants, such as Pelargonium, thrive in a sunny window but even these, in common with all other plants, should have the pot and soil surface shaded in the hot summer months. If this is not done, the soil may be baked and the roots killed.

● **HOT DRY AIR** With central heating, and with most forms of artificial heat, the air lacks moisture and conditions are not favourable for most indoor plants. Delicate plants may die under such winter conditions, and it is necessary to increase the Relative Humidity of the surrounding air by one of the techniques on page 229.

● **DRAUGHTS** When a door *and* window are opened in a room, and when the temperature outside the room is lower than within, then a cross-current of air occurs and these draughts are an important cause of plant failure. For this reason, avoid standing plants in a direct line between door and windows.

Another spot which is subject to draughts is the windowsill where there are cracks in the window frame. If delicate plants are to be grown on a windowsill, it is essential to block up all cracks.

● **NO LIGHT** Poor light conditions in an average room do not usually kill; the result is generally pale, weak growth and no flowers. There is a level, however, at which the amount of light is not sufficient to support house plant life and this can occur in dark passages, corners of large rooms, hallways, etc. If you wish to keep plants in such areas, return them at regular intervals to a moderately well-lit spot for a fortnight's holiday.

Cultural faults

UPPER LEAVES FIRM BUT YELLOW

This is generally due to the use of CALCIUM in the compost of lime-hating plants or the use of HARD WATER for watering such plants.

LEAVES DULL AND LIFELESS

TOO MUCH LIGHT is the probable culprit; another possibility is RED SPIDER MITE (see page 244). Even healthy green leaves can be rendered dull and lifeless by dust and grime — follow the cleaning instructions on page 232.

SPOTS OR PATCHES ON LEAVES

If spots or patches are crisp and brown, UNDERWATERING is the most likely cause. If the areas are soft and dark brown, OVERWATERING is the probable reason. If spots or patches are white or straw-coloured, the trouble is due to WATERING WITH COLD WATER, WATER SPLASHES ON LEAVES, AEROSOL DAMAGE, TOO MUCH SUN or PEST/DISEASE DAMAGE (see pages 244 – 245). If spots are moist and blister-like or dry and sunken, the cause is DISEASE (see page 245). Several PESTS can cause speckling of the leaf surface (see page 244).

BROWN TIPS OR EDGES ON LEAVES

If edges remain green, the most likely cause is DRY AIR. Another possible reason is BRUISING — people or pets touching the tips can be the culprit, so can leaf tips pressing against a wall or window. If edges are yellow or brown, the possible causes are many and varied — OVERWATERING, UNDERWATERING, TOO LITTLE LIGHT, TOO MUCH SUN, TOO LITTLE HEAT, TOO MUCH HEAT, OVERFEEDING, DRY AIR or DRAUGHTS. To pinpoint the cause, look for other symptoms.

LEAVES CURL AND FALL

Curling followed by leaf fall is a sign of TOO LITTLE HEAT, OVERWATERING or COLD DRAUGHTS.

WILTING LEAVES

The most usual cause is either SOIL DRYNESS (caused by underwatering) or WATERLOGGING (caused by impeded drainage or watering too frequently). Other possible causes are TOO MUCH LIGHT (especially if wilting takes place regularly at midday), DRY AIR, TOO MUCH HEAT, POT-BOUND ROOTS or PEST DAMAGE (see page 244).

SUDDEN LEAF FALL

Rapid defoliation without a prolonged preliminary period of wilting or discolouration is generally due to a SHOCK to the plant's system. There may have been a large drop or rise in temperature, a sudden increase in daytime light intensity or an intense cold draught. DRYNESS at the roots below the critical level can result in this sudden loss of leaves, especially with woody specimens.

LEAF FALL ON NEW PLANTS

It is quite normal for a newly repotted plant, a new purchase or a plant moved from one room to another, to lose one or two lower leaves. Keep MOVEMENT SHOCK to a minimum by repotting into a pot which is only slightly larger than the previous one, by protecting new plants on the way home from the shop and by never moving a plant from a shady spot to a very bright one without a few days in medium light.

LEAVES TURN YELLOW AND FALL

It is quite normal for an occasional lower leaf on a mature plant to turn yellow and eventually fall. When several leaves turn yellow at the same time and then fall, the most likely cause is OVERWATERING or COLD DRAUGHTS.

LOWER LEAVES DRY UP AND FALL

There are three common causes — TOO LITTLE LIGHT, TOO MUCH HEAT or UNDERWATERING.

PLANT GROWING SLOWLY OR NOT AT ALL

In winter this is normal for nearly all plants, so do not force it to grow. In summer the most likely cause is UNDERFEEDING, OVERWATERING or TOO LITTLE LIGHT. If these factors are not responsible, and the temperature is in the recommended range, then the plant is probably POT-BOUND (see page 238).

SMALL, PALE LEAVES; SPINDLY GROWTH

This occurs in winter and early spring when the plant has been kept too warm and the compost too wet for the limited amount of light available. Where practical, prune off this poor quality growth. If these symptoms appear in the growing season, the most likely cause is either UNDER-FEEDING or TOO LITTLE LIGHT.

FLOWER BUDS FALL

The conditions which cause leaf drop can also lead to loss of buds and flowers. The commonest causes are DRY AIR, UNDERWATERING, TOO LITTLE LIGHT, MOVING THE POT and INSECT DAMAGE (see page 244).

NO FLOWERS

If the plant has reached flowering size and blooms do not appear at the due time of year, several factors can be responsible. The most likely causes are lighting problems — TOO LITTLE LIGHT or WRONG DAYLENGTH. Other possibilities are OVERFEEDING, DRY AIR, THRIPS (see page 244) or REPOTTING (some flowering plants need to be pot-bound before they will flower).

VARIEGATED LEAVES TURN ALL-GREEN

The simple explanation here is that the foliage is not receiving sufficient light. Remove the all-green branch (if practical) and move the pot closer to the window.

FLOWERS QUICKLY FADE

The commonest culprits are UNDERWATERING, DRY AIR, TOO LITTLE LIGHT and TOO MUCH HEAT.

ROTTING LEAVES AND STEMS

This is due to disease attack where growing conditions are poor. The fault often lies with OVERWATERING in winter or LEAVING WATER ON LEAVES at night.

HOLES AND TEARS IN LEAVES

There are two basic causes — PHYSICAL DAMAGE by pets or people (merely brushing against an opening leaf bud can occasionally be responsible) or INSECT DAMAGE (see page 244).

GREEN SLIME ON CLAY POT

A sure sign of watering problems — OVERWATERING or BLOCKED DRAINAGE is the cause.

WHITE CRUST ON CLAY POT

There are two possible causes — use of excessively HARD WATER or OVERFEEDING.

Pests

Pest attacks are less common indoors than in the garden, but if they do occur and are allowed to get out of hand then serious damage can result. Apply the appropriate remedy as soon as the first signs are seen.

APHID (Greenfly)

Small, sap-sucking insects, usually green but may be black, grey or orange. All plants with soft tissues can be attacked; shoot tips and flower buds are the preferred site. Flowering pot plants are especially susceptible. The plant is weakened and sticky honeydew is deposited. Spray with permethrin — alternatively use malathion or derris. Repeat as necessary.

CATERPILLAR

Caterpillars of many types can infest the plants in a conservatory but these pests are rarely found on specimens in the living room. The tell-tale sign is the presence of holes in the leaves; some species of caterpillar spin leaves together with silken threads. Pick off and destroy individual caterpillars — spraying with fenitrothion or derris is usually not necessary.

CYCLAMEN MITE

Minute mites, looking like a film of dust on the underside of leaves. Cyclamen, Impatiens, Pelargonium and Saintpaulia are susceptible. The infested plant is stunted; leaf edges are curled, stems are twisted, flower buds wither. Unlike red spider mite, this pest will flourish in humid conditions. Spraying with standard insecticides is not effective — destroy infested leaves.

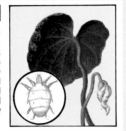

EARWIG

A familiar garden and household pest with a dark brown body and pincer-like tail. It is rarely if ever seen on house plants as it hides during the day, feeding at night on leaves and flower petals. Ragged holes are produced and leaves may be skeletonised. Pick off the insects — look under the leaves and shake the flowers. Spraying with malathion is rarely necessary.

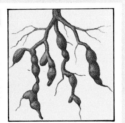

EELWORM

Fortunately these microscopic, soil-living worms are not common house plant pests. If a plant collapses for no apparent reason remove it from its pot — large, corky swellings on the roots are a sure sign of root knot eelworm attack. Destroy the plant immediately — do not put it on the compost heap. In future use sterilised compost and buy plants from a reputable supplier.

FUNGUS GNAT

The small, black, adult insects which fly around the plant are harmless, but they lay eggs on the compost and the tiny, black-headed maggots they produce can be harmful. The maggots normally feed on organic matter in the compost but they will occasionally devour young roots. Fungus gnats can be troublesome in over-damp conditions — water with malathion solution.

MEALY BUG

Small pests covered with white, cottony fluff. Large clusters can occur on the stems and under the leaves of a wide variety of plants. A serious attack leads to wilting, yellowing and leaf fall. A light infestation is easily dealt with — wipe off with a damp cloth or a babycare cotton bud. A severe infestation is difficult to control — spray weekly with malathion or systemic insecticide.

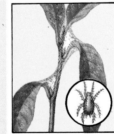

RED SPIDER MITE

Minute, sap-sucking pests which can infest the underside of leaves of nearly all house plants growing in hot and dry conditions. The upper surface becomes speckled with yellow blotches and the leaves fall prematurely; white webbing is sometimes produced between the leaves and stems. Daily misting will help to prevent attacks; spray with derris, malathion or systemic insecticide as soon as the first signs are seen. Repeat as necessary.

SCALE

Small, brown discs attached to the underside of leaves, especially along the veins. These immobile adults are protected from sprays by the outer waxy shells, but they can be wiped off with a damp cloth or a babycare cotton bud. After removal spray the whole plant with malathion. If a plant is allowed to become badly infested the leaves turn yellow and sticky with honeydew; eradication is difficult or impossible at this stage.

THRIPS

These tiny, black insects are a minor pest of house plants, but Begonia, Codiaeum and Fuchsia are sometimes disfigured. They fly or jump from leaf to leaf, causing tell-tale silvery streaks, but the worst damage is to flowers which are spotted and distorted. Growth is stunted. Control is not difficult — spray with permethrin, malathion or derris at the first sign of attack and repeat as necessary.

VINE WEEVIL

The adult beetles attack leaves, but it is the 1 in. creamy grubs which do the real damage. They live in the compost and rapidly devour roots, bulbs and tubers. Control is difficult or impossible — the root system will have been seriously damaged by the time the plant has started to wilt. Water immediately with lindane. Use as a precautionary measure if beetles are noticed on Cyclamen or Primula leaves.

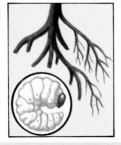

WHITEFLY

Tiny, white moth-like insects which can be troublesome, especially to Begonia, Fuchsia, Impatiens and Pelargonium. The adult flies are unsightly; the greenish larvae on the underside of the leaves suck sap and deposit sticky honeydew. Badly infested leaves turn yellow and drop. Whitefly can occur in great numbers and rapidly spread from plant to plant. Eradication is difficult — spray with permethrin and repeat at 3-day intervals.

Diseases

The appearance of disease is usually a sign of poor growing conditions. Speedy action is essential — cut out the affected area as soon as it is seen, use a fungicide if one is recommended and correct the cultural fault.

ANTHRACNOSE

Sunken black spots appear on the foliage of Palms, Ficus and other susceptible plants. Dark brown streaks may occur at the leaf tips. This disease is associated with warm and very moist conditions, and it is therefore much more likely in the greenhouse than in the living room. Remove and burn infected leaves, spray the plant with systemic fungicide and keep it on the dry side without misting for several weeks.

BLACK LEG

A disease of stem cuttings, especially Pelargonium. The base of the cutting turns black, due to the invasion of the Botrytis fungus. Remove the infected cutting as soon as possible. The cause is overwatering or overcompaction of the compost which has prevented proper drainage. Make sure that the Seed and Cutting Compost is kept drier next time you take Pelargonium cuttings; do not cover with glass or polythene.

BOTRYTIS (Grey Mould)

Familiar grey, fluffy mould which can cover all parts of the plant — leaves, stems, buds and flowers if the growing conditions are cool, humid and still. All soft-leaved plants can be affected — Begonia, Cyclamen, Gloxinia and Saintpaulia are particularly susceptible. Cut away and destroy all affected parts. Remove mouldy compost. Spray with systemic fungicide. Reduce watering and misting; improve ventilation.

CROWN & STEM ROT

Part of the stem or crown has turned soft and rotten. When the diseased area is at the base of the plant it is known as basal rot. The fungus usually spreads rapidly and kills the plant — the usual course is to throw the pot, compost and plant away. If you have caught the trouble early you can try to save it by cutting away all diseased tissue. In future avoid overwatering, underventilating and keeping the plant too cool.

DAMPING OFF

The damping off fungi attack the root and stem bases of seedlings. Shrinkage and rot occur at ground level and the plants topple over. The golden rules are to use sterilised compost, sow thinly and never overwater. At the first sign of attack remove collapsed seedlings, improve the ventilation and move the seedlings to a cooler spot. Water the remainder with Cheshunt Compound.

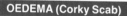

LEAF SPOT

Brown, moist spots appear on the foliage of Citrus, Dracaena, Dieffenbachia and other susceptible plants. In a bad attack the small spots enlarge and merge, killing the whole leaf. Both bacteria and fungi can cause this effect — the best general treatment is to remove and burn infected leaves, spray the plant with systemic fungicide and keep it on the dry side without misting for several weeks.

OEDEMA (Corky Scab)

Hard corky growths sometimes appear on the underside of leaves. This disease is not caused by either a fungus or bacterium; it is the plant's response to waterlogged compost coupled with low light intensity. Badly affected leaves will not recover so they should be removed. Transferring the plant to a better lit spot and reducing the frequency of watering will result in healthy new foliage.

POWDERY MILDEW

A fungus disease which grows on the surface of leaves, spotting or coating them with a white powdery deposit. Unlike Botrytis this complaint is neither common nor fatal, but it is disfiguring and can spread to stems and flowers. Remove badly mildewed leaves and spray the plants with systemic fungicide or dinocap. Alternatively lightly dust the leaves with sulphur. Improve ventilation around the plants.

ROOT ROT (Tuber Rot)

A killer disease to which Cacti, Succulents, Begonia, Palms and Saintpaulia are particularly prone. The first sign is usually the yellowing and wilting of the leaves which is rapidly followed by browning and collapse. The cause is fungal decay of the roots due to waterlogging and you can only save the plant if the trouble is spotted in time and you follow the Root Rot Surgery technique on page 246.

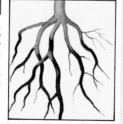

RUST

An uncommon disease which need not concern the ordinary house plant owner. The only plant you are likely to see infected with rust is the Pelargonium — brown concentric rings of spores on the underside of the leaves. It is difficult to control — remove and burn infected leaves, improve the ventilation around the plants and spray with mancozeb. Do not propagate cuttings infected with this disease.

SOOTY MOULD

A black fungus which grows on the sticky honeydew which is deposited by aphid, scale, whitefly and mealy bug. The unsightly mould does not directly harm the plant, but it does reduce growth and vigour by blocking the pores and shading the surface from sunlight. Remove sooty mould by wiping with a damp cloth; rinse with clean warm water. Control future attacks by spraying promptly against the pests which produce honeydew.

VIRUS

There is no single symptom of virus infection. The growth may be severely stunted and stems are often distorted. The usual effect on leaves is the appearance of pale green or yellow spots or small patches. Coloured flowers may bear large white streaks. The infection was brought in by insects or was already present in the plant at the time of purchase. There is no cure — throw away the plant if you are sure of your diagnosis.

First aid for house plants

House plant varieties have changed over the years, but one would expect their problems to be quite unchanging. This surprisingly is not so — the menace of coal gas fumes has disappeared in recent years but it has been replaced by an equally serious but completely different menace — the hot, desert-dry air of the centrally-heated room. Even pests and diseases change — Pelargonium rust was virtually unknown until a few years ago.

The problems that can occur are many and varied. Inspect the plants regularly, especially under the leaves. You may detect the first signs of rot because you forgot to reduce watering as winter approached, or you may notice symptoms of light deficiency if you have redecorated using much darker wallpaper. Use pages 242–245 to put a name to the problems you see, then take prompt action. The secret of green fingers is to look for and act on the first signs of trouble.

PREVENTION IS BETTER THAN CURE

Don't bring trouble in with the compost
Never use unsterilised soil. Buy a specially-prepared compost, which you can be sure will be pest- and disease-free. Alternatively sterilise soil if you wish to prepare a home-made compost.

Don't bring trouble in with the plants
Inspect new plants carefully and take any remedial action which may be necessary before putting them with the other plants.

Don't put plants in the danger spots:
- Between an open window and a door
- Near an air-conditioning heating duct
- On the TV or radiator unless extra humidity is provided
- On a windowsill with poor-fitting frames
- In an unlit corner or a dark passageway
- Between closed curtains and the window during frosty weather

Remove dead flowers and dying leaves
Hygiene is important. Fallen leaves can become covered in grey mould, and this will spread rapidly to healthy leaves if conditions are cool and humid.

Prevent trouble by following the rules
Look up the plant in the A–Z guide — nearly all problems arise from inadequate care.

Act promptly when there is trouble
Don't wait. Move the plant to a better location or spray the leaves if such treatment is recommended.

GOOD SPRAYING PRACTICE

Use the right product
Make sure that it is recommended for the pest or disease to be controlled, and make sure that there is no warning against spraying the plant to be treated.

Buy a brand recommended for house plants
Where possible obtain a product which is specially recommended for use indoors — check that it will not harm surrounding furnishings or fabrics.

Spray the right way
Before spraying read the instructions — avoid using too little or too much. Cover fish bowls and aquaria before you start. Spray thoroughly both above and below the leaves. Wash out the sprayer after use.

Spray the right plants
With the quick-moving invaders, such as aphid and whitefly, spray all the neighbouring plants. With slow-moving pests, such as scale and mealy bug, only plants which are infested need be sprayed.

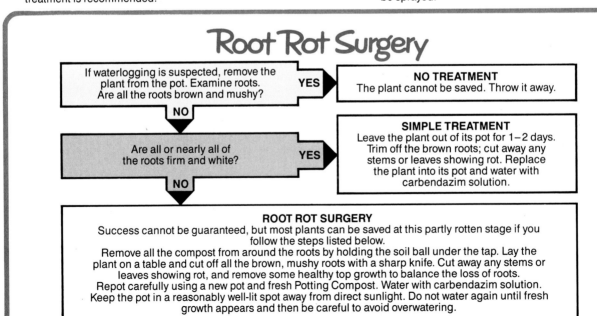

Root Rot Surgery

If waterlogging is suspected, remove the plant from the pot. Examine roots. Are all the roots brown and mushy? — **YES** → **NO TREATMENT** The plant cannot be saved. Throw it away.

NO ↓

Are all or nearly all of the roots firm and white? — **YES** → **SIMPLE TREATMENT** Leave the plant out of its pot for 1–2 days. Trim off the brown roots; cut away any stems or leaves showing rot. Replace the plant into its pot and water with carbendazim solution.

NO ↓

ROOT ROT SURGERY
Success cannot be guaranteed, but most plants can be saved at this partly rotten stage if you follow the steps listed below.
Remove all the compost from around the roots by holding the soil ball under the tap. Lay the plant on a table and cut off all the brown, mushy roots with a sharp knife. Cut away any stems or leaves showing rot, and remove some healthy top growth to balance the loss of roots.
Repot carefully using a new pot and fresh Potting Compost. Water with carbendazim solution.
Keep the pot in a reasonably well-lit spot away from direct sunlight. Do not water again until fresh growth appears and then be careful to avoid overwatering.

CHAPTER 16

HOUSE PLANT GROWER'S DICTIONARY

ACID MEDIUM A compost which contains little or no lime and has a pH of less than 6.5.

AERIAL ROOT A root which grows out from the stem above ground level. Aerial roots are commonly seen on mature specimens of Monstera deliciosa.

AIR LAYERING A method of propagating single-stem plants, such as Ficus elastica decora, which have lost their lower leaves. See page 235 for details.

ALTERNATE Leaf form, where the leaves are arranged singly at different heights on the stem. Compare *opposite* and *whorled*.

ANNUAL A plant which completes its life cycle within one year of germination. Compare *biennial* and *perennial.*

ANTHER The part of the flower which produces pollen. It is the upper section of the *stamen.*

APICAL At the tip of a branch.

AQUATIC See Picture Dictionary (page 248).

AREOLE A small well-defined area, usually hairy and cushion-like, found on the stem of cacti. From them arise spines or *glochids.*

AROID A plant belonging to the Araceae or Arum-lily family. Popular aroids include Aglaonema, Anthurium, Dieffenbachia, Monstera and Philodendron.

AXIL The angle between the upper surface of a leaf or leaf stalk and the stem that carries it. A growth or flower bud ("axillary bud") often appears in the axil.

BEARDED A petal bearing a tuft or row of long hairs.

BICOLOUR A flower with petals which bear two distinctly different colours.

BIENNIAL A plant which completes its life cycle in two seasons. Compare *annual* and *perennial.*

BLADE The expanded part of a leaf or petal.

BLEEDING The loss of sap from plant tissues which have been cut.

BLIND The loss of the growing point, resulting in stoppage of growth. Also, failure to produce flowers or fruit.

BLOOM A natural mealy or waxy coating covering the leaves of some house plants.

BONSAI The art of dwarfing trees by careful root and stem pruning coupled with root restriction.

BOTTLE GARDEN A form of *terrarium* in which a large and heavy glass container such as a *carboy* is used.

BRACT A modified leaf, often highly coloured and sometimes mistaken for a petal. Examples of house plants with showy bracts are Poinsettia, Aphelandra and Bougainvillea.

BREAK Production of a side shoot after removal of the growing point.

BULB A storage organ, usually formed below ground level, used for propagation. A true bulb consists of fleshy scales surrounding the central bud, but the term is often loosely applied to *corms, rhizomes* and *tubers.*

BULBIL An immature small bulb formed on the stem of a plant; e.g Lily.

BULBLET An immature small bulb formed at the base of a mature bulb; e.g Hyacinth.

CALYX The outer ring of flower parts, usually green but sometimes coloured.

CAPILLARY ACTION The natural upward movement of water in confined areas, such as the spaces between soil particles.

CARBOY A large and heavy glass vessel, originally designed for the storage of chemicals but now commonly used as a container for bottle gardens.

CHLOROSIS An abnormal yellowing or blanching of the leaves due to lack of chlorophyll. See Chapter 15 for possible causes.

CLADODE A modified stem which has taken on the form of a leaf; e.g the needle-like "leaves" of Asparagus Fern.

COLOURED LEAF See Picture Dictionary (page 248).

COMPOST Usual meaning for the house plant grower is a potting or seed/cutting mixture made from peat ("soilless compost") or sterilised soil ("loam compost") plus other materials such as sand, lime and fertilizer. Compost is also a term for decomposed vegetable matter.

COMPOUND FLOWER A flower made up of many *florets*; e.g Chrysanthemum.

COMPOUND LEAF A leaf made up of two or more *leaflets* attached to the leaf stalk; e.g Schefflera.

CONSERVATORY A structure composed partly or entirely of glass, attached to the house and within which a large number of plants are grown and enjoyed.

CORM A swollen, underground stem base used for propagation; e.g Crocus.

COROLLA The ring of separate or fused petals which is nearly always responsible for the main floral display.

CRESTED Cockscomb-like growth of leaves, stems or flowers. Other name — *cristate.*

CRISTATE Cockscomb-like growth of leaves (e.g Pteris cretica cristata), stems (Cereus peruvianus monstrosus) or flowers (Celosia cristata).

CROCK A piece of broken pot used to help drainage. See page 239.

CROWN The region where shoot and root join, usually at or very near ground level.

CULTIVAR See *Naming House Plants*, page 200.

CUTTING A piece of a plant (leaf, stem or root) which can be used to produce a new plant.

DAMPING OFF Decay of young seedlings at ground level following fungal attack. See page 245.

DEAD-HEADING The removal of faded heads of flowers.

DECIDUOUS See Picture Dictionary (page 248).

DISTILLED WATER Pure water free from dissolved salts. Formerly made by distillation, now produced chemically by demineralisation.

DIVISION A method of propagating plants by separating each one into two or more sections and then repotting.

Picture Dictionary

Pots

IMPERIAL SIZE	METRIC EQUIVALENT
2½ in.	65 mm
3½ in.	90 mm
5 in.	130 mm
7 in.	180 mm
10 in.	250 mm

Flowers

SIMPLE FLOWER

Anther — Throat
Filament
Eye

COMPOUND FLOWER

Florets

BRACT FLOWER

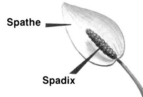

True flowers
Bract

SPATHE FLOWER

Spathe
Spadix

SINGLE

The normal number of petals are present, arranged in a single row

HOSE IN HOSE

Petals are arranged so that one flower appears to be growing within another

DOUBLE

Many more petals are present than in the single form. The latin name is 'flore pleno'

Leaves & Stems

Most leaves and stems are non-succulent.
Succulent house plants have leaves and/or stems which are thick and fleshy.
Most house plants are **Evergreen**, retaining their leaves throughout the year. The remainder are **Deciduous,** losing their leaves at the end of the growing season.

— **TENDRIL**

AERIAL ROOT

Axil
SIMPLE LEAF

Leaf base attached to stem **Node**

COMPOUND LEAF
Leaf stalk
Leaflet

FROND

OFFSET

GREEN LEAF

Depending upon the variety, the colour may be any shade from pale green to nearly black

VARIEGATED LEAF

Green leaf which is blotched, edged or spotted with yellow, white or cream

COLOURED LEAF

One or more colours apart from green, white or cream are distinctly present

RUNNER

Creeping stem which produces small plantlets along its length. Sometimes called a **Stolon**

Natural Habitat

EPIPHYTE
Plant which grows above ground attached to trees or rocks

AQUATIC
Plant which grows partly or wholly in water

TERRESTRIAL
Plant which grows in the soil

ROOT BALL
Matted roots plus enclosed compost within the pot

Roots

Not all the plant parts below soil level are roots. **Rhizomes** are creeping stems. **Bulbs** are short stems surrounded by rows and rows of fleshy leaves. **Tubers** and **Corms** are swollen stems which produce new plants. Some plants, such as Dahlias, produce swollen roots which are also known as **Tubers**.

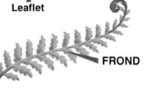

DORMANT PERIOD The time when a plant has naturally stopped growing and the leaves have fallen or the top growth has died down. The dormant period is usually, but not always, in winter. Compare *resting period*.

DOUBLE FLOWER See Picture Dictionary (page 248).

DOUBLE POTTING An American term for placing a potted plant in a larger pot with damp peat in between. See page 229.

DRAWN Excessively tall and weak growth, caused by plants being grown in too little light or too closely together.

ENTIRE LEAF An undivided and unserrated leaf.

EPIDERMIS The transparent protective skin which covers non-woody plants.

EPIPHYTE See Picture Dictionary (page 248).

EXOTIC Strictly speaking, a plant which is not native to the area, but popularly any unusual or striking house plant.

EYE Two unrelated meanings — an undeveloped growth bud or the centre of a flower.

F₁ HYBRID A first generation offspring of two pure-bred strains. An F₁ hybrid is generally more vigorous than an ordinary hybrid.

FAMILY See *Naming House Plants*, page 200.

FLORET A small flower which is part of a much larger compound flower-head; e.g Cineraria.

FLOWER SPIKE A flower-head made up of a central stem with the flowers growing directly on it.

FORCING The process of making a plant grow or flower before its natural season.

FROND A leaf of a fern or palm.

FUNGICIDE A chemical used to control diseases caused by fungi.

FUNGUS A primitive form of plant life which is known to the house plant grower as the most common cause of infectious disease — powdery mildew, sooty mould and grey mould are examples.

GENUS See *Naming House Plants*, page 200.

GERMINATION The first stage in the development of a plant from seed.

GESNERIAD A plant belonging to the Gesneriaceae or African Violet family. Popular gesneriads include Saintpaulia, Gloxinia, Streptocarpus and Columnea.

GLABROUS Plant surface which is smooth and hairless.

GLAUCOUS Plant surface which is covered with a bluish-grey bloom.

GLOCHID A small hooked hair borne on some cacti.

GRAFTING The process of joining a stem or bud of one plant on to the stem of another.

GROUND COVER A plant used to provide a low-growing carpet between other plants.

GROWING POINT The tip of a stem, which is responsible for extension growth.

HALF HARDY An indoor plant which requires a minimum temperature of 50°–55°F for healthy growth. Compare *hardy* and *tender*.

HARDENING OFF Gradual acclimatisation to colder conditions.

HARDY An indoor plant which can withstand prolonged exposure to temperatures at or below 45°F. Compare *half hardy* and *tender*.

HEEL A strip of bark and wood remaining at the base of a side shoot cutting pulled off a main shoot. Some cuttings root more readily if a heel is attached.

HERB A plant grown for flavouring or medicinal purposes.

HERBACEOUS A plant with a non-woody stem.

HONEYDEW Sticky, sugary secretion deposited on plants by insects such as aphid and whitefly.

HUMIDIFIER A piece of equipment used to raise the humidity of the air in a room.

HYBRID A plant with parents which are genetically distinct. The parent plants may be different *cultivars, varieties, species or genera* but not different *families*.

HYDROPONICS A method of growing a plant in water containing dissolved nutrients.

HYGROMETER An instrument used to measure the Relative Humidity of the air.

INFLORESCENCE The arrangement of flowers on the stem.

INORGANIC A chemical or fertilizer which is not obtained from a source which is or has been alive.

INSECTICIDE A chemical used to control insect pests.

INTERNODE The part of the stem between one *node* and another.

KNOCKING OUT The temporary removal of a plant from its pot in order to check the condition of the root ball.

LATERAL SHOOT A side branch growing from the main stem.

LATEX Milky sap which exudes from cut surfaces of a few house plants, such as Ficus elastica decora and Euphorbia.

LEAF MOULD Partially decayed leaves used in some potting mixtures. It must be sieved and sterilised before use.

LEAFLET A leaf-like section of a *compound leaf*.

LEGGY Abnormally tall and spindly growth.

LOAM Good quality soil used in preparing compost. Adequate supplies of clay, sand and fibre must be present.

LONG DAY PLANT A plant which requires light for a longer period than it would normally receive from daylight in order to induce flowering; e.g Saintpaulia.

MACRAMÉ Decoratively knotted rope or cord forming a harness-like structure for hanging pots.

MICROCLIMATE The warmth and humidity of the air in close proximity to a plant. It may differ significantly from the general climate of the room.

MICRO-CUTTING A plant produced by micropropagation — a modern technique using tiny pieces of the parent plant on a sterile nutrient jelly.

MIST PROPAGATION The ideal method of propagation under glass, using automatic mist generators and soil heaters.

MOUTH The open end of a bell-shaped or tubular flower.

MULTICOLOUR A flower with petals which bear at least three distinctly different colours.

MUTATION A sudden change in the genetic make-up of a plant, leading to a new feature. This new feature can be inherited.

NEUTRAL Neither acid nor alkaline; pH 6.5 – 7.5.

NODE The point on a stem where a leaf or bud is attached.

OFFSET A young plantlet which appears on a mature plant. An offset can generally be detached and used for propagation.

OPPOSITE Leaf form, where the leaves are arranged in opposite pairs along the stem. Compare *alternate* and *whorled*.

ORGANIC A chemical or fertilizer which is obtained from a source which is or has been alive.

OSMUNDA FIBRE The roots of the fern Osmunda regalis, used for making Orchid Compost.

OVER-POTTING Repotting a plant into a pot which is too large to allow successful establishment.

PALMATE LEAF Five or more lobes arising from one point — hand-like.

PEAT (Peat moss in the U.S.) Partially decomposed sphagnum moss or sedge used in making composts. Valuable for its pronounced air- and water-holding capacity and its freedom from weeds and disease organisms.

PENDENT Hanging.

PERENNIAL A plant which will live for three years or more under normal conditions.

PERFOLIATE Paired leaves which fuse around the stem.

PETIOLE A leaf stalk.

pH A measure of acidity and alkalinity. Below pH 6.5 is acid, above pH 7.5 is alkaline.

PHOTOSYNTHESIS The food-making process which occurs in the leaf. This process requires water, air and adequate light.

PHYLLODE A leaf stalk expanded to look like and act like a leaf.

PINCHING OUT The removal of the growing point of a stem to induce bushiness or to encourage flowering. Also known as *stopping*.

PINNATE LEAF A series of leaflets arranged on either side of a central stalk.

PIP Two distinct meanings — the seed of some fruits (e.g Orange) and the rootstock of some flowering plants (e.g Convallaria).

PISTIL The female reproductive parts of the flower.

PLANT WINDOW Double window with plants grown in the space between.

PLUNGING The placing of a pot up to its rim outdoors in soil, peat or ashes.

POT-BOUND A plant growing in a pot which is too small to allow proper leaf and stem growth.

POTTING ON The repotting of a plant into a proper-sized larger container which will allow continued root development.

PRICKING OUT The moving of seedlings from the tray or pot in which they were sown to other receptacles where they can be spaced out individually.

RESTING PERIOD The time when a plant has naturally stopped growing but when there is little or no leaf fall. Compare *dormant period*.

RHIZOME A thickened stem which grows horizontally below or on the soil surface.

ROOT BALL See Picture Dictionary (page 248).

RUNNER See Picture Dictionary (page 248).

SELF-COLOUR A flower with single-coloured petals.

SEPAL One of the divisions of the *calyx*.

SERRATE Saw-edged.

SESSILE A stalkless leaf or flower which is borne directly on the stem.

SHARP SAND Coarse, lime-free sand.

SHORT DAY PLANT A plant which requires light for a shorter period than it would normally receive from daylight in order to induce flowering; e.g Chrysanthemum and Poinsettia.

SHRUB A woody plant with a framework of branches and little or no central stem. Compare *tree*.

SINGLE FLOWER See Picture Dictionary (page 248).

SPADIX A fleshy flower spike in which tiny *florets* are embedded.

SPATHE A large *bract*, sometimes highly coloured, surrounding or enclosing a *spadix*. The spathe flower is characteristic of the *aroids*, such as Anthurium and Spathiphyllum.

SPECIES See *Naming House Plants*, page 200.

SPORE A reproductive cell of non-flowering plants, such as ferns.

SPORT A plant which shows a marked and inheritable change from its parent; a *mutation*.

STAMEN The male reproductive parts of a flower.

STANDARD A plant which does not normally grow as a tree but is trained into a tree-like form.

STERILISED SOIL A rather misleading term, as steam- or chemically-sterilised soil is only partially sterilised. Harmful organisms have been killed but helpful bacteria have been spared.

STOLON See *runner*.

STOPPING See *pinching out*.

STOVE PLANT A plant which requires warm greenhouse conditions in winter.

STRAIN A selection of a *variety, cultivar* or *species* which is raised from seed.

SUB-SHRUB A plant which at the adult stage has woody stems near the base and a framework of soft green growth.

SUCCULENT See Picture Dictionary (page 248).

SUCKER A shoot which arises from an underground shoot or root of a plant.

SYSTEMIC A pesticide which goes inside the plant and travels in the sap stream.

TAP ROOT A strong root, sometimes swollen, which grows vertically into the soil or compost.

TENDER An indoor plant which requires a minimum temperature of 60°F. Occasional short exposure to temperatures below this level may be tolerated. Compare *hardy* and *half hardy*.

TENDRIL A thread-like stem or leaf which clings to any nearby support.

TERMINAL The uppermost bud or flower on a stem.

TERRARIUM A partly or entirely closed glass container used to house a collection of indoor plants.

TERRESTRIAL See Picture Dictionary (page 248).

TOPIARY The art of clipping and training woody plants to form geometric shapes or intricate patterns. Box and Myrtle are suitable types.

TRANSPIRATION The loss of water through the pores of the leaf.

TREE A woody plant with a distinct central trunk. Compare *shrub*.

TUBER A storage organ used for propagation. It may be a fleshy root (e.g Dahlia) or a swollen underground stem.

VARIEGATED LEAF See Picture Dictionary (page 248).

VARIETY See *Naming House Plants*, page 200.

WHORLED Leaf form, where three or more leaves radiate from a single *node*.

XEROPHYTE A plant which is able to live under very dry conditions.

CHAPTER 17

PLANT INDEX

Acknowledgements

As the author of The House Plant Expert I wish to express my gratitude for the help received over the years from a small group of people. They devoted much time and care to this work, and they are acknowledged in the paperback edition.

My special thanks go to the team which helped me to produce this Gold Plated version. Two people stand out — John Woodbridge for his design skills and his effective leadership of the production team, and Gill Jackson for her remarkable organisational, secretarial and proofing skills. In addition, I am grateful to Gerard McEvilly, Joan Hill, The Saintpaulia and Houseplant Society, Matthew Biggs, Hans Fliegner and Mark Sparrow of the Royal Botanic Gardens, Kew, Tony Ball of P A Moerman Ltd, Mr & Mrs John Ainsworth of Tokonoma Bonsai, Pathfast Ltd, Pauline Dobbs, Jacqueline Norris, Angelina Gibbs, Joan Hessayon and Constance Barry.

Additional paintings for this edition were produced by Deborah Achilleos, Norman Barber and Garden Studio. Photographs came from several sources, including Heather Angel, A-Z Botanical Collection Ltd, Pat Brindley, Carleton Photographic, Gary Chowanetz/EWA, Michael Dunne/EWA, Mary Evans Picture Library, Gwen Goodship, Robert Harding Picture Library, Iris Hardwick Library, Private Collection/The Bridgeman Art Library (p 39), Roy Miles Fine Painting, London/The Bridgeman Art Library (p 40), Tom Rochford III, Harry Smith Horticultural Photographic Collection, Neil Lorimer/EWA and Michael Warren.